THE CAMBRIDG
SAYYID AHMAD KHAN

Sayyid Ahmad Khan (1817–1898), *Sir Sayyid/Syed* for many, is well known for his pivotal role in the foundation of Muhammadan Anglo-Oriental College that became Aligarh Muslim University in 1920. The university's role in giving shape to a progressive Muslim community is the living legacy of Sayyid Ahmad Khan. He was a multidimensional personality – a pioneering thinker, an erudite scholar and a prolific writer, a rationalist theologian, community organizer, secularist leader, as well as a modernizer, deeply rooted in the Indian tradition. He serves as an inspiration even today, 200 years after his birth. He personified the reformist spirit of Raja Ram Mohan Roy and the fervent zeal to uplift his people as embodied by Mahatma Gandhi. Globally, one can place him alongside leading Muslim intellectuals of his time, such as the political activist Jamaluddin al-Afghani (1838–1897), modernist reformer and thinker Muhammad Abduh (1849–1905), and theologian Bediuzzaman Nursi (1877–1960). While there are ample scholarly and academic books, biographical narratives, and descriptive histories on the above-mentioned personalities, serious and dedicated scholarship on Sayyid Ahmad that captures the breadth of his activities and legacies is absent. This book, with contributions from some of the leading scholars in the field, critically examines Sayyid Ahmad's life and contributions in the context of his and our current times. Engaging with his multifaceted work offers a better understanding of the challenges Indians faced during colonialism as well as enables a constructive way for addressing difficult problems of today.

Yasmin Saikia teaches history and holds the endowed Hardt-Nickachos Chair in Peace Studies at Arizona State University. She has authored *Fragmented Memories: Struggling to Be Tai-Ahom in Assam* (2004) and *Women, War and the Making of Bangladesh: Remembering 1971* (2011). Her most recent work is a co-edited book, *Northeast India: A Place of Relations* (2016). Her research and teaching interests are multidisciplinary, including peace studies, cultural and intellectual history, religious history with a focus on Muslim South Asia, gender and violence, and memory and identity.

M. Raisur Rahman teaches history at Wake Forest University. He is the author of *Locale, Everyday Islam, and Modernity: Qasbah Towns and Muslim Life in Colonial India* (2015). Trained as a historian of South Asia, his academic focus has been on the literary, social, and intellectual histories of Muslims in modern India. He currently serves as the President of South Asian Muslim Studies Association.

THE CAMBRIDGE COMPANION TO
SAYYID AHMAD KHAN

Edited by
Yasmin Saikia
Arizona State University

M. Raisur Rahman
Wake Forest University

CAMBRIDGE
UNIVERSITY PRESS

University Printing House, Cambridge CB2 8BS, United Kingdom

One Liberty Plaza, 20th Floor, New York, NY 10006, USA

477 Williamstown Road, Port Melbourne, VIC 3207, Australia

314 to 321, 3rd Floor, Plot No.3, Splendor Forum, Jasola District Centre, New Delhi 110025, India

79 Anson Road, #06-04/06, Singapore 079906

Cambridge University Press is part of the University of Cambridge.

It furthers the University's mission by disseminating knowledge in the pursuit of education, learning and research at the highest international levels of excellence.

www.cambridge.org
Information on this title: www.cambridge.org/9781108483872

© Cambridge University Press 2019

This publication is in copyright. Subject to statutory exception and to the provisions of relevant collective licensing agreements, no reproduction of any part may take place without the written permission of Cambridge University Press.

First published 2019

Printed in India by Rajkamal Electric Press

A catalogue record for this publication is available from the British Library

ISBN 978-1-108-48387-2 Hardback

ISBN 978-1-108-70524-0 Paperback

Cambridge University Press has no responsibility for the persistence or accuracy of URLs for external or third-party internet websites referred to in this publication, and does not guarantee that any content on such websites is, or will remain, accurate or appropriate.

Contents

List of Figures vii
Notes on Contributors ix
Acknowledgements xiii
A Note on Spellings and Transliteration xvii
Chronology of Sayyid Ahmad Khan xix

Introduction 1
YASMIN SAIKIA AND M. RAISUR RAHMAN

Part I. *Sayyid Ahmad Khan: The rise of a historical figure*

1. Sir Sayyid on History: The Indian Rebellion of 1857 and Rethinking the 'Rebellious' Muslim Question 17
YASMIN SAIKIA

2. Indian Muslims Are the Most Loyal Subjects of the British Raj: Sir Sayyid Ahmad Khan and the Caliphate 38
CARIMO MOHOMED

3. Sir Sayyid on 'The Present State of Education among Muhammadan Females' 55
GAIL MINAULT

4. *Naicari* Nature: Sir Sayyid Ahmad Khan and the Reconciliation of Science, Technology, and Religion 69
DAVID LELYVELD

Part II. *Musalman-e Hind: Indian Muslim in a plural environment*

5. Creating a Community: Sir Sayyid and His Contemporaries 89
M. RAISUR RAHMAN

6. Envisioning a Future: Sir Sayyid Ahmad's Mission of Education 108
MOHAMMAD SAJJAD

7. Religion, Science, and the Coherence of Prophetic and Natural Revelation: Sayyid Ahmad Khan's Religious Writings 138
CHARLES M. RAMSEY

8 Defending the 'Community': Sir Sayyid's Concept of *Qaum*   159
   FRANCES W. PRITCHETT

9 Understanding Sir Sayyid's Political Thought   175
   MIRZA ASMER BEG

Part III. *Sir Sayyid today: Enduring legacies*

10 Bridging the Past and the Present: How Sir Sayyid Speaks
    to the Twenty-First Century Protestors   195
    MOHAMMAD ASIM SIDDIQUI

11 Darwin or Design? Examining Sayyid Ahmad Khan's
    Views on Human Evolution   214
    SARAH A. QIDWAI

12 Loss and Longing at the *Qila Mu`alla*: *Āṣār-us Ṣanādīd*
    and the Early Sayyid Ahmad Khan   233
    MRINALINI RAJAGOPALAN

13 A Living Legacy: Sir Sayyid Today   255
    AMBER H. ABBAS

    Conclusion   273
    YASMIN SAIKIA AND M. RAISUR RAHMAN

Suggested Further Readings   281
Index   283

Figures

1. *Naicari Jogi, Oudh Punch*, 4 August 1884   69
2. An alumni of Aligarh Muslim University (AMU) and recipient of the Bharat Ratna, Dr Zakir Husain, who later served as the Vice President (1962–7) and the President of India (1967–9), is seen on the AMU campus (note the Jama Majid of AMU in the background) with Dr Rajendra Prasad, the first President of India (1952–62)   130
3. A photograph of some notable personalities at AMU, including the poet Fani Badauni and Maulana Hasrat Mohani   130
4. An image of a plaque on the AMU campus depicting the family tree of Sayyid Ahmad Khan and showing his lineage to Prophet Muhammad and his daughter Fatima   131
5. *Bijnor Rebellion* book cover   131
6. The last message of Sayyid Ahmad Khan, referenced on page 273 in the book   131
7. Sayyid Ahmad Khan, seated, with four Aligs. One of the rare photographs that show how seamlessly he incorporated Western suit into his persona, the way he adopted Western learning and ideas.   131
8. Document signed by Sayyid Ahmad Khan that shows his occupation of the land on which he established the Scientific Society   132
9. Indian and British staff of the MAO College in a group photograph   132
10. A map of MAO College, Aligarh, in 1895   133
11. Book cover of *Asbab-e Baghawat-e Hind*. Published by Matba Mufid-e Aam, Aligarh, 1903.   133
12. Dining room of Sir Sayyid Hall in AMU   133
13. European faculty of the MAO College, along with their wives. Photographed in 1898.   134
14. MAO College football team, 1897–8   134
15. An early photograph providing an overview of MAO College   135
16. The photograph includes Viqar-ul Mulk, Mohsin-ul Mulk, Deputy Nazir Ahmad, Altaf Husain Hali, Shibli Numani, and T. W. Arnold   135

viii   Figures

17 A facsimile image of *Tahzib-ul Akhlaq*, or *Muhammadan Social Reformer* — 136
18 A group photograph of Sayyid Ahmad Khan with students and staff of MAO — 136
19 Seal of the MAO College, Aligarh — 137
20 Strachey Hall, one of the iconic buildings of MAO College, was the first building to come up on the campus. It was completed in 1885 and named after Sir John Strachey — 137
21 Entrance to Sir Sayyid Hall (North). The entrance Bab-e Ishaque seen in this picture was the main entrance and was named after Nawab Mohammad Ishaq Khan, Secretary of Trustees — 137
22 Astrological chart for the Red Fort from *Āṣār-us Ṣanādīd* (DS486.D3 A61847) — 240
23 Delhi Gate of the Red Fort from *Āṣār-us Ṣanādīd* (DS486.D3 A61847) — 243
24 Diwan-e ʿAm of the Red Fort from *Āṣār-us Ṣanādīd* (DS486.D3 A61847) — 244
25 Naqqar Khana of the Red Fort from *Āṣār-us Ṣanādīd* (DS486.D3 A61847) — 246
26 Iron Pillar at the Quwwat-ul-Islam Mosque from *Āṣār-us Ṣanādīd* (DS486.D3 A61847) — 248

Notes on Contributors

Amber H. Abbas is Assistant Professor of History at Saint Joseph's University, Philadelphia. Her research focuses on the period of transition associated with the 1947 Independence and Partition of India, and its particular impact on South Asian Muslims. Her published articles and forthcoming monograph deal with Aligarh Muslim University and the demand for Pakistan.

Mirza Asmer Beg is Professor of Political Science at Aligarh Muslim University. His work has been published in *The Round Table: The Commonwealth Journal of International Affairs, Economic and Political Weekly, Seminar, South Asian Studies, Studies in Islam*, and *Indian Journal of Politics*. He has published one monograph and edited three volumes. He was a visiting Fulbright scholar at Southern Illinois University, USA, in 1999 and is a fellow of the Salzburg Global Seminars, Austria.

David Lelyveld is Professor of History (Retired) at William Paterson University in the United States. He is the author of *Aligarh's First Generation: Muslim Solidarity in British India* (1978, repr. 2003) and co-editor of *A Wilderness of Possibilities: Urdu Studies in Transnational Perspective* (2005). His most recent publications deal with the social and political history of Urdu and its differentiation from Hindi. His current project is Sir Sayyid and Macaulay's Curse, a three generation study of an Indian Muslim family.

Gail Minault is Professor Emerita of History and Asian Studies at the University of Texas at Austin. She is the author of *The Khilafat Movement: Religious Symbolism and Political Mobilization in India* (1982), *Secluded Scholars: Women's Education and Muslim Social Reform in Colonial India* (1998), and *Gender, Language, and Learning: Essays in Indo-Muslim Cultural History* (2009).

Carimo Mohomed is based in Lisbon, Portugal. His research interests include history of political ideas in the Islamic world, particularly in South Asia, and the relation between religion and politics in cultural and civilizational contexts. His research and publications focus on Sayyid Ahmad Khan and Muslim India. Mohomed serves as Executive Member of the International Political Science Association Research Committee 'Religion and Politics' and sits on the Editorial Board of the *International Journal of Islamic Thought*.

Frances W. Pritchett is Professor Emerita of Modern Indic Languages at Columbia University. She has taught and published on modern South Asian literature, especially Urdu poetry. Her books include *Nets of Awareness: Urdu Poetry and Its Critics* (1994), *The Romance Tradition in Urdu: Adventures from the Dastan of Amir Hamzah* (1991), and (with Khaliq Ahmad Khaliq) *Urdu Meter: A Practical Handbook* (1987).

Sarah A. Qidwai is a PhD candidate at the University of Toronto's Institute for the History and Philosophy of Science and Technology, where she is working on a dissertation on the history of science and Islam in colonial India.

M. Raisur Rahman is Associate Professor of History at Wake Forest University. Trained as a historian of South Asia, his academic focus has been on the literary, social, and intellectual histories of Muslims in modern India. For the last two decades, he has closely studied the Muslim social and cultural ethos, and the salience of Urdu literary culture in the United Provinces – now Uttar Pradesh – in order to understand Indian and Muslim self-making that builds on interconnections and intersections. He is the author of Locale, *Everyday Islam, and Modernity: Qasbah Towns and Muslim Life in Colonial India* (2015).

Mrinalini Rajagopalan is Associate Professor in the Department of the History of Art and Architecture at the University of Pittsburgh. She is particularly interested in the impact of British colonialism on the built environment of modern South Asia. She is the author of *Building Histories: The Archival and Affective Lives of Five Monuments in Modern Delhi* (2017) and co-editor of *Colonial Frames, Nationalist Histories: Imperial Legacies, Architecture, and Modernity* (2012).

Charles M. Ramsey teaches at Baylor University. Prior to joining Baylor, he was Assistant Professor of Religion and Public Policy at Forman Christian College in Lahore, Pakistan. He has co-translated and annotated *Sir Sayyid's Commentary of the Gospel: Tabyīn al-kalām, Part 3* (2017), co-edited *South Asian Sufis: Devotion, Deviation, and Destiny* (2014), and has authored several articles on Sayyid Ahmad Khan.

Yasmin Saikia is Professor of History and holds the endowed Hardt-Nickachos Chair in Peace Studies at Arizona State University. Her book *Fragmented Memories: Struggling to Be Tai-Ahom in Assam* won the Srikanta Datta best book prize from the Nehru Memorial Museum and Library, New Delhi, in 2005, and her book *Women, War and the Making of Bangladesh: Remembering 1971* won the Oral History Association Biennial Book Award in 2013 in the US. She also co-edited *Northeast India: A Place of Relations* for Cambridge University Press in 2016. Her research and teaching interests are multidisciplinary, including peace studies, cultural and intellectual history, religious history with a focus on Muslim South Asia, gender and violence, and memory and identity.

Mohammad Sajjad is Professor at the Center for Advanced Study in History, Aligarh Muslim University. He is the author of *Muslim Politics in Bihar: Changing Contours* (2014), *Contesting Colonialism and Separatism: Muslims of Muzaffarpur since 1857* (2014) and several scholarly articles. He is a regular contributor to several print and digital media platforms.

Mohammad Asim Siddiqui is Professor of English at Aligarh Muslim University. His areas of interest include literary theory, particularly structuralism and feminism, Indian and Pakistani writing in English, and Cultural Studies. He is the co-author of *Jahan-e-Syed* (2017), a photographic and historical overview of Sayyid Ahmad Khan's life and work. Siddiqui's popular and scholarly articles have appeared in *The Guardian, Asiatic, Social Scientist, Third Frame: Literature, Culture and Society, Journal of English Language and Literature, The Indian Express* and *The Hindu*. He was a Fulbright Fellow at New York University in 2007.

Acknowledgements

The *Cambridge Companion* on Sayyid Ahmad Khan or *Sir Sayyid/Syed* germinated in a conversation with Qudsiya Ahmed, Editor, Cambridge University Press, India, in 2016. We are deeply thankful to her for her sustained encouragement to make this book a reality. The responsibility to write about Sir Sayyid was a daunting task for both of us. Sir Sayyid is the most brilliant and unusual reformer of India who was perhaps the first to adopt the method of non-violence for transforming the lives of millions through education, not for the purposes of politics or power but for self-improvement. To tell this story needed more than an account of his recorded accomplishments. It was necessary for us to engage with the deep sentiments and reverence of the people who associate with the Aligarh Movement that Sir Sayyid spearheaded. More than a hundred years since Sir Sayyid has passed away, even today he inspires and shapes the lives and worldviews of hundreds and thousands of individuals across generations. Taking cue from this spirit, we approached numerous friends and colleagues to present their research at a daylong 'pre-conference' at the annual meeting of South Asia conference held in Madison, Wisconsin, in October 2016. We would like to thank South Asian Muslim Studies Association (SAMSA) under whose auspices this meeting was convened. We would like to expresses our deepest thanks to David Lelyveld for many discussions on Aligarh and Sir Sayyid and for contributing a chapter. For their contributions to this volume and for making it a worthwhile task, we are grateful to Gail Minault, Frances Pritchett, Mirza Asmer Beg, Mohammad Sajjad, Asim Siddiqui, Mrinalini Rajagopalan, Amber Abbas, Carimo Mohomed, Sarah Qidwai, and Charles Ramsey. We want to express a special thank you to Roger D. Long for his support, encouragement, and assistance in hosting the pre-conference on Sir Sayyid in Madison. Irfan Omar and Ruqayya Khan helped us by engaging in multiple formal and informal conversations on Sir Sayyid.

We thank Qudsiya Ahmed and her colleagues at Cambridge University Press for their amazing team work that helped us to move this book forward in a timely manner. Aniruddha De, in particular, was exceptional. His never failing timely response to our emails, prompt work, and careful reading and rereading of the text made the chapters stronger and better. The continuous support and earnest dedication of all the staff members involved in the production of the book has resulted in this volume and we offer our special thanks to them. Roohi Narula, at Wake Forest University, helped us prepare the 'timeline' on

Sir Sayyid included in this book. Faisal Saleem and Asim Siddiqui procured the pictures with copyright permission from Aligarh Muslim University (AMU) for the book. We are very grateful to all of them.

There are several others from AMU who provided support at different stages of the project. In particular, we thank Naved Masood for his continuous guidance and feedback, Rahat Abrar for providing us some last minute information, and Tariq Mansoor, the current Vice Chancellor of AMU, for offering assistance in preparing the book. For making available their resources, we are in debt of the staff of Maulana Azad Library, Sir Syed House, Sir Syed Archives, and the support staff of the AMU guest house for facilitating our visits to campus.

Raisur Rahman, not a formal Alig as he has never been officially affiliated with AMU, has always admired the welcoming environment of this iconic institution in facilitating his work over the past two decades. It is AMU's steadfast appeal as an institute of historical eminence and its impressive list of alumni that has guided him to work on the highly inspirational figure of Sir Sayyid. He would like to thank his friends and colleagues associated with AMU and at his home institution. Wake Forest University has provided him with a caring community and, during 2017–2018, awarded him with Reynolds research leave that enabled him to dedicate time to this book. For his education and academic pursuits, he is thankful to his parents, late Najma Bano and Azizur Rahman, his siblings, and his teachers in India and the United States. No words of thanks would be adequate for the unconditional support he has received from his wife Kulsum Zaidi and from their two children, Ayaan and Zoya, young readers aware of the fact that an author needs to focus on writing book have often kept themselves occupied for hours to allow him to work on this volume which they might read one day. The fact that this book will have quite a few pictures has made them excited to see it in print.

Yasmin Saikia, an 'old girl', has never lost her connection with AMU. Sir Sayyid was and continues to be the beacon that inspires her academic endeavors and gives meaning to her intellectual life. It is Sir Sayyid's education mission of empowering the vulnerable and the downtrodden that she embraced in becoming a teacher herself and it guides her scholarly work and outlook. Her deepest gratitude is to her AMU teachers, Abdullah Hall seniors, friends and staff, and the AMU alumni network in the United States who constitute her 'Aligarh family.' She thanks Arizona State University for supporting her research, writing and travel to India. Chad Haines, her partner and husband, has been the most dependable source of support and his willing adoption into the AMU family has provided a seamless continuity to be in the United States and in Aligarh without a gap. Yasmin's sister, Shabnam Ahmed, also an 'old girl', has been the keeper of Abdullah Hall memories and she thanks her for the many late night conversations about Aligarh, as if they had never left the place.

We dedicate this book to Aligs around the world and those who believe in the power of education in changing lives, in keeping with Sir Sayyid's lifelong mission.

Yasmin Saikia
Paradise Valley, AZ
USA

M. Raisur Rahman
Winston-Salem, NC
USA

September 2018

A Note on Spellings and Transliteration

Our contributors belong to varied disciplinary backgrounds and follow different conventions of spellings and transliteration based on their own respective fields. As the editors, we decided to honor individual disciplinary preference over a universal and uniform style of transliteration of Urdu words and terms. In some of the chapters diacritical marks are evident, while others do have them. While being respectful to those who have chosen to follow their preferred conventions, we have ensured that there is uniformity of spellings and style across the rest of the chapters. When applicable, we have used '-e' over '-e-' or '-i-' as a connector, such as *Musalman-e Hind*; '-ul' or '-us' over '-ul-' or 'us-' or 'ul-' such as *Viqar-ul Mulk* or *Asar-us Sanadid*. We have chosen to avoid using diacritics in cases where the authors have not opted them in.

For spellings, we have used the Indian/South Asian conventions such as *Jamaluddin al-Afghani* over *Jamal al-Din al-Afghani*. However, when it comes to spelling *Sayyid*, which is spelled in different ways such as *Syed* or *Saiyid*, we settled on *Sayyid* after a careful deliberation and consultation with our valuable colleagues. *Sayyid* is the spelling used in the book title and consistently throughout the book, unless it is part of a book title or a quotation. Similarly, we have used *Muhammad* over other renditions of its spellings and *Ahmad* over *Ahmed*.

For any discrepancies and errors, we remain responsible.

Yasmin Saikia   **M. Raisur Rahman**

Chronology of Sayyid Ahmad Khan

1817	Born in Delhi, 17 October, to Sayyid Muhammad Muttaqi and Aziz-un Nisa.
1828	Death of Khawaja Fariduddin, maternal grandfather and *wazir* in the court of Emperor Akbar II, who played an important role in Sayyid Ahmad's early education.
1836	Marries Parsa Begum Mubarak.
1837	Starts *Sayyid-ul Akhbar*, Urdu weekly newspaper.
1838	Death of father, Sayyid Muhammad Muttaqi.
1839	Appointed as *naib munshi* at Agra in February.
1841	Appointed as *munsif* at Manipuri, December 24.
1842	Receives the title of *Jawad-ud Daula Arif Jung* from the Mughal court. Completes *Jila-ul Qulub bi Zikr il Mahbub*, a book dealing with the religious and cultural components of Islam.
1844	Completes *Tuhfa-e Hasan* and *Tashil fi jar-e Saqil*, books on the cultural component of Islam.
1847	The first edition of *Asar-us Sanadid* (The Remnants of Ancient Heroes) is released.
1849	Completes *Kalamat-ul Haqq*. First son, Sayyid Hamid, is born.
1850	Completes *Risala Sunnat dar radi bid`at*. Second son, Sayyid Mahmood, is born.
1852	Completes *Namiqa dar bayan masla tasawwur-e Shaikh* and *Silsilat-ul Mulk* (Chain of Kings).
1854	Second edition of *Asar-us Sanadid* appears, showing a remarkable change in Khan's style and narrative.
1855	Appointed permanent *sadr amin* at Bijnor, 13 January. Edits *Ain-e Akbari* (The Constitution of Akbar), a document recording the administration of Akbar's empire.
1857	Revolt breaks out, 10 May. Mother, Aziz-un Nisa, passes away.
1858	Appointed *Sadr-us Sadur* in Moradabad in April. Publishes *Tarikh-e Sarkashi-e Bijnor*, a history of the Bijnor revolution.
1859	Publishes *Asbab-e Baghawat-e Hind*, or *The Causes of the Indian Revolt*. Establishes a madrasa at Moradabad.
1860	Publishes *Loyal Muhammadans of India*. Conducts relief work for famine in North West Frontier Provinces.

1861	French translation of *Asar-us Sanadid* by Garcin de Tassy is released. Death of his wife, Begum Mubarak.
1862	Transferred to Ghazipur. Edits *Tarikh-e Firoz Shahi*, a history of Firoz Shah, the fourteenth-century ruler of the Tughlaq dynasty.
1863	Publishes a pamphlet on education.
1864	Elected an Honorary Member of the Royal Asiatic Society of Great Britain, 4 July. Lays the foundation of a madrasa at Ghazipur, but transfers it to Aligarh.
1865	30 December, sends a memorandum to the Government about the intention to establish the Scientific Society for publishing books on agriculture.
1866	Starts the *Aligarh Gazette*, previously known as *Scientific Society Magazine*.
1867	Sends a memorandum to the Viceroy for establishment of a vernacular university, 1 August. Starts homeopathic dispensary and hospital at Banaras, 25 September.
1869	Leaves Banaras for England, 1 April. Receives the insignia of Companions of the Order of the Star of India (C.S.I.), 6 August.
1870	Leaves London for Bombay, 6 September. Starts writing *Tahzib-ul Akhlaq*, a periodical aimed at socially and morally reforming the Muslims of the subcontinent, 24 December. Establishes the Committee for the Better Diffusion and Advancement of Learning among Muslims of India, 26 December.
1873	Presents a scheme for establishing a college in February.
1875	Inauguration of the Muhammadan Anglo Oriental College, 24 May. Regular teachings starts, 1 June.
1876	Retires from service. Starts writing commentary on the Qur'an.
1878	Nominated member of the Viceroy's Legislative Council.
1883	The Muhammadan Civil Service Fund Association is founded. Muhammadan Association Aligarh is established.
1886	Muhammadan Educational Conference is established.
1887	Nominated as a member of the Civil Service Commission by Lord Dufferin.
1888	Establishes the Patriotic Association at Aligarh. Receives Knight Commander of the Order of the Star of India (K.C.S.I.).
1889	Receives the degree of LL.D *honoris causa* from Edinburgh.
1898	Dies at Aligarh, 27 March, at the age of eighty.

Introduction

YASMIN SAIKIA AND M. RAISUR RAHMAN

Sitting high above ground in a basket suspended between two scaffolds parallel to the enormous Qutb Minar, Sayyid Ahmad Khan (1817–1898), a young *munshi* (clerk) of the English East India Company, read and tried to reproduce the indecipherable inscriptions on the tower in his book *Asar-us Sanadid* (*Traces of Noblemen*, also called *Great Monuments of Delhi*).[1] The determination, courage, and resourcefulness demonstrated here were the hallmarks of Sayyid Ahmad's life, which was full of formidable challenges. With his imaginativeness and a keen sense of history, along with his conviction that evidence of progress is within the Muslim community, Sayyid Ahmad embarked on a progressive vision for Muslim community development in British India. His rationalist approach combined with an ethical outlook and passion transformed the lives of Muslims in India and abroad forever.

Sayyid Ahmad was born on 17 October 1817 in Mughal Delhi. He belonged to an aristocratic Muslim family who traced their genealogical roots to Prophet Muhammad.[2] In 1864, Sayyid Ahmad moved to Aligarh – a small town, approximately 100 miles southeast of the capital city – where he spent the rest of his life. In Indian nationalist historiography, Sayyid Ahmad appears, at times, as a promoter of Hindu–Muslim unity in his early years – to him, Hindus and Muslims were 'the two eyes of the beautiful bride that is Hindustan'. By contrast, Pakistani historiography remembers him as the architect of the two-nation theory, which eventually led to the creation of Pakistan. It is strange to attribute to him a historic event not anticipated during his time: he passed away in 1898 – forty-two years before the Muslim League raised the demand for the creation of Pakistan. Regardless of this contrasting retelling of history (one from India and the

---

[1] Altaf Husain Hali, *Hayat-e Javed*, trans. David J. Matthews (Delhi: Rupa & Co., 1994), p. 51.
[2] George Farquhar Irving Graham, *The Life and Work of Syed Ahmed Khan* (Calcutta: Thacker, Spink & Co., 1909).

other from Pakistan), Sayyid Ahmad can be considered a true historical marker for Muslims in South Asia. Even today, he remains the unchallenged champion of Muslim modernization and community reform. Throughout his lifetime, Sayyid Ahmad envisaged a modern Muslim society by making efforts to promote modern Western education, scientific knowledge, rational thinking, religious pluralism, political accommodation, and participatory community associations founded on ethics and justice. The history he made holds Muslims to a public memory that remains inspirational even today. His thoughts and actions motivated a rational, scientific, and reformed outlook that considerably shaped the concept of *Musalman-e Hind*, the Indian Muslim.

Sayyid Ahmad was a multifaceted personality: he was a historian, ethicist, arbitrator and diplomat, administrator, advocate, writer, religious and scientific scholar, community organizer, and, most importantly, passionate educationist. His intense passion for a modern Muslim community led to the idea of secular education – a project he began in 1857 and continued until he died in 1898. Sayyid Ahmad had many new ideas for holistically improving the education and thus the lives of Muslims in India. The Muslims did not readily accept some of these ideas because they were not only novel but also controversial for the community. As a firm believer in consensus building through dialogue and discussion and by working at various capacities with his peers, Sayyid Ahmad established a path for Muslim reformation in India.

Although a believer in the Hindustani identity, Sayyid Ahmad did not think of cultural systems as fixed entities. For him, religion was only a set of beliefs, not an institution for political conflict, and using religion for political gain would have been bigotry. Because of his rational approach to find answers to everything with studied evidence, he would never accept such a narrow position. Since he believed that Hindus and Muslims were from the same cultural world – of and from Hindustan – the cultural and social wellbeing of Hindustan was a primary concern to him. In this scope of thinking, he included the British in Hindustan, whom he did not see as foreigners, but as representatives of another cultural system with much potential to contribute to India's advancement. Through this catholic approach to the different religious communities, Sayyid Ahmad could appreciate the transcendence of God beyond religion. He saw that religions were pathways, and the final truth was with God alone. Acknowledging the validity of the different worship systems of religions, he elaborated on this concept in his dispatches during his voyage to England in 1869: he wrote,

I saw the way God was prayed to.... Some men bow down to idols; others address Him seated on chairs, with heads uncovered; some worship Him with head covered and beads on, with hands clasped in profound respect; many abuse Him, but He cares nought for this. He is indeed the only one who is possessed of the attribute of catholicity.[3]

He remained open to this way of thinking about religion as journeys to the indivisible God until his last breath. According to him, a society reflecting the aforementioned understanding should represent a degree of heterogeneity. Hindustan, the land of multiple religious practices, enabled this type of composite society. This was an idea he instilled in his new educational institution, the Muhammadan Anglo-Oriental (MAO) College, founded in 1877.[4] The first graduate of MAO College, Ishwari Prasad, was a Hindu, who became an eminent historian.

The decade of the 1850s had a catalytic effect on Sayyid Ahmad. This decade included the last few years of the existence as well as the end of the mighty Mughal Empire. Following in the footsteps of many of his contemporaries of the *ashraf* (high born) background, Sayyid Ahmad mourned the decline of the Mughal Empire. The emperor's subjects could no longer ignore the imminent socioeconomic losses. For them, the present suddenly seemed like a dark cloud looming over the Indian sky; there was nothing but gloom. Sayyid Ahmad – whose ancestors were endowed by the Mughal rulers with land grants, titles, and honours – now began to reconsider the continuation of these privileges. Nevertheless, his elevated social standing equipped him with such capacity that he could face multiple challenges. He took advantage of his network with the elite, the educated, and the wealthy, while simultaneously reconciling with the loss of the Mughal royal power and possible resultant decline of the Muslim gentry. The Indian Rebellion of 1857 and the attack on his home in Delhi enforced this awareness further. His deep connection with the Mughal ruling power led to the qualms about leaving the Mughal world in Delhi for pursuing service and excellence under the Company Raj. However, unlike many others who were unable to think beyond the conflicting moment of the past

---

[3] Graham, *Life and Work*, p. 84.
[4] The Muhammadan Anglo-Oriental School founded in 1875 became a college by the same name in 1877 and in 1920 became Aligarh Muslim University.

and the present, Sayyid Ahmad leaped forward and carved out a new space for himself and his community. For this, he put his education to good use. He was trained in Urdu, Persian, Arabic, mathematics, astronomy, as well as religious subjects, such as Islamic jurisprudence, and had imbibed the courtly traditions of courtesy and diplomacy. Thus, to do away with the cloud of distrust and pave a path of good relationship between the Indian Muslims and their newly emerging English rulers, he decided to mediate on behalf of his *qaum*.

Sayyid Ahmad did not concentrate on saving the Mughals because he understood that British power was on the rise. The British brought a transformed political context, along with new utilitarian political dispensation of jobs and career advancement, all of which had replaced the old Mughal nobility. Sayyid Ahmad was an excellent representative for his social class of Mughal gentry – a composite community. He understood the need of investing in comprehending what made the British superior to the Mughals and then teaching his own community how to develop such qualities in order to be successful themselves. He began acting on this understanding at a personal level. He joined the service of the English East India Company in 1837, starting as a *munshi* and then rose to the rank of a subordinate judge (*sadr amin*), the office beyond which Indian natives were not promoted until 1860, when Indians were employed at the civil service ranks for the first time. Reaching the peak position in the hierarchy of an Indian's employment in the English East India Company service at the time, Sayyid Ahmad potentially developed an organic solidarity with the British, owing to his close association with them, such as that shown by Raja Ram Mohan Roy (1772–1833).

Two incidents that occurred in the 1850s, in addition to the experience of working for and with the British, had a lasting impact on Sayyid Ahmad's mind, resulting in his subsequent actions. After he finished reading an illustrated, scholarly edition of *Ain-e Akbari* – a highly informative Mughal text written by Abul Fazal, the court historian of Emperor Akbar (1556–1605), which is considered the 'Constitution of Akbar', detailing his administrative system – Sayyid Ahmad undertook the laborious task of translating the text to Urdu. On completion, he requested his friend, the acclaimed poet Mirza Ghalib (1797–1869) to write a foreword (*taqriz*) for this translated version. Ghalib agreed but provided the *taqriz* as a Persian poem castigating the imperial Mughals for their inability to rule. Furthermore, he chastised Sayyid Ahmad for not reading the winds of change, advising him to learn from the British who had surpassed their oriental counterparts in every field: 'What is the point of celebrating Akbar's rule at a time when the constitution of the modern world is being written in Calcutta (capital of British India)?' Taking this message to heart, Sayyid Ahmad finally realized the absence of something fundamental in the Muslim mind, which needed immediate attention and correction for his community to survive. Although he continued pursuing his interests in historical texts and wrote *Asar-us Sanadid*, detailing the ruinous monuments of Delhi, he decided to focus on understanding the British rulers and identifying their scientific and technological development skills, which helped them establish an empire in India. Moreover, within India, the Hindus and other non-Muslim communities had adopted English education and advanced into government and civil services, but his *qaum* remained uninitiated into modern education: they did not engage with the British, and based on superficial knowledge, concluded that modern Western education would result in the loss of their religion and Christianization. They were afraid and confused in their ignorance. The need for progress and awareness regarding the present changes in scientific knowledge and modern education became his mission, which he embarked on immediately after the 1857 rebellion.

The 1857 rebellion and its failure had significantly affected the north Indian Muslims. The British believed that the Muslims were the main conspirators of the rebellion, who tried to overthrow them; brutal punishments followed. The last Mughal emperor, Bahadur Shah Zafar II, was exiled to Rangoon (Yangon) and the British ensured the demise of the Mughal dynasty; the crown prince along with several other members of the royal family were executed. There were no Mughal heirs to the throne of Delhi. Indeed, the bloody end of the Mughal Empire by a mere foreign commercial company was as bizarre as it was cruel. Sayyid Ahmad, who was an employee of the Company, realized that the Muslims had to endure this pain until they moved ahead by learning the ways of the British, speaking their language, and engaging the subtleties of their thinking; for all this, English education was a must.

He felt that the British also needed to learn and appreciate their Indian Muslim subjects. To make sense of this necessity, he wrote an account of the rebellion, called *Tarikh-e Sarkashi-e Bijnor* (*The History of the Bijnor Rebellion*), which was based on his personal experiences as a sub-judicial officer, and his rationality as a historian found expression in another study called the *Asbab-e Baghawat-e Hind* (*The Causes of the Indian Revolt*). In both the aforementioned pieces, Sayyid Ahmad indicated the need for the British to learn about the Indian culture and people. Although he expressed solidarity with the British, he implored them to not mythologize the

Muslims as rebels but deepen their relationship with their Indian subjects through good governance and by including Indians, particularly the educated Muslims, in local governance because they were skilled at understanding the issues and problems of the people on the ground.

Sayyid Ahmad readily cooperated with the British; to emphasize his point, he published another pamphlet in 1860, called *The Loyal Muhammadans of India*, wherein he presented his case on behalf of the Muslims, who were considerably confused and prejudiced because of little contact with their rulers. Thus, he expressed regret that his *qaum* was misguided. Distancing himself from the participants of the rebellion, he cited examples of numerous Muslims, including his own sons, who served British interests and were favourably disposed to the British government. He regretted that the Muslims who sincerely performed their services remained mostly unacknowledged, while those Muslims involved in the rebellion and comprising just a small minority were flagrantly visible in the British eyes. With little evidence, the British had painted an entire community with a broad stroke and heaped on the epithet 'rebel', he complained in his writings publicly. For Muslims, he had another message, urging them to overcome their emotional reactions, discipline their responses even if they were discriminated, and enter into reasonable discussion with the British for improving their condition. He believed that the Muslims had to accept the British dominance and work with them towards resolving their own deprived status.

Although the proactive positioning of the Muslims as loyal and good subjects abated the immediate problem for a short while, it could not cure the down-sliding backwardness of the Muslims. Who would be the patrons of the Muslims and pull them out of their moribund condition, he wondered. No one seemed willing to save the Muslims. After writing the treatises on the rebellion and clearing the Muslims of their alleged involvement in the diabolical design to oust the British, he rationally concluded that only through education and social reform could his community elevate to a position based on their own work and thus benefit the entire Indian community. To resolve the problem faced by the Muslims, Sayyid Ahmad encouraged the formation of voluntary associations, scientific societies, and educational bodies because he believed these organizations were the best avenues not only for shaping policy but also for learning to work with others (even those who have conflicting opinions). He realized that the Muslims needed to eradicate their mental, psychological, and cultural blocks against the British. By implementing educational advancement and founding the

MAO College based on the principle of volunteer work, 'an effective instance of reform from below'[5] could be established.

Sayyid Ahmad became a firm advocate of increasing Indian involvement in government and civil services, much like his contemporaries, the early nationalists such as Surendranath Banerjee (1848–1925) and Dadabhai Naoroji (1825–1917). Believing that change affected through diverse layers of government, wherein legislative, judicial, educational, commercial, and voluntary organizations combined and functioned at varied capacities, to be the best way to reach consensus on problems and search for solutions, he supported the nationalists' appeals for enhanced Indian involvement in the management of Indian administration.

Eventually, through his rational and studied approach towards resolving problems, Sayyid Ahmad won the trust of the British. The British recognized him as an ally. He was nominated to the Viceroy's Executive Council in 1878. Ten years later, in 1888, when he received the Knight Commander of the Order of Star of India (KCSI), Sayyid Ahmad Taqvi bin Sayyid Muhammad Mutaqqi became Sir Sayyid Ahmad Khan. Since then, all those in South Asia whose lives Sayyid Ahmad touched or continues to shape refer to him as *Sir Sayyid* or *Sir Syed* – a term denoting respect, honour, and endearment simultaneously. For an Alig (an alumnus of Aligarh Muslim University [AMU], a university that spawned from the MAO College), it is sacrilegious to call him simply Sayyid Ahmad or Sayyid Ahmad Khan – names we have used throughout the book, privileging academic treatment over emotional register, but with due respect to such sentiments. Herein, some authors have also used *Sir Sayyid*, as it is customary among the scholars studying the Aligarh Movement and South Asian Islam.

Many of Sayyid Ahmad's Muslim contemporaries considered his attachment and loyalty to the British as a problem, not an asset. During the establishment of the MAO College, he had faced stiff opposition from a large section of the Muslim community, which was not in favour of modern English education. Consequently, he appealed to his critics to reflect on the changes in the world of scientific knowledge and education and consider these seemingly foreign factors with a peaceful and reasoned discourse. However, refusing to accept his persuasive reasons, his peers acquired a *fatwa* from Mecca declaring him a *kafir* (infidel). Undeterred by this, in 1864, he established the Aligarh Scientific Society for promoting scientific

---

[5] Sheila McDonough, *Muslim Ethics and Modernity: A Comparative Study of the Ethical Thought of Sayyid Ahmad Khan and Mawlana Mawdudi* (Waterloo, Canada: Canadian Corporation for Studies in Religion, 1984).

and technological knowledge by making English scientific books available in the vernacular. In *Tafsir-ul Qur'an* (Qur'anic exegesis), published in a series over 1880–1904, he adopted a rational outlook towards understanding the Qur'an. While touching upon many topics, his main thrust in the *Tafsir* was to show the compatibility of the Qur'an and the new arts and sciences. He continued to promote Western science and technology, thus inviting the wrath of the orthodox clergy who derogatorily labelled him a *naicari*, who intended to corrupt Muslim minds and turn them agnostic.

Other non-Muslim Indians considered him a turncoat who had abandoned his pursuit for Hindu–Muslim unity and joined communitarian politics to pursue his interests of improving the Muslim condition and increasing his proximity to the British. He disapproved the pan-Indian nationalist organization Indian National Congress (INC), founded in 1885; this was considered an anti-Indian move. Several sources, including Jawaharlal Nehru and W. C. Smith, defended Sayyid Ahmad, suggesting that he opposed INC because of its aggressive anti-British tenor. Sayyid Ahmad believed in the politics of justice and participatory association of equals. How could the uneducated Muslims irk the British, the dominant force in India, he asked. It took him nearly two decades to win the trust and assistance of the British for establishing the MAO College. He was convinced that first the Muslims needed to equip themselves with knowledge and training for addressing the real problems affecting them. For this, he knew that political organizations or loyalty to a single body was not the solution because affinity groups, such as INC where everyone had the same ideas was not going to be a problem-solving association. Different from the latter-day politics of Muhammad Ali Jinnah (1876–1948), who viewed the INC as a predominantly Hindu organization, Sayyid Ahmad did not even consider the Hindu–Muslim question; he rather approached the Hindus to assist him and oppose INC politics by founding the United Indian Patriotic Organization in 1888. His opinion regarding the INC was similar to that of the Maharaja of Banaras. Unfortunately, in 1893, he renamed United Indian Patriotic Organization as Muhammadan Defence Association, thus making his contemporaries misjudge his interests.

For Sayyid Ahmad, the Indian Muslims were part of the national and international cultural mainstream. During the Hindi–Urdu language controversy, he sided with his own Urdu-speaking community. Did this make Sayyid Ahmad someone who solely privileged Urdu-speaking community? To answer this question, we must first understand his lifelong commitment to Urdu language and literature, just as we need to understand the nuanced position that Mahatma Gandhi (1869–1948) undertook over the language question. Although he prioritized Muslim interest, Sayyid Ahmad did not envision it to be antithetical to Hindustani or Hindu interest, as evidenced by his position on the Hindi–Urdu controversy. He argued that Urdu and Hindi were actually the same language. Moreover, Urdu being the *lingua franca* of India deserved government support. Nevertheless, he did not promote Urdu in exclusivity of Hindi by opining that good and accessible Urdu should not be Arabized or Persianized. Although Urdu had become a dynamic and useful language through his publications and writings, he never attempted to make it a language confined to the Muslims alone.

His journey to London in 1869 deepened his conviction regarding his work for the betterment of the Muslims, as penned in his travelogue *Musafiran-e Landan*. He believed that travelling widened one's understanding and interaction with different people, enabling exchange and learning. Deeply touched by the civility and education of the British men and women he met during his stay in London, he began encouraging Indians to emulate their learning for improving their conduct and lives. He was awestruck by the scientific temperament evident in the metropolis. His trip to London led to his own self-discovery; he implemented what he learned in the vision of his college.

He founded the MAO College as a residential university, as per the Oxbridge system. At the MAO College, students and teachers from varied backgrounds lived together, which he believed would foster community feelings and friendships emerging from this association would better and further dignify the Indian community. On 8 January 1877, Lord Lytton, the Viceroy of India, laid the foundation stone of the college. With British aid, Sayyid Ahmad put the small town of Aligarh on the map of India. From the beginning the college had an inclusive outlook. In 1880 there were seven Hindu students and eight Muslim students and in 1881 an equal number of eight Hindu and eight Muslim students. The pattern remained uniform in the subsequent years. In fact, in 1885 and 1887 there were more Hindu students than Muslim students enrolled in the college. Only in 1888 did the number of Muslim students increase to thirty-nine while Hindu students remained steady at thirty. The same can be said about the staff of the college. In 1886, the school had four Hindu teachers of the total six teachers and in 1894 there were two Hindu teachers out of seven Indian teachers.[6] Two of his friends and compatriots, Nawab Viqar-ul Mulk (1841–1917) and

---

[6] Shan Muhammad, *Sir Syed Ahmad Khan: A Political Biography* (Meerut: Meenakshi Prakashan, 1969), p. 235.

Mohsin-ul Mulk (1837–1907), along with many donors, patrons, parents, and students from different communities, be it Hindu, Muslim, or Sikh, assisted him in realizing his dream of imparting modern education. The MAO College was not a mere educational institution, it opened windows of social and cultural opportunities for its students. Initially, the MAO College was an institution that served upper class and upper-caste men. The Nawabs' and landlords' sons were easily admitted and accommodated. However, we must understand that even Cambridge University, on which Sayyid Ahmad planned to model his institution, was completely elitist in this era. The MAO College was also a product of its time. Nevertheless, the college did become more open, diverse, and inclusive with time. With the expansion of the student body, the MAO College transformed itself into a plural community, wherein all were imparted education in the liberal arts and sciences.

Sayyid Ahmad's fundraising efforts also reflect the plural character of the institution. Examples of such efforts included investing of personal funds, appearing publicly as a beggar to collect money, and agreeing to dance at the state fair to raise money; these and other such anecdotes are recounted even today. Through these efforts, he enlisted the support of many British donors, such as Lord Northbrook, the Viceroy of India, who donated 10,000 rupees, which then was quite a sizeable amount. For his cause, Sayyid Ahmad also reached out to not only his lay supporters but also the princely rulers. Collectively, these efforts allowed him to enforce a new network of Indian supporters. Numerous Hindu donors, including the Maharajas of Banaras, Patiala, and Vizianagaram, also joined his cause. At the time of Sayyid Ahmad's death in 1898, the college had 285 Muslim and 64 Hindu students. After a campaign to convert it into a university, the MAO College became AMU after an act passed by the Government of India in 1920. AMU serves as a catalyst or model for similar developments across South Asia. The Aligarh Movement for the sociocultural and political regeneration of the Muslims originated in and spread out from this institution.

During Sayyid Ahmad's lifetime, there was an uproar regarding the moral decay and degeneration of the Muslim society, similar to that seen currently. Addressing these issues openly and rationally, Sayyid Ahmad hoped to improve the social conditions of his fellow Muslims. Through the *Scientific Society Magazine* and *Tahzib-ul Akhlaq (Muhammadan Social Reformer)*, he began discussing the problems that the rapidly changing Muslim community was encountering, such as polygamy, religious fanaticism, and hypocrisy – all of which he condemned. He urged people to emulate culturally advanced nations and select the good, but reject the undesirable. Through *Tahzib-ul Akhlaq*, he sought total Muslim reformation – by not only imparting lessons on table manners and public behaviour but also advocating balanced religion and human progress. For him, religion was about love and service to humanity, not a hurdle to progress.

His passion for scientificity and a rational understanding of the biological world inspired him to engage in interfaith dialogue. In his *Tabyin-ul Kalam* (Commentary on the Bible), he attempted a comparative study of religions; by contrast, in *Tafsir-ul Qur'an*, he offered new interpretations of the Qur'an considering the contemporary changes and realities. The orthodox elements of the Muslim community resented all these publications. Those who disagreed with him called him an 'atheist', 'agnostic', *kafir*, and even *dajjal* ('false messiah' or 'the antichrist' in Islamic eschatology). Despite these assaults, Sayyid Ahmad remained steadfast and resolute, while continuing his work for what he believed to be in his people's best interest. Explaining and summarizing his deeds, speeches, and writings of religious and secular nature that helped articulate his ideals, dreams, and vision in this limited space is difficult.

Sayyid Ahmad wrote a commentary on the Bible reflecting his approach towards religious and scriptural pluralism. This attempt at comparatively studying religions in India was the first of its kind in the nineteenth century, as K. A. Nizami has indicated.[7] He also credits Sayyid Ahmad for having laid the foundation of a new *ilm-ul kalam* (scholasticism). In a recent essay,[8] Charles M. Ramsey argues that Sayyid Ahmad rejected dispensational supersession, which is the notion that a legislative prophet's authority supplants an earlier authority. That is, all prophets appearing in different places and periods originated from the same source. In *Tabyin-ul Kalam*, Sayyid Ahmad also considered the authenticity of Psalms, Pentateuch, gospels, and other Christian religious texts.

Sayyid Ahmad combined engaging with other religious faiths with his conviction to liberate religion of superstitions, particularly those hindering progressive thinking. Much like Raja Ram Mohan Roy, he considered miracles a deviation from factual reality and believed in the reconciliation of science, technology, and religion. He also attempted to find common ground

[7] Khaliq A. Nizami, *Sayyid Ahmad Khan* (Delhi: Publications Division, Ministry of Information and Broadcasting, Government of India), pp. 120–1.
[8] Charles M. Ramsey, 'Sir Sayyid and the Religious Foundations for a Pluralist Society', in *Sir Syed Ahmad Khan: Muslim Renaissance Man of India – A Bicentenary Commemorative Volume*, edited by A. R. Kidwai, pp. 288–307 (Delhi: Viva Books, 2017).

between 'modern science' and religion. Although he accepted Darwinism, he established a well-considered approach outlining its continuity with previous Islamic theories of development. He compared his position to the theory of evolution by natural selection. Similarly, he emphasized reason as his guiding principle; this explains his distrust of miracles and angelology, without refuting revelation. Thus, Sayyid Ahmad's approach towards religion aimed at finding common ground between religions, without unsettling long-held beliefs and simultaneously challenging discrepancies, despite reason and rationalism.

K. A. Nizami opined that Sayyid Ahmad's approach towards social reform was twofold: persuading people to abandon their old habits and customs, which impeded their social advancement, and encouraging them to take up the new scientific and rational approach. G. F. I. Graham, Sayyid Ahmad's biographer, included him among the foremost Muslims with a force of character, influence over his fellowmen, and literary ability. Theodore Beck, who was the first principal of the MAO College, was one of his greatest admirers.

In his *magnum opus* on the first generation of Aligarh students, historian David Lelyveld showed the multiple sides of Sayyid Ahmad and the institution he created.[9] Lelyveld demonstrated the intermediary nature of the college having picked up the best elements from the British and Muslim cultures to create something new for the community. The newly emerged curriculum favoured English education; nevertheless, Islamic theology remained a part of this educational programme. Together, they generated a consciousness that helped create and foster the 'Indian Muslim'. The game of cricket, *mushairah*s (poetic assemblies), the debating society, student union elections, and several other extracurricular activities inculcated public roles and political ambitions among its students. Its impact can be noted through the significant role of Aligs within and beyond India and South Asia. The legacy Sayyid Ahmad envisioned and established lives on.

A social reformer, educationist, institution-builder, politician, prolific writer, and religious thinker, Sayyid Ahmad was a tireless worker whose actions determined the fate of the millions of Indians. His MAO College served as a movement opening vistas for Indians; it improved their understanding of their role in the modern world through English education and, more practically, improved the socioeconomic condition

---

[9] David Lelyveld, *Aligarh's First Generation: Muslim Solidarity in British India* (Princeton: Princeton, University Press, 1978).

of his community. From its inception as the MAO College to its current form as AMU, Sayyid Ahmad's educational mission emerged as a beacon of hope for Muslims, women, other minority groups, and the less privileged. Sayyid Ahmad had inspired the idea of mediation for finding a balance between the community and the British in the colonial era; even now, in the postcolonial nation-state of India, AMU continues to teach Sir Sayyid's concept of pluralism and rationality. The *Musalman-e Hind* or 'Indian Muslim' community was born out of the particular historical backdrop of 1857 and Sayyid Ahmad's vision. The Indian Muslim is one who straddles Indianness and Muslimness without paradox, just as Sayyid Ahmad donned the black Western suit, sported a long, white flowing beard, and put on a *fez* cap – this imagery can alleviate the current environment of suspicion and hatred. For Sayyid Ahmad, the prognosis of the Indian Muslim is someone who is aware of the surrounding, takes ownership, maintains dignity, and is part of the plural society and evolves with changing times. This *Companion* is a small step to engage with this larger-than-life individual. His ideology and attendant historical transformations warrant wider attention than most scholarly and non-scholarly debates have paid. On *Sir Sayyid's* bicentenary birth celebrations, his ideas are far more relevant in the twenty-first century than ever before, to understand the Muslim question better – in India and globally.

Part I

Sayyid Ahmad Khan: The rise of a historical figure

1 Sir Sayyid on History

The Indian Rebellion of 1857 and Rethinking the 'Rebellious' Muslim Question

YASMIN SAIKIA

INTRODUCING SIR SAYYID

Sayyid Ahmad, in Pierre Bourdieu's term, was a 'collective individual' who cannot be encapsulated in a single narrative. We can view his extraordinary life through different lenses, but each lens will seem inadequate. A towering figure revered and held in high esteem by his contemporaries in the late nineteenth century because of his unparalleled Muslim reform work that he undertook singlehandedly; Sayyid Ahmad still looms large in the collective imaginaire of the South Asian Muslims. Postcolonial scholars such as Hafeez Malik, Shan Muhammad, Christian Troll, Aziz Ahmed, and Mushirul Hasan have written extensively on Sayyid Ahmad's reformist activities and accomplishments. Others such as Ayesha Jalal, Francis Robinson, and K. M. Ashraf find in his reformist agenda the source for latter-day Muslim political 'separatism' and 'communalism', germinating the idea of an exclusive Muslim identity, leading to the creation of Pakistan. By contrast, Ajay Sinha provides a completely different interpretation, qualifying Sayyid Ahmad as a 'forceful voice in the nationalist struggle against British colonial rule' and one of the earliest 'cosmopolitan' Indians.[1] Such a figure although he can be located in a time and a place is simultaneously beyond the fixed time and a place. He stands as his own evidence of a person who gave shape to a new history and was shaped by the historical structures and events of his time. He is 'history in person', in the terms of Holland and Lave, who continuously engaged with context and process creating pathways of new possibilities for self and others.[2] His story inspires us even today.

[1] Ajay Sinha, 'Response: Modernism in India: A Short History of a Blush', *The Art Bulletin* 90, no. 4 (2008): 561–8.
[2] Dorothy Holland and Jean Lave, *History in Person: Enduring Struggles, Contentious Practice, Intimate Identities* (Oxford: James Currey, 2001).

What would have the Indian Muslims been today without Sayyid Ahmad Khan? This question warrants some reflection, particularly concerning the present day representation of the Muslims as an obscurantist community involved in terrorism and in need of a new makeover.[3] In the late nineteenth century, Sayyid Ahmad Khan launched a community reform movement, which transformed the image of Muslims from violent and rebellious into that of a forward-looking community.[4] By using tools of the British masters – modernization and Western education – Sayyid Ahmad Khan paved a path for a new Muslim future in India. The failure of the 1857 rebellion had

---

[3] In current-day India, with a roughly 175 million Muslim population, only a small percentage qualifies as economically middle class. The Muslim communities are the poorest and most disadvantaged as the 'Sachar Committee Report' established in 2005. The Muslim condition was no better a hundred years ago, when Sayyid Ahmad Khan was alive. Rather than addressing and implementing programmes to improve the condition of the downtrodden Muslim, the effort is to represent Muslims as violent and pre-modern. At Jawaharlal Nehru University in Delhi, India, a new course on 'Islamic Terrorism' was approved for teaching about Muslim violence (see http://indianexpress.com/article/education/soon-at-jnu-study-on-islamic-terrorism, accessed on 19 May 2018). By contrast, the image of the obscurantist Muslim becomes a matter of public discussion as evidenced in the vociferous public and courtroom discussions for banning triple *talaq* (whereby Muslim men could divorce their wives by verbally announcing their intention to divorce three times). This practice was deemed a cruel gender-biased practice of Indian Muslims. Even Muslim food practices, such as eating beef is under attack. Animal slaughter or *halal* is viewed as 'barbaric' and efforts are underway to ban *halal* slaughter houses. The ban on *halal* and *kosher* meat is already effective in many European countries that follow the stunting method.

[4] Akeel Bilgrami considers that Muslims had experienced 'reformation' in the form of social movements for renewal (*tajdid*), such as the one led by Sayyid Ahmad. However, this was not really in the line of transformation like Western societies, which went through a thorough reformation supported by industrialization (see Akeel Bilgrami, 'Rushdie and the Reform of Islam', *Economic and Political Weekly* 25, no. 12 (1990): 605–8). In 'The Islamic Road to the Modern World', a review of *The Islamic Enlightenment: The Struggle Between Faith and Reason, 1798 to Modern Times* by Christopher de Bellaigue and *Freedom in the Arab World: Concepts and Ideologies in Arabic Thought in the Nineteenth Century* by Wael Abu-'Uksa, Malise Ruthven addresses the issue of Islamic reform and enlightenment beyond the Middle East in the nineteenth century (*New York Review of Books*, 22 June 2017, available at http://www.nybooks.com/contributors/malise-ruthven/, accessed on 14 June 2017).

galvanized him into action. The superior administrative and organizational skills of the British as well as their fighting power and modern technological tools, all of which enabled their success in 1857, convinced Sayyid Ahmad that military struggle against this mighty force was futile. The Muslim community needed to work differently, in cooperation with the British, for their positive transformation. This conviction compelled him to evaluate the value of both the British rule and Western education. The intensity of Sayyid Ahmad's thought for Muslim reform found expression in the development of a comprehensive plan generating new opportunities in advancing the Muslims. He introduced the Muslims to Western education within an Indian Muslim cultural environment. Sheila McDonough qualifies this as his 'acculturationist' approach, which immediately yielded positive results for the Muslims in the nineteenth century; its legacy continues even today.[5]

To achieve his Muslim reform goals, Sayyid Ahmad founded the Muhammadan-Anglo Oriental (MAO) School at Aligarh in 1875; it became the MAO College in 1877 and later became the foundation site for Aligarh Muslim University (AMU) in 1920. A hundred years later, AMU still stands as testimony to Sayyid Ahmad's dedicated work of improving Muslim community through modern education and social reform. His message of community development through education is accepted throughout South Asia.[6]

This chapter focuses on a single moment of history – the failed rebellion of 1857 – and Sayyid Ahmad's transformed outlook for building the Indian Muslim future thereafter. Sayyid Ahmad was convinced that the structure of British power was entrenched after the rebellion. The Indians, particularly the Muslims, were humiliated and marginalized, and the dethronement of the Mughal Emperor, Bahadur Shah Zafar II had finally ended the facile image of Muslim political power. For Sayyid Ahmad, this was not a time for mourning, but for establishing agency. Understanding that the chasms between the British and the Muslims needed to be overcome, he began taking a harder look at the recent Muslim history in India. The picture was

---

[5] Sheila McDonough, *Muslim Ethics and Modernity: A Comparative Study of the Ethical Thought of Sayyid Ahmad Khan and Mawlana Mawdudi* (Waterloo: Wilfrid Laurier University Press, 1984), p. 2.

[6] In India, Pakistan, Bangladesh, and even Afghanistan, one finds schools named after Sir Sayyid Ahmad Khan. *Sir Syed* is a brand name for secular, modern schools aimed at progressive and holistic education of Muslims, particularly for boys.

unflattering and the reality dismal – requiring incredible courage to even dream future possibilities. Acknowledging the recent events, creating a site for reconciliation between the British rulers and their Muslim subjects, and claiming Muslim agency for change became his priority.

His first gesture towards this was of welcoming the proclamation of Queen Victoria as the Empress of India in 1858. He commended the British for their success in establishing their authority in India. He followed this gesture by yet another gesture, which was, once again, conciliatory like the previous one; however, this time he was more passionate and penetrating in his analysis. By using the tool of writing (an instrument of his choice), he communicated to the British regarding their failure at establishing a representative, culturally sensitive government in India, claiming that this was the root cause for the 1857 rebellion. He urged the British to include Indians in the governance and decision-making institutions of the government, disguising it as an opportunity for improving the system as well as the relationship of the British rulers with their Indian subjects. This bold appeal and a trail-blazing request, asking the British to take Indians into their confidence for ruling India, preceded the petition of the Indian National Congress (INC) for representing Indians in local and municipal bodies by nearly three decades.

Keenly aware that the British–Muslim partnership required a semblance of respect, Sayyid Ahmad needed to represent the Muslims as a loyal, progressive, and capable community, not as *jihadi* and 'rebellious' conspirators (as the British colonial masters typified them). Sayyid Ahmad devoted his energy, time, and money to achieve this outcome. In Derridian terms, Sayyid Ahmad offered 'a new horizon' of possibilities and transformed the Indian Muslim future. In his narrative of the 1857 rebellion, Sayyid Ahmad's summarizes politics, personal sacrifice, courage, and dreams – in short, embodiment and expression of hope – of the Indian Muslims.

The current chapter focuses on the writings of Sayyid Ahmad on the 1857 rebellion, which inspired the Muslims to participate in their own development, reconstruct a positive community image, and assume agency in transformation.

SOURCES OF TRADITION AND HISTORY-TO-BE

Sayyid Ahmad used a novel approach for Muslim reform. By using the cumulative tradition of ethical Islamic thinking (heavily drawn from al-Miskawahy's *Tahzib-ul Akhlaq* or 'Reform of Morals') and selecting from the vast storehouse of the concepts on good governance, he addressed the concerns of the Indian Muslims to the British by adopting a tone and style of compromise. Coming from a family of Mughal court diplomats, with the traditional knowledge of the necessity of *akhlaq* or good cultivated manners to resolve disputes, Sayyid Ahmad was well versed in public diplomacy. At a personal level, Sayyid Ahmad tried to emulate a characteristic of Prophet Muhammad: the capacity to settle disputes and reconcile former opponents. He used his skills of refined manners and astute diplomacy for opening the channels of mediation to remove the feelings of distrust that the British had towards the Muslims. Simultaneously, he clarified to the Muslims that revenge against the British was not a solution. Because political power was in their hands (which he believed they deserved), the British were bound to their Indian subjects. He further believed that using this connection was the only way forward. For enabling progress, his mission became the promotion of the use of Indian Islamic knowledge and practices, such as respect for authority and dialogue.

In his journal *Tahzib-ul Akhlaq*, subtitled in English as *The Muhammadan Social Reformer* (1870–1876), he emphasized the importance of ethical thinking and practices based on *akhlaq* and communicated the relationship between social reform and character refinement for creative institution building. He implored his Muslim audiences to think about the future. The ethical project of community building becomes particularly evident in his commentary on the Bible (*Tabyin-ul kalam fi'l tafsir-ul tawrd wa'l injil cala millat-ul Islam*), in which he discussed the possibility of a different method of Muslim–British interaction. Rather than emphasizing the strangeness and distance, he established the common bonds of contact between the Muslims and Christians based on an ethical view of religion, presented as a liberating space for moving beyond fear and hatred. Simultaneously, he decentred the supremacy of Western hierarchical position and Christianity as the only true faith.

An ethical thinker, Sayyid Ahmad knew the importance of looking beyond the immediate constructs of power and Western modernism of the colonial rulers and focussing on an ideal behaviour for reaffirming the values necessary for embarking on a common endeavour of progress. Drawing from the Islamic concepts including obedience, loyalty, generosity, inclusivity, and tolerance, he rationalized a social contract between the ruler and the ruled. He also opined that to chart a new path for individual and collective progress, ethical values were necessary. As an individual, he was faithful to the aforementioned values – which had shaped Muslim morals since the emergence of Islam in the seventh century – and used them to make it into a community project after 1857. When he called for change, modernization, and friendship with the British rulers, he invoked these as a Muslim, upholding traditional Islamic ethical values, urging his audiences to act and do what is right: be obedient to the ruling authority and using their energy for community improvement without involving in political machinations. In his estimation, each Muslim must act on what is right because they would be responsible for their own actions, with God being the only judge of it.

Throughout his career as a reformer, Sayyid Ahmad held on to the belief of the overarching good of British institutions. For him, Western education had become both a quest and an instrument for improving the Muslim condition, even though he himself had not received schooling in English. Thus, for him, education was not simply utilitarian, but a formative platform for improved life.[7] By using the masters' tools, Western education, he hoped the Muslims would be able to grasp the opportunities available in British India. In some ways, Sayyid Ahmad was a true 'gentleman' rebel with a cause, who transformed and empowered the Muslim community with their own voice to answer their British rulers, using the knowledge they had gained from the British. Nevertheless, for Sayyid Ahmad, Western education was not a weapon of revenge against the British, but a rational approach towards gaining power and participation in the public sphere with a courteous conduct.

Envisaging a Muslim history of progress to-be with British aid, he worked hard to overcome the inimical relationship between the British and Muslims and sought friendship between them; simultaneously, he sternly reminded the British rulers that they must adhere to the principles of justice when governing India. Post rebellion, Sayyid Ahmad's approach had a deep impact on the shaping of the British thoughts and policies towards Muslims as well as on the emotions and perspectives that the Muslims had towards the British rulers.

The relationship of the Muslims with other communities was built on friendship at its core; this included their friendships with the Hindu

---

[7] See Yasmin Saikia, 'Strangers, Friends, and Peace: The Women's World of Abdullah Hall, Aligarh Muslim University', in *Women and Peace in the Islamic World: Gender, Influence and Agency*, edited by Yasmin Saikia and Chad Haines, pp. 275–308 (London: I.B. Tauris, 2015).

communities and even the British colonial masters.[8] The language of common concerns, sameness, and shared experiences of history, including the 1857 rebellion, created the memories of friendship. Though uncontrived, Sayyid Ahmad genuinely believed that this friendship was foundational to wear out the storm of rumoured enmity between the Muslims and the British and emphasized the good and the possibility of creating good governance for achieving positive transformation. His mission and conduct provided access to rethink the story of modern Indian history, the Indian Muslims' response to change, and ethical community building beyond violence.

In the next section, I discuss in detail his publications on the 1857 rebellion and his creative use of this event for initiating a reform platform, along with his robust modernist vision expressed in his writings (in Urdu, translated into English by his English friends and admirers). Through his writings, Sayyid Ahmad connected the Indian Muslims and Hindus with their British masters for the emergence of a new colonial humanity. Thus, Sayyid Ahmad opened a space for a future possibility for all Indians, particularly Muslims, to regain their civilizational dignity – which was his lasting and continuous legacy.

TEXT AND CONTEXT

Sayyid Ahmad was the first Indian to produce an account of the rebellion of 1857.[9] Two expository treatises called *Tarikh-e Sarkashi-e Bijnor* (*History*

---

[8] Rajat Kanta Roy makes an important argument of the overlapping relationships between the Muslims and Hindus before the rise of Western style nationalism in the Indian subcontinent, which transcended normative religious boundaries. See his *The Felt Community: Commonality and Mentality before the Emergence of Indian Nationalism* (New Delhi: Oxford University Press 2003).

[9] He mentions this in *Causes* (Sayyid Ahmad Khan, *Causes of the Indian Revolt*, trans. by two European friends, Banaras: Medical Hall Press, 1873), available at http://www.columbia.edu/itc/mealac/pritchett/00urdu/asbab/ accessed on 24 June 2017), p. 1. Only a few years ago, India celebrated 150 years of the rebellion. Various scholarly and popular discussions were organized and numerous books on the rebellion published. Even Bollywood commemorated the event by making a film called *Mangal Pandey*, the biopic of the first Indian soldier who defied and raised the banner of mutiny against the British. In all these productions, few seemed to recall that Sayyid Ahmad was the first Indian to produce an account of the rebellion. In Biswamoy Pati's review essay on the rebellion, he makes a passing reference to Sayyid Ahmad's writing on the rebellion as 'a tract to counter [British] allegation' of 'Muslim conspiracy'. He

of the Bijnor Rebellion) in 1858 and *Risalah-e Asbab-e Baghawat-e Hind* (*Causes of the Indian Rebellion*) in 1859 as well as one narrative pamphlet called *Risalah Khair Khawahan Musalmanan* (*An Account of the Loyal Muhammadans of India*) in 1860. Taken together, all three publications present an eyewitness account of the 'riotous' events, wherein Sayyid Ahmad connects the events to a deeper history of the relationship (or gaps) between the Indian subjects and British administration. He appeals to the British to give up the persecution policy and trust the Muslims for their 'loyalty'. Simultaneously, he advises the Muslims to adopt a practical outlook and be responsible in their duty as British subjects for etching a progressive future.

The ruler–ruled relationship and the critical issues related to the past, present, and future shapes of Muslim history after 1857 remained intricately entwined, at least in the British mind; undoing resentment and bitterness for the Muslims required careful handling. Symbolic and real actions for negotiating the place of the Muslims as participants in the colonial administrative landscape were needed. By using his writings and other works, Sayyid Ahmad prepared his audience to embrace the role and display their transformation capacity – through a dialogic process: the Muslims needed the British to believe in their reformed outlook and the British had to 'see' Muslims as useful in their administration. Sayyid Ahmad played a unique role as the facilitator of this new history of relationship, immediately after the rebellion of 1857.

History narrates the local history of the rebellion at Bijnor. Therein, the record of the daily activities of the 'rebels' reliably recounts how the riots started, along with the erratic and short-sighted planning and action of different groups divided on the grounds of religion and ethnicity (for example, Muslim Pathans versus Hindu Rawas versus Hindu Gujjars) and

---

qualifies V. D. Savarkar as 'perhaps the first Indian to write about 1857' (see Biswamoy Pati, 'Historians and Historiography: Situating 1857', *Economic and Political Weekly* 42, no. 19 (2007): 1686–91). Sachin Sen's 1994 writing on Muslim political thought reduces Sayyid Ahmad's reform and historical writing as nothing more than 'the Moslem bourgeoisie' attempt to 'compet[e] with the Hindus in the hope of securing crumbs of favor from the ruling [British] race'. He concludes that 'Sir Syed was first and last a religious reformer' and did not attribute to him the pioneering work of historical memory that he created on the 1857 rebellion as its first local narrator (see Sachin Sen, 'Moslem Political Thought since 1858', *The Indian Journal of Political Science* 6, no. 2 (1944): 97–108).

the violence they indulged against each other with the consequent outcomes. By contrast, *Causes* presents the reasons behind the rebellion itself and suggests solutions for overcoming the distance between the British rulers and their Indian subjects, particularly the Muslims. Both these narratives are of salient importance for understanding the events of 1857 at both the micro and macro levels. Through his voice, Sayyid Ahmad straddles both the victims and perpetrators viewpoints and their shifting positions throughout the rebellion. He neither takes sides nor blames a single community for the rebellion. He demonstrates the problems and suggests a future course of action to move beyond the horrific calamities. At a personal level, as the *sadr amin* (civil sub-judge) of Bijnor, he remained loyal to his office during the rebellion and performed the tasks required of him, but his narrative is not devoid of emotion.

As a Muslim, Sayyid Ahmad felt that he needed to explain the violence committed by several members of the Muslim community and the violence of the different groups of the Hindus against the Muslims, even if both the British and the Hindus eventually blamed the Muslims for being the leading conspirators in the rebellion.[10] Instead of playing a blame game, Sayyid Ahmad considered this event an opportunity to rectify past mistakes

---

[10] Several of Sayyid Ahmad Khan's Hindu contemporaries in Bengal also commented on the rebellion. Rajani Kant Gupta, a disciple of Bankim Chandra Chattopadhyaya, produced a multi-volume book titled *Sipahi Yuddher Itihas* (The History of the Mutiny) in Bengali (Calcutta, multiple volumes, 1876–1897; vol. 5 [1897] is important for our consideration here). In the book, he emphasizes the fidelity of Hindus and asserts that in most cases, the Muslims were the architects of this 'mischief'. Similarly, Sambhu Chandra Mukherjee and Kishan Chandra Mitra presented the revolt as a localized movement and blamed the Muslims for making an attempt to restore the Mughal Empire by revolting against the British. Raja Siva Prasad, an employee of the British, ruled out political ambition and qualified the 1857 rebellion as an incident of loot and plunder of the criminal classes in concert with the mutineers. According to him, the Hindus were obedient to the sovereign authority of the British because they did not see the Muslims as the rightful rulers of India. It appears that the Hindu beneficiaries of the British were loyal to their masters and did not want to distance themselves from the gains they had made by blaming the British. By contrast, it was convenient for them to blame the other within – the Muslims. Sayyid Ahmad held a similar position of not openly blaming the British, but he did not point fingers at the Hindus for the rebellion. There is a distinctive difference between these two approaches (see Ramesh Rawat, 'Perception of 1857', *Social Scientist* 35, nos 11/12 [2007]: 15–28).

and provide the government suggestions regarding constructive policies for establishing just governance. In his writings on the 1857 rebellion, he considers the rebellion as a foundational moment establishing the Muslim voice as participants in the development of India and presenting them in a spirit of critical inquiry. His writings also offer a practical visionary approach for envisaging a new future.[11]

The two publications on the rebellion by Sayyid Ahmad aimed at two different audiences: *History* was mainly for an Indian audience (or so it seems) based on the use of the pronoun 'we' in addition 'us' that abound in the narrative,[12] whereas *Causes* was written for the British rulers.[13] Both publications were a combined set written within a year of each other. In his book *Hayat-e Javed* (An Immortal Life), Altaf Hussain Hali notes that even as the rebellion unfolded, Sayyid Ahmad was convinced that the rebels would not succeed and the British would return to power. Deeply aware that a momentous history was shaping, he collected documents and materials he could access as a British officer and then wrote about the rebellion. However, before detailing on the two primary texts, I provide a small discussion on *The Loyal Muhammadans*, his third publication.

---

[11] By contemporary history, I do not mean post-1945 history. There is an assumption that World War II was a break from the past, driving a new course of history thereafter. I use 'contemporary history' as a conceptual term. History aiming to make sense, contextualize, and provide historical explanation about some aspects of the recent past and provide a historical understanding of the trends leading to that history and its outcomes that are of current relevance (see Peter Catterall, 'What If Anything Is Distinctive about Contemporary History', *Journal of Contemporary History* 32, no. 4 [1997]: 441–52). Sayyid Ahmad's two treatises on 1857 can be included within this genre of contemporary history. Irfan Habib's essay on the 1857 rebellion and 'its coming' situates the notion of contemporary history as understood by the contemporaries of that time (see Irfan Habib, 'The Coming of 1857', *Social Scientist* 26, nos 1/4 [1998]: 6–15).

[12] Sayyid Ahmad Khan, *History of the Bijnor Rebellion*, trans. Hafeez Malik and Morris Dembo, available at http://www.columbia.edu/itc/mealac/pritchett/00urdu/asbab/bijnor/ (accessed on 26 June 2017). I also consulted the published and translated edition by Jaweed Ashraf, *History of the Insubordination in Bijnor District* (Delhi: Gaur Publishers and Distributors, 2012).

[13] Besides the online version of *Causes*, I consulted the published and translated edition by Jaweed Ashraf, *Causes of the Indian Rebellion, 1857* (Delhi: Asha Jyoti Books Sellers and Publishers, 2007).

Sayyid Ahmad wrote the pamphlet *The Loyal Muhammadans* for the British audience. He highlights to his English readers the services rendered by the Muslims during the rebellion and discusses why the rebellion did not qualify as *jihad*[14] by establishing that *jihad* cannot be fought against the protectors by the protected and that the Muslims living under the protection of the British in India were not undertaking *jihad*. A popular outbreak, the rebellion, did not remain confined to one class or creed. To show the contributions of the loyal Muslims, he named Muslim individuals who risked their lives and reputation to protect English lives, property, and dignity. With confidence, he wrote, 'To blame the Muslim community as a whole for the horror and calamities at that terrible time … was to a very great extent unjust.'[15] Making a point of religious affinity, he declared, 'If in Hindustan there was one class of people … who … were fast bound with Christians … in the bonds of amity and friendship, those people were the Muhammadans.'[16] Sayyid Ahmad hoped that his defence of the Muslims would assure the British that the Muslims were respectful of British political authority and that they were bound by their religion to be loyal subjects. Because this was the last in the series of his writings on the 1857 rebellion, Sayyid Ahmad built on the previous two publications and proved his point that the Muslims were not driven to be the 'Other' in British India, but they were cooperative subjects keen to contribute to an administration that must be good for all in India. The Muslims could be trustworthy subjects, enabling good governance.

In the remaining part of this section, I focus first on *History* and then on *Causes* to discuss the effects of these writings on the British–Muslim relationship before and after 1857. The main plot of *History* is embedded in the chronological narration of the violence that occurred from 12 May 1857 to 28 April 1858. Presented in seven chapters as an eyewitness report, Sayyid Ahmad develops a convincing argument that the violence in Bijnor was not a rebellion as such, but insubordination to the British administration. The real problems leading to the violence and chaos were the ambitions of the

---

[14] For further reading on the misuse of the term *jihad* for the 1857 rebellion, see Iqtidar Alam Khan, 'The Wahhabis in the 1857 Revolt: A Brief Reappraisal of Their Role', *Social Scientist* 41, nos 5/6 (2013): 15–23.

[15] George Farquhar Irving Graham, *The Life and Work of Sir Syed Ahmed Khan* (Edinburg: William Blackwood and Sons, 1885), p. 58, available at https://archive.org/stream/lifeworkofsyedahoograh#page/n9/mode/2up (accessed on 15 May 2017).

[16] Ibid., p. 60.

Hindu and Muslim feudal groups and their ungratefulness to the British rulers. He opines that the villagers, the people incited to commit violence, were not the men who could read the consequences of their own actions or understand defiance they were eliciting against the British rulers. They did not know who to follow during this chaotic time. The oscillating claims of leadership by the Muslim Nawab Mahmud Khan and his rivals, including Chaudhri Nain Singh, Chaudhri Jodh Singh, and Chaudhris of Halduar, invigorated feudal loyalties; this led to intracommunity violence between the followers of the different Chaudhris and those of the Rawa and Gujjar Hindus as well as intercommunity violence between the Muslims and Hindus. In Chapter 3 of *History*, Sayyid Ahmad indicates that such a history did not have a past and thus it must be read as new evidence of developing local enmity. He asserts, '[B]efore this fighting there had never been a dispute, nor feelings of hatred, not even a religious altercation, between Hindus and Muslims of this district.'[17]

The departure of the British officers from Bijnor on 7 June 1857 indicated the beginning of community violence. The Muslims and Hindus looted and plundered the villages, mosques, and temples; abducted women from rival groups; and engaged in multiple killings. Sayyid Ahmad was deeply affected by these tragic losses. In his writing, recalling the time before the violence, he considers the British administration as a neutral presence, maintaining community peace. He writes that the Muslim violence during the rebellion was not a matter of planning and deep thinking: to make 'war against the English Government nor fighting with the English Government' was the intention of the villagers. The rioting Muslims were 'mobilized simply out of greed for loot'. The lack of preparation and insufficient knowledge of artillery of the rebels convinced Sayyid Ahamd that 'no man will die in all this fighting from an artillery ball'.[18] The rebels were defeated with the return of the British forces, concluding the local rebellion against the British authority in Bijnor. Even when the Nawab announced full land tax remission to incite the Muslims to join his army and fight against the British forces, the Muslims 'ran away'.[19] Sayyid Ahmad writes that they 'threw their shoes, uniforms and weapons' and 'abandoned the fight'.[20] These men certainly were not soldiers neither did they belong to any institution

---

[17] *History*, trans. Ashraf, chapter 3, p. 6.
[18] Ibid., chapter 4, section 6, p. 20.
[19] Ibid., chapter 5, section 31, p. 19.
[20] Ibid., chapter 6, p. 5.

such as the army; thus, they lacked discipline and did not follow authority. Sayyid Ahmad concluded that the Bijnor episode was neither mutiny nor planned rebellion.

On 28 April 1858, the triumphant collector of Bijnor, Alexander Shakespeare, and his officers returned. Sayyid Ahmad writes that this 'brought peace to the entire district through their great effort and planning'.[21] He elaborates his point by writing that the British order and discipline were both signs of the legitimate authority of the rulers. He admonishes both the Muslim and Hindu groups for the violence, unambiguously stating that the turmoil was a punishment from God for their 'ungratefulness'. The return of the British to power had re-established the correct relationship, which required the Indian subjects to be obedient to this authority. However, he does criticize the British as well by stating that the government should do their part, paying more attention to the condition of the common people so that they can live freely with honour. He recommends that the British and the Indians should work together for both individual and collective improvement and create a new future. Sayyid Ahmad believed that because of its many excellent natural powers, India can become superior – if not equal – to England, provided Indians achieve their civilizational call.[22]

Indeed, *History* powerfully comments on the 1857 events, making the unceremonious collapse of the Mughal political power and the establishment of English crown rule a respectable historical narrative. The desperate attempts of the feudal lords to create a political space for themselves during the rebellion; the ordinary Indian villagers joining in the struggle hoping to loot; and the final end to the mayhem, with the British return – all are presented without rancour, but in hope and acknowledgement that the British could improve the lives of the Indian communities further. Telling this honest story of the Indian failure and using it, as an entry point to make an appeal for reform required an artful mastery of understanding of the happenings, along with optimism undefeated by violence. Sayyid Ahmad conveys to his Muslim audience that they must obey British authority to envision the future of the Muslim communal self while accepting the loss of power of the Muslim political self. The Muslims needed to work in partnership with others to find a place for themselves in British India. Thus, he wrote the narrative in both tone

---

[21] *History*, trans. Ashraf, chapter 6, section 7, p. 5.
[22] He writes about this in his letters during his visit to England in 1869. Quoted in Graham, *Life and Work*, p. 180.

and language of immediacy with the right effect of hindsight observation to describe what had occurred actually.

In *Causes*, he further investigates the 1857 rebellion and its reasons. Written in multiple voices – part chronicler of history, part petitioner, part negotiator – Sayyid Ahmad's ethical concern for good governance is dominant in *Causes*. Through *Causes*, he refutes the theory of the British that the Muslims were to blame for the rebellion and presents his argument to clear his Muslim community of this accusation. He argues that blaming the Muslims for the rebellion was insufficient because the religious differences between the British rulers and the Indian subjects were not the only reason for the rebellion. Something else was fundamentally troubling the people. Religious concerns were part of that 'something else', which was the root cause of the rebellion. He questions this root cause and provides solutions necessary to reach closure for a better future. Of the five hundred copies of *Causes* printed in India, and except for two one sent to the Government of India and a personal copy, the bulk were sent to England.[23]

In *Causes*, he warmly welcomes the Queen's proclamation of 1858 as a new chapter for the betterment of India. Next, he declares the reasons for the rebellion, which 'did not originate from a single cause but from a complication of causes', and approaches the way forward by first addressing the tensions the people of India were experiencing because of the changes implemented by the British, which were producing negative results in the social, cultural, and economic lives of the Indian subjects. He then recalls the stereotypical reasons for the rebellion and then discounts neither the rebellion happened due to outside assistance – from the Persians or Russians – nor through the internal plotting of the Muslims to lead a *jihad* against the British to support the Mughal king in Delhi. Furthermore, he asserts the army had not colluded to rebel due to the greased cartridges or occupation of Awadh. He writes that the single reason for the rebellion was the nonadmission of native Indians as Legislative Council members.[24] At first glance, this reason seems bewildering for explaining the rebellion. However, on reading Sayyid Ahmad's explanation further, it becomes clear that the British rulers' failure to include and hear the voices of the people 'meant the government did not know how its projects were received by the

[23] The original pamphlet was written in Urdu; many translations into English were done by the Government of India, the India Office, and several members of the Parliament, but it was never made publicly available (see http://www.columbia.edu/itc/mealac/pritchett/00urdu/asbab/, accessed on 22 May 2017).
[24] *Causes*, trans. Ashraf, p. 7.

people', thus widening the gap between the Indian subjects and the British government. This distance was accentuated by fears on both sides, and the laws passed were considered degrading and ruinous for the people of India. Fear and alienation became powerful forces, which made people rise against the oppression.

Sayyid Ahmad then establishes five causes connected to the root issue of the non-representation of the Indians in the law-making council and its consequences. One of the first causes was the government's failure to take wholesome interest in the wellbeing of its subjects, ignorant of their conditions as well as modes of thought and life. Another cause was the interference of Christian missionaries by creating the apprehension of forced conversion and transforming the epistemic foundation of Indian culture and life. In addition to religious and social uncertainties, the Indian people considered the new rules and regulations that changed gender relations through female empowerment thus degrading Indian men, even in the intimate spaces of their homes, to be abhorrent. There were many other causes on his list: the disruption of caste concerns in jail and military institutions, land tax policies and institution of heavy revenue rates, disregard to the connections of land, social identity and personal honour (*izzat*), as well as growing fears of unemployment and strained economic conditions, all made the people panic. Of the aforementioned list, the fourth cause accentuated the fears of the people, such that it was immediately evident in the rebellion. With assertion, Sayyid Ahmad criticizes the distance between the British rulers and their Indian subjects, which widened the gaps making the British inaccessible, such that it was the 'most offensive to all the people of India, but most especially so to the Muhammadans'.[25] As the lack of communication became sufficiently evident, Indians began seeing the British as foreigners who had usurped their land and economy, now determined to change them religiously and culturally. Sayyid Ahmad questions the government for undermining the *izzat* of the local gentry, degrading the people, and holding them in contempt. He asserts that the Indian audience responded to the call for recruits to join the rebellion because it was a traditional norm to enter the service of powerful nobles willing to pay: 'Thousands of poor men, wanting service, flocked in and took it.... Hindus were concerned therein as Muhammadans, and the proof of this will be found in what took place all over Hindustan.'[26]

[25] *Causes*, trans. Ashraf, p. 25.
[26] Ibid., pp. 27–8.

Finally, he states the fifth cause: The British created a single army by mixing Hindus and Muslims, disturbing caste and religious consideration and causing friction among the Indian communities. Added to this was the introduction of cartridges laced with pig and beef fat, which was an affront to the religious sentiments of the soldiers. The refusal of the soldiers to use them was met by the punishment of being disbanded; this Sayyid Ahmad notes with disappointment as 'an act utterly devoid of justice on the part of the government'.[27] For Indians, the rebellion spread without a plan or strategy but became a site to express passion and loyalty to their brethren, such that 'even those who wanted to remain faithful to their salt were carried away by the majority'.[28] In a pithy final statement of *Causes*, Sayyid Ahmad notes, 'When it became known that the army had revolted, the people also became riotous. They no longer were in awe of the government.'[29]

In the now exposed theatre of the British government, defiance had become an act of bravery. The sense of history, kindred relationships among Indian communities, and distance Indian people felt from the British government, all became the site for making a new history through rebellion. Although the rebellion failed, it helped establish the ability of these people to question the rulers. Sayyid Ahmad's publication *Causes* thus represents a new-found voice of an Indian subject speaking directly to the master, appealing for change.

When evaluating *Causes*, language is a critical concern. Although Sayyid Ahmad wrote this pamphlet aiming to correct the misrepresentations of Muslims as rebels, his tone remained ethical, and he did not forsake his good manners and diplomatic skills. Sayyid Ahmad registers the concerns of the Indian people, but while praising the British for the many wonderful things about their administration. Simultaneously, he reminds the British that fairness in administration must display requisite justice through same treatment for all. In his view, the racist and arrogant attitude of the British was dangerous: it caused anger and violence among their despised Indian subjects. He further asserts that their arrogance made the British incompetent, making them unable to understand and accurately address the needs of the governed.

By exemplifying previous government measures valuing inclusiveness, he recommends necessary changes through a two-way process: the British to stop thinking of the Muslims as rivals and rebels and accept them

---

[27] *Causes*, trans. Ashraf, p. 29.
[28] Ibid., p. 30.
[29] Ibid., pp. 30–1.

as trustworthy subjects, who could aid their administration in India if they are empowered with legislative powers of governance. Furthermore, he estimated that educated Muslims would be allies of the British administration. This approach was not an admission of subservience, but it was a claim to partnership – a gesture to connect the British and the Indians for effective governance and relationship building. Consequently, the Indian Muslims could change and acculturate themselves to modern ways of the British.

For an ethical thinker like Sayyid Ahmad, this process meant selecting and incorporating what is good for other communities and conditioning them to the Indian Muslim attitude. The changes he believed would benefit the Muslims included social manners, secular education for economic improvement, Western knowledge, awareness and improvement of business acumen, and an entrepreneurial spirit. He placed emphasis on using reason for evaluating old habits and reforming the moribund traditions through debate and discussion to make way for the new.

For a reform to uplift the *ashraf* (elite) community, Sayyid Ahmad used a wide-ranged approach. However, he remained hopeful that the *ajlaf* (lower) communities would have opportunities for development in British India as well. This is evident in his critical response to W.W. Hunter's book *The Indian Mussalman: Are They Bound by Conscience to Rebel against the Queen?* (1871), published in the *Pioneer* (later reprinted in the *Aligarh Institute Gazette* from 28 November 1871 to 23 February 1872). In this response, he advances his argument on behalf 'of my fellow countrymen' and 'in opposition to Dr Hunter'.[30] To dispel the fears of the British against the lower-class Muslim rebels, perceived to be working under the influence of Wahhabi puritanical fervour, he again engages the issue of *jihad*, providing a succinct argument regarding the reason that *jihad* was not viable in British India where the practice of Islam is not restricted. He notes that after 1857, the Hindu and Muslim rebels – 'a band of desperate men, composed of mutineers and others' – 'fled for their lives' to the remote Northwest frontier fearing severe punishment from the British. Their fight, he opines, was against 'the oppression and severities of the Sikh rulers' and to assume that they were fighting a religious war was 'too absurd for

---

[30] Reprinted and published in Graham, *Life and Work*, pp. 205–43. Also, see *Writings and Speeches of Sir Syed Ahmad Khan*, comp. and ed. Shan Muhammad (Bombay: Nachiketa Publications Limited, 1972), p. 67.

belief'.[31] Sayyid Ahmad criticizes Dr Hunter: 'Dr Hunter stands convicted of either intentionally misleading the public or of profound ignorance.'[32] This, he followed with a question: 'Does Dr Hunter mean that none of us Muhammadans who remained in India are good and zealous Musalmans?' He finally concludes using a conciliatory tone, citing from both the Qur'an and Bible. Invoking verse 85, Chapter V from the Qur'an, he reminds his readers that the Muslims must be friends with true Christians because they are 'not elated with pride' and then uses Jesus's words that 'men should do to you ... even so to them'. Then, by adding his own voice as an act of duty to speak for justice, he appeals to the government to change punishment policies for their Indian subjects.[33]

Evidently, Sayyid Ahmad considered the failed 1857 and it consequences a turning point, which motivated him to become an actor in the sociopolitical landscape. His method was nonviolent but visionary. Most strikingly, even in such a perilous time, he could conceive a way forward. Instead of blaming the British for considering the Muslims to be rivals in political power, Sayyid Ahmad invoked help and support of the British masters to lead by the example of good governance. This was his unique imagination and strategy to create a new future for the Indian Muslims emerging from the morasses of their ruin. By connecting past history with present crisis, Sayyid Ahmad's narrative became a site to cultivate friendship between the perpetrators and their victims.[34] This was no ordinary approach. It was a voice of change not as a nostalgic journey into the past of Muslim glory but as a purposeful one for the future empowerment of the depressed Muslims.

THE MAN, HIS MISSION, AND HIS LEGACY IN HISTORIOGRAPHY

In the post-1857 India, Sayyid Ahmad approached the Muslim condition pragmatically, layering it with ethical thinking derived from an Indian context and Islamic values, thus producing a unique way of thinking as an Indian Muslim (*Musalman-e Hind* in his terms). For him, an Indian Muslim

---

[31] *Writings and Speeches*, ed. Muhammad, p. 76.
[32] Graham, *Life and Work*, p. 232.
[33] *Writings and Speeches*, ed. Muhammad, pp. 81–2.
[34] Haroon Khan Sherwani, 'The Political Thought of Sir Syed Ahmed Khan', *The Indian Journal of Political Science* 5, no. 4 (1944): 306–28.

was intimately connected and part of the Hindu; thus, he concluded that the Muslims and the Hindus constituted one *qaum* (people) by the virtue of living in the same country.[35] In *History*, he addresses the shared Hindu and Muslim world of India in detail. In his 1883 speech in Patna on the eve of the formation of the INC, he reiterated these thoughts:

> Friends, just as the higher caste Hindus came and settled in this land once, forgot where their earlier home was and considered India to be their own country, we also did exactly the same thing – we also left out former climes hundreds of years ago, we also regard this land of India our own.... Both my Hindu brethren and my Muslim co-religionists breathe the same air, drink the waters of the sacred Ganges and the Jamuna, eat the products which God has given to this country, live and die together.... I say with conviction ... then in all matter of everyday life, the Hindus and the Muslims really belong to one community.... If the two live in concord with one another, the bride will remain forever resplendent and becoming.[36]

Thus, when he approached the issue of improving the Muslim condition with British support and goodwill, he did not present it as a Muslim-only issue; he included that the subject communities, including both the Muslims and Hindus, deserved good governance. By contrast, Sayyid Ahmad had no ambition for the Muslims outside India. Muhammad Sarwar notes that Maulana Obaidullah Sindhi, a revolutionary anticolonial freedom fighter, credited Sayyid Ahmad for stopping the Muslim migration from India to Egypt after 1857. Sayyid Ahmad refused to leave for either Egypt or Arabia, as did many others, claiming that Hindustan (India) was his *watan* (home).[37] This won him not only Muslim and Hindu allies but also severe critics from both communities. Sir Sultan Muhammed Shah Aga Khan III, Sayyid Mehdi Ali (known as Nawab Mohsin-ul Mulk), Maharajas

---

35 Quoted in Sherwani, 'Political Thought,' pp. 319–20.
36 *Majmu'a Resolution Hai*, from 1886 to 1895 (publisher unknown, Agra, 1896), pp. 149–51.
37 Unlike Sayyid Ahmad, Mohammad Qasim Nanotvi and Rasheed Ahmad Gangohi left for Arabia after 1857. On their return to India, they founded the Deoband Madrasa, a counter movement against the progressive MAO approach. See Obaidullah Sindhi, *Ifadat wa Malfuzat*, compiled by Muhammad Sarwar (Lahore: Sind Sagar Academy, repr. ed. 2014).

of Patiala and Vizianagaram and several middle-class Hindus, Sikhs, and Muslims aided Sayyid Ahmad in developing his programme of Muslim education at Aligarh. The financial, emotional, and educational support of these well-wishers facilitated the establishment of the MAO College. Sayyid Ahmad Khan simultaneously attracted severe criticism from some of his Muslim contemporaries, such as the well-known pan-Islamic revolutionary Jamaluddin al-Afghani and the poet Akbar Allahabadi; even the Islamic reformer Shibli Numani, who was once his friend and a teacher at MAO College, parted ways with him. Al-Afghani criticized him for his Indianist and modernist outlook as well as his friendship with the British. Maulana Abul Kalam Azad, a foremost Muslim leader of INC, considered Sayyid Ahmad's reticence towards INC and his failure to encourage the Muslim youth to participate in this organization as 'his grave blunder'.[38] Sayyid Ahmad emphasized *ijtihad* (independent reasoning) and disapproved *taqlid* (adherence to the four authoritative schools of Islamic jurisprudence); this set him apart from the traditional `ulama, who saw in his modernist intellectual stance an attack on their learning and privileged status in the Muslim society. Nevertheless, two decades after Sayyid Ahmad's death, in 1910, the `ulama from the Deoband Madrasa met with the westernized AMU students to discuss their common role as Indian Muslims.[39] Sayyid Ahmad's ethical outlook and his reflective actions for the community wellbeing guided the amalgamation of disparate groups for the common cause of India's freedom. Hindu leaders who did not want the Muslims to advance alongside the Hindu community did not appreciate this. In his keynote address of the Indian Political Association in 1944, Professor Sachin Sen blamed Sayyid Ahmad Khan for 'thirst[ing] for the extension of State protection and patronage to Moslems so that they might run shoulder to shoulder with Hindus in the race of life'. Furthermore, he considered 'the founding of the Moslem League in 1906 and the Deputation headed by H. H. the Aga Khan before Lord Minto in 1906 urging for separate electorate' as the product of the Aligarh Movement, spearheaded by Sayyid Ahmad. He concluded by asserting that Sayyid Ahmad is the father of Muslim

---

[38] Convocation Address at Aligarh Muslim University, 20 February 1949, quoted in *Abdul Kalam Azad: Selected Speeches and Writings* (Delhi: Ministry of Information and Broadcasting, Government of India, rev. 1989), pp. 75–83.

[39] Muhammad Hajjan Shaikh, *Maulana Ubaid Allah Sindhi: A Revolutionary Scholar* (Islamabad: National Institute of Historical and Cultural Research, 1986), pp. 17–22.

separatist politics and that 'Moslem politics has hardly walked out of the track chalked out by' him.[40]

CONCLUSION

On repeated assessments, we can note that Sayyid Ahmad's representations do not change his image but rather provide a new way of thinking about his work and accomplishments every time. A pioneer Muslim reformer, he did not have much in the way of establishing a path to tread on; however, what he created for Indian Muslims was both unique and extraordinary. He dreamt of the future for Muslims as full, engaged citizens, at a time when his contemporaries could not even grasp the meaning of subjecthood under colonial rule. 'Twilight', a metaphor used by the author Ahmed Ali, encapsulates the mood of the time as the Muslims fumbled in anxiety – unable to understand what future lay ahead. For avoiding the existential threat of annihilation, a search for the 'Muslim self' was essential. Becoming deeply conscious of the new order of white man's rule, Sayyid Ahmad feared that his *qaum* was in imminent danger of losing their preeminent position, not only because of the end of the Mughal rule but also due to the threat from the numerically larger and the English educated Bengali government employees, who would have certainly undermined the Muslims. As noted, his response was always pragmatic. He focused on the business of actualizing his mission, which was protecting, preserving, and promoting the interests of his *qaum*. His tenacity for improving the Muslim condition defined his life's work. The episode of Sayyid Ahmad hanging from a basket for deciphering the inscription of Qutb Minar speaks volumes of his tenacity, imaginativeness, and resourcefulness – all the qualities demonstrated, repeatedly, throughout his life. Indeed, his commitment to act on and implement his theory of Muslim improvement changed the course of Muslim history in India.

---

[40] Sen, 'Moslem Political Thought,' p. 103.

2 Indian Muslims Are the Most Loyal Subjects of the British Raj

Sir Sayyid Ahmad Khan and the Caliphate

CARIMO MOHOMED

INTRODUCTION

Currently, the fear and suspicion of Muslim communities, living as minorities in different parts of the world, are growing. In addition, the issues related to 'caliphate', 'Islamic governance', 'Islamic state', and the political and religious loyalties of these communities remain a concern.

In the recent past, a series of scattered events involving Muslims as the perpetrators occurred in different parts of the world. These were highly mediatized. This mediatization polarized the discourses on 'Islam'. This trend seems to have (re)started after the fall of the Soviet Union and then reinforced by the events of 11 September 2001 – the most recent defining moment for the representation of Islam and Muslim societies.

Just because an organization calls itself the Islamic state, even though most of its victims – in Iraq, Syria, and the neighbouring countries – are Muslims, many people have started believing that all Muslims are members of such organizations. This idea has grabbed the imagination of Western societies, particularly the politicians trying to capitalize on it. Examples of such biased individuals include the members of some 'liberal' and 'freedom' political parties in the European Union as well as the current US president, Donald Trump, who has shown that immigration, even if legal, is an issue of concern to a large segment of the US electorate. For historians, inflammatory remarks concerning Muslims and migrants of a 'different' heritage, recall immigration 'restrictionists' whose jingoist rhetoric would have seemed buried for good, but which has not.

Soares and Osella[1] showed that the stereotypes regarding Islam and Muslims have actually been remarkably resilient. The figure of a 'mad mullah', who radicalized the 'uneducated, naïve, but largely benign, Muslim

[1] Benjamin Soares and Filippo Osella, 'Islam, Politics, Anthropology', *Journal of the Royal Anthropological Institute* 15, no. s1 (2009): S1–S23.

masses', in nineteenth-century British accounts of Muslim anticolonial politics, or the twentieth-century French accounts of allegedly dangerous 'Sufis' and 'Wahhabis', who threatened to lead ordinary Muslims in their West African colonies astray. These are the genealogical antecedents of contemporary characterizations of 'radical' Islam and Muslims in most Western media, public culture, and even the academic world.

During his time, Sir Sayyid Ahmad Khan also dealt with similar issues. By using his views on the caliphate, in this chapter, I assess how Sayyid Ahmad tried to historically explain the institution of Islam and quell the fears of the British administrators regarding the loyalties of the Muslim community. I also try to establish a parallel with the current events.

Herein, primary sources are mainly used and the strategy proposed by Muhammad Arkoun[2] (1928–2010) and Quentin Skinner[3] is employed; that is, primary and secondary texts will not be read, not for discussing the facts themselves, but for 'problematizing' the epistemis and epistemological framework underlying the articulation of each discourse.

From Arkoun's perspective, 'historical epistemology' has a priority over the purely descriptive, narrative presentation of what Islam teaches or what Muslims say, do, or achieve as social and historical protagonists. He questions the extent to which these protagonists are aware of the ideological dimensions of their discourse and historical actions. He then identifies the cognitive structures they use for the purpose of interpreting their religion, applying it to their actual life or reshaping it on the basis of historical pressures. Finally, he elucidates the extent to which they develop a critical relationship with their past and present to have better control over their future and then questions the relevance, effectiveness, and creativeness of such a relationship.

According to Skinner, concepts alter over time and thus cannot provide us with anything more than a series of changing perspectives on the world we live in. Our concepts are part of what we bring to the world in an effort to make sense of the world itself. This process gives rise to shifting conceptualizations, which constitute the very core of an ideological debate. With such conceptual changes occurring continually, regret and denial become insignificant.

---

[2] Mohammed Arkoun, *Islam: To Reform or to Subvert?* (London: Saqi Books, 2006), pp. 16–17.

[3] Quentin Skinner, 'Retrospect: Studying Rhetoric and Conceptual Change', in *Visions of Politics. Volume 1: Regarding Method*, pp. 368–413 (Cambridge: Cambridge University Press, 2002).

Herein, I also explain why some concepts came to prominence during a particular historical period. Concepts – or what we express through them – have a history. They rise and they fall, and in some cases, they finally disappear from sight, reflecting deeper transformations in social life.

A main concern herein is the ideas proposed by Sayyid Ahmad, not the Islamic or similar ideas. Although the study of theology and texts is important, the political dynamics and historical context in which a given discourse ascends, gains acceptance, or loses salience are far more significant. The concepts such as caliphate, Islamic governance, and Islamic state continue to show resilience, even in societies that pride themselves for having separated the political and religious allegiances long ago; however, this separation is only rhetorical.

BACKGROUND OF THE PROBLEM

In 1832, the Reverend Midgeley John Jennings (d. 1857) arrived in India, and in 1852, became chaplain of the Christian population of Delhi, hoping to convert the local population to Anglican Christianity, thus ending with the local 'false religions'. Many evangelical British in India, expecting to not only rule and manage the country but also 'save' her by using their influence through the British East India Company and converting the country, shared this sentiment.[4] For them, the British Empire was proof that God was on their side, and they believed that the propagation of faith would augment even more that empire. Some evangelical personalities, such as the Reverends Henry Martyn (1781–1812), Joseph Wolff (1795–1862), and particularly Carl Pfander (1803–1865), were important missionaries with an aggressive posture of 'frontal attack' against Islam, exemplified by the publication of books such as the *Mizan-ul Haqq, or Balance of Truth* (first published in 1829)[5] and *Remarks on the Nature of Muhammadanism* (1840).[6]

---

[4] For further details, please refer to Penelope Carson, *The East India Company and Religion, 1698–1858* (Woodbridge, Suffolk: Boydell Press, 2012) and Avril Ann Powell, *Muslims and Missionaries in Pre-Mutiny India* (Richmond, Surrey: Curzon Press Ltd., 1993).

[5] Carl G. Pfander, *The Mizan ul Haqq, or Balance of Truth* (London: The Religious Tract Society, 1910).

[6] Carl G. Pfander, *Remarks on the Nature of Muhammadanism: Traditions* (Calcutta: Baptist Mission Press, 1840).

After the Indian Rebellion of 1857, although the great majority of the insurgents were Hindus, the last Mughal emperor, Bahadur Shah Zafar II (1775–1862), was put on trial by the British and charged with being behind an international Muslim conspiracy stretching from Istanbul, Mecca, and Iran to the walls of the Red Fort in Delhi. During the 1857 rebellion, Sayyid Ahmad was a civil sub-judge in Bijnor. The journal he wrote between May 1857 and April 1858 was published as a monograph with the title *Tarikh-e Sarkashi-e Bijnor* (History of the Mutiny in Bijnor). In 1859, Sayyid Ahmad published a book in Urdu called *Risalah-e Asbab-e Baghawat-e Hind* (Causes of the Indian Mutiny), which was later translated into English. Therein, he criticized the mutiny of the previous years, while arguing that the mutiny occurred due to only one cause followed by its consequences: Indian natives blamed the British government for diminishing their position and dignity, for maintaining them in a lower position, and for the daily suffering and abuse at the hands of the officials.

During 1860–1861, Sayyid Ahmad published his *Risalah Khair Khawahân Musalmanân* (An Account of the Loyal Muhammadans of India), wherein he defended Indian Muslims as the most loyal subjects of the British Raj because of their disposition and religious principles. For him, the existing resentment was due to mutual prejudices and ignorance. His effort to mediate between Christianity and Islam developed in his work *Ahkam-e Ta'am-e Ahl-e Kitab* (Rules for Eating with the People of the Book), which deals with the social contact among Muslims, Christians, and Jews. In a commentary on the Bible therein, he tries to establish that all three religions were derived from the same source and that their similitude would be quickly recognized by whoever studied and compared them.

In the appendix of *Muhammadan Commentary on the Bible* (*Tabîyyan-ul kalâm fî'l tafsîr-ul tawrâ wa'l injîl calâ millat-ul Islam*), he includes the *fatwa* issued by Jamal ibn al-`Abd Allah `Umar-ul Hanfi, the Mufti of Mecca, stating that as long as some Islamic rites are maintained in India, it will be *Dar-ul Islam*. His aim was to hold back the *fatwa* issued by some Indian `ulama saying that India has become *Dar-ul Harb*.

Sir William Muir (1819–1905) wrote *The Life of Mahomet*[7] in response to a veteran missionary's request. This text amplified the thesis that Islam was a backward religion, based on information drawn from the study of some Muslim sources. This publication was acclaimed as a great help in the missionary enterprise. Therein, Sir William Muir talks about divorce,

---

[7] William Muir, *The Life of Mahomet* (London: Smith, Elder, & Co, 1861).

polygamy, and slavery. Sayyid Ahmad refuted this text with his collection of twelve essays called *Essays on the Life of Mohammed and Subjects Subsidiary Thereto*.[8]

In 1871, the Viceroy Lord Mayo (1822–1872) commissioned William Wilson Hunter (1840–1900) to write and publish his *The Indian Musalmans*,[9] with the aim of safeguarding British power in India. Based on the various trials after the mutiny, Hunter revealed a causal relationship between the Wahhabi activities and the permanent instability at the Northwest Frontier. According to him, this was a well-organized movement, with its leaders claiming all functions of sovereignty over their constituents. Extraordinarily strong and permanent bonds connected the members of this 'secret order'. The headquarters in Patna and the controlling machinery throughout rural areas for the 'spreading of insatisfaction, sent a multitude of zealots carefully indoctrinated with treason and equipped with vast literature about the duty to wage war against the British. An uninterrupted flow of money and fiery recruits determined to extirpate the infidel crossed the border'.[10]

The title and subtitle of Hunter's book are very informative: for Hunter, a monolithic entity called the 'Indian Musalmans' existed, and he wanted to know if *they*, as a whole, were bound in conscience to rebel against the Queen. Hunter painted a picture that caused a protest from Sayyid Ahmad, who characterized the book as misleading and historically inaccurate: In a recension to *The Indian Musalmans*,[11] Sayyid Ahmad pointed out many inaccuracies in Hunter's views on Wahhabi precepts and charted out a

---

[8] Syed Ahmed Khan Bahador, *A Series of Essays on the Life of Mohammed, and Subjects Subsidiary Thereto* (London: Trübner & Co, 1870).

[9] Sir William Wilson Hunter, *The Indian Musalmans: Are They Bound in Conscience to Rebel Against the Queen?* (London: Trübner & Co, 1871). In the same year, another book with the same title, *Indian Musalmáns: Being Three Letters Reprinted From the 'Times'* (London and Edinburgh: Williams and Norgate, 1871), was published by William Nassau Lees (1825–1889), a fellow of the University of Calcutta.

[10] If we replace 'secret order' with 'Islamic State', or Patna with Raqqa, Hunter's text could be a current opinion by some social 'scientists' and 'experts' commenting on current events, be they in the USA, Europe, or the Middle East.

[11] Syed Ahmad Khan, 'Review on Hunter's *Indian Musalmans* (1872)', in *Writings and Speeches of Sir Syed Ahmad Khan*, comp. and ed. Shan Muhammad, pp. 65–82 (Bombay: Nachiketa Publications, 1972).

critical history of that movement from 1823 until the publication of Hunter's book in 1872. For Sayyid Ahmad, the permanent trans-border hostility against British rule had to do with the continuing presence in the border of a large, non-loyal, and terrified population, comprising both the Hindus and Muslims who had run away from British territory after the mutiny to escape the wrath of the conqueror, and this had no connections with the Wahhabi fomentations. This absconding population sought shelter among the tribes and started a new life in an unknown environment; thus, it was not strange that these migrants received visitors and money from their families and others in India. Finally, the tribal enmity against authority noted near the Indus River had been recurrent in Indian history. This has been illustrated by the expeditions sent in the past by the Mughal Emperors Akbar (1542–1605), Shah Jahan (1592–1666), and Aurangzeb (1618–1707), all of whom had failed in their goal of subjugating the insurgents.[12]

For Sayyid Ahmad, the demonization of Islam and distortion of the related history in the West had directly caused political adversity towards Indian Muslims. Thus, a more objective approach to the past would have made the Western people end their strong aversion towards Islam and its followers and ensure that even the Muslims rediscovered their own identity and ideals. History was an instrument in the Muslim renaissance, an attitude which influenced Muslim reformers, such as Shibli Nu`mani (1857–1914), Zaka' Allah (1832–1911) and Maulawi Mehdi `Ali (Mohsin-ul Mulk) (1837–1907).

After the events of 1857–1858, Sayyid Ahmad concluded that Indian Muslims needed to accommodate the British – a line of thought which influenced several Muslims, including Chiragh `Ali (1844–1895), who defended that the 'state' was separated from the 'church' in Islam.

By using the equations 'state' equals 'politics' and 'church' equals 'religion' as well as secularism and *laïcité* as main ideological features of late nineteenth century in Western Europe (with the 'separation' of 'state' and 'church' and that of 'politics' and 'religion'), Sayyid Ahmad tried explaining to his readers that politics and religion were separated in Islam as well.

Although Islam does not have a 'church' (in this case, a Catholic one), which is also a political institution, that equation persisted, as if the 'state' were the only 'locus' for 'politics' and the 'church' that for 'religion'. The

---

[12] Again, with some minor differences, Sayyid Ahmad's observations could be applied to the situation in the so-called Middle East after the invasions of Afghanistan and Iraq.

suspicion that Indian Muslims were or could be disloyal particularly worried Sayyid Ahmad. Therefore, he always tried maintaining loyalty towards the British, as illustrated by his views on the caliphate.

SAYYID AHMAD ON THE CALIPHATE AND PAN-ISLAMISM

The Islamic caliphate was formally abolished in 1924. However, it had already ceased to exist as a unitary and effectively administered political institution many centuries earlier. The ever-widening gap between political ideals and historical realities is also reflected in the varying conceptualizations and theories regarding the caliphate developed by Islamic religious scholars and Muslim and Western intellectuals in the past and currently. The recent events in the Islamic world indicate that the idea of caliphate still appeals to Muslims of varying persuasions and continues to be a subject of debate in the Western academic and political circles.[13]

In 1924, the modern concept of the Islamic state emerged in response to the demise of the last caliphate in Turkey. Muhammad Rashid Rida (1865–1935) initiated this move, for protesting the Turkish decision to turn the caliphate into a purely spiritual authority post World War I, in 1923 through his the published book *Al-Khilafa aw al-Imama al-'Uzma* (The Caliphate or the Grand Imamate). In this book, he argues that the caliphate

[13] For further details, please refer to Vernie Liebl, 'The Caliphate', *Middle Eastern Studies* 45, no. 3 (2009): 373–91. As Abderrahmane El Moudden points out, most reflection on the concept of the caliphate occurred in the context of high political stakes involving this very issue. This somewhat affected the overall research on this theme. For instance, in 1919, the Italian scholar Carlo Alfonso Nallino (1872–1938) published a study in which he tried to demonstrate that the Ottoman Sultan had no valid claim to the caliphate. This occurred almost simultaneously with Italy rejecting any Ottoman say whatsoever – Islamic or historical – in Tripolitan affairs. Likewise, in the early 1920s, the British Orientalist Thomas W. Arnold (1864–1930) set out to demonstrate that the formal transfer of the caliphate from the last scion of the Abbasids to the Ottoman Selim I in Cairo in 1517 did not occur. We should not overlook that some years before, Great Britain had been eagerly seeking alternatives to the Ottoman Sultan–Caliph Abdül Hamid II. For further details, please refer to Abderrahmane El Moudden, 'The Idea of the Caliphate between Moroccans and Ottomans: Political and Symbolic Stakes in the 16th and 17th Century-Maghrib', *Studia Islamica* 82 (1995): 103–12; Thomas W. Arnold, *The Caliphate* (Oxford: Clarendon Press, 1924); Carlo Alfonso Nallino, *Notes on the Nature of the 'Caliphate' in General and on the Alleged 'Ottoman Caliphate'* (Rome: Direzione Generale degli Affair Politici [Press of the Foreign Office], 1919).

has always been and should continue to be a combination of spiritual and temporal authorities. He called for an Arab *khilafat durura* (caliphate of necessity or urgency) and maintained that this would give both Muslim and non-Muslim Arabs a state of their own.[14]

About a decade later, the intellectual evolution of the concept of *al-Islam din wa dawla* moved forward by another step. The political context was marked by British colonialism, with the Indian–Pakistani writer Abu'l `Ala Mawdudi (1903–1979) as its major proponent. As a result, some Indian Muslims vocally reacted to the termination of the Ottoman caliphate by establishing the Khilafat Movement, among other actions.[15] Most of Mawdudi's political ideas developed in India during the turbulent period of 1937–1941. In contrast to many who saw the emergence of Pakistan as grounds for optimism, Mawdudi did not advocate for a Muslim state – a state for the Indian Muslims – but an Islamic state – an ideological state run only by true believers on the basis of the Qur'an and the *Sunna*.

In 1925, the Egyptian `alim `Ali `Abd-ul-Raziq (1888–1966) published the book *Al-Islam wa Usul al-Hukm* (Islam and the Foundations of Government), in which he talked about the historical institution of the caliphate, criticizing it and defending the consensus of the community as the transformational power of juridical and political change. He created great controversy by explicitly stating that there was no basis for the caliphate in either the Qur'an or the *Hadith*.[16]

Some forty years before this, Sayyid Ahmad had already explored and given his opinion on the caliphate by using nearly the same arguments `Ali `Abd-ul-Raziq used. To understand the reason and time that Sayyid Ahmad

---

[14] For further details see Jean-François Legrain, *L'idée de califat universel et de congrès islamique face à la revendication de souveraineté nationale et aux menaces d'écrasement de l'empire ottoman. À propos du Traité sur le califat de Rachîd Ridâ* (Lyon: Maison de l'Orient et la Méditerranée, 2006).

[15] For further details on the Khilafat Movement, please refer to Naeem Qureshi, *Pan-Islam in British Indian Politics: A Study of the Khilafat Movement, 1918–1924* (Leiden: Brill, 1999); K. H. Ansari, 'Pan-Islam and the Making of the Early Indian Muslim Socialists', *Modern Asian Studies* 20, no. 3 (1986): 509–37; and Gail Minault, *The Khilafat Movement: Religious Symbolism and Political Mobilization in India* (New York: Columbia University Press, 1982).

[16] Ali Abd Ar-Raziq, *Al-Islam Wa Usul Al-Hukm: Bahth Fi-l Khilafa Wa-l Hukuma Fi-l Islam* (Islam and the Foundations of Governance: Research on the Caliphate and Governance in Islam) (Cairo, 1925), Spanish translation used: *El Islam y los fundamentos del poder* (Granada: Editorial Universidad de Granada, 2007).

decided to address this issue, we must be aware of the following. In 1878, the Ottoman Sultan Abdül Hamid II (1842–1918) newly emphasized his claims as the caliph to counter the Tsar's invocation of 'orthodoxy and slavdom' as well as deal with the constant interferences of Britain and France in internal Ottoman affairs, countries which used the protection of the Christian population in the Ottoman Empire as an excuse.[17] Because of this new emphasis, Muslim subjects living in European and Christian colonial and imperial states, such as those of Russia, France, and Great Britain, were suspected of mutiny by their rulers.[18] Sayyid Ahmad always tried maintaining loyalty to the British – an allegiance well documented by his views on the caliphate.

Some Indian Muslims had forged an emotional link with the Ottoman Empire. A considerable section recognized the Ottoman claim as the universal Islamic caliphate – a recognition that was religious, but with several political implications. All was well until Britain continued pursuing a pro-Ottoman policy and encouraged this attitude among Indian Muslims. As British policy manifestly shifted, tension began developing between the two loyalties.[19]

In a communication,[20] Sayyid Ahmad stated that Islam, in which he had full and abiding faith, preached radical principles and opposed all forms of monarchy – whether hereditary or limited. Although it approved of the rule

[17] For further details, please refer to Benjamin Braude (ed.), *Christians and Jews in the Ottoman Empire: The Abridged Edition* (Boulder: Lynne Rienner Publishers, 2014), especially pp. 43–8.

[18] For a detailed account on British debates on the Ottoman's right to the Caliphate and the Arabs' opposition regarding the Sultan's claims, see Tufan Buzpinar, 'Opposition to the Ottoman Caliphate in the Early Years of Abdülhamid II: 1877–1882', *Die Welt des Islams*, n.s., 36, no. 1 (March 1996): 59–89, and Sean Oliver-Dee, *The Caliphate Question: the British Government and Islamic Governance* (Lanham: Lexington Books, 2009).

[19] For Shibli Nu`mani, there was a sense of the community of Islam – the universality of the *millat* – which made him take interest in the vicissitudes of the Ottoman Empire. The difference between him and Sayyid Ahmad was that Sayyid Ahmad had a concrete political loyalty towards the British, whereas Nu`mani had a spectral religious loyalty towards the Turks. For further details, please refer to Mehr Afroz Murad, *Intellectual Modernism of Shibli Nu`mani: An Exposition of His Religious and Political Ideas* (New Delhi: Kitab Bhavan, 1996), pp. 89–115.

[20] Compiled by Siraj-ud-din Ahmed, *The Truth about the Khilafat* (Lahore: Ripon Press, 1916).

of a popularly elected president, it denounced the concentration of capital and insisted on dividing properties and possessions among legal heirs on the demise of their owners. Nevertheless, he stated that the religion, which taught him these principles, also inculcated certain others. He believed that if God willed subjection of the Muslims to another race – which granted its subjects religious freedom, governed them justly, preserved their peace, as well as protected their life and belongings, as the British did in India – then they should wish their rulers well and allegiance.

For him, Prophet Muhammad was endowed with three attributes: First, prophecy. The commandments of God were revealed to the Prophet, which ended with his death, and in this sense, no one ever was, is, or can be his caliph or deputy. Second, communication. The Prophet communicated or announced to the people what was revealed to him. In this attribute, all Muslim[21] lawyers, learned men, and men of tradition who inculcated the articles of Muslim faith could be considered caliphs of the Prophet. Hence, some commentators of the Qur'an included the words "those who are in authority among you" including the twelve Imams and the Muslim lawyers. Lastly, government of the country. The Prophet ruled the country, enforced the revealed commandments and looked after their proper observance, as well as protected the people of the country and repulsed the enemy by force.

In the third attribute, according to Sayyid Ahmad, those who possessed and governed a country had the power to enforce and keep the rules of faith alive. They could also defend the country against its invaders through their strength and resources. Only these people could be considered caliphs or deputies of the Prophet, provided they were gifted with the virtues and manners of the Prophet and followed the dictates of the religion and possessed external and internal holiness. Some commentators of the Qur'an included the words "those who are in authority among you," Muslim generals under whom were large multitudes of people.

From this point of view, Muslim sovereigns of a country may regard themselves as caliphs. However, they could be caliphs or sultans of only the country they ruled and their Muslims subjects, and not of Muslims or countries not governed by them. This is because it was necessary for a caliph to be the ruler of the country, be able to give retaliation orders and enforce punishment, defend the faith, protect the country and its people from their enemies, and maintain peace and order within. Hence, if a Muslim sovereign did not possess these powers and could not exercise such authority in a particular country, he should not be called the caliph over that country or

---

[21] Where Sir Sayyid Ahmad Khan uses *Muhammadan*, I use *Muslim*.

its Muslim inhabitants. Thus, for Ahmad Khan, Indian Muslims were the subjects of the British Government, under whose protection they lived, regardless of whether the Sultan of Turkey was the caliph or was from the Prophet's tribe.

Sayyid Ahmad may be considered a defender of Westphalian sovereignty (in which a ruler has exclusive sovereignty over their territory). For him, the sultan was only the caliph in his own country (which he governed) and only for the Muslims of this country (who owed him allegiance). Only in his country could he inflict punishment of death or retaliation and maintain the laws of religion. By contrast, the sultan was not the caliph in a country where he did not have the supreme authority and control and thus could not give orders for death or retaliation, maintenance of the faith, or protection of its Muslim inhabitants.

For Sayyid Ahmad, Indian Muslims were the subjects of the British Government, under whose protection they lived.[22] The government had given them peace and allowed them all religious freedoms. Although the English rulers professed the faith of Christ, their government presented no difficulties to a Christian who converted to Islam and vice versa. Notably, the Christian missionaries had nothing to do with the government:[23] They wandered about preaching their religion, akin to the hundreds of Muslims delivering public sermons on Islam. For every Muslim converted to Christianity,[24] there was a Christian converted to Islam.

The British Government had given adequate liberty to its Muslim subjects in the matters of faith. In addition, it safeguarded their lives and properties as well as permitted their rights to marriage, divorce, inheritance, wills, gifts, and endowments allowed by the Islamic law, such that even Christian judges were obliged to adjudicate according to the law of Islam.[25]

---

[22] Here, Shibli Nu`mani was also clear in what the loyalty of Indian Muslims towards the British referred to – see Murad, *Intellectual Modernism of Shibli Nu`mani*, pp. 89–95 and 112–3.

[23] Here, Sayyid Ahmad Khan was deluding himself: religion was a powerful instrument for different European powers to expand their empires. For further details on this please refer to Kevin Ward, Philippa Levine and Frank Trentmann (eds), *Beyond Sovereignty. Britain, Empire and Transnationalism, c. 1880–1950* (London: Palgrave Macmillan, 2007), especially pp. 103–25.

[24] A very famous example was Abdul Masih (1776–1827).

[25] For further details on this, please refer to Alan M. Guenther, *Syed Mahmood and the Transformation of Muslim Law in British India* (Montreal: Institute of Islamic Studies McGill University, 2004).

Thus, Indian Muslims had a religious duty of remaining faithful to and wish well for the British Government, without doing or saying anything practically or theoretically inconsistent with this loyalty and goodwill. For Sayyid Ahmad, the Ottoman Sultan Abdül Hamid II neither ruled India nor he had any sort of authority over the Indian Muslims. He considered that for Indian Muslims, he was a Muslim sovereign, with whom they would consequently sympathize, but not the caliph, according to the Muslim law or religion. He had the rights of a caliph only in his country and over the people of his territorial domain.

History has also proven that whenever a Muslim sovereign assumed the title of the caliph, his caliphate extended only to the extent of his dominions and subjects. A country beyond the range of his government had nothing to do with his caliphate, imamate, and sultanate. There have been times when more than one caliph existed. The Ottoman Sultan was indeed the guardian of the sacred places of the Holy Kaaba, Medina, and Jerusalem, but this had no connection to him being the caliph.[26] In short, no Muslim sovereign was a caliph for Muslims not living in the caliph's dominions.[27]

The implications of the positions taken by Sayyid Ahmad led to various developments – either encouraging or conflicting. In his work, Chiragh `Ali, an associate of Sayyid Ahmad, illustrates the radical potential of the new modernism and rejects the whole structure of medieval society as outmoded. He also vigorously defends Islam against the criticism of Christian missionaries and other Europeans, but through analysis and interpretation of the Qur'an, rather than by defending existing Muslim practices. In this defence, he presents arguments through rational historical analysis.

While dismissing the claims that Islam presents its followers with a binding political and social structure revealed in the Qur'an and the *Sunna*, Chiragh `Ali proved that the *Sunna* is not a reliable source for interpreting Islam and that the Qur'an, the sole reliable source for an analysis of Islam, stipulates no sociopolitical structure. His dismissal of the *Sunna* and the *Hadith* as authentic sources of Islam implied that no basis for 'Muslim

---

[26] Like today, the fact that the king of Saudi Arabia styles himself as the 'Custodian of the Two Holy Mosques' does not mean that all Muslims owe him any allegiance – no one in their sound mind would say that all Christians are Italians or Argentineans just because Pope Francis lives in Italy or is from Argentina.

[27] 'The Views of Sir Syed on the Caliphate', in *Writings and Speeches of Sir Syed Ahmad Khan*, comp. and ed. Shan Muhammad, pp. 255–60.

Common Law' existed and that the true development of Muslim societies depended on the development of a 'secular' state legal system, separating 'church' from 'state' and 'religion' from 'politics'. This implication was noted at a time when the modern state (here, the 'nation-state'), with 'secularism' as its ideology, was becoming the political norm along with the naïve idea that 'politics' was fully embodied in the 'state', whereas 'religion' was fully embodied in 'church': this is not only a political organization but also an institution characteristic of only a small part of humankind.

Chiragh `Ali adopted a modernist stance combined with rejection of all classical sources of Islamic law and thought, except for the Qur'an itself. He supported his positions through a rigorous (speculative) analysis of the Islamic law and viewed everything else in the Islamic traditions in its historical context. Chiragh `Ali and others like him could thus argue that the Prophet neither established a formal legal system nor required his followers to do so. Therefore, the Muslims were free to develop legal systems that were according to the specific conditions of their own times, without being bound by systems developed by Muslims in other times or places, thus opening doors for a radically modernist form of Islam.[28]

CONCLUSION

When I had first outlined this chapter, I had a very clear idea of the issue I wanted to address: All the talk on the caliphate, Islamic state, and so on is nothing new. Sayyid Ahmad had already addressed it, which is yet another example of him being ahead of his time. Herein, I aimed to contextualize his thought and move in the direction of what this book proposes to do: think of his projects in the context of how he speaks to us today and how best we may use Sayyid Ahmad's ideas for addressing important issues of contemporary concern.

Considering the current events, one may not see the point of writing an essay on the views of Sayyid Ahmad regarding the caliphate, because there is always some 'scholar', 'expert', 'demagogue', or 'politician' – Muslim or not – who talks either of an 'Islamic state' as something that already existed in the time of the Prophet or of a 'Muslim threat'. Nevertheless, Sayyid Ahmad talks to us from two viewpoints: historical and pragmatic – with the former being easier than the latter.

---

[28] For further details on this, please refer to Carimo Mohomed, 'A Historiographical Approach to the Qur'an and Shari'a in Late 19th Century India: The Case of Chiragh `Ali', *História da Historiografia* 17 (2015): 209–25.

Historically, as Quentin Skinner asserts, the idea that a supreme political authority can be the authority of the state was originally a consequence of a theory of the civil association – a theory with both absolutist and secular ideological allegiances. This theory, nevertheless, was the product of the earliest major counterrevolutionary movement in modern European history, the movement of reaction against the ideologies of popular sovereignty, which was developed in the Dutch and French religious wars of sixteenth and seventeenth centuries initially and then reinstated in the course of the English constitutional upheavals of the mid-seventeenth century. The ideology of state power as well as the new terminology used for its expression provoked a series of doubts and criticisms. Some initial hostility came from conservative theorists who were anxious to uphold the venerable ideal of 'one king, one faith, one law' and repudiated any suggestion that the public authority's aims should be purely civil in character. Thus, they sought to reinstate a closer relationship between their allegiance towards church and towards state. Some critics also clarified that sovereigns were of far higher standing than mere representatives were, and they insisted that the powers of the state must be understood to inhere in them, not in the person of the state.

Once the term 'state' became accepted as the master noun of political discourse, numerous other concepts and assumptions based on the analysis of sovereignty had to be reorganized or even given up. The concept of political allegiance underwent a consequential process of redefinition. A subject or *subditus* had traditionally sworn allegiance to his sovereign as a liege lord, but with the acceptance that sovereignty was lodged not with rulers but the state, the 'familiar' view that citizens owed their loyalty to the state itself come into being.[29]

Political institutions and practices, which had evolved in the West, were considered by Western intellectuals and statesmen as the sole models of political modernity, which had to be adopted by worldwide. Of these models, the model of the modern nation-state was particularly important. This model, with the expansion in print media and education, led to the rise of a new group of Muslim intellectuals claiming authority to interpret Islam as well as act as spokesmen for the community, a fragmentation of religious authority which facilitated the rise of numerous intellectuals

---

[29] Quentin Skinner, 'From the State of Princes to the Person of the State', in *Visions of Politics. Volume 2: Renaissance Virtues*, pp. 368–413 (Cambridge: Cambridge University Press, 2004).

seeking exercise *ijtihad* (independent reasoning) to provide solutions to contemporary problems and were active in acquiring new sociopolitical ideas from the West as well as reinterpreting their own traditions considering these new ideas.

For every individual, the meaning of 'religion' is different: an identitarian affiliation, a spiritual affirmation, or just faith. Nevertheless, all these factors impact the society in the political process, which does not exhaust itself in the 'state'. Some Muslims have often considered Islam a total world view comprising religion and politics, but this unity has rarely been realized. This view on the totalizing aspect of Islam appears particularly in the periods of political instability than in those of political stability. In 1996, Ira M. Lapidus[30] wrote that the history of the Middle East and the wider Muslim world reveals various institutional situations. The supposed Muslim norm of the integration of state (political organization) and religious authority and the identification of state and religious community actually characterize only a small segment of Middle Eastern and other Muslim populations. Despite the common statement (and the Muslim ideal) that the institutions of state and religion are unified with Islam as the total way of life defining political as well as social and family matters, most Muslim societies do not conform to this ideal. They have been built around separate institutions of state and religion.

The historical actuality of the division of Muslim societies into a realm of political authority and that of religiocommunal affairs has other contemporary reverberations. In addition to Islam, the long-established state–religious-community differentiation has legitimized political power. In particular, besides religious validation, the Ottoman Empire achieved a *de facto* legitimacy as a conquering state and defender of Muslims. Ottoman (and Iranian) rulers were also conceived as vice-regents of God – that is, direct agents of God's authority on Earth. Beyond the theory of Islamic states was the reality of legitimate non-Islamic monarchies. An inevitable reality is that religious communities embody a corresponding tradition of political passivity, along with the tendency to accept political actualities and state power based on conquest and preserved by force. In this tradition, the realm of Islamic authenticity lies within an individual's soul and their behaviour in small communities.

---

[30] Ira M. Lapidus, 'State and Religion in Islamic Societies', *Past and Present* 151, no. 1 (1996): 3–27.

Irfan Ahmad[31] argues that the debate on the Islamic state has been conducted mostly in the field of Islamic studies or area studies. Not surprisingly, the theological factors have weighed heavily in these debates. While being sensitive to theology, social scientists should use approaches giving importance to the political factors and historical context, in which philological interpretation is made or unmade, as well as critically subject theological arguments to historical–political matrices shaping them, and more importantly, the product of interpretation. The use of an exclusively theological approach to the canonical texts, such as the Qur'an, has considerable limits. The Qur'an is not a pristine text yielding meanings by itself. The distinct social condition and biography of its reader produces its meanings.

Considering that Islam was the state from the very beginning imposes a distinctly modern term on a pre-modern social formation. Equally misleading are the dominant assumptions, widespread across academic disciplines, that the so-called 'theological' character of Islam forces it to fuse religion and politics and that, before the European encroachment in the late eighteenth century, Muslims rarely studied politics in isolation from their religion are equally misleading.[32] This essentialist view on Muslim political literature neglects *akhlaqi* texts ('mirrors of princes'), aiming to instruct on the right political conduct in specific political contexts and concerning not only ethically good actions but also resolution of statecraft-, political culture-, and philosophy-related issues. A tradition of dissidence, 'mirrors of princes', redefines *Shari`a* in a philosophical, non-sectarian, and humane way as a kind of protest against an overly legalistic approach. In many important ways, these ethical–philosophical texts transcend the conventional positions of *Shari`a* and address concerns of the larger humanity. According to their history and practices, most Indian Muslim rulers did not follow *Shari`a*; rather, they framed secular laws, *zawabit* (administrative, standards, principles), independent of *Shari`a*. Moreover, the meaning of *Shari`a* has varied. This body of juridical rules propounded by theologians and of *akhlaq* texts has been anything but stable.[33]

[31] Irfan Ahmad, 'Genealogy of the Islamic State: Reflections on Maududi's Political thought and Islamism', *Journal of the Royal Anthropological Institute* 15, no. s1 (2009): S145–62.

[32] Hamid Enayat, *Modern Islamic Political Thought: The Response of the Shi'i and Sunni Muslims to the Twentieth Century* (London: I. B. Tauris, 2009), p. 3.

[33] For further details on this, please refer to Muzaffar Alam, *The Languages of Political Islam: India, 1200–1800* (Chicago: University of Chicago Press, 2004).

With regard to practice in the twenty-first century, how can we implement Sayyid Ahmad's recommendations? Sayyid Ahmad lived in a period when Muslims (in this case, Indian Muslims) became subjects of a Christian–Western power and when politicians as well as historians and social scientists raised suspicions regarding their political allegiances of this community. Currently, Muslims are not confined – as in the nineteenth century – to their 'traditional' homelands and the 'suspicions' remain high. What would Sayyid Ahmad recommend to his fellow Muslims born and living in countries where the rulers are clearly anti-Muslim? Should they comply? Because Sayyid Ahmad favoured the British Government, as it granted religious freedom, would he be in favour of disobedience in those cases where the leaders are anti-Muslim? What about countries that are considered Islamic, where the state sometimes declares parts of its population as non-Muslim, with all the political consequences, or where the state is ally of governments with an anti-Muslim sentiment?

Answering these questions will indeed be a difficult task for Sayyid Ahmad.

3 Sir Sayyid on 'The Present State of Education among Muhammadan Females'

GAIL MINAULT

The title of this chapter refers to the testimony that Sir Sayyid Ahmad Khan gave before the Indian Education Commission in 1882:

> The question of female education much resembles the question of the oriental philosopher who asked whether the egg or the hen were first created. Those who hold that women should be educated and civilised prior to the men are greatly mistaken. The fact is that no satisfactory education can be provided for Muhammadan females until a large number of Muhammadan males receive a sound education. The present state of education among Muhammadan females is, in my opinion, enough for domestic happiness, considering the present social and economic condition of the life of the Muhammadans of India.

This statement before a government body makes it clear that Sir Sayyid had a definite priority, that is, the development of his college at Aligarh, designed to reform the education of Muslim men. In urging this priority to the government, he no doubt hoped for more resources to be directed towards his institution. But did that mean he was against women's education? Not necessarily. Sir Sayyid, in fact, has been praised for his support of women's education, although anyone reading the above quote would have to question that generalization.

What were Sir Sayyid's actual views towards women's education, and what did he mean by its 'present state'? To answer these questions, one needs to consult a variety of his writings on the topic – not just his testimony before a British government body, where his motives were to urge wise expenditure. Among such writings are his biography of his maternal grandfather, *Sirat-e Faridiyya*, wherein he discusses his own mother's education, and his articles on the subjects of women and their rights and status, which are part of his collected writings. Only after considering in greater detail his opinions and the contexts in which he rendered them can one have a clear idea of whether or not Sir Sayyid supported women's education.

Sir Sayyid had an unusual childhood. He was raised in the household of his maternal grandfather Khwaja Fariduddin Ahmad (1747–1828), a high official in the Mughal court, who also served the British in various capacities. He was also a learned mathematician and astronomer. In *Sirat-e Faridiyya*, Sir Sayyid recounts reciting his Persian lesson before this formidable figure and receiving a tongue-lashing for bungling his translation from Sa`di's *Bustan*.[1] Sir Sayyid's mother, Azizunnissa Begam (1780?–1857) was the eldest daughter of the household and had received a basic religious education at home – the type given to upper-class, purdah-observing women of the time. She had read the Qur'an and some basic Persian books (including Sa`di's *Gulistan* and *Bustan*). She also had an influence on Sir Sayyid's intellectual development. He mentions reciting his lessons from the *Gulistan* to her and the fact that she had a scourge, made of thongs of woven rope with a wooden handle, to chastise him, although she never used it on him. He notes, 'She must surely have got angry with me on many occasions.'[2] Sir Sayyid also describes her religious faith: she not only knew the Qur'an but was a disciple of Shah Ghulam Ali, a Sufi mystic of the Naqshbandi Mujaddidi order. Ghulam Ali was a reformer who, among other practices, refused to hand out amulets as protection against illness. Like her Sufi religious guide, Azizunnissa believed that such customs went against the Islamic belief in God's absolute power. She was pious and charitable to those less fortunate, and thus served as a moral example in Sir Sayyid's life. He echoes an adage popular at the time: 'a good mother is better than a thousand teachers.'[3] From Sayyid Ahmad's account, it is clear that he was raised in a household of considerable literary and scientific culture, and that he owed much of his moral fibre to his mother's example. He knew from this experience that even in purdah, a woman could be literate, gracious, compassionate, and religiously exemplary.

Azizunnissa's example, so firmly embedded in Sir Sayyid's early consciousness, probably contributed to his later judgement that women's education was sufficient for 'domestic happiness'. Sir Sayyid resisted the idea

---

[1] Sayyid Ahmad Khan, *Sirat-e Faridiyya* (Agra: Mufid-i-Am Press, 1896), repr. in M. Ismail Panipati (ed.), *Maqalat-e Sir Sayyid*, vol. 16 (Lahore: Majlis-e Taraqqi-e Adab, 1965), pp. 629–96; Christopher Shackle (trans.), 'English Translation of Sir Sayyid Ahmad Khan's "Sirat-e-Faridiya"', *Islamic Culture* 46, no. 3 (1972): 307–36 (Shackle's translation hereafter cited as *SF*; this reference is from *SF*, pp. 325–26).

[2] *SF*, p. 330.

[3] Ibid., p. 331.

of women's education outside their home – at least for women of his social class – because he knew that there were women, like his mother, who, even without much formal education, contributed to the moral improvement of their families and society.

Sir Sayyid's writings specifically dealing with women in Indian society shed further light on his mixed feelings about women's capacity for improvement, on the one hand arguing for the equality of men and women as human beings and as believers, but on the other despairing at women's deficiencies and arguing in favour of changes initiated by men. In an article on women's rights 'Auraton ke Huquq', published in 1871, he argues that the position of women in Islamic law recognizes women's abilities in a host of ways: A Muslim woman can enter into contracts (including her necessary consent to marriage), inherit and control property, dispose of property, sue and be sued, and establish endowments. In brief, a Muslim woman is recognized as a legal equal to a man, argues Sir Sayyid, except with regard to the limitations she accepts in her marriage contract or those that are divinely imposed by nature on man and woman as biological differences. By contrast, he notes that in Western countries, including Britain, a woman after marriage becomes part of her husband's legal person, and her property is under his control. Without her husband's permission, she cannot enter into contracts and agreements, dispose of property, or initiate a lawsuit. He recalls an 1870 debate in the British Parliament over a bill to abolish the condition that women, upon marriage, be deprived of control over their own property. In the debate, a Member of Parliament (MP) commented that the impact of marriage on a woman is like punishment for a crime: 'when you are convicted, your property is confiscated'. Many MPs laughed at this comment but agreed that the condition under consideration was hurtful and unjust to women.[4]

After laying out this contrast, Sir Sayyid concludes that the laws of Islam clearly consider men and women as equals – more so than any other religion or laws of any other country. He notes that it is surprising, therefore, that in Western countries, Muslim women's status is greatly pitied compared with that of their own women. In fact, the situation should be exactly the opposite. Trying to explain this paradox, Sir Sayyid sidesteps the question of purdah, noting that there are many different opinions about this matter.

---

[4] Sayyid Ahmad Khan, 'Auraton ke Huquq', originally published in *Tahzib-ul Akhlaq* (Aligarh: 15 Jamadi ul-Awwal 1288 AH, 1871), repr. in Panipati (ed.), *Maqalat*, vol. 5, pp. 194–9 (Lahore: Majlis-e Taraqqi-e Adab, 1962).

Still, he grants that the observance of purdah in India is excessive. What concerns him, however, are men's attitudes towards women's well-being, concern for their happiness and dignity, and ideas about companionship between spouses in different countries. In other words, despite their legal rights, the social attitudes of men towards women in Muslim countries, most of all in India, are abysmal. We should not deny this, he argues, but rather improve our social attitudes in the light of Islam. In effect, we should treat our women better because we already have the law on our side.[5] This summary of a complex argument demonstrates Sir Sayyid's wrestling with different aspects of 'the woman question' in both Britain and India, after he had returned from a visit to Britain in 1869–1970, and he was articulating the differences in both laws and social attitudes that he had observed.

In a short article titled 'Pardah',[6] Sir Sayyid elaborates on Muslim differences of opinion about women's seclusion. There are men who think that it is based on the Qur'an and thus essential, but others view it as outmoded custom and thus a barrier to civilizational advancement. Most women themselves consider it ordained by their religion, and thus any attempt to change it would doubtless be a losing battle. As for himself, Sir Sayyid does not worry about being labelled old-fashioned, but he thinks that men who do not follow the Qur'an in other aspects of their lives should not argue on that basis in this instance. As for those who want to be like the English by doing away with purdah, that is a mistaken idea. First, let men improve to the point where they are the intellectual match of the English, and only then can they pay attention to the status of their women. There are ambiguities in both these articles, but both include the unequivocal point that Indian men need to change their attitudes and behaviours before any improvement in the status of women will be possible.

Elsewhere in his writings, Sir Sayyid was fond of repeating the dictum of the Prophet Muhammad that Muslims, both men and women, should seek knowledge from sources far and wide. In the essays reviewed here, Sir Sayyid elaborates on that tradition, claiming that in the great early days of Islam, women had been educated. Since they could inherit property, they had to be able to manage it. Thus, they had to be able to read (not only scriptures), write, and calculate. He believed that because Islamic civilization had fallen on evil days, the status and rights of women had become abridged. This was not true Islam, but the result of adherence to bad custom.

---

[5] Khan, 'Auraton ke Huquq', repr. in Panipati (ed.), *Maqalat*, vol. 5, pp. 194–9.
[6] Sayyid Ahmad Khan, 'Pardah', in Panipati (ed.), *Maqalat*, vol. 5, pp. 186–7.

Sir Sayyid connects these ideas in another article devoted to the state or condition of Indian women 'Hindustan ki Auraton ki Halat', published in 1876.[7] Therein, Sir Sayyid reiterates his thesis that as long as the state of Indian men is in need of reform, the state of Indian women is a matter for later consideration. Women are way behind men in mental development and thus are weaker, even though they belong to the same species as men. Girls are not as fortunate as boys, in that they observe purdah from an early age, and so their horizons are limited. Just like a bird locked up in a cage who never can learn to fly, so a girl's humanity is blighted. This would seem to be an argument against purdah. Sir Sayyid, however, does not follow this line of reasoning, for purdah, according to him, is not an obstacle to the home education of women. Rather, he turns to a discussion of customary observances and household rituals that define the limits of many women's imaginations. Again, many of these were observances that his own mother eschewed. He discusses some of the customs to which women cling, for they believe that to change them will bring about calamity. They hold that the influence of ghosts and *djinn*s causes misfortune. Rather than calling on *hakim*s or doctors, they fall prey to the foolish advice of folk practitioners and their amulets and rituals of exorcism. Groups of women will attend a birth, and if it is difficult, they will raise a hue and cry, believing that this will frighten the baby into letting go its hold inside the mother. They argue and give conflicting advice to the mother in labour until she is confused and exhausted. They refuse her nourishment, or even simple broth to drink, to restore her energy. In his description, Sir Sayyid quotes an account by an (unnamed) Englishwoman who attended a village birth and argued with the midwife about the delivery. She was told that there was such a difference between Indian women and foreign women that her practices would only result in disaster. She insisted, however, on allowing the woman to lie down, and untied the binding cloth around her abdomen. Consequently, her baby was soon born without complications.[8] Sir Sayyid cites this ethnographic account as an example of the backward mentality and inappropriate behaviour that limit the lives of Indian women.

---

[7] In the two previous articles, Sir Sayyid focuses on Indian Muslim women, but in this one, as indicated by the title, he addresses the status of Indian women in general, though his verdict is comparable. Sayyid Ahmad Khan, 'Hindustan ki Auraton ki Halat', originally published in *Akhbar-e Scientific Society*, 14 April 1876, Aligarh, repr. in Panipati (ed.), *Maqalat*, vol. 5, pp. 188–93.

[8] Citation from an Englishwoman (in Urdu), in Panipati (ed.), *Maqalat*, vol. 5, pp. 191–2.

Sir Sayyid's articles on the condition of Indian women in the 1870s and 1880s display a deep ambivalence. On the one hand, he considered that women are equal to men as fellow humans and enjoy a legal status in Islam that is better than that in the laws of Western countries. On the other hand, during his visit to Britain, he noted that Englishwomen enjoyed a higher regard and greater participation in society than was current in India. He does not blame purdah for the perceived backwardness of Indian women, but rather their adherence to false and useless customs. This condition was difficult to overcome and made the lives of Indian women miserable and the lives of their men very difficult. Women were thus the main cause of the backwardness of society, but paradoxically also its main victims. This discourse of custom did not originate with Sir Sayyid, but was common among religious and social reformers, both Hindu and Muslim, in late nineteenth-century India.[9] Sir Sayyid was concerned with the state of Indian women as a hindrance to social and educational reform, but he saw the solution as involving first the enlightenment of men, who could then enlighten their women. His constant refrain throughout these writings and in his testimony before the Indian Education Commission in 1882 was first to educate and civilize the men and the enlightenment of the women would follow. His college at Aligarh, founded in 1875, was in his view an obvious vanguard in that reform and the ideal beneficiary of British largesse.

In the early 1890s, Sir Sayyid reiterated these opinions on women's education in a personal letter to Sayyid Mumtaz Ali (1860–1935), a young man from Lahore who considered himself a disciple of Sir Sayyid, even though he had not been educated at Aligarh. Sir Sayyid refers to a letter he had received from Mumtaz Ali advocating women's education and notes that while he wishes that girls could receive a high quality and worthy education, he is convinced that under present conditions, to educate girls would only increase their sorrow and oppression. He also notes that in Indian society, women cannot remain unmarried, but given the backward and poorly civilized nature of the men, who treat their wives as no better than slave girls, it is better that young wives not be too educated. Indeed, given the poor quality of the men, if a girl were accomplished and cultured, she would be miserable. It would be far better that she not realize how

---

[9] For a further discussion of this point, see Gail Minault, 'Women, Legal Reform, and Muslim Identity', *Comparative Studies in South Asia, Africa, and the Middle East* 17, no. 2 (1998): 1–10, repr. in Gail Minault, *Gender, Language, and Learning: Essays in Indo-Muslim Cultural History*, pp. 64–83 (New Delhi: Permanent Black, 2009) (hereafter cited as Minault, *GLL*).

oppressed she is. He reiterates that it is thus premature to discuss women's education before men's education is better developed, for that would be disastrous for the women concerned. This is why he has not worked for women's education so far. He thinks that there is no great harm in the fact that educated young men cannot find educated women as wives. They will love them according to their social custom and may even educate them, and the wives will follow their example. He repeats that educating boys first is much more important. To have women more educated than their husbands would be damaging to the women's well-being. This is apparently what Sir Sayyid means by 'domestic happiness'.[10]

It is worth noting that in this letter to an admirer who had sought his advice concerning various proposals to improve girls' education, Sir Sayyid's tone is more personalized. He expresses concern for women's happiness, or at least forbearance, in marriage. Sir Sayyid, nevertheless, remains opposed to women's education, save that which they could acquire at home from enlightened families or husbands.

By the 1890s, however, a number of Sir Sayyid's Aligarh students and graduates were discussing the desirability of girls' education, precisely because they desired educated wives for themselves or wanted education for their daughters. The older custom of educating purdah-observing girls at home, by means of governesses, was only possible for the wealthy. Thus, schools and curricula suitable for girls were increasingly becoming part of public debate in social and educational reform associations. The All-India Muhammadan (later, Muslim) Educational Conference, founded by Sir Sayyid in 1886, as a forum for discussion of the improvement of education among Indian Muslims, avoided the topic of women's education under his leadership. By 1896, however, a number of students and professors at Aligarh College who favoured the promotion of Muslim women's education founded the Women's Education Section of the Educational Conference. Chief among the organizers was Sayyid Karamat Husain, the Professor of Law at Aligarh, and later, a judge at the Allahabad High Court and founder of two girls' schools in Allahabad and Lucknow.[11] Mumtaz Ali was chosen

---

[10] Mumtaz Ali published Sir Sayyid's letter in *Huquq un-Niswan* (Lahore: Dar ul-Isha'iat-i-Punjab, 1898), pp. 57–59.

[11] On Karamat Husain's career, see Gail Minault, 'Sayyid Karamat Husain and Education for Women', in *Lucknow: Memories of a City*, ed. Violette Graf, pp. 155–64 (Delhi: Oxford University Press, 1997), repr. in Minault, *GLL*, pp. 182–93; and Gail Minault, *Secluded Scholars: Women's Education and Muslim Social Reform in Colonial India* (Delhi: Oxford University Press, 1998), pp. 188–92, 216–28.

as the Secretary of the Women's Education Section, tasked with developing plans for a normal school to train teachers for Muslim girls, and served until 1902.

Eventually, Mumtaz Ali's attention turned towards a career in publishing. He also sought Sir Sayyid's advice in that endeavour. He had written a treatise in defence of women's rights in Islamic law, *Huquq un-Niswan*, and may have taken his inspiration from Sir Sayyid's article 'Auraton ke Huquq',[12] for he visited Sir Sayyid in Aligarh sometime in the 1890s to show him the manuscript of his work, perhaps hoping for the elder man's approbation. Sir Sayyid started to peruse it, but looked increasingly shocked and disturbed. As he leafed through it, his face turned red and his hands began to tremble. Finally, he tore up the manuscript and threw it into the wastepaper basket. Fortunately, at that moment, a servant arrived to announce lunch. As Sir Sayyid left the room, Mumtaz Ali retrieved his mutilated manuscript from the trash.[13] Undaunted, on another occasion, he wrote to Sir Sayyid asking his advice concerning a name for his proposed newspaper for women. Sir Sayyid replied, grumbling that Mumtaz Ali had not asked his advice on whether to start the journal or not, and warned him that if he started such a publication, he would not only earn public opprobrium but would ultimately fail. If he persisted in this folly, however, he should name it *Tahzib un-Niswan*, a direct reference to Sir Sayyid's own social reform journal, *Tahzib-ul Akhlaq* (The Social Reformer). At the end of his life, it seemed, Sir Sayyid admired Mumtaz Ali's courage if not his chosen cause. A few weeks after receiving the old man's letter, in early 1898, Mumtaz Ali heard the news of his death. He started publishing his newspaper for women a few months later. His collaborator in the writing and editing of *Tahzib un-Niswan* was his wife Muhammadi Begam (1878?–1908), who had been educated at home by her father and brothers. Mumtaz Ali also waited until after Sir Sayyid's death to publish *Huquq un-Niswan*.[14]

The question remains: what was 'the present state of education among Muhammadan females'? Sir Sayyid did not define a curriculum for girls in

---

[12] Discussed earlier.
[13] Abul Athar Hafiz Jalandhari, 'Maulvi Sayyid Mumtaz Ali', *Tahzib un-Niswan* 38 (1935): 615–6; Sayyid Mumtaz Ali, *Huquq un-Niswan*.
[14] Mumtaz Ali, 'Tahzib un-Niswan', *Tahzib un-Niswan*, 21 (1918): 425; Minault, *Secluded Scholars*, pp. 110–22; unpublished biography of Muhammadi Begam by her sister, Ahmadi Begam, photocopy in author's possession.

his day because he consistently tried to downplay its urgency. Nevertheless, among his allies in the Aligarh Movement and others who considered themselves his disciples, there were many discussions in print and in public of real and ideal plans for women's education during his time. Maulvi Nazir Ahmad Dehlavi (1833?–1912) published the novel *Mir`at-ul `Urus* in 1869, which described the ideal, home-educated, modern Muslim woman in the character of Asghari, who reforms her household, keeps her husband in line, and then, founds a school at her home to educate the girls of her neighbourhood.[15] The poet Altaf Husain Hali (1837–1914) published in 1874 *Majalis un-Nissa*, fictionalized conversations among women on the subject of women's education. The central character in this story, Zubaida Khatun, is given an ideal moral, literary, and practical education by her parents, and then, she teaches her son to be an exemplary and resourceful citizen of the modern world.[16]

In addition to these fictional heroines, there were real women who had been educated at home in families with literary traditions, such as Sir Sayyid's mother, Azizunnissa, or in middle-class families, where literacy was considered a must for the men and a virtue for the women. The men of such families might be *maulvi*s (teachers or government servants of middling rank), or *vakil*s and *hakim*s (practitioners of law and medicine), or religious clerics who purveyed religious literacy, at least the knowledge of the Qur'an, to village boys and girls. The wives and widows of such men sometimes served as *ustani*s (governesses) to higher-class families, while their daughters received basic lessons in the Qur'an starting around the age of four, at home, along with their brothers. Beyond the knowledge of the scriptures, some girls learned to read Persian and/or Urdu (because their scripts are similar to the Arabic of the Qur'an). Girls at home had little time for other study, as most of their waking hours were taken up by helping their mother cook, sew, and look after their younger siblings, or helping to supervise the servants charged with those tasks. In this way, daughters learned what they most needed to know for their future roles as wives and mothers. For them, it was useful to know a few moral maxims and some basic mathematics in order to keep household accounts, but

---

[15] It remains in print in numerous editions, Nazir Ahmad, *Mir'at ul-`Arus*, Eng. tr. by G. E. Ward as *The Bride's Mirror* (London: Henry Frowde, 1903), repr. with an afterword by Frances W. Pritchett (New Delhi: Permanent Black, 2001).

[16] Translated by Gail Minault as *Voices of Silence: English Translation of Hali's Majalis un-Nissa and Chup ki Dad* (Delhi: Chanakya Publications, 1986). For a summary of these two fictional heroines as role models, see Minault, *Secluded Scholars*, pp. 31–55.

the standard wisdom regarded a literary education as superfluous for girls. Furthermore, it was considered dangerous for a girl to know how to write. The prohibition against writing was based on classical Persian texts, but it was also the product of an anxiety that if a girl knew how to write, she might write letters to a forbidden person – defined as any man, related or unrelated, who might be an eligible marriage partner – thereby violating the rules of purdah and damaging family honour.[17]

There were, of course, exceptions to these generalizations, but often, they only proved the overall rule. The Begams of Bhopal belonged to a dynasty that produced no male heirs for three generations, so women ruled this small central Indian state and princesses of the house of Bhopal were educated. Sultan Jahan Begam (1858–1930) outlined her lessons in her autobiography. The princesses were taught the Qur'an, Persian, English, Pushto (as the dynasty was of Pathan descent), arithmetic, handwriting, riding, and fencing. Sultan Jahan maintained strict purdah for most of her life, and she herself as well as others pointed to her case as evidence that women in purdah could be well educated. While it is true that veiled women could be educated, the Begams of Bhopal were atypical.[18]

More typical were women who acquired their education against great odds. Abadi Banu Begam (1852–1924), otherwise known as 'Bi Amman', became well-known as the mother of the Ali Brothers, Shaukat and Mohamed Ali, who were Muslim political leaders in the early twentieth century. She was from an administrative family in the Muslim principality of Rampur. Because she had learned the Qur'an as a child, she knew the Arabic script in a rudimentary fashion. She taught herself to read Urdu by asking one of her nephews to read to her from a book of stories. She then committed it to memory and reread it to herself – partly from memory and partly by sounding out the letters. She therefore could read, and in addition was a great storyteller, but she never learned to write. Widowed at a young age, she raised her five sons and one daughter, and was such a devotee of learning – reported her son Mohamed – that she pawned her gold ornaments in order to guarantee that her sons had a good education.[19]

---

[17] This reconstruction of girls' education in Sir Sayyid's time is a summary based on Minault, *Secluded Scholars*, pp. 19–31, the sources for which were biographical or autobiographical.
[18] Sultan Jahan Begam, *An Account of My Life (Gohur-i-Iqbal)*, Eng. tr. Charles Herbert Payne (London: John Murray, 1912), pp. 23–4.
[19] Mohamed Ali, *My Life, A Fragment* (repr. Lahore: S. M. Ashraf, 1966), pp. 4–5, 12–17.

The Present State of Education among Muhammadan Females 65

Especially remarkable was Ashrafunnissa Begam (1840–1903), called Bibi Ashraf, who wrote an account of how she learned to read and write, which shows the amazing degree of self-discipline and determination required, even in a literate family. Bibi Ashraf came from a family of modest means, but one in which the women were taught to read, but never to write. Her father was a *vakil*, employed away from home in the princely state of Gwalior. Bibi Ashraf and her siblings were thus raised in her grandfather's house, where an *ustani* would come to teach the girls to read the Qur'an. This arrangement lasted until the *ustani*, a widow, remarried. This happened when Bibi Ashraf was six years old and only halfway through the sacred book. The grandfather was so shocked by the *ustani*'s remarriage (despite widow remarriage being permitted in Islam) that he banned the woman from the house, and the Qur'anic lessons ceased. Bibi Ashraf's grandmother, however, encouraged her to read and reread the sections of the Qur'an that she had already studied, and she persisted until she completed the sacred book on her own. She still could not read Urdu and wanted to do so in order to participate in poetic recitations during the sacred month of Muharram at *Sh'ia* rituals in the household. She asked a relative for the texts of some of the poems offered at such rituals, saying that she would have them copied so she could practise reading and reciting them. She got the texts, some paper, and took some coal blacking from the kitchen (to make ink to copy the texts) and then, in secret, went up to the roof at midday – when everyone else in the household was resting – to copy the texts, which she could not understand. She then found a teacher, a male cousin who needed help studying the Qur'an, and exchanged that service for help in learning to read some of the Urdu elegiac poetry that she had copied so diligently. After a while, she found that she could read and understand these poems well. Thereafter, it was simply a matter of practice – reading and copying out everything that came to hand. Eventually, the other women in the household found out that she could write, and thus Bibi Ashraf became the family scribe who wrote their letters. Later in life, after marriage, motherhood, and widowhood, Bibi Ashraf became a teacher at a girls' school in Lahore. Her faith and determination combined to make her an inspiring role model for her students.[20]

---

[20] C. M. Naim has translated and commented upon Ashrafunnissa's story in 'How Bibi Ashraf Learned to Read and Write', *Annual of Urdu Studies* 6 (1987): 99–115; Muhammadi Begam, *Hayat-e Ashraf* (Lahore: Imambara Sayyid Mubarak Begam, n.d.). Bibi Ashraf's biographer, Muhammadi Begam, was the wife of Mumtaz Ali and the editor of *Tahzib un-Niswan*.

Bi Amman, Bibi Ashraf, and Muhammadi Begam, all came from families with a tradition of service to government, where the boys were educated and the girls exposed to a modicum of literacy. Even in these families, however, girls had to use stealth and determination to acquire the ability to read prose and poetry in Urdu and, sometimes, subterfuge to learn to write.

The Women's Education Section of the Muhammadan Educational Conference, meanwhile, continued to advocate the founding of schools for Muslim girls, including a normal school to provide teachers for such schools. Little had been accomplished, however, beyond discussions at annual meetings and debates over desirable curricula. In 1902, at the annual meeting of the conference, Shaikh Abdullah (1874–1965), an Aligarh lawyer, was named the Secretary of the Women's Education Section, replacing Mumtaz Ali. Shaikh Abdullah vowed to raise funds for the normal school and urged the conference to establish it in Lahore. This was partly to mollify Mumtaz Ali and partly because of vocal opposition to establishing a school for girls and women in Aligarh, so close to the boys' college.[21] Shaikh Abdullah had been educated at Aligarh College, where he also studied law, and was inspired by the views favouring women's education of his law professor, Sayyid Karamat Husain.[22] Shaikh Abdullah's talents for organizing and fundraising had also endeared him to Aftab Ahmad Khan, a leader of the Aligarh College Duty Society and of the Aligarh Old Boys' (Alumni) Association. Following Shaikh Abdullah's marriage in 1902 to a young woman with some home-based education (and a sister of one of his Aligarh College classmates), he began considering concrete ways to promote education for Muslim women. Aftab Ahmad encouraged him to take on the task of revitalizing the Women's Education Section, while Begam Abdullah encouraged him in these efforts.[23] The normal school idea was eventually deemphasized, for lack of support, but together, Shaikh and Begam Abdullah founded Aligarh

---

[21] Shaikh Abdullah, *Mushahidat wa Ta'asurat* (The Autobiography of Shaikh Abdullah) (Aligarh: Female Education Association, 1969), pp. 210–11; Muhammadan Educational Conference Proceedings, 1902, pp. 227–32; 1905, pp. 194–5.

[22] Mentioned above as instrumental in the founding of the Women's Education Section, and of girls' schools.

[23] David Lelyveld, *Aligarh's First Generation: Muslim Solidarity in British India* (Princeton, NJ: Princeton University Press, 1978), pp. 192–3, 287–9, 330–1; Shaikh Abdullah, *Sawanih-e `Umri-e Abdullah Begam* (Biography of Begam Abdullah) (Aligarh: Privately published, 1954), pp. 14–16.

Girls' School in 1906. They had to overcome great opposition, not only because of the school's proximity to Aligarh College, but also from parents who opposed sending their daughters out of the house to school. They were ultimately successful thanks to Shaikh Abdullah's persistence in seeking patronage – both from the government and (significantly) from the Begam of Bhopal. Begam Abdullah supervised the school and assiduously cultivated the goodwill of the many parents who had to be convinced of the safety of their daughters and the value of the education they were receiving.[24] The Abdullahs made careful arrangements for strict purdah both at the school and in transporting the students to school. The curriculum included the 'three Rs' as well as religious instruction, prayers at the required times and training in needlework and household management. Aligarh Girls' School grew slowly, but prospered. By 1914, it had added a hostel to accommodate boarding students who came from beyond Aligarh. The school became an intermediate college in 1925, started degree classes in 1937, and eventually became the Women's College of Aligarh Muslim University.[25] The Abdullahs' accomplishments in founding a significant women's educational institution parallel those of Mumtaz Ali and Muhammadi Begam in founding the first important Urdu journal for women.

Returning to Sir Sayyid's views on the state of Muslim women's education, it is clear that Sir Sayyid's focus on making Aligarh College a successful institution of modern education for Indian Muslim men placed the education of Muslim girls and women in a lower priority. Nevertheless, the Aligarh Movement produced lively debate concerning the desirability of women's education, including questions about how and where it would be offered (at home or in schools), what sort of curriculum it would include, and what effects it would have on women, religion, and family life. Without the work of Sir Sayyid, if seems fair to speculate, these debates and the efforts to start girls' schools, publish women's magazines and other books deemed suitable for women to read, and other manifestations of the movement for women's enlightenment in the late nineteenth and early twentieth centuries, might have been much slower to materialize. Sir Sayyid was

---

[24] Abdullah, *Sawanih-e 'Umri-e Abdullah Begam*, pp. 18–20.
[25] For the history of Aligarh Girls' School, see Gail Minault, '*Sharif* Education for Girls at Aligarh', in *Modernization and Social Change among Muslims in India*, ed. Imtiaz Ahmad (Delhi: Manohar, 1983), pp. 207–36, repr. in Minault, *GLL*, pp. 194–219; and Minault, *Secluded Scholars*, pp. 228–49.

a man firmly of his own time. He was acutely aware of the difficulties of founding institutions and changing public opinion, and his priorities were clear. He was convinced that 'no satisfactory education can be provided for Muhammadan females until a large number of Muhammadan males receive a sound education'. He did not realize that those Muslim women might have minds of their own.

4 *Naicari* Nature
Sir Sayyid Ahmad Khan and the Reconciliation of Science, Technology, and Religion
DAVID LELYVELD

Figure 1 *Naicari Jogi, Oudh Punch*, 4 August 1884. Available at http://dsal.uchicago.edu/digbooks/digpager.html?BOOKID =NC1718.08&object=43 (accessed on 21 September 2018).

In April 1869, Sayyid Ahmad Khan set out on a journey to England, filled with cheerful curiosity and friendliness, which was largely reciprocated by his British copassengers on the P&O steamship, the RMS *Baroda*, as it made its way across the Indian Ocean towards Egypt. One evening, a young British lieutenant came and sat beside him. '*Tum* London *jātē ho?*' he asked abruptly, using the condescending familiar second person. Sayyid Ahmad, already fifty-one, might have been addressed with more courtesy. The latter replied with a terse affirmative, '*Hāṅ*.' The lieutenant introduced himself as a specialist in gunnery and land surveying, not a missionary, but he wanted to talk about religion. He then launched into a lengthy discourse about the superiority of Christianity.

> [He] asked me to contemplate what the Christian race had done; how the English had been blessed by God above all other nations; how they surpassed all other nations in the arts and sciences and philosophy; what a wonderful thing the ship we were in was, and how she speeded through the waters by the appliances of science. 'You have seen,' he said, 'the wonders of the railway and the telegraph. No other nation is so powerful in war as mine. If any other religion were the true one, God would have blessed it as He has mine.[1]

For Sayyid Ahmad, this unwelcome confrontation – the claim that things of this world could prove truth or error in religion – seems to have hovered over the rest of his year-and-a-half-long pilgrimage into the world of European modernity. The encounter with the lieutenant ended unpleasantly and was not renewed, but it may well have played a part in redirecting the focus of Sayyid Ahmad's intellectual life and work as a founder of educational and social organizations.

Christianity had long served to justify European expansion, but as Michael Adas has shown, it was only with the great leaps of technology in the nineteenth century and the rise of industry that Europeans could claim

---

[1] George Farquhar Irving Graham, *The Life and Work of Syed Ahmed Khan* (Edinburgh: William. Blackwood and Sons, 1885), pp. 121–2. This is Graham's free translation. For the original Urdu, which presumably the lieutenant was speaking, see Sayyid Aḥmad Ḵẖān, *Sar Sayyid kā safar nāmah, musāfirān-e Landan*, ed. Aṣghar ʿAbbās (ʿAlīgaṛh: Ejūkeshnal Buk Hā'ūs, 2009), p. 56. See also Sayyid Ahmad Khan, *A Voyage to Modernism*, ed. and trans. Mushirul Hasan and Nishat Zaidi (Delhi: Primus Books, 2011), pp. 79–80, though unaccountably this version promotes the lieutenant to lieutenant general.

superiority on the basis of both science and technology.[2] Until his voyage to England in 1869, Sayyid Ahmad's interest in religion, on the one hand, and science and technology, on the other, had moved on separate tracks. Although he had written a number of tracts on religious matters and was probably exposed to Christian–Muslim disputations in Agra in the early 1840s as well as to contemporary scientific ideas in Delhi,[3] it was only after 1857 that he began to develop his ideas about the compatibility of Islam with Christianity and with contemporary European thought. Both the Urdu and English versions of the pamphlet published shortly after the rebellion, *Asbāb-e sarkashi-e Hindustān* (Causes of the Indian Revolt), 1859, included quotations from the New Testament extolling love and forgiveness.[4] Over the following three years he embarked on an ambitious study of the Bible in the light both of Islamic thought and contemporary European scholarship.[5] His concern here was to establish a claim that the Bible, despite questions

---

[2] Michael Adas, *Machines as the Measure of Men: Science, Technology, and Ideologies of Western Dominance Michael Adas* (Ithaca: Cornelll University Press, 1989), pp. 133–98. Thanks to Gail Minault for suggesting that I make reference to this work.

[3] Christian W. Troll, *Sayyid Ahmad Khan: A Reinterpretation of Muslim Theology* (New Delhi: Vikas Publication. House, 1978), pp. 36–57, 61–9, 150–4. I am indebted throughout this paper to Troll's book, which treats Sayyid Ahmad's religious ideas with formidable scholarly thoroughness and subtlety. On Sayyid Ahmad's early exposure to Christian–Muslim religious controversies see also Avril A. Powell, *Muslims and Missionaries in Pre-Mutiny India* (Richmond, Surrey: Curzon Press, 1993), pp. 166–7.

[4] Sayyid Ahmad Khan, *Āsbāb-e sarkashi-e Hindūstān ka javāb mazmūn* (Syud Ahmed Khan, *An Essay on the Causes of the Indian Revolt*) (Agra: J. A. Gibbons, Mofussilite Press, 1859). There are two English translations, one by Nassau Lees (Calcutta: FF. Wyman, Home Secretariat, 1859). The more familiar one (Banaras: Medical Hall Press, 1873) omits the Christian quotations. All this can be found on Frances Pritchett's website along with the Urdu text and a new 'literal' translation at http://www.columbia.edu/itc/mealac/pritchett/00urdu/asbab/index.html (accessed on 8 October 2018).

[5] Sayyid Aḥmad K͟hān, *The Muhammadan Commentary on the Holy Bible (Taba'īn al-kalām fī tafsīr al-Taurāt wa al-Injīl ʿalá millat-i al-Islām)*, Part I (Ghazeepore: Printed and published by the author at his private press, 1862), Part II (Aligarh, 1866). See Troll, *Sayyid Ahmad Khan*, pp. 58–99. Published in double columns with the English on one side and Urdu on the left; the English was prepared by an unnamed translator and often varies significantly from the Urdu.

about the accuracy of its textual transmission, is fundamentally consistent with the Qur'an, which is by definition the true and eternal word of God: '... whatever has been revealed by God to his prophets is all true'. Actually, Sayyid Ahmad, as opposed to his English translator, says that 'we must trust it' – *'ham imān lāyē haiṅ'* and 'affirm it with our hearts' – *'dil sē taṣdīq kareṅ'*. That is a statement of obligation of faith rather than an objective truth claim.[6] In any case, Part I of his *Muhammadan Commentary on the Holy Bible*, published in 1862, relies entirely on the scriptures themselves, at least as those interpreted by contemporary Christian scholarship. It does not make an appeal to external criteria, such as natural science. Thus, the extensive chronological table therein starts with 'Creation', dated 4000 BC.[7]

By 1863, one year after the publication of Part I, Sayyid Ahmad began altering his approach by applying the English word 'nature' as a criterion for interpreting the *Book of Genesis*.[8] He quotes Thomas Hartwell Horne, his major source for biblical scholarship: '... some futile objections have been made against the chronology of this book, because it makes the world less ancient than is necessary to support the theories of some modern self-styled philosophers....'[9] Sayyid Ahmad appears to accept Horne's position, except that he goes on to defend the reading of scripture, at least in part, as 'allegorical' (*tamṣīli*) and 'figurative' (*tashbīh, miṣāl*), rather than factual. He says that because divine revelation aimed 'to regulate our morals' (*tahẓīb-e akḫlāq*), the message had to be 'available to all mankind in proportion to their capacities' and remain valid and understandable 'in every stage of the gradual progress of learning and science'.[10]

Everyone now knows, Sayyid Ahmad continues, that the earth is spherical and 'only ... those who are unwilling to accept the results of modern scientific discoveries' hold on to the ideas of Aristotle and continue to assert 'the theory of the Earth being motionless, and of the firmament,

---

[6] Khān, *The Muhammadan Commentary*, Part I, pp. 62–3.

[7] Ibid., Appendix 1, p. 8.

[8] Ibid., Part II, has an inner title page for the commentary on Genesis, dated Ghazipur, 1863. I am indebted to Professor Asghar Abbas for calling this section and its use of the word 'nature' to my attention.

[9] Ibid., p. 30; see Troll, *Sayyid Ahmad Khan*, p. 79. Thomas Hartwell Horne, *An Introduction to the Critical Study and Knowledge of the Holy Scriptures* (London: Printed for T. Cadell and W. Davies, 1818) has been revised and reprinted many times in England, Ireland, the United States, and Canada, most recently in 2013 by Cambridge University Press.

[10] Khān, *The Muhammadan Commentary*, Part II, pp. 31–2. See fuller discussion in Troll, *Sayyid Ahmad Khan*, pp. 107–9.

sun, moon and stars revolving around it'.[11] As the *Commentary* moves through the narrative of creation, Sayyid Ahmad considers the nature of 'day' and 'night' as well as 'light' and 'dark', speculating that before the 'beginning' only God existed and the 'law of nature' (using the English words for this term) had not yet come into force. 'We cannot know what was the duration' of the first three 'days' of Creation because 'they are days such as were caused by the quite miraculous power of God without the operation of any natural or visible causes such as those of our day.... We acknowledge that Nature [*naicar*] is the Work of God, and Revelation [*waḥi*] is his Word [*kalām*]; that no discrepancy should ever occur between them for asmuch [sic] as both proceed from the same Source'.[12]

Notwithstanding this gesture to the 'progress of learning and science', Sayyid Ahmad's interest in science and technology before his journey to Europe had been, to a large extent, a separate matter. His maternal grandfather, Khwaja Fariduddin Ahmad, had travelled to Lucknow in the late eighteenth century to study with the celebrated Allama Tafazzul Husain Khan – who, among other things, is said to have translated Newton's *Principia* into Persian. Such interests were carried on by Khwaja Farid's son, Khwaja Zain Uddin, who crafted scientific instruments, particularly for astronomical observation.[13] All this made a great impression on Sayyid Ahmad, and as a young man he produced a translation of Khwaja Farid's treatise on the proportional compass, translated an illustrated text on mechanics, and used trigonometry to measure the height of the Quit Minar. Another venture into 'science' was a treatise Sayyid Ahmad published in 1845 to prove on the basis of principles of motion, if not quite on Newtonian ones, that the sun revolves around the earth. What is interesting about this essay is that it makes practically no reference to God or scripture. Twenty years later, as we have seen, he had changed his mind about the relationship of the earth, the moon and the sun.[14]

---

[11] Khān, *The Muhammadan Commentary*, Part II, pp. 45–6.
[12] Ibid., p. 66.
[13] Sayyid Aḥmad Khān, *Sīrat-e Farīdīyah* (Agra: Matba`-i Mufīd-i `Ām, 1896); Christopher A. Bayly, *Empire and Information: Intelligence Gathering and Social Communication in India, 1780–1870* (Cambridge: Cambridge University Press, 1996), pp. 85, 184–5.
[14] Mawlānā Muḥammad Ismā`īl Pānīpatī (ed.), *Maqālat-e Sar Sayyid*, vol. 16 (Lahore: Majlis Taraqqī-yi Adab, 1965), pp. 75–206, 485–500; Troll, *Sayyid Ahmad Khan*, pp. 147–9. See also Iftikhār `Ālam Khān, *Sir Sayyid aur jadidiyat* (Delhi: Educational Publishing House, 2014), pp. 186–7.

One of Sayyid Ahmad's responses to the 1857 Rebellion was his effort to bring the advancements of contemporary science and technology to a north Indian Urdu language public. In 1864, Sayyid Ahmad founded the Scientific Society, first in Ghazipur and then moved it to Aligarh. Its main task was to publish Urdu translations and original works on science, technology, and agriculture, along with a journal, that later came to be known as *The Aligarh Institute Gazette*. Printed on Sayyid Ahmad's private press in moveable type, all these publications appeared in both English and Urdu, often in a double-column format. The journal carried news and information about meteors and earthquakes, chemistry and physics, electricity, telegraphs, railways, and photography.[15] One of the society's publications was an Urdu translation of a popular work on 'Natural Philosophy'. In addition, the Society. The society also offered public lectures and maintained a laboratory and garden for various experiments and demonstrations, such as the popularization of the new American invention, the tube well. One of the lectures the society organized was on 'Natural Science' by Dr Charles Kilkelly, a civil surgeon in Aligarh. The subscribing members of the society were Muslims, Hindus, and sympathetic British officials.[16]

Sayyid Ahmad's journey to England took place just half a year before a transformative human alteration of Earth's geography: the opening of the Suez Canal. He traveled the route through Egypt to the Mediterranean by railway, which also was a recent development that had greatly eased the itinerary between India and Europe. Along the way, Sayyid Ahmad had the opportunity to spend time with the man most responsible for formulating and promoting the canal, Ferdinand de Lessups. Filled with admiration, Sayyid Ahmad shared a writing table on the ship with the Frenchman, but

---

[15] Shafey Kidwai, *Cementing Ethics with Modernism: An Appraisal of Sir Sayyed Ahmed Khan's Writings* (New Delhi: Gyan Pub. House, 2010), p. 224.

[16] Iftikhār `Ālam Khān, *Sir Syed aur Scientific Society* (Delhi: Maktaba Jamià, 2000), available at https://rekhta.org/ebooks/sir-syed-aur-scientific-society-ek-bazyaft-iftikhar-alam-khan-ebooks (accessed on 8 October 2018). Iftikhār `Ālam Khān, *Sir Sayyid aur Hindūstāni niẓām-e zirā`at* (Delhi: Educational Publishing House, 2014), pp. 46–95. My thanks to Professor Alam Khan for these books and further advice. One of the books translated and published by the Scientific Society was Charles Tomlinson, *Introduction to the Study of Natural Philosophy, for the Use of Young Beginners* (London: John Weale, 1853), listed in *Ru`idad Scientific Society* (Allahabad, 1865), p. 20, viewed at http://www.sirsyedtoday.org/books/?cid=33 (accessed on 21 September 2018).

the language barrier – though de Lessups had some rudimentary Arabic – prevented them from sharing much in the way of conversation.[17]

For all his excitement about new technologies, Sayyid Ahmad turned the greater part of his attention during his time in London to the study of religious texts, responding in particular to an evangelically inspired critic of Islam, Sir William Muir, who also happened to be the Lieutenant-governor of the North-West Provinces and the major sponsor of Sayyid Ahmad's ability to make the trip in the first place. If refuting Muir had been a prior motive of the journey – as he and his biographers later said – it had not been mentioned in his application for leave and funding.[18] But once he had arrived in England, his attention turned in large part to religion, rather than science and technology. His correspondence with Sayyid Mehdi Ali (later known as Mohsin-ul Mulk) reveals the passion and urgency that propelled his efforts to defend Islam.[19] Muir, however, appears to have been untouched by the scientific and technological transformations of modern Europe because his writings on Islam comprise textual criticism and ethical evaluations grounded only in his own religious commitments.[20] Sayyid Ahmad's response to Muir was fought on much the same grounds – relying on the textual authority of the scriptures, supplemented by lengthy quotations from more sympathetic English writers, notably Gibbon and Carlyle.[21]

---

[17] K̲h̲ān, *Sar Sayyid kā safar nāmah, musāfirān-e Landan*, p. 99.

[18] Correspondence of Syed Ahmed Khan Bahadur, C.S.I., Subordinate Judge and Judge of Banaras Small Claims Court, relating to the grant of a special allowance during furlough and of an advance on his return to duty, National Archives of India (NAI) - Home/Judicial B - 9 July 1870 - #28.

[19] Muḥammad Ismā`īl Pānīpatī (ed.), *Maktūbāt-e Sar Sayyid*, vol. 1 (Lahore: Majlis-e Taraqqi-e Adab, 1976), pp. 413–80. Some of these are translated in *A Voyage to Modernism*, ed. and trans. Hasan and Zaidi.

[20] Avril A. Powell, *Scottish Orientalists and India: The Muir Brothers, Religion, Education and Empire* (Woodbridge, UK: Boydell Press, 2010), pp. 158–68, 195–212.

[21] Syed Ahmed Khan Bahador, *A Series of Essays on the Life of Muhammad and Subjects Subsidiary Thereto* (London: Trübner and Co., 1870). Powell, *Scottish Orientalists*, pp. 195–212. The book was published first in English with acknowledged assistance from unnamed others. The Urdu text is *al-Khuṭbāt al-Aḥmadīyah fī Al-`Arab wa-al-sīrat al-Muḥammadīyah* (Lāhore: Muslim Printing Press, 1870 [Hathi Trust Digital Library]). There are significant differences between the English and Urdu texts that call for further analysis.

For Sayyid Ahmad, truth was a matter of affiliation with authority. In Part I of *Commentary*, he maintains that knowledge must depend on the authority of the transmitters of that particular knowledge, namely *isnād* (the chain of authorities), as certified by the biographical accounts of their piety and integrity. Sayyid Ahmad exemplifies this by using the pedagogical lineage of his own teacher, his teacher's teacher, and so on, reaching back to Prophet Muhammad.[22] Perhaps, based on this intellectual pedigree, he considered himself entitled to offer his own judgements – as in his discussion of the lifespan of Adam and Noah and the worldwide extent of the biblical flood, which are all accepted as historical fact.[23] In *Essays on the Life of Muhammad*, the book he published in London, Sayyid Ahmad identifies 'true religion' with the 'law of nature' (*qānūn-i qudrat*), 'in conformity to which all objects around us, whether material or immaterial, receive their existence, and which determines the relation which they bear to each other'. In response to Muir's attack on polygamy- and divorce-related Islamic rules, he argues that they conform to this same 'law of nature', which he identifies with 'the will and intention of the Creator'.[24] This was hardly an argument based on contemporary European thought, but rather one reminiscent of that of Shah Wali Ullah, the great eighteenth-century theologian, who Sayyid Ahmad counted in his intellectual pedigree.[25]

Sayyid Ahmad came to believe that knowledge develops over time. The ideas established in the past may have been superseded today. Likewise, the ideas considered authoritative today may well be overridden in the future. However, the selection criteria for this, such as deciding whom to believe and to what extent should one exercise their own reason and independent investigation, remains unclear. Regardless, the choice between the Prophet and Newton – or Darwin or oneself – is impossible referring to only the Qur'an and few valid *hadis*, all of which the Prophet transmitted from God, the source of all knowledge. If there is something in the Qur'an that 'may seem to us to contradict truth or reality, there are two explanations...: either we have made an error in understanding the meaning of these verses, or we are mistaken in our understanding of what is truth and reality'.[26]

---

[22] Khān, *The Mahomedan Commentary*, Part I, pp. 58–9.
[23] Ibid., Part II, pp. 318–49, 359–60, 364.
[24] Khan Bahador, *Essays on the Life of Muhammad*, V, pp. 147–8; *al-Khuṭbāt al-Aḥmadīyah*, pp. 3–4, 157.
[25] Marcia K. Hermansen (trans.), *The Conclusive Argument from God: Shāh Walī Allāh of Delhi's Hujjat Allāh al-bāligha* (Leiden: E.J. Brill, 1996), pp. 123–6.
[26] 'Fifteen Principles Submitted by Sayyid Ahmad Khan to the ʿUlama of Saharanpur' (1873 or 1874), in Troll, *Sayyid Ahmad Khan*, p. 276.

Although he aimed to discover new ways to read the revealed truth considering scientific progress, Sayyid Ahmad had limited access to contemporary scientific theory, because he was not literate in English and had to rely on translations, oral and written, to pick up ideas about contemporary science and technology. His own educational formation was founded on a substantial, if uneven, acquaintance with the rich tradition of Islamicate science and philosophy in Arabic and Persian. As with his nearly silent interaction with Ferdinand de Lessups, the result was what Faisal Devji has called 'apologetic modernity': 'attempts to enter into conversation with someone speaking a different language'.[27]

Sayyid Ahmad did not need the European Enlightenment or Victorian science to discover the 'progress' (taraqqi) of knowledge. A century ago, Shah Wali Ullah, probably the most influential intellectual antecedent of Sayyid Ahmad, had developed the concept of stages of human advancement, irtifāqāt – through which emerges meaning, understanding, and a moral social order. For Shah Wali Ullah, the 'world of images' (ʿālam al-miṣāl) was the realm of prior ultimate truth.[28] The things of this world were manifestations of this permanent constitution of existence, fitrat. For Sayyid Ahmad, nevertheless, the images were literary functions to communicate meaning to a prescientific age. He also believed that the phenomena of this world have objective existence, accessible to scientific observation, apart from whatever they may be, as signs of God's eternal order. He translated fitrat using the English word 'nature'.

'Nature is perhaps the most complex word in the language,' writes Raymond Williams; and much the same can be said about fitrat, qudrat, ṭabīʿat, the Arabic words that Sayyid Ahmad often used as synonyms.[29] His decision to use the English word may have signalled his affiliation towards British intellectual hegemony and towards the present over the past, but the underlying concept owed at least as much to the Islamic tradition, which, like the European, reached back to Plato and Aristotle. Indeed, Sayyid Ahmad pointed out Muslims wrote in Arabic to preserve and develop classical philosophy and science. He also relied on this Islamicate intellectual history

---

[27] Faisal Devji, 'Apologetic Modernity', *Modern Intellectual History* 4, no. 1 (2007): 61–76, 62.
[28] Marcia K. Hermansen, 'Translator's Introduction', in *The Conclusive Argument from God*, pp. xv–xxiii.
[29] Raymond Williams, *Keywords: A Vocabulary of Culture and Society* (rev. ed.) (New York: Oxford University Press, 1983), p. 219.

to establish that empirical science and independent reason had, at least in an earlier age, a profound presence among Muslims. It was at least as possible for Muslims as for Christians to find ways to reconcile science and religion. However, it was also necessary to disentangle these overlapping and conflicting intellectual traditions.[30]

In London, Sayyid Ahmad's earlier interest in science and technology fell under the shadow of his religious concerns: defending Islam and Muslims in the eyes of the British rulers in India and protecting the new generation of Muslims, who may draw away from their religion by the attractions of European ideas and institutions. He had indicated the second concern as early as 1863 in a Persian lecture delivered to a Muslim audience in Calcutta and reiterated it in the introduction to his *Essays on the Life of Muhammad*.[31] When he returned to India in 1870, his two major projects, the journal *Tahzīb-ul akhlāq* and (what became) the Muhammadan Anglo-Oriental (MAO) College, both had superseded the Scientific Society – which continued as a publishing operation but otherwise ceased to exist.[32] *Tahzīb-ul akhlāq*, also known as *The Muhammadan Social Reformer*, rarely published any articles on science and technology, except by substantiating Sayyid Ahmad's exegesis of the Qur'an. Although early schemes for the college called for a strong curriculum in the sciences,[33] science and technology were notably absent from both the college and its affiliated publications at least until Sayyid Ahmad's death in 1898.

Sayyid Ahmad's use of the English term 'nature', transliterated into Urdu as *naicar*, in his writings led to critique on not only his ideas but also the institution, the Aligarh College, which had become his most profound

---

[30] Ẓafar Ḥasan, *Sar Sayyid aur Ḥālī kā naẓariyah-yi fiṭrat* (Lāhaur: Idārah-yi Saqāfat-i Islāmiyyah, 1990), pp. 255–92. I am indebted to Professor Asghar Abbas for this reference.

[31] Muḥammad Ismā'īl Pānīpatī (ed.), *Khuṭbāt-e Sar Sayyid* (Lahore: Majlis-e Taraqqī-e Adab, 1972), pp. 72–3 (Urdu translation); Khan Bahador, *Essays on the Life of Muhammad*, p. xii.

[32] Officially the Society lasted till about 1886, the year that the Muhammadan Educational Congress (later Conference) was founded. See ˋAsghar Abbās, *Sar Sayyid kī Sā'intifik Sosā'iṭī* (Aligarh: Educational Book House, 2015), p. 30. Many thanks to Professor Asghar Abbas for sending me this valuable book compilation of the society's records.

[33] Yusuf Husain Khan (ed.), *Selected Documents from the Aligarh Archives* (Aligarh: Published for the Department of History, Aligarh Muslim University [by] Asia Pub. House, 1967), pp. 230–5.

project. Just before founding the college in 1875, Maulvi Ali Bakhsh wrote to Sayyid Mehdi Ali (the future Nawab Mohsin-ul Mulk) that he did not oppose the establishment of an institution for promoting modern education among Muslims *per se*, but opposed only Sayyid Ahmad's *millat-e naicariya*.[34] In the final decades of his life, Sayyid Ahmad embraced the term 'nature' more prominently and developed it – though inconsistently – in his writings.

Although he had spent his professional career as a judge, there is little evidence in his later writings to indicate that he was concerned with the natural law as a specifically legal philosophy with respect to the judicial administration of British India. Some hint of such a philosophy may be noted in the judicial opinions of his son, Sayyid Mahmood, concerning the British formula, 'justice, equity and good conscience', applied to the Muslim law in the British courts. Sayyid Mahmood maintained that one could use independent legal and moral reasoning within the confines of Muslim law, without having to resort to external sources.[35] By contrast, Sayyid Ahmad applied his theories of interpretation to other matters; for instance, he analyzed whether eating chicken slaughtered by Christians, sharing meals with them, or wearing shoes in the mosque was permissible within the *Shari`a*.[36] These concerns were a feature of the 'social reform' promoted in his journals. Chiefly concerned with ethics, these articles relied on textual analysis, particularly of the Qur'an, while considering what Sayyid Ahmad called *fitrat-e insān* (human nature).

Sayyid Ahmad grounded his understanding of *naicar* in what he understood to be the 'modern sciences', `*ulūm-e jadīda*, but they served to buttress religious authority in much the same ways that earlier Muslim scholars had studied stars, animals, plants, and the human body. The procedures for observation and analysis, he recognized, had changed. Now,

[34] Khan (ed.), *Selected Documents from the Aligarh Archives*, p. 212; Āl-i-Aḥmad Surūr, 'Sar Sayyid kē ek mukhālif', in *Na'e aur purane caragh* (Lucknow: Idarah-e Farogh-e Urdu, 1963), pp. 120–9, available at https://rekhta.org/ebooks/nay-aur-purane-charagh-aal-e-ahmad-suroor-ebooks?lang=ur (accessed on 8 October 2018).

[35] Alan Guenther, 'Searching for 'Justice, Equity, and Good Conscience': A Muslim Re-interpretation of Law in British India' (n.d.), available at https://www.academia.edu/5600739/Searching_for_Justice_Equity_and_Good_Conscience_A_Muslim_re-interpretation_of_law_in_British_India (accessed on 17 July 2018).

[36] Pānīpatī (ed.), *Maqālat*, vol. 1, 181–3; vol. 15, 368–72 (from his *Tafsir* on Sura Al-Ma`ida).

there were instruments like microscopes and telescopes and protocols of experimentationthat made the findings of scientists more reliable, and there were new ways of organizing information in a comparative framework.[37] But Sayyid Ahmad claimed that such scientific findings served all the better to validate a theistic perspective on the world as a unified, rule-based, and beneficent order designed, created, and maintained by an all-powerful and all-seeing God. At *qiyāmat* (Day of Judgement), 'naturalists', who felt reverence and awe for this divine order on the basis of such scientific findings, might well enter *jannat*, the eternal garden, as much as any Jew, Christian, or Wahhabi would.[38]

Sayyid Ahmad's most ambitious intellectual project was to read the Qur'an through the lens of what he considered *naicar* and 'modern sciences'. The Qur'an can be shown to be entirely consistent with the 'law of nature' (*qānūn-e fitrat*) because it is God's eternal, unbreakable promise (*wa`da*). 'Much of this law of nature God has told us and some of it man has discovered, even if man has not discovered much.' By using the English word 'supernatural', he states that miracles (*mo`jizāt*) do not exist. Since the time of the Prophet, whatever appears to be deviating from the factual reality can all be explained through metaphors, allegories, or Arabic idioms. The Prophet's role in receiving the word of God could be characterized as something like a special talent (*malaka*), not a miracle. 'As for the nature of man's soul ... and what happens to it after death ..., all these things are beyond the comprehension of man.'[39] Nevertheless, God does not deviate from the unified regularity of 'nature', and thus 'nature' and Islam are indistinguishable.

In his commentary on Sura Yusuf, for example, Sayyid Ahmad claims that dreams can be explained by the modern sciences of 'psychology' and 'physiology', so Yusuf's ability to interpret them was no more than a special aptitude. Yusuf could also predict the years of famine and plenty because he understood the flood patterns of the Nile.[40] As Faisal Devji has shown,

---

[37] 'al-dalīl wa al burhān', *Maqālat*, vol. 3, pp. 286–300.
[38] 'naichari', *Maqālat*, vol. 15, pp. 154–9.
[39] Muhammad Daud Rahbar, 'Sir Sayyid Ahmad Khān's Principles of Exegesis Translated from His *Tahrhīr fī usūl al-tafsīr*', *The Muslim World* 46, no. 2 (1956): 104–12; 'Qur'ān majīd kī tafsīr kē usūl', in *Maqālat*, vol. 2, pp. 227–58.
[40] Sayyid Ahmad Khān, *Tafsīr al-qur'ān: va huva al-hady valfurqān*, vol. 5 (Lahore: Matba`-i Nawal Kishor, n.d.), p. 57; (lithograph) as reproduced in *Sir Sayyid ki tafsīr-e Qur'ān*, Part II (Patna: Khuda Bakhsh Oriental Public Library, 1995). See David Lelyveld, 'Young Man Sayyid: Dreams and Biographical Texts', in

Sayyid Ahmad offered an industrialized version of the concept of *ruḥ* (spirit) as a type of steam or electricity.[41] To justify his arguments, rather than deploying the findings and procedures of contemporary European science, Sayyid Ahmad looked mainly to the classics of Islamic scholasticism, such as Ibn Sina, Al-Razi, and his more immediate intellectual influence, Shah Wali Ullah. His appeal to 'nature' was hardly a grand epistemological shift, but rather a rearguard action to revive and advance the rationalist strain in the Islamic intellectual tradition. By appealing to 'science', he sought to reassure young Muslims who might be drawn towards religious scepticism by the contemporary ideas associated with British dominance.

Sayyid Ahmad's interpretations of the Qur'an were – and still are – criticized as mechanical or materialistic, without any space for divine intervention or transcendence. But, in his essay 'Naicar', which led off the resumption of publication of the journal *Tahzīb-ul akhlāq* in 1879 after a hiatus of several years, he uses a different tack. Leaving aside the claims of science, he passionately appeals to the wonder and beauty of the world: wind and water, thunder and lightning, palm trees, cattle, bees and honey, grapes and wine. He then implores the readers to join in a concerted effort of social transformation and concludes with a couplet from Hafiz: 'for you the tree of paradise, for me the figure of the beloved; each person sets his attention to the extent of his own spirit (*himmat*)'.[42]

If Sayyid Ahmad himself could not quite reach the heights of lyrical poetry, he enlisted others, particularly Altaf Husain Hali, to take up the task of 'natural poetry'. This is a verse version of Sayyid Ahmad's essay in Laurel Steele's prose translation:

> The army of clouds approaching and the companies of wind are behind them. Rain-filled clouds are overhead; the winds of paradise are coming. The gardens have had a refreshing bath, the fields are robed in green. Trees and stones are clothed in a single uniform: the whole world is made out of lapis lazuli. Mountains are covered with

---

Muslim Voices Community and the Self in South Asia, ed. Usha Sanyal, David Gilmartin, and Sandria B. Freitag (New Delhi: Yoda Press, 2013), pp. 253–72.

[41] Faisal Devji, *Muslim Zion* (Cambridge, MA: Harvard University Press, 2013), pp. 209–12.

[42] 'naichar', *Maqālat*, vol. 15, pp. 146–53. The quote is from Hafiz's *ghazal* no. 56.

تو و طوبی و ما و قامت یار

فکر هر کس به قدر همت اوست

flowers and the trees are decked out like a bridegroom. The marshes are filled with water, the jungle is echoing, the cuckoos and peacocks are calling on every side.[43]

For Sayyid Ahmad as well as for Hali, the authority of 'nature' was more a matter of religious emotion than of scientific observation. Speaking in Lahore during his 1884 Punjab tour, Sayyid Ahmad declared that the uneducated who 'from their hearts believe in Islam without knowing the proofs for its truth according to the principles of logic and philosophy' were *'ahl-e jannat'* and better Muslims than he was.[44] If, as Frances Pritchett states, Hali was 'haunted by the invisible presence of Wordsworth and his poetics', then this was hardly an endorsement of science and technology.[45]

But, as Javed Majeed has pointed out, Hali never actually mentioned Wordsworth; rather, his allegiance was to 'the natural sciences of the nineteenth century', characterized by observations, experimentation, and importantly, technological transformations of agriculture and landscape through such large-scale human interventions, such as construction of canals.[46] As Majeed states, these actions were of the colonial state and assertions of the kind of superiority and dominance that Sayyid Ahmad encountered in his conversation with the young lieutenant on the ship. Nevertheless, technology is not the same as science, and the lieutenant's claims on behalf of Christianity suggest that British domination was not so much a manifestation of the 'European Enlightenment' as was it an exercise of wealth and brute power.

In the Lahore tour, the impending task was to mobilize Muslims – at least some of them – for the future and for worldly success under rapidly changing circumstances. 'Nature' was not only a rallying cry but also a

---

[43] Laurel Steele, 'Hali and His *Muqaddamah*: The Creation of a Literary Attitude in Nineteenth-Century India', *Annual of Urdu Studies* 1 (1981): 1–45, available at http://dsal.uchicago.edu/books/annualofurdustudies/pager.html?volume=1&objectid=PK2151.A6152_1_007.gif (accessed on 17 July 2018).
[44] Translated in Troll, *Sayyid Ahmad Khan*, p. 309.
[45] Frances W. Pritchett, *Nets of Awareness: Urdu Poetry and Its Critics* (Berkely: University of California Press, 1994), p. 166.
[46] Javed Majeed, 'Nature, Hyperbole and the Colonial State: Some Muslim Appropriations of European Modernity in Late Nineteenth Century Urdu Literature', in *Islam and Modernity: Muslim Intellectuals Respond*, ed. John Cooper, Ronald Nettler, and Mohamed Mahmoud (London: I.B. Taurus, 1998), p. 18.

target for satire and condemnation. In the same year as the Punjab tour, 1884, a cartoon appeared in *Oudh Punch*, depicting Sayyid Ahmad as a 'naicari jōgī' – a snake charmer gathering cobra-headed packets of monetary donations, *canda*.[47] In another speech during this tour, to raise support for the Aligarh College, Sayyid Ahmad offered a purely utilitarian response to his critics: 'Call me what you like, infidel heretic, *naicari*. I am not asking you to intercede for me before God.... Whatever I say is for the benefit of your own children.'[48]

Sayyid Ahmad's critics took such remarks as evidence of expediency, expressions of a desire for the benefits of worldly achievement, even under the circumstances of imperialist domination. In 1884, Sayyid Jamaluddin al-Afghani from Cairo attacked Sir Sayyid in Arabic, while addressing him as 'Ahmad Khan', for 'hovering around the English in order to obtain some advantage from them....' He further stated, 'He called openly for the abandonment of all religions ... and cried "nature nature", in order to convince people that Europe only progressed in civilization, advanced in science and industry....' Three years earlier, while still in Hyderabad, al-Afghani had published a Persian discourse portraying the *mazhab-e naicari* as atheistic, materialist, and Satanic.[49] However, no evidence indicates that al-Afghani actually read what Sayyid Ahmad Khan wrote – or that Sayyid Ahmad was even aware of al-Afghani's attacks. Actually, not much difference appears between the two with respect to their validation of contemporary science – or its absence. Both emphasized the historical role of Islamicate science as foundation for contemporary European science. Al-Afghani asserted a functionalist concept of religion in disciplining the social order, whereas Sayyid Ahmad – at least sometimes – tended to bifurcate science from religion as well as personal religious belief and practice from the social projects of education and mobilization among Indian Muslims.[50]

---

47 Available at http://dsal.uchicago.edu/digbooks/digpager.html?BOOKID=NC1718.08&object=43 (accessed on 21 September 2018).
48 Sayyid Iqbāl ʿAlī, *Sayyid Aḥmad Khān kā safar nāmah-yi Panjāb* (Lahore: Majlis Taraqqī-yi Adab, 1973 [1884]).
49 Nikki R. Keddie, *An Islamic Response to Imperialism: Political and Religious Writings of Sayyad Jamāl Ad-Din 'Al-Afghānī'* (Berkeley: University of California Press, 1983), pp. 130–80. See also Anwar Moazzam, *Jamāl Al-Dīn Al-Afghānī, a Muslim Intellectual* (New Delhi: Concept, 1984), pp. 81–99.
50 Javed Majeed, *Muhammad Iqbal: Islam, Aesthetics and Postcolonialism* (New Delhi: Routledge, Taylor & Francis Group, 2009), pp. 123–27; see David Lelyveld, 'Disenchantment at Aligarh', *Die Welt Des Islams* 22, no. 1 (1982):

The real difference between Sayyid Ahmad and al-Afghani was a political one: Sayyid Ahmad believed that the British rule was the vehicle of intellectual and social progress for India, but al-Afghani made efforts to call upon Muslims of the world to unite to resist European hegemony. In either case, the ultimate goal was to share in the benefits of modernity – not to defer to it as the cultural monopoly of foreign rulers. Gyan Prakash argues that if purported universal reason embodied in science and technology served to legitimate imperial power, then claiming knowledge as one's own right and heritage was also possible.[51] If Lieutenant Lawrence could claim the ship as proof of Christian, or at least British, superiority, the argument that Indians had participated in such technological developments before British power and greed had snatched away access to their share remains valid.[52]

A generation after Sayyid Ahmad, Muhammad Iqbal stated, 'But we must not forget that what is called science is not a single systematic view of Reality. It is a mass of sectional views of Reality – fragments of a total experience that we do not seem to fit together.... In fact, the various natural sciences are like so many vultures falling on the dead body of Nature, and each running away with a piece of its flesh.'[53] The intricate multiplicity of procedures and findings in various fields of what we call science and the often very varied skills and mechanisms we call technology do not lend themselves to a unified category of knowledge, let alone to the emotions and motivations associated with what we call religion. For Iqbal, as for Sayyid Ahmad, it is the moral and emotional force of a religious tradition that motivated intellectual commitment and discovery among individuals and communities. Majeed suggests that the writings of Sayyid Ahmad and Hali were not limited to uncritical – if distant – admiration for the nineteenth-century European science and its role in exercising and justifying British

---

85–102; also David Lelyveld, 'Sir Sayyid's Religion', in *Sir Sayyid Day Aligarh Magazine* (Northern California: AMU Alumni Associations of New Jersey and Pennsylvania, 2015), pp. 17–19.

[51] Gyan Prakash, *Another Reason: Science and the Imagination of Modern India* (Princeton: University Press, 1999).

[52] Amitav Ghosh, *The Great Derangement: Climate Change and the Unthinkable* (Gurgaon: Penguin, 2016), pp. 139–45.

[53] Allama Muhammad Iqbal, *The Reconstruction of Religious Thought in Islam*, repr. ed. (Lahore: Sh. Muhammad Ashraf, Lahore, 1965), pp. 41–2. In some respects this brief passage anticipates the ideas of Bruno Latour, as in his *Politics of Nature: How to Bring the Sciences into Democracy* (Cambridge: Harvard University Press, 2009).

imperialism. The mixture and confusion of ideas about religion, science, and history, express a profound 'ambivalence' about modernity and a good deal of nostalgia for an ideal past, particularly that associated with the Prophet and the foundations of Islam.[54] However, ambivalence, scepticism, or downright rejection of modernity was hardly limited to Aligarh or to Muslims, but was widely shared within Europe, and perhaps, most profoundly in India by Mahatma Gandhi. From the more recent perspective of a world on the brink of nuclear war, human-induced climate degradation, or worse, the Victorian optimism with respect to the onward march of knowledge and prosperity seems a lot less attractive. Still, there is much to be said for Sayyid Ahmad's commitment to evidence and open-minded reasoning in the service of humanity and 'nature'. Now that we have reached this point, it is only through more and better science and a wider concept of the universal that human history has any future at all.[55]

---

[54] Majeed, 'Nature, Hyperbole and the Colonial State', pp. 29–35.
[55] See Dipesh Chakrabarty, 'The Climate of History: Four Theses', *Critical Inquiry* 35, no. 2 (2009): 197–222.

Part II

Musalman-e Hind: Indian Muslim in a plural environment

5 Creating a Community

Sir Sayyid and His Contemporaries

M. RAISUR RAHMAN

In his short essay published in the Urdu quarterly *Fikr-o Nazar*, Khaliq Ahmad Nizami (1925–1997), an erudite scholar and eminent historian at Aligarh Muslim University (AMU), makes an interesting observation: 'Sir Sayyid, in India, had made efforts to prove the uniformity of conceptions of religion and scientific theories. Maulana Abul Kalam Azad has called it unnecessary and even though did not mention the name of Sir Sayyid but ... [he] has referred to the same trends of thoughts.'[1] The ideas, thoughts, and movement represented by Sir Sayyid – as he is known popularly – continued to be debated, challenged, embraced, and opposed during and after his lifetime. Maulana Abul Kalam Azad (1888–1958) was barely 10 years old when Sayyid Ahmad Khan died in 1898. The reference to Azad in this context was but a small part of the engagement Sir Sayyid drew. Succeeding leaders continued to invoke Sayyid Ahmad's thoughts and legacies. One can critique the shortcomings of his work but can hardly disagree that the nature of the tasks he undertook during his time and in the space he inhabited was pioneering. The reception of Sayyid Ahmad's ideas has never been unilinear – neither in his times nor in ours. In fact, as he went along trying to convince his cohorts of the ideas he was deeply committed to in the late nineteenth century, he garnered adversaries and critics alike.

Sayyid Ahmad found strong support in some of his lieutenants such as Nawab Mushtaq Husain Viqar-ul Mulk (1841–1917) and Sayyid Mehdi Ali Mohsin-ul Mulk (1837–1907), both of whom were very close to him – the founder of the Aligarh Movement – and carried on his message shoulder to shoulder, even more vigorously after his death. Those opposing Sayyid Ahmad included both conservatives and liberals, who curtly disapproved of his engagement with Western learning, critiqued his opposition to the Indian National Congress (INC) politics, criticized his deism, and called

---

[1] 'Aligarh Tehrik ka Pas-e Manzar', *Fikr-o-Nazar*, nos 1–3 (January–December 1985), pp. 26–32, 30.

him *naicari* ('naturalist'), a pejorative term meaning someone who had swallowed European agnostic naturalism. Regardless of the support, criticism, or outright rejection, Sayyid Ahmad was a persistent worker, thinker, negotiator, writer, orator, and leader, who tirelessly worked towards his goals, determined not to be cowed down in his vision and mission. He was deeply aware that he could have been nowhere close to his goals had he not succeeded in building a community and engaged with it. Notably, at the outset, the community that he alluded to was much more fluid and supple than what later writings implied. His sense of community was not set in stone. Contrary to popular perceptions in both India and Pakistan today, his community did not include only Muslims or the members of his economic or social group. The community that he spoke to could be members of the aristocracy, people he shared his faith with, the British rulers who aided him in his educational goals, his Hindu peers who donated for his cause, or everyone in the Indian subcontinent across divisions.

Through his writings, speeches, correspondence, and personal interactions, Sayyid Ahmad continually strove to engage with friends and foes alike, clarifying his positions, rationalizing his actions, or simply articulating his intentions. This chapter focusses on how his ideas were received, debated, and argued by his contemporaries to understand the challenges that he and his ideas and actions faced during and after his lifetime as well as how he and his supporters dealt with the multiple contestations. In other words, the following narrative explores the story of Sayyid Ahmad's efforts in fashioning a community, out of both sustenance and antagonism. Keeping with how he continued addressing various groups as his community, this chapter focusses on those counted as his supporters and detractors, such as the `ulama (Muslim religious leaders) and non-`ulama, the British, as well as his Hindu compatriots. The purpose is to understand where Sayyid Ahmad found himself amidst his contemporaries, how he engaged or dealt with them, and what did creating a community entail for him in view of the grand task that he had undertaken. In some ways, such analyses signpost the challenges Sayyid Ahmad faced and how he dealt with them. Lastly, this chapter situates Sir Sayyid within the larger world of late-nineteenth-century actors – the Muslims, Hindus, and British alike.

BUILDING COMMUNITY: THE TRIUMVIRATE

Among his closest allies, Sayyid Ahmad had none but those who wholeheartedly embraced his mission for education. His core group was made up of the non-`*ulama* who stood for and by him since the germination of the idea of the Muhammadan Anglo-Oriental (MAO) College and continued to work hard even beyond Sayyid Ahmad's lifetime advancing the ethos of the Aligarh Movement. Among them were Nawab Mushtaq Husain Viqar-ul Mulk of Amroha and Sayyid Mehdi Ali alias Nawab Mohsin-ul Mulk of Etawah. Their dedication to Sayyid Ahmad and his cause increased after the passing of their mentor, as they tried to not only play their own parts but also fill in their mentor's shoes. In fact, the entire Aligarh Movement was spearheaded by the triumvirate consisting of Sir Sayyid, Nawab Mohsin-ul Mulk,[2] and Viqar-ul Mulk, the three ostensibly comprising his closest community. Sayyid Ahmad 'wanted the college to act as a bridge between old and the new, the East and the West'[3] and wholeheartedly relied on these two individuals as his pillars of strength. While committed to imparting instruction in Western learning, Sayyid Ahmad was no less devoted to the significance of Oriental learning and to the need to pass it along to the future generations. In this conviction, the aforementioned triumvirate remained steadfast, despite occasionally differing with one another.

Viqar-ul Mulk served as the honorary secretary of the MAO College from 1909 to 1912 and worked with Mohsin-ul Mulk as a member of the college's Board of Trustees. He contributed organizationally, administratively, and clerically to help with the daily operations of the college, while choosing to reside on campus from 1879 to 1882 to ensure that parents felt safe and confident about their children staying in the residential campus.[4] Born in Amroha, Viqar-ul Mulk earned an engineering degree from the Roorkee College in 1861[5] and undertook government service, where he worked alongside Sayyid Ahmad as a colleague. He spent a considerable amount

---

[2] For an excellent biography on Nawab Mohsin-ul Mulk written by Muhammad Amin Zuberi (1872–1958), one of his contemporaries, see Muhammad Amin Zuberi, *Hayat-e Mohsin: yani Sawaneh Umri Nawab Mohsin-ud Daulah Mohsin-ul Mulk Maulvi Sayyid Mehdi Ali Khan* (Karachi: Academy of Educational Research, All Pakistan Educational Conference, 1994). Zuberi wrote similar biographies on Viqar-ul Mulk, Sayyid Ahmad Khan, Maulana Altaf Husain Hali, and Sayyid Mahmud.

[3] Khaliq Ahmad Nizami, *Sayyid Ahmad Khan* (Delhi: Publications Division, Government of India, 1966), p. 84.

[4] David Lelyveld, *Aligarh's First Generation: Muslim Solidarity in British India* (Princeton, NJ: Princeton University Press, 1978), pp. 198, 262.

[5] Muhammad Amin Zuberi, *Tazkirah-e Viqar: Mukhtasar Halaat Nawab Viqar-ud Daulah Viqar-ul Mulk Maulvi Mushtaq Husain Khan Bahadur Intesar Jung* (Aligarh: Muslim University, 1938), p. 3.

of time working as an administrator in Aligarh, including the charge of publishing *Tahzib-ul Akhlaq*, a publication that was started in the first place to dispel Muslim suspicion of Western learning. He also looked after the *Aligarh Institute Gazette* and other miscellaneous publications, thus taking some pressure off Sayyid Ahmad. He served on the College Fund Committee, when it was constituted, and joined Sayyid Ahmad in fundraising activities. Through his thought-provoking articles on the condition of Muslims, their religious issues, and the changing times, he engaged in the debate reinforcing Sayyid Ahmad's position over what Muslims needed to do in terms of their education.[6] Although his reverence for Sayyid Ahmad remained firm, Viqar-ul Mulk did not hesitate to openly differ with him on issues, such as the increasing influence of the British in the college and Sayyid Ahmad's criticisms of pan-Islamism. Sayyid Ahmad later recommended him to Nawab Salar Jung I, the Prime Minister of the state of Hyderabad, who appointed him as the Inspector of Courts in which capacity he fared very successfully. It was here that he worked at the highest levels of the bureaucracy and earned the title of *Viqar-ul Mulk* (Honour of the Sovereign) in 1890.[7]

However, staying away from Aligarh between 1875 and 1892 did not deter Viqar-ul Mulk from his commitment to promote the MAO College. He continued using the network he had developed while in Hyderabad for the college. Once Sir Asman Jah, the Prime Minister of Hyderabad state from 1887 to 1894, visited Aligarh for a few hours in 1888. By the time he left, Viqar-ul Mulk had succeeded in raising the annual grant for the college by 250 rupees per annum. He also raised an enormous sum from his friends and relatives as an endowment for the college and collected substantial donations from the people of Hyderabad for constructing Asman Manzil, an MAO College campus building.[8] His endeavours were crucial, particularly at the time of crisis, when the operating expenditures of the college were on the rise and fund collections were shrinking.[9] On finishing his tenure in Hyderabad, Viqar-ul Mulk chose to return to Aligarh to further Sir Sayyid's vision of promoting education among Indian Muslims, having declined an offer to serve as the Prime Minister of the state of Bhopal.[10]

---

[6] Mushtaq Husain, 'Haiyat-e Jadidah: Haiyat-e Jadidah aur Maujezah-e Qurani', *Tahzib-ul Akhlaq* 1, no. 2 (1871): 23–4.
[7] Zuberi, *Tazkirah-e Viqar*, pp. 12–58.
[8] Ibid., p. 99.
[9] Lelyveld, *Aligarh's First Generation*, pp. 134–42.
[10] Mushtaq Ahmad (ed.), *Khutoot-e Viqar-ul Mulk* (Aligarh: Aligarh Muslim University Press, 1974), pp. 183–4.

He appeared before the Hunter Commission of 1882 appointed by the British Indian Government to review the state of education in India and suggest necessary measures for its progress. Here, Viqar-ul Mulk spoke his mind openly, advocating for a more practical curriculum, more residential universities, and affordable education.[11] In particular, he pointed out the ongoing demand for converting the MAO College into a university. The idea of a Muslim university had been conceptualized in 1873 by Sir Sayyid and his friends, but it had never been vigorously pursued until the campaign was revived during 1910–1912 by leaders, including Viqar-ul Mulk.[12] In 1911, a Muslim University Foundation Committee was organized, replacing Sir Sayyid Memorial Fund Committee. Aga Khan served as committee president and Nawab Viqar-ul Mulk was elected as secretary, to serve at its headquarters in Aligarh.[13] Viqar-ul Mulk coordinated several committees across India working towards establishing a Muslim university. Hundreds of thousands of rupees were collected under his supervision. Viqar-ul Mulk also continuously participated in the All India Muhammadan Educational Conference. In short, his services furthered the legacy of Sayyid Ahmad's vision for an educational institution. The transformation of the MAO College to AMU in 1920, one of the visions of Sayyid Ahmad, would not have been possible without his supporters, like Viqar-ul Mulk.

Another key figure in the coterie of Sayyid Ahmad was Mohsin-ul Mulk, who met Sayyid Ahmad in Etawah, where Sayyid Ahmad was a *tehsildar*. Soon after Sayyid Ahmad initiated and formed a committee to deliberate on the formation of the MAO College, he became a key collaborator and remained a long-term associate. During his visit in London, Sayyid Ahmad had written to Mohsin-ul Mulk stating that madrasas focussing on Arabic language and traditional curriculum would not do the community any good. He further extolled the British educational system that served as an aspirational model for him. To see how children were taught there and how their community would attain honour was an inspiration for him.[14] This is what he shared with his close lieutenant, who remained deeply convinced

---

[11] Zuberi, *Tazkirah-e Viqar*, pp. 131–2.
[12] Gail Minault and David Lelyveld, 'The Campaign for a Muslim University, 1898–1920', *Modern Asian Studies* 8, no. 2 (1974): 145–89, 146, 160–1.
[13] Zuberi, *Tazkirah-e Viqar*, pp. 289–90; Minault and Lelyveld, 'The Campaign', p. 61.
[14] Sayyid Ahmad to Mehdi Ali, London, 10 September 1869, in Shaikh Muhammad Ismail Panipati (ed.), *Maktubat-e Sir Sayyid*, vol. 1 (Lahore: Majlis-e Taraqqi-e Adab, 1976), p. 90.

with the idea until his death in 1907. Before being named Mohsin-ul Mulk, Sayyid Mehdi Ali was recommended by Sayyid Ahmad to the Nizam of Hyderabad. Here, Mehdi Ali served in various capacities for nineteen years and earned the title of Mohsin-ul Mulk (Helper of the Sovereign). Upon his retirement in the early 1890s, Mohsin-ul Mulk returned to Aligarh to join Sayyid Ahmad in his educational mission.

Mohsin-ul Mulk believed that given the changed social and political realities, the sort of education that the Muslims needed was exactly the one promoted by Sayyid Ahmad. Like Viqar-ul Mulk, he passionately served as an honorary secretary of the MAO College after Sayyid Ahmad's death and regularly contributed to *Tahzib-ul Akhlaq*, earning a place for himself within the Aligarh circles, but also receiving threats from those opposed to Sayyid Ahmad. He travelled to places as far as Karachi and Rangoon to raise funds for the college. Upon the death of Sayyid Ahmad when the college was undergoing a crisis, Mohsin-ul Mulk's leadership came to the rescue. He, along with Viqar-ul Mulk, led the institution to more success. Biographer Shan Muhammad refers to him as 'a faithful interpreter of Syed's ideas, and it was he who first understood Syed and realized the sincerity of his mission'.[15]

Shan Muhammad further asserts that there were two obstacles in front of Sayyid Ahmad while founding AMU: lack of funds and hostility of conservative sections of the Muslim community. Mohsin-ul Mulk was able to effectively deal with them both. He raised adequate money to pay off the financial debts of the college, and through his written and oratory skills, he had won great appreciation from the Muslim community. He also performed specific tasks of Sayyid Ahmad and fulfilled them dutifully. In response to the demands raised by some Hindu leaders of Banaras for the promotion of Devanagari script, Mohsin-ul Mulk developed in 1900 the Urdu Defense Association, a body for the advocacy of Urdu as the *lingua franca*, and thereby advanced Sayyid Ahmad's position on the issue.

Both Viqar-ul Mulk and Mohsin-ul Mulk were strong examples of the kind of coterie of friends and advisers Sayyid Ahmad could build and with whose help and commitment he was able to actualize his educational mission and reformist vision. This was the beginning of the sense of community, which grew even further to meet and overcome various challenges. The kind of support Sayyid Ahmad received from these two eminent figures, however, should not give the false impression that he did not face challenges and hostilities.

---

[15] Shan Muhammad, *Sir Syed Ahmad Khan: A Political Biography* (Meerut: Meenakshi Prakashan, 1969), p. 95.

CONFRONTING CHALLENGES, BRIDGING DISTANCES

Sir Sayyid aimed to not only combine curriculum or model his institution along the British system but also reform theology and practices among the Muslims.[16] His laborious interpretation of the Qur'an and launch of *Tahzib-ul Akhlaq* can be seen in this light. The radicality of his approach that sought to replace the old system of learning with the new Oxbridge style of imparting education was something that the traditional `ulama had a hard time grappling with. This is where he faced most opposition as the `ulama were unwilling to relinquish the selection of texts that would go into the curriculum. Sir Sayyid's goal was to eliminate the role of the `ulama as the arbiters of Islamic doctrine and practice in favour of 'educated Muslim gentlemen'.[17] For the `ulama, establishing a religious department next to a secular one was difficult, and this was precisely what Sayyid Ahmad wanted to do. Moreover, the `ulama neither supported nor agreed on what will be the nature of theology at the MAO College. The local imam of Aligarh, Lutfullah, showed his unwillingness to join the college. The Deobandis opposed the establishment of college because it was going to be open for Shia Muslims as well. A Barelwi named Ali Bakhsh went to Mecca to obtain a *fatwa* against the founding of the college, yet Maulvi Abdullah Ansari accepted the position of `alim in residence who gave Friday sermons and was charged by Sayyid Ahmad with privately speaking with any student 'wavering in religious belief'.[18] Seemingly, for Sayyid Ahmad and his group, figuring out a way to find common ground (if there was one) was a constant struggle, requiring substantial effort.

The new theology that emerged from Sayyid Ahmad's rationalist approach implied with it a re-evaluation of the traditional social ethics of the Muslim community. Just as among the Hindus and Hindu social reformers of the nineteenth century, Muslims were increasingly becoming aware of the need to purge their religion of practices that had crept in and had no place within Islamic doctrines. In some ways, event today, the Muslims of India continue to face these challenges, including the custom of triple *talaq* (instant divorce), which was still in practice without any legal or juridical basis, until recently when it started being probed more widely.

---

[16] David Lelyveld, 'Disenchantment at Aligarh: Islam and the Realm of the Secular in Late Nineteenth Century India', *Die Welt des Islams* 22, nos 1/4 (1982): 85–102.
[17] Ibid., p. 93.
[18] Lelyveld, *Aligarh's First Generation*, pp. 94–6.

Sayyid Ahmad launched *Tahzib-ul Akhlaq* (*Muhammadan Social Reformer*) to aid the Muslims to reform their old customs and adopt modern ways of life. Sayyid Ahmad, no doubt, attracted the wrath of all. To conservatives, he was a liberal as he sought to find good even among the British; to the liberals, he was a conservative since he was not a thoroughgoing imitator of the Western ways.[19]

The `ulama, especially the Deobandis, vehemently opposed Sayyid Ahmad's ideas on his modernist philosophy and its lasting legacy in the field of education, which sought to combine Islamic subjects with secular, modern, Western learning. Within the larger debate on Islam and modernity, Muhammad Qasim Zaman notes (and rightly so) that 'questions of educational reform are among the thorniest'.[20] In this regard, a major argument made by the `ulama is that the sort of virtues the Muslims need to cultivate come from the Islamic religious tradition itself, not from the West, and that mixing Islamic knowledge with modern forms of learning represents a thinly veiled attack on Islam.[21] The `ulama continued to offer learning and education to those seeking them, mostly based on *Dars-e Nizami*, a curriculum named after its founder Mulla Nizamuddin Firangi Mahalli, which was widely popular among madrasas across the Indian subcontinent. It consists of two broad areas of subjects – *manqulat* and *m`aqulat*. In *manqulat* ('revealed' science category), they taught recitation and exegesis of the Qur'an, along with the study of *hadith* and *fiqh* and sometimes, *tasawwuf*. In *m`aqulat* ('rational' science category), they taught grammar, etymology, logic, mathematics, philosophy, rhetoric, astronomy, and *tibb*.[22] Sayyid Ahmad offered an alteration in this arrangement by injecting Western sciences; this was bound to ruffle some feathers.

Still, the `ulama in toto were opposed to Sayyid Ahmad's vision. Many – `ulama and non-`ulama alike – adopted his rational modern outlook and combined their religious piety with a transformed approach to education. Several came close to him with lifelong support, conviction, and friendship.

---

[19] Remarks of Kennedy, 'District Collector of Aligarh at the Turn of the Century', *Aligarh Institute Gazette* (1888): 557.

[20] Muhammad Qasim Zaman, *Modernist Islamic Thought in a Radical Age: Religious Authority and Internal Criticism* (Cambridge: Cambridge University Press, 2012), p. 143.

[21] Zaman, *Modernist Islamic Thought in a Radical Age*, p. 143.

[22] Ghulām Muhyi'd Dīn Sufi, *Al Minhaj: Being the Evolution of Curriculum in the Muslim Educational Institutions of India* (Lahore: Shaikh Muhammad Ashraf, 1941).

The most outstanding example among such supporters was Maulana Shibli Numani (1857–1914), the founder of *Darul Musannifin* (House of Writers) in Azamgarh to which he belonged and the principal of *Nadwatul 'Ulama*, a prominent madrasa in Lucknow. Shibli had taught Persian and Arabic at Aligarh for several years. After visiting Constantinople, Egypt, and Syria in 1892 – travels he recorded in an exceptional travelogue – Shibli noted that education in these places had the same problem as in India: the new education lacked a feeling of association or religious component, whereas the traditional education did not impart skills of use or relevance in changed times.[23] This could be a reason that he began further appreciating Sayyid Ahmad's efforts at striking a balance between the two sets of education systems and the inherent worth of this entire enterprise. However, Numani soon developed differences with Sayyid Ahmad on the question of how each of them viewed Western values: Numani was more interested in reforming Muslims from within, which led him to *Nadwatul 'Ulama* and an increasing dedication to pan-Islamism after having visited many Muslim countries. His admiration for Aligarh, nonetheless, remained intact.

Another person who was an active supporter of Sayyid Ahmad's reform efforts was Maulvi Zaka Ullah (1832–1910) of Delhi. He viewed education as a means to awaken the Muslims. After his retirement from Muir Central College in Allahabad as Professor of Persian and Mathematics, he offered his services to teach Mathematics at the MAO College. A major task he undertook was of translating works on science and mathematics into Urdu. He even gave an open offer to Sayyid Ahmad that the college could publish any of his translated works for the benefit of the teachers and students.[24] Although this indicated a basic contention between the two – Sayyid Ahmad wanted education to be imparted in English language and not in the vernacular – Zaka Ullah's relationship with or admiration for Sayyid Ahmad did not diminish.

Sayyid Ahmad continued to make friends and earn respect from a host of people, who joined him mostly because of their shared concern for the Muslim community. Khwaja Altaf Hussain Hali (1837–1914), an eminent Urdu poet, writer, and biographer, was inspired by Sayyid Ahmad's zeal for

---

[23] Maulana Shibli Numani, *Safarnama-e Rum wa Misr wa Shaam* (Dehli: Qaumi Press, 1901), p. 153.

[24] This offer was made via latter written to Sayyid Ahmad Khan dated 26 February 1873. In Yusuf Husain (ed.), *Selected Documents from the Aligarh Archives* (New York: Asia Publishing House, 1967), p. 239.

his fellow Muslims. At the request of Sayyid Ahmad, Hali wrote his epic poem *Musaddas-e Madd-o Jazr-e Islam* (An Elegiac Poem on the Ebb and Tide of Islam), commonly known as *Musaddas-e Hali*. This poem examines the social and moral degradation marring the contemporary Muslim society. David Lelyveld has rightly termed it as 'a popular statement of ideas associated with the Aligarh Movement'.[25] Hali's principal contributions were his poems and articles, which he regularly contributed to *Aligarh Institute Gazette* and *Tahzib-ul Akhlaq* – a feat to which he devoted himself. His participation in the Muslim Educational Conference and efforts at reforms within the community were significant too. Like other people close to Sayyid Ahmad, Hali had his share of differences on specific subjects, such as female education, but the two of them worked harmoniously. This stood in contrast to the people who bluntly accused Sayyid Ahmad. His emphasis on rationalism and attempts to justify the theory of evolution led many, particularly some conservative segments, to label him as a *naicari*. He also became subject to well-publicized attacks from orthodox Muslims. Two of his most vocal critics included Ali Bakhsh Khan and Sayyid Imdad Ali, who were not opposed to English education but to the spread of religious reform.[26] Many *fatwa*s declaring Sayyid Ahmad to be a *kafir* (infidel), agnostic, atheist, and *dajjal* (a monster described in Qur'an to appear before the Day of Judgement) were issued.[27] Sayyid Ahmad's response ranged from anger to assurance that his co-workers were men of immovable orthodoxy. Moreover, he wanted to step aside to minimize controversies, so that he could focus on the basic task of promoting education.

RAPPROCHEMENT WITH THE BRITISH

Sayyid Ahmad's interactions with the British is an intriguing question. Commonly and widely understood as a 'loyalist Muslim', his intellectual reflections and personal dispositions with the British were not simply a matter of respect and deference. Although he was extremely impressed with British ways of life and education particularly after his return from London, his position was not uncritical. In the same letter he wrote on 15 October 1869 from London to the Secretary of the Scientific Society at Aligarh, which appeared in Urdu in the *Aligarh Institute Gazette* later, we find different streaks of his thoughts. He writes, 'All good things, spiritual

---

[25] Lelyveld, *Aligarh's First Generation*, p. 241n.
[26] Ibid., pp. 131–4.
[27] Muhammad, *Sir Syed Ahmad Khan*, p. 69.

and worldly, which should be found in man, have been bestowed by the Almighty on Europe, and especially on England.' Although he admired their politeness, knowledge, good faith, cleanliness, skilled workmanship, accomplishments, and thoroughness – alongside their religiosity – he further added, 'I undoubtedly maintain that the general behaviour of Englishmen towards the natives is the reverse of polite, and that this should certainly cease.'[28] Most of the factors that impressed him in England were similar to those that enthralled him during his travels to England. He admirably described the steamship RMS *Baroda* he boarded from Bombay, while praising its baths, engines, and cabins. The saloon, he wrote, is 'heaven!'[29] In his travelogue *Musafiran-e Landan*, Sayyid Ahmad comes across as a person awestruck with the technological prowess of the Western world.[30] He was also deeply impressed with the Oxbridge model and, on returning to India, attempted to replicate it in the MAO College. This did not mean that his relationship with the British was smooth and harmonious, all along the way.

With regard to the time Sayyid Ahmad was out to prove Muslim allegiance towards the British in the aftermath of the Indian Rebellion of 1857, W. W. Hunter came up with a contrasting thesis in his work *The Indian Musalmans*, wherein he held Muslims as treacherous to the British rule. In response, Sayyid Ahmad defended his co-religionists by providing a short account of Indian Wahhabism, which Hunter had held responsible for the rebellion. In addition, he argued that the Muslims under the British rule had all religious freedoms, so they had no reason to rise in a rebellion. All of this, Sayyid Ahmad presented very gently, while calling Hunter's work politically a grave mistake and, to some extent, a historical misinterpretation.[31]

Undoubtedly, he did not want to irk the British officials whose help he was seeking to advance his educational mission. S. Brooke of Jabalpur replied to Sayyid Ahmad's letter on 10 January 1873, wherein Brooke stated that he would try to make Sayyid Ahmad's case in front of Shahjehan Begum of Bhopal and 'press on her consideration of as worthy an object as the proposed new Mohammedan College'.[32] Similarly, his relations with the British principal of the MAO College, Theodore Beck, was more nuanced than expected. Although Beck carried on the administration of the college, Sayyid

---

[28] George Farquhar Irving Graham, *The Life and Work of Syed Ahmed Khan* (Delhi: Idarah-e Adabiyat-e Delli, 1974 [1885]), pp. 185–8.
[29] Ibid., p. 118.
[30] Sayyid Ahmad Khan, *Musafiran-e Landan* (Lahore: Majlis-e Taraqqi-e Adab, 1961).
[31] Muhammad, *Sir Syed Ahmad Khan*, pp. 120–8.
[32] Husain, *Selected Documents*, p. 215.

Ahmad always had the final word on matters of critical importance. Thus, Sayyid Ahmad certainly allied with the British, admired their institutions, and even looked up to the British society as a model to be emulated, but his position was nuanced, far more than that of a mere 'loyalist'.

ENGAGING HINDU COMPATRIOTS

Sayyid Ahmad's interactions with the Hindu intelligentsia and reformers made sure that he attracted various Hindu supporters, despite the opposition of the Arya Samajists.[33] Unsurprisingly, the very first graduate of the college, an institution that was founded along the ideals of providing community education to the Muslim youth, was Hindu – the noted historian Ishwari Prasad (1888–1986). Although early in his life, he believed that Hindus and Muslims were akin to 'two eyes of the beautiful bride, India', he preoccupied himself solely with Muslim interests in the later phase. This change in his viewpoint may indicate that he had not completely given up on what more recent accounts would tout as his departure from the secular outlook. Any such approach based on binary models is hardly defensible in the light of what can be referred to as the historical contexts that changed more rapidly than expected.

Although much of Sayyid Ahmad's work surrounded Muslim interests, as a reformer and educationist, he did draw the support of his Hindu compatriots. Some of his most important supporters who proved critical to his projects were not Muslims. On 4 January 1873, in response to Sayyid Ahmad's request, Raja Jaikishan Dass of Aligarh enthusiastically wrote,

> Mr. Lawrence, the Collector, Dr. Jackson, the Civil Surgeon, Mr. Hunt, the Executive Engineer as well as Mohomed Inayat Ullah Khan, and Moulvi Mohomed Yoosuff have all agreed to act as members of a special committee for the selection of a suitable site as Allygurh for the Muhammadan College. And as for myself, I very thankfully accept the membership of the Committee.[34]

---

[33] Lala Lajpat Rai started his career with a serious attack on Sir Sayyid. Although he was initially impressed with the liberal ideology of Sayyid Ahmad, he was disheartened with Sayyid Ahmad's collaboration with the British. 'Open Letters to Sir Sayyid Ahmad Khan', in *Lala Lajpat Rai: Writings and Speeches*, ed. Vijay Chandra Joshi, vol. 1, pp. 1–25 (Delhi: University Publishers, 1966).

[34] Husain, *Selected Documents*, p. 214.

Raja Jaikishan Dass not only supported Sayyid Ahmad's efforts but also actively mobilized resources and individuals towards the task. Similarly, Raja Vijeanagur of Calcutta promised Sayyid Ahmad a subscription of three thousand rupees – a fairly handsome amount.[35] Although the specific purpose this money was used for remains unclear, people like Raja Vijeanagur were within the network that Sayyid Ahmad could create for himself and his cause. Such successes in enlisting the support of the Hindu *taluqdar*s was possible because of the way he presented his cause; this further debunks any narrow understanding of Sayyid Ahmad as someone who championed solely for Muslim education. In a letter to Rani Raja Gobind Singh of Pargana Sikandarrao, District Aligarh, dated 29 July 1965, Sayyid Ahmad states,

> Since the *rausa* (magnates) of this district have started constructing a building for the sake of benevolence and the wealthy Indians on donation, rather it is reaching its completion the purpose of which is that Indians can always gather in it for the progress of learning and where the wealthy Indians could have educational conversations, and it is for this task the *rausa* of this district and those of Bulnadshahr have donated money. But the entire amount that is needed could not be collected.[36]

He further adds that because the building was being constructed for the wealthy people of the district, donating money for the cause would have been beneficial. Although he was writing this letter much before the foundation of the MAO College, when he was still operating the Scientific Society, his approach was much more inclusive. On the same day, he wrote at least two more letters with the same argument to *taluqdar*s Rao Sahib Lakshmi Chand and Raja Sahib Sarpati Singh.[37] As the Secretary of the Scientific Society at Aligarh, he also connected with Pundit Harsookh Rai, Secretary of the Society for the Diffusion of Useful Knowledge at Lahore. These wide-ranging contacts must have increased his appeal; thus, when it came to the founding of the college in the 1870s, he could garner the support of the aforementioned *taluqdar*s.

Sayyid Ahmad ensured that the doors of the MAO College were open to all. As K. A. Nizami put it, 'he envisaged a community institution and

---

[35] Husain, *Selected Documents*, p. 216.
[36] Ibid., pp. 66-7.
[37] Ibid., pp. 66-8.

not a communal [one]',[38] even though the institution primarily aimed at catering to the needs of the Muslims. Numerous donors contributed to the various projects, such as the construction of the rooms. The Managing Committee of the MAO College in 1887 consisted of 11 members out of which 3 were Hindus. In the early years of the college, the number of Hindu and Muslim students was practically the same. In 1880, it was 7 Hindu and 8 Muslim students. By 1888, it increased to 30 Hindu and 39 Muslim students.[39] In 1898, when Sayyid Ahmad passed away, there were 285 Muslim and 64 Hindu students were enrolled in different classes. Thus, Sayyid Ahmad ensured that his college was for all Indians because he had originally stipulated that good education should be available to all, not the Muslims alone.

NATION, COMMUNITY, AND THE GLOBAL MUSLIMS

The efforts of Sayyid Ahmad to engage with different layers of community he inhabited included modernists (like himself) who were not in complete agreement with him, Muslims who disagreed with his anti-imperialist and anti-pan-Islamic politics, and Hindus who sided with him with regard to their opposition to the INC. Sayyid Ahmad's involvement with these people displays that as a leader, he was open to dialogue and negotiation in order to arrive at his goals amicably. Additionally, Sayyid Ahmad had to deal with much more nuanced groups in his attempt to create a community that he could depend on for both support and critique.

Sayyid Ameer Ali (1849–1928), an eminent lawyer, judge, and prolific writer on matters concerning the Muslims of his time, both agreed and disagreed with Sayyid Ahmad's thoughts. Like Sayyid Ahmad, he was concerned about the lack of English education among Indian Muslims. In 1882, he wrote,

> The study of English is a vital question for the Muslims. It means whether the Muslims are to be enabled to emerge from the desperate condition into which they have fallen and take their proper place among the Indian nationalists, or whether they are allowed to sink still lower in material prosperity.[40]

---

[38] Nizami, *Sayyid Ahmad Khan*, p. 85.
[39] Muhammad, *Sir Syed Ahmad Khan*, p. 235.
[40] Syed Razi Wasti (ed.), *Memoirs and Other Writings of Syed Ameer Ali* (Lahore: People's Publishing House, 1968), p. 174.

Sayyid Ameer Ali expressed his differences with Sir Sayyid's approach, particularly regarding the future of Indian Muslims, but both converged on the question of building a community. In a speech he delivered on 19 June 1903, on the occasion of the annual dinner of the MAO College, Sayyid Ameer Ali said that he and Sayyid Ahmad had 'agreed most emphatically' on the future advancement of the Muslims of India that depended on the formation of character in early part of one's life, which was an aim that Sayyid Ahmad had set out for himself while establishing the college.[41] As opposed to Sayyid Ahmad, who went ahead with the establishment of the college as a venue to provide education, Sayyid Ameer Ali always believed that the Muslims should first organize themselves politically. Then only could they secure a resolute political future by using instruments, such as the separate electorates, provided to them by the Indian Councils Act of 1909 and to a few other communities in 1919.

For Sayyid Ahmad, the Muslim community's educational advancement and its attendant economic advancement preceded their political interests. This issue earned him several critics – at home and abroad. Two specific political positions displeased his detractors. First, he emerged as one of the strongest critiques of pan-Islamism. Noted Islamic thinker and modernist Sayyid Jamaluddin al-Afghani (1839–1897), a major advocate of pan-Islamic unity as a mobilizer for anti-colonialism, believed that Sayyid Ahmad's anti-pan-Islamic ideas were a sign of servility to the British and would isolate Indian Muslims from the rest of the Muslim world. In the late 1870s, during his stay in India – when he was exiled from Egypt by the Khedive Tewfiq Pasha – al-Afghani viewed Sayyid Ahmad as a major adversary, whose extreme rationalism was another bone of contention for him, leading to heresy and falsification of the words of the Qur'an. However, the two personalities converged when it came to their belief that Islam was capable of an evolutionary process within the present and future history of humankind.[42] Their approach towards the necessity of modernism was also the same. Both al-Afghani and Sayyid Ahmad feared the misuse of religious orthodoxy, which could have brought the community down. Both were also deeply inspired by the Tunisian and Ottoman statesman, Khayr al-Din Pasha (1820–1890), in their adoption of modernism and the significance

---

[41] Shan Muhammad (ed.), *The Right Hon'ble Syed Ameer Ali: Political Writings* (New Delhi: Ashish Publishing House, 1989), p. 174.
[42] Aziz Ahmad, 'Sayyid Ahmad Khan, Jamal al-Din al-Afghani and Muslim India', *Studia Islamica* 13 (1960): 55–78, 58.

of the freedom of expression in revolutionizing ideas and minds of the Muslims.[43] Sayyid Ahmad, thus, was ideologically linked to the leading Muslim thinkers of his time.

Several co-religionists during and after the lifetime of Sayyid Ahmad, such as Muhammad Ali (1878–1931), M. A. Ansari (1880–1936), Maulana Abul Kalam Azad (1888–1958), Altaf Husain Hali, Shibli Numani, and Muhammad Iqbal, supported pan-Islamism in its anti-imperialist spirit.[44] By contrast, Sayyid Ahmad promoted views that were non-confrontational. He supported writers on Islam, such as Bosworth Smith, whose approach was conciliatory with regard to Islam and the West.[45] While visiting London during 1869–1870, Sayyid Ahmad published *A Series of Essays on the Life of Muhammad* (1870) refuting most of William Muir's arguments. In a letter addressed to Mohsin-ul Mulk on 20 August 1869, he expressed his anguish leading him to write these essays: 'These days, I am a bit troubled. I am reading William Muir's book on the Prophet ... his injustice and bigotry has cut my heart into pieces.'[46] Sayyid Ahmad had diverted most of his energies to establishing good relations with the British, particularly in the context of the aftermath of the 1857 rebellion, and had tried not to displease them further. This led to his second political position of shunning the anticolonial efforts within the Indian political spectrum.

Most political stances of Sayyid Ahmad Khan were geared towards benefitting his community in his social and educational goals. Since 1857, Sayyid Ahmad had worked on developing a better understanding between the British and Indian Muslims. *Asbab-e Baghawat-e Hind* (*The Causes of the Indian Rebellion*), his deeply analytical pamphlet on the causes of the 1857 rebellion, has mostly been read as a political analysis of the reasons that led to the revolt. More than a political piece, it is a well-thought reflection of the ruler–ruled relationship. This piece of writing seems to be as much a social and cultural commentary as it is a political analysis. His innate desire to bring the two groups of people to a reconciliation was driven by the fact that Muslims had already been running behind their peers and what they needed was an ongoing relationship with the British

---

[43] Ahmad, 'Sayyid Ahmad Khan, Jamal al-Din al-Afghani', pp. 59–60.
[44] Mangesh Kulkarni (ed.), *Interdisciplinary Perspectives in Political Theory* (New Delhi: Sage Publications, 2011), p. 93
[45] Humayun Ansari, *The Infidel Within: Muslims in Britain since 1800* (London: C. Hurst & Co, 2004), p. 73.
[46] Muhammad Ismail Panipati (ed.), *Maktubat-e Sir Sayyid*, vol. 1 (Lahore: Majlis-e Taraqqi-e Adab, 1976), p. 431.

and efforts to advance themselves by attaining higher English education. When the INC was formed in 1885, he could not foresee a change in his course altogether. Shan Muhammad writes that after the birth of the INC, 'for some time Syed maintained strict silence, but soon this changed into active opposition'.[47] He took to public speeches as well as devoted columns of *Aligarh Institute Gazette* to oppose the INC. His opposition was combined with his devotion to the British as well as his failure to leave his aristocratic mindset, which inhibited him from the thought of sharing platforms of governance with those from non-elitist backgrounds. He asked the Muslims to eschew politics for education and warned the people that if the INC's agitation went unchecked, it might end in another mutiny, finally ending in 'a disastrous catastrophe'.[48] Moreover, this was a warning for everyone, not just the Muslims.

Sayyid Ahmad quickly came to lock his horns with the Muslims who joined the nationalist movement led by the INC. The third session of the INC, held in Madras in 1887, was presided over by Badruddin Tyabji (1844–1906) of Bombay. Tyabji exhorted all people to join the INC movement to serve the common benefit of all communities and even persuaded Sayyid Ahmad to enter into communication with him:

> I have not been able to thoroughly understand the grounds on which this abstention is sought.... I understand your objection to be that of the Hindus being more advanced than ourselves who would profit more by any concessions made by the Government.... If any proposal is made which would subject the Mussalmans to the Hindus or would vest the exclusive power in Hindus to the detriment of the Mussalmans, I should oppose it with all my strength, but the Congress proposes to do no such things.[49]

Just as Badruddin Tyabji appealed everyone to join the Congress, Sayyid Ahmad's plea was not confined to only his Muslim followers. Several influential Hindu figures vehemently opposed the INC politics as well. These personalities included the landed gentry of the United Provinces, such as Kunwar Durga Pershad (*taluqdar* of Sarwan Baragaon), Kunwar Narindra Bahadur (*taluqdar* of Sandila), and Uday Pertap Singh (raja of Bhinga in

---

[47] Muhammad, *Sir Syed Ahmad Khan*, p. 144.
[48] Ibid., p. 146.
[49] Ibid., p. 147.

Awadh). In fact, the Maharaja of Banaras termed the men of INC as self-elected leaders, not public delegates and denounced the idea of representative institutions as an occidental idea.[50] Although Sayyid Ahmad's ideas agreed with such compatriots, his main motive was, of course, to cater to the needs of the Muslim community. In a letter to Badruddin Tyabji, dated 18 February 1888, he wrote:

> We do not mean to 'retard the national progress of India' or 'to prevent other people from enjoying rights for which they are qualified....' Your remark that 'it is our duty if possible to raise ourselves in the scale of progress' is quite true, yet you should not forget that saying of our old Philosopher 'that before we get the antidote from Iraq the snakebitten person will die'.[51]

This response clearly shows that Sayyid Ahmad privileged the educational and social standing of the Muslims over the larger political quest addressed by the INC and its leaders, such as Badruddin Tyabji.

By foregrounding Muslim interests, Sayyid Ahmad was not foregoing the larger interests of the people of India. K. A. Nizami states that Sir Sayyid was convinced that the time for political agitation had not come yet and 'it was incumbent upon all Indians, to whatever religion they might belong, to concentrate all their energies on ceaseless activity to spread education and learning amongst the people'.[52] His civic engagement with Tyabji was a testimony to why his politics was not in conflict with that of the INC. This is further evidenced in, among many others, the following statement, Sayyid Ahmad wrote a year before his death: 'Without any doubt, as I want friendship, unity and love between two communities [Hindus and Muslims], leaving aside the religious distinction, similarly I want mutual cooperation, love, sympathy and brotherhood socially, in spite of the political differences.'[53] While he was trying to do away with any misgivings between the communities, Sayyid Ahmad expected for due consideration of mutual political interests.

---

[50] *Showing the Seditious Character of the Indian National Congress and the Opinions Held by Eminent Natives of India Who Are Opposed to the Movement* (Allahabad: The Pioneer Press, 1888), p. xxxiv. Also Muhammad, *Sir Syed Ahmad Khan*, pp. 149–50.
[51] Cited in Muhammad, *Sir Syed Ahmad Khan*, p. 148.
[52] Nizami, *Sayyid Ahmad Khan*, p. 143.
[53] *The Aligarh Institute Gazette*, 12 June 1897.

CONCLUSION

The MAO College at Aligarh, a manifestation of Sayyid Ahmad Khan's reformist ideology, was revolutionary for the notion of education among the Muslims of the colonial India. Along with his collaborators, Sayyid Ahmad always tried to combat attitudes that considered English education and European ideas as obstacles in the way of the religious learning of Islam.[54]

It was but natural for Sayyid Ahmad to find groups that were fervidly opposed, passionately reassuring, and those torn between ideas. He was able to garner support from the non-'ulama, the British, and the Hindus. It was his idea that produced students like Khwaja Abdullah, a law graduate and a *munsif* at Pawayan in the Shahjahanpur district, who within a few years of Sayyid Ahmad's death wrote an essay titled 'How Far Can We Reconcile Islam with Modern Ideas?' which published in the *Aligarh Monthly* in 1904. This essay was a scathing criticism of a preceding article published in the same periodical, emphasizing that 'Islam is irreconcilable with modern ideas'.[55] Khawja Abdullah's response refuted the arguments made in the previous article by asserting the need for social reform in Islam and challenging the notion that English-knowing Muslims are indifferent to religion.

Taken together, Sayyid Ahmad left a legacy of how to build a community and use it to maximize one's vision and mission. In his lifetime, Sir Sayyid had established a set of warm, abiding relationships with people throughout north India, as reflected in the collection of letters that he wrote to many people and the letters he received. They reveal the diversity of his friendships.[56] After his death, he left behind an army of supporters who continue to advance his work on education and the ethos of reform.

---

[54] Lelyveld, *Aligarh's First Generation*, p. 87.
[55] *The Aligarh Monthly* II, IX (September 1904): pp. 114–22.
[56] Lelyveld, *Aligarh's First Generation*, p. 64.

6 Envisioning a Future
Sir Sayyid Ahmad's Mission of Education
MOHAMMAD SAJJAD

INTRODUCTION

The gentry to which Sir Sayyid Ahmad (1817–1898) belonged considered education a vehicle for cultivating the mind, while service under the state mainly a duty for men born in the concerned families; in other words, they believed that military and executive service under the state was *noblesse oblige*. Initially, Sir Sayyid Ahmad's thoughts on education were, quite predictably (and naturally), lofty and idealistic. He feared that education was primarily treated as a mere tool of livelihood. Rather than continuing his familial tradition of serving in the Mughal court (for which his rather rambling education had prepared him), he chose to serve the East India Company: this arguably marked the beginning of the process through which the youth from old elite families came to terms with the increasingly disorienting new world. During their lifetime, humans go through distinct phases wherein their conceptions of higher and nobler ultimate purposes of education undergo modifications and adaptations. Originally, education is the process of cultivating thinking and intellect; there is a discernible trend of the process coming closer to the realities of Sir Sayyid's time when the reins of command and control ceased to be even nominally with the ancient regime of the Mughals – the baton passed indubitably to the East India Company. Thus, to test Western education's ability to cultivate minds and enhance the learners' future material well-being, Sir Sayyid Ahmad started experiments of establishing Western educational institutions at Moradabad in 1859 and Ghazipur in 1862. However, the character-building ability of this type of education was affected by the mediocre curriculum of universities to which his labour of love, the Muhammadan Anglo-Oriental (MAO) College, was affiliated.

Over the years, educational projects metamorphosed to involve various paradigms – from using Persian as a dominant medium for attaining knowledge to including useful sciences (*kaar aamad* or *mufeed uloom*), such as agriculture, soil sciences, and allied disciplines, suitable for upgrading the overwhelmingly agrarian economy, and establishing conventional universities with the elusive vernacular as the medium of instruction. Thus, Sir Sayyid Ahmad initiated the translation of Western knowledge from various disciplines, such as philosophy, political economy, logic, and history; however, after making some progress, the pragmatic entrepreneur realized that the time available for translation was very short, and hence he stopped the translation work. This transition signifies the change in Sir Sayyid Ahmad's mindset: his intellectual aspirations and pursuit of excellence were tempered by the needs of his time and realization that his *qaum* (community) had to maintain a presence closer to the levers of power, which now meant the relatively higher echelons of public services that had now been opened to Indians. However, to be eligible, the aspirant was required to have Western education, which was in favour of the then-prevalent college education model: the colonial powers had resolved to recruit native Indian youths in somewhat 'superior' tiers of executive and judicial administration if the aspirants had obtained Western/collegiate education. As the 1870s advanced, this policy of exposure to Western learning became less of a preference and more of a mandatory requirement.

Sir Sayyid Ahmad's compromise of establishing the MAO College in Aligarh (1877), however, was not an act of tame surrender to the routine: if he had to conform to the 'routine' in imparting higher education (primarily) to the Muslim youth, it had to be under the best possible circumstances. The MAO College adopted the Oxbridge model of residential colleges both in form and substance, to the extent that the local circumstances in nineteenth-century north India permitted.

Sir Sayyid Ahmad's story of this evolving and metamorphosing project gleans from his writings and utterances, primarily documented in his journals (*Aligarh Institute Gazette* and *Tahzib-ul Akhlaq*), along with his speeches, correspondences, and other sources from which the rest of the narrative is drawn. The current chapter seeks to outline the course of these evolving, self-correcting paradigms in the mind of this founder of the Aligarh Movement, as he understood the realities of the time imposed on his *qaum*. To the author's knowledge, no such outline of a narrative encompassing a variety of seemingly disparate endeavours leading to well-defined goals has been published thus far.

This short chapter aims to reveal the reason that the mission was such a mobile target for someone like Sir Sayyid Ahmad who had a trained judicial mind with uncanny clarity of vision. Through the process of elucidation, this chapter attempts to join the various strands of thought and action – primarily concerning education – of our protagonist in the last four decades of his eventful career. Herein, neither are new facts reported nor known facts reassessed. Nevertheless, this chapter does hope to further elucidate the reasons that education remained the sheet anchor of Sir Sayyid Ahmad's life's mission, although it may have led to a 'larger end'.

SIR SAYYID AHMAD'S EARLY CAREER: COMING TO TERMS WITH MODERNITY

Sir Sayyid Ahmad had only passing exposure to 'formal' education; however, none of it occurred in *Dilli Kalij* (Delhi College), which had already introduced a new course in English language and sciences in the 1820s. The college was located just about a mile from his *haveli*.

Nevertheless, this was compensated by his eclectic (but not exactly catholic) domiciliary education; it traversed disparate fields ranging from Arabic grammar to Persian literature, astronomy, Islamic jurisprudence, and orthodox Greek medicine. At the same time, Sir Sayyid Ahmad underwent physical training in wrestling, indigenous martial arts, archery, and swimming – the forte of his father, Mir Mutaqqi (d. 1836/38). One of the greatest intellectual influences and role models of Sir Sayyid Ahmad was his maternal grandfather, Khwaja Fariduddin (1747–1826/28). Fariduddin was a polymath and a versatile personality, who combined mental acuity with administrative acumen. He thus became a senior official with the East India Company at Calcutta and the company's emissary to Persia.

Until 1857–1858, Sir Sayyid Ahmad's writings did not indicate any interest in education, given his peripatetic career as a judge under the East India Company in various districts of present-day western Uttar Pradesh.

The events of 1857 severely affected Sir Sayyid Ahmad's family in Delhi. During the uprising in 1857, Sir Sayyid Ahmad was posted in Bijnore, where he saved lives of English men and women, attempted to quell the 'revolt', and his difficulties after the place of his posting was overrun by 'rebels' from outside; however, these facts are not central to this presentation. The aftermath of those disturbed times led to many consequences. Although it seems that the functionaries of the restored government looked to him as a saviour, ample circumstantial evidence indicates that this was a catharsis that made Sir Sayyid Ahmad realize that the world around him had changed irrevocably; he could foresee a period where a white man presided over the country. This clear foresight also brought a realization: the new order endangered his *qaum* to losing its pre-eminent position – a sense of apprehension possibly exacerbated when he saw Bengali government employees educated in English language in the areas that he was serving.

In his renewed publications, he began unravelling the causes of the 'Indian rebellion' or chronicling the noble deeds of 'loyal' Muslims during the course of the disturbances, thus seeking to exculpate his community as much as possible under the dire circumstances. However, the pragmatic Sir Sayyid Ahmad finally began actualizing his mission; this could be best described as protecting, preserving, and promoting the interests of his *qaum*.[1] To achieve his objective, he used the then-available tools: when the crown formally succeeded the East India Company's rule, he began convincing the government about the trustworthiness of 'his people' and prepared them for the changed life in numerous ways, mainly the process of educating its youth.

MADRASA IN MORADABAD (1859): A FALTERING FIRST STEP

While writing tracts on the 'revolt' and explaining the role of the Muslim elite, Sir Sayyid Ahmad seems to have begun envisioning an educational enterprise, leading to the establishment of a Persian madrasa in Moradabad. For all practical purposes, the madrasa was based on the pedagogy of his childhood, with a major departure from the old pattern: unlike the private arrangement in his *haveli*, knowledge was imparted in a public location. In the madrasa, the language taught and used as the medium of instruction for a few elementary subjects was Persian because the pupils were mostly children from local notable Muslim and Hindu families, along with a few from plebeian families. The sons of Sir Sayyid Ahmad, Hamid (1849–1894) and Mahmud (1850–1903), also studied in this rather tentative institution.

Although no direct evidence supports this, it is a fairly reasonable assumption that the madrasa's establishment was a sequel to the first public meeting organized by Sir Sayyid Ahmad on 28 July 1859 in Moradabad. This well-attended 'rally' was a thanksgiving event where the Muslims of Moradabad expressed gratitude to the Almighty for the restoration of peace and assumption of sovereignty by the Queen Empress. The setting up of the madrasa must be an outcome of a rudimentary movement set in motion

---

[1] *Qaum* can be translated as 'nationality'. Overall, to Sir Sayyid, it meant the religious community of Muslims, mainly of noble descent. At times, for Hindus and Muslims, as a collectivity it could also denote caste, or even an 'alien' linguistic group such as the Bengalis. In the Educational Conference (1891), Sir Sayyid also used the word 'nationality'; see Muhammad Imamuddin (ed.), *Mukammal Majmua Lectures wa Speeches from 1863 to 1898* (Lucknow: Munshi Nawal Kishor Press, 1900), p. 534.

for coming to terms with the changing times, with education as a possible element of the process. In *Risalah-e Asbab-e Baghawat-e Hind* (1858), Sir Sayyid Ahmad notes that surreptitious attempts of the missionary schools to proselytize and degrade local faith to be one of the precipitating causes of unrest leading to the events of 1857. Thus, by 1858, Sir Sayyid Ahmad had realized the need for education imparted in schools established by the local communities.

The few accounts available on this infant, brief experiment in Moradabad indicate that a departure from the old pattern was made at least in one crucial respect – a course in history was introduced. Neville (1911) attributes the adoption of Persian language to indicate intense abhorrence of Western things by the local notables, thus implying that Sir Sayyid Ahmad considered the adoption of an 'acceptable medium of instruction' as expedient. However, this explanation is quite implausible;[2] it can be dismissed as speculation because during the stay of Sir Sayyid Ahmad in Moradabad (until 1862), the madrasa was merged with an existing government school without an evident enrolment loss in the new school. The experiment was clearly a tentative step in his 'mission education'; this speculation is confirmed by his address to a communally mixed gathering of fathers of students in the madrasa, in which he urged them the advantages of education at a madrasa over the kind of domiciliary education he received as a child of a prominent family.[3] His main arguments for the experiment were that the quality of teachers at the madrasa would be better than that of a domiciliary teacher because their remuneration would be much higher than that an individual family could afford and that the company of their compatriots would provide better motivation to the students to pick up learning.

This short-lived initiative warrants more scholarly attention than it has received so far. Here, Sir Sayyid Ahmad made a bold departure from the everyday paradigm of home-schooling the sons of the gentry – Muslims and Hindus alike. He boldly, but cautiously, tested waters without straying too far from the 'comfort zone' of the families, such that their children received the education their fathers and grandfathers did, but in an institutional setting. The merger of the madrasa with an existing government school soon after its inception potentially indicates Sir Sayyid Ahmad's realization that the use of Persian language as the medium of instruction was a thing

---

[2] Henry Rivers Neville, *Moradabad: A Gazetteer*, vol. XVI (Allahabad: Superintendent Government Press, 1911), p. 97.

[3] Rehmani Begum, *Sir Syed Ahmad Khan: The Politics of Educational Reform* (Lahore: Vanguard, 1985), p. 61.

of the past. As noted below, this replacement of Persian language in 1837 was not accompanied by a considerable change in preference for government schools (*madaris-e sarkari*) as the appropriate institutions for education of the children from good, or *sharif* (elite), families.

MADRASA IN GHAZIPUR (1862): GATHERING MOMENTUM

In 1862, Sir Sayyid Ahmad moved from Moradabad to Ghazipur because of his official transfer. Soon after the move, he seems to have begun establishing a network of local Hindu and Muslim notables to create modalities for addressing issues of all-round progress of society, including the setting up of a school. This was, however, preceded by the registration of a Translation Society, founded mainly for translating English works on subjects such as history, natural science, political economy, and agriculture into Urdu. This society had a link to the madrasa in Moradabad regarding at least one of its objectives: to prepare textbooks in the vernacular.

In March 1864, a little later after the establishment of the Translation Society, a school named the Victoria College was founded; this cross-communal alliance, with almost equal number of Muslim and Hindu students, was a fairly radical departure from the timid testing of waters in Moradabad. Persian was relegated as one among several languages – it was optionally taught along with Sanskrit and Arabic. Of course, Sir Sayyid Ahmad included his old favourite, history, but with elementary science as the added curricular component. The introduction of the study of English was the icing on the cake. At each grade level, two separate sections were created – one for teaching Arabic and the other for teaching Sanskrit – with other subjects being common to both sections.

An important piece of evidence, Sir Sayyid Ahmad's inaugural address on establishment of the school, indicates his motivation in promoting the kind of education he was espousing for the future younger generations of Hindus and Muslims. Essentially, his view was that Western learning, including knowledge of the English language, will prepare the youth for appointment at important positions in the government. In particular, he envisioned the possibility of (educated) Indians as part of bodies such as the Viceroy's Council under the Government of India Act 1858.[4] He highlighted the practical aspects of education to be imparted in the to-be-operational school and indicated that the knowledge of English would aid local people

---

[4] Sir Sayyid's Speech at the Victoria School, Ghazipur, 11 March 1864; see Muhammad Imamuddin, *Mukammal Majmua*.

in understanding the government's legislations, rules, and policies and the rationale of the levied taxes.[5] Sir Sayyid Ahmad had intellectual interest in the large project of harmonizing (or at least, reconciling) Islam with Christianity and in looking at the logic of doctrines and tenets of his own faith; however, for him, the basic mission of formal education – as he unveiled in Ghazipur – was a straightforward pragmatic manifesto, with practical benefits and tangible economic and political gains being the end-result of this model. Thus, for him, education was clearly just an element of a larger complex.

Similar to that in Moradabad, the institution at Ghazipur was soon merged with the local government school, apparently to create a platform where 'good' families of Hindus and Muslims may send their sons to receive a mix of modern and classical education. After the familiarity with the new pattern overcame the existing apprehensions, this pro tempore institution was to be merged with the official educational mainstream through 'inoculation'.

THE 'VERNACULAR' IMBROGLIO

Sir Sayyid Ahmad held a conundrum of a position for long: acquisition of knowledge through local languages (including classical languages) is a qualitatively better method of understanding the nuances of various academic disciplines. In his writings, he indicates the unfavourable results of the comparison of the capacity of thinking of the younger generation exposed to college education with that of people of his own generation, schooled classically (by using Persian, in close association with the masters in extra-institutional formats).[6] In the initial burst of activities, the Translation Society began translating English works on philosophy, economics, and history into Urdu for providing the 'native' intelligentsia with what Sir Sayyid Ahmad considered the 'best' in the world of mind in the West. The publication of original mathematics textbooks in Urdu,

---

[5] Annual Report, Scientific Society, 9 January 1864, in Asghar Abbas (comp.), *Sir Sayyid Ki Scientific Society* (Urdu) (Aligarh: Educational Book House, 2014), p. 61.

[6] Sir Sayyid's Essay, 'Arz Daasht-e-Sir Syed ba-raaye Vernacular University', *Aligarh Institute Gazette*, 9 August 1867, repr. in Ismail Panipati (ed.), *Maqalat-e Sir Sayyid*, vol. 8, 2nd ed. (Lahore: Majlis-e-Taraqqi-e-Adab, 1991), p. 55. Also see Altaf Husain Hali, *Hayat-e Javed* (Kanpur: Naami Press, 1901, repr. Delhi: Taraqqi Urdu Bureau, 1982), pp. 134–8.

written by 'Munshi' Zakaullah (1832–1910), clearly indicated a preference for teaching through the medium of Urdu. In a comprehensive proposal for establishing a 'Vernacular University' on the lines of the University of Calcutta, with the 'vernacular', rather than English, as the medium of instruction, Sir Sayyid Ahmad unveiled his 'agenda' for higher education.[7] For him, the 'vernacular' was Urdu written in the Persian script; the proposal was formulated and then pushed for government approval on these lines.

By now, Sir Sayyid Ahmad realized no exact meeting of minds occurred between him (and many of his colleagues, some of them from the majority community) and many other members of the Translation Society, led by 'Raja' Shiva Prasad, who did not dispute the use of the 'vernacular' as the medium of instruction, but advocated that the script of the language of instruction should be in both Nagri and Persian.[8] Here, we encounter a 'research gap': there is no accurate number, or even a reliable estimated one, of literates in the two scripts. However, circumstantial evidence suggests that with the fairly abundant village-level Zamindari and slightly higher number of Halqa schools in the Agra Province, established from the late 1840s onwards (under the utilitarian impetus of Lieutenant Governor John Thomason), the number of Nagri literates was higher than that of Persian literates.[9] The circumstance for this situation would appear to be the availability of teachers literate in Nagri alone at the level of the typical village, where teaching – such as it was – could only be performed by *pujari*s (temple priests), whose learning was solely in Nagri, in which the extant versions of scriptures were available. Thus, the project was abandoned; however, the detailed reasons for the abandonment remain unclear. A probable reason was that a divided house of promoters could not formulate a joint proposal and Shiva Prasad found support from his boss, Mathews Kempson, the provincial head of the education department, because, as seen a little later, the bitterness between Sir Sayyid Ahmad and Kempson had an adverse outcome in 1872, when a proposal mooted by a committee headed

---

[7] 'Arz Daasht-e-Sir Syed ba-raaye Vernacular University', *Aligarh Institute Gazette*, 9 August 1867, repr. in Panipati (ed.), *Maqalat-e Sir Sayyid*, p. 55. Also see Hali, *Hayat-e Javed*, pp. 134–8.
[8] For the Nagri–Urdu controversy, see Christopher R. King, *One Language, Two Scripts* (Bombay: Oxford University Press, 1994).
[9] Syed Nurullah and Jayant Pandurang Nayak, *History of Education in India* (London: Macmilan, 1951); also see Francis Robinson, *Separatism among Indian Muslims: The Politics of the United Provinces' Muslims, 1860–1923* (Cambridge: Cambridge University Press, 1974), p. 72.

by Sir Sayyid Ahmad for a chain of residential Muslim schools fell through in the teeth of opposition from the same Mathews Kempson.

Even with the dearth of information, there are two equally plausible explanations. First, Sir Sayyid Ahmad, a man with robust pragmatism and foresight, foretold a situation of continuous strife between the two aforementioned scripts – with Muslims and the Urdu elite being at a numerical disadvantage. Second, he noted that familiarity with the English language as a school subject alone was insufficient because government recruitment policies were steadily shifting towards the induction of personnel who could perform business transaction and communicate with their superiors in English.

However, in 1869, in his 33-page pamphlet, *Strictures upon the Present Educational System in India*, Sir Sayyid Ahmad critiqued the government educational system and fully supported education 'at all levels in the vernacular'.[10] Thus, the abandonment of the Vernacular University project was a tactical withdrawal, not a revisiting of pre-existing beliefs; it was the concession of the pragmatist to certain practical expediencies. The visionary Sir Sayyid Ahmad continued to hold the position to which he had reached after much apparent agony. Although principles may retain their validity, processes required tailoring to the imperatives of here and now.

UTILITARIAN VERSUS PIOUS EDUCATION

For understanding Sir Sayyid Ahmad's vision of the type of education he considered useful for Indians (more so, Muslims), how he distinguished the need to make a learner come to terms with their inhabited world from religious learning is noteworthy. Furthermore, he distinguished between the two streams more for pragmatic requirements than for conceptual clarity, the end being to induce the well-off sections of the community to open their purses for the 'new education' he clearly saw as the imperative of the times.

In his society, the closely related education and piety facilitated the flow of funds for financing institutions for theological learning. In brief, Sir Sayyid Ahmad clearly foresaw that charity for religious education was detrimental to his emerging projects and thus it impeded a future where the community's well-being and its attainment of modern education were welded together.

Although these concerns chronologically appeared a little later, they began appearing in the foreground since the time his educational projects

---

[10] Sir Sayyid Ahmad Khan, *Strictures upon the Present Educational System in India* (London: Henry. S & Co., 1869).

became more dependent on funding from his co-religionists, after the vernacular dichotomy caused cross-communal resource mobilization to become increasingly challenging. He clearly stated his thoughts on this in his speech in Patna on 27 January 1883, in which before he came to the point that the progress of the community was 'entirely dependent on education', he spoke at length on the way Muslim charities were concentrated towards religious causes including assistance to institutions of religious education.

Similarly, during his speech in Ludhiana on 23 January 1883, he announced that people must visit Muslim countries where modern education has made such a positive impact on the progress of the local community (presumably, the Ottoman Empire).[11] He added that for the good of his community, the excessive charity given to religious institutions must be diverted towards the (more worthy) cause of the kind of education he was advocating.[12]

Many of these observations are from the time Sir Sayyid Ahamd had completely withdrawn from providing discourses on the rational basis of Islam and begun reinterpreting many of the dogmas of faith in the light of 'modern' thought prevailing in the nineteenth century. This emphasizes the pragmatism at the bedrock of his educational mission: he could withdraw from the polemics he apparently treasured until the end in the larger cause of education. Furthermore, he did not mind indicating these points indirectly if it helped improve material assistance for his project. In summary, his discourse about religious versus educational philanthropy was mainly for accomplishing the mission for a bright future, for which resources were to be harnessed.

SCIENTIFIC SOCIETY AND TRANSLATIONS

Was the Scientific Society (formed in Ghazipur and subsequently shifted to Aligarh) in furtherance of Sir Sayyid Ahmad's educational mission, or did it have larger objectives beyond things that were purely educational in the narrow sense of the term?

---

[11] Ismail Panipati (ed.), *Maqalat-e Sir Sayyid*, vol. 5 (Lahore, 1961), pp. 49–50.

[12] Muhammad Imamuddin, *Mukammal Majmua*, pp. 183–92. To this effect of preferring an education for the betterment of this worldly lives than to remain anxious about the other world, see Sir Sayyid's Meerut speech (1896), in *Writings and Speeches of Sir Syed Ahmad Khan*, comp. and ed. Shan Muhammad (Bombay: Nachiketa, 1972), pp. 123–7, and Muhammad Imamuddin, *Mukammal Majmua*, p. 593.

Unfortunately, this question has no clear answers in the literature. The Scientific Society was formed in 1864 as a successor to the Translation Society; this suggests a change in emphasis and widening of scope of activities. The earlier translations by the Scientific Society are attributable to the need for texts for teaching certain disciplines in Urdu. Over a dozen textbooks of mathematics that certainly fit the 'curricular' category were translated; however, soon, the translation work ceased completely, with the discourse shifting towards shorter writings, particularly with the introduction of the *Aligarh Institute Gazette*, the official journal of the Scientific Society. In this periodical, a truly versatile range of subjects was covered. 'Practical technology', as termed by Lelyveld (1978), particularly in topics such as agricultural growth, farm machinery, and animal husbandry, was increasingly emphasized.

In the 'post-Ghazipur period', the Scientific Society was the forum expressing opinions of Sir Sayyid Ahmad on matters concerning education. These opinions varied from reiteration of his earlier views on suitability of the vernacular as the medium of imparting education at all levels to specific demands – with the plea to the government to hand over the responsibility of supervising the affairs of local schools to committees of notables of the school being the most important. This demand was conceded with a rider that the District Committee's role will be advisory, not supervisory. In addition, in Aligarh, the District Committee was an extension of the Scientific Society for all practical purposes.

The Scientific Society added an extracurricular dimension to education; it was an adjunct to Sir Sayyid Ahmad's institution building in education. In 1886, the Scientific Society passed this baton to the All India Muhammadan Educational Conference (AIMEC), which not only carried forward the non-institutional dimension but also acquired the added burden of political orientation of the community. However, all this happened only after Sir Sayyid Ahmad's journey to Britain.

SOJOURN TO ENGLAND (1869–1870): A WATERSHED

The defining point of Sir Sayyid Ahmad's story is his trip to England, undertaken reportedly on the suggestion of his friend Colonel Graham (b. 1840), apparently with the main objective of penning a rebuttal of William Muir's opinionated and biased account of the Prophet of Islam. This trip conveniently coincided with the time his younger son, Sayyid Mahmud, obtained a government scholarship for university education in England. Although biographers have not investigated whether the visit had an ancillary purpose of preparing a blueprint for an educational project of larger dimensions, it is clearly evident that a series of reports in *The Pioneer* on the decreasing proportion of Muslim employees in government offices since 1868 continuously engaged his attention during this sojourn.

In his correspondence with his associate Mehdi Ali 'Mohsin-ul Mulk' (1837–1909) regarding the decreasing proportion of Muslim employees in government offices, Sir Sayyid Ahmad indicated that this was the stage when he started veering round to the view that for their future well-being, the educational paradigm of Muslims would have to substantially follow the 'European pattern', which had already been introduced back home, where the recipients of such education were ever more likely to open the portals of government service to his community. His observations of the academic and extracurricular routines of the Christ College, Cambridge, where his son was enrolled, also spurred his interest in the way education was being imparted in the better institutions of England and Scotland. He then started visiting educational institutions and interacting with their teachers and the management to understand the intricacies of their systems.[13]

In *Strictures upon the Present Educational System in India*, however, Sir Sayyid Ahmad indicated that he was then in a dilemma; intellectually he still had uncertainties regarding the model because he asserted that the government 'system of schools had failed to achieve either popular mass education or the stimulation of intellectual creativity'.

He then argued that the vernacular was indispensable for imparting knowledge and the existing notion about imparting knowledge through English medium to Indians was 'nothing but a delusion', which was 'further increased by the ... three Universities of Calcutta, Bombay, and Madras'. He also articulated the ineffectiveness of downward filtration theory envisaged in Woods' (1854) educational despatch.

Thereafter, evidence indicates an inner conflict between what Sir Sayyid Ahmad thought to be the most effective method of imparting education to the Muslim youth (the vernacular) and the pragmatic imperatives of not straying much from *diffusion of knowledge* was formed to examine the kind of the model of university education as followed in three Indian universities with English as their linguistic vehicle. His writings after returning from England emphasize the idea of self-reliance of the community by establishing its own institutions, with virtues, such as right deportment (*shaayestagi*) and character building (*tarbiyat*). In *Strictures upon the Present Educational System in India*, he points towards continuing adherence to the postulates

---

[13] Johannes M. S. Baljon, *The Reforms and Religious Ideas of Sir Sayyid Ahmad Khan* (Lahore: Orientalia, 1958 [Leiden: Brill, 1949]), p. 48.

while being impressed with his observations in England. This potentially indicates the natural dichotomy resulting from what he felt and what he saw.

Even in 1882, before the Education Commission (the Hunter Commission) was established, Sir Sayyid displayed deep concern for modern education through the vernacular while his own MAO College was virtually getting modelled on the lines of the Oxbridge model.

ENVISIONING THE MAO COLLEGE: THE RUN UP

In 1872, a Select Committee for education required by the Muslim community was established; for reasons that will be explained below, the creation of this committee was a preliminary exercise towards establishing the *cause celebre* of Sir Sayyid Ahmad – the MAO College. However, this move should be considered in detail, independent of the developments in Sir Sayyid Ahmad's life, such as those in 1882, and his writings and speeches on this subject. As noted later, the scheme set forth by the committee and the effects of the views of officers like Kempson on its recommendations ultimately led the project to a concrete outcome, not as a general pattern of institutional arrangement but as the establishment of a standalone college, which was difficult to replicate in the future; indeed, replication seldom happened during Sir Sayyid Ahmad's lifetime.

The committee deliberated on why Muslim elite families were so reluctant to allow their children join government schools even though the material benefits of this kind of education were becoming increasingly evident to this gentry with a long tradition of performing service under the state. An underlying assumption, soon confirmed by the committee as a major factor leading to this reluctance, was the realization that schooling in government institutions meant that these elite-class children were to rub shoulders with those of the 'lower class'. Notably, on several occasions, Sir Sayyid Ahmad argued against such class prejudice of his 'target' audience, but to no avail. In the committee, he emphasized that because the new dispensation had introduced the idea of equality before law, such 'superior airs' were simply unacceptable: if the people of the two social classes could travel in the same coach of the trains, then why could not their children study in the same school?[14]

[14] *Report of the Members of the Select Committee for the Better Diffusion and Advancement of Learning among the Muhammadans of India, 1872*, Part I, section 7, in *Aligarh Movement: Basic Documents, 1864–98*, ed. Shan Muhammad (Meerut: Meenakshi Prakashan, 1978), p. 352.

Through this committee, Sir Sayyid Ahmad emphasized on both *talim* (knowledge or formal education) and *tarbiyat* (character building), that is, to be something conducive of 'upbringing of children, in such a manner that they [would] grow up to be humane, just, honest, self-respecting, and dutiful. While education signals a path to a bright and cheerful future, its value would be nullified without a gentle and benevolent culture and the civic virtues, which he regarded as the moral basis of a community'.[15] In addition, he insisted that regardless of their position in the social hierarchy, parents must direct and inspire their children towards doing noble actions.[16]

However, in practical terms, his priority seems to have remained education of the privileged. In the committee report, he (speaking for the committee) dedicated an entire section to quite explicitly emphasizing this aspect. He believed that by the age of 10 years, every boy from a noble (*sharif*) family must be sent to a boarding school, located in or near big cities, with amenities such as gardens, lawns, sports facilities, library, dining halls, health centre, and mosques with requisite religious functionaries: this was a vision of the extra-domiciliary variety – away from the digressions of home. Briefly, the framework of recommendations had to conform to the education pattern laid down by the government, but with as many adaptations as possible within the following constraints: these purely residential institutions were to meet the requirements of character building, religious instruction, and a choice of medium of instruction.

The committee's scheme – which was practically the brainwork of Sir Sayyid Ahmad – was sent for examination to the then Director of Public Instruction, the Government of the Northern-Western Province, Simon Mathews Edwin Kempson (1831–1894) – a main antagonist of the Vernacular University controversy. For reasons not relevant for the present chapter, Kempson had frequently and strongly contradicted Sir Sayyid Ahmad on several issues, in addition to his opposition to using the vernacular at the Vernacular University. As Robinson (1974) points out, Kempson also adhered to the 'approach of bureaucratic efficiency' against the paternalistic policies pursued by the Utilitarians of the 1860s.[17] He believed that the government schools were sufficient for educating children from various sections of society and that an adequate number of Muslim children were studying in such schools.

---

[15] Mushirul Hasan and Nishat Zaidi (trans. and ed.), *A Voyage to Modernism: Sir Syed Ahmad Khan* (Delhi: Primus, 2011), p. 11.
[16] Muhammad Imamuddin, *Mukammal Majmua*, p. 566.
[17] Robinson, *Separatism among Indian Muslims*, p. 102n4

Every Muslim-specific school, established and administered by the community with government grants-in-aid, was mandatorily subjected to the educational administration of the government. To justify the case of 'Muslim-only residential schools' in the required manner, the committee criticized the existing government and 'aided' schools – while asserting that its residential schools were a better solution. The committee also stressed that the quality of government and government-aided institutions deteriorated because of micromanagement by the education department, for which it did not have adequate infrastructure. It also advocated that local schools should be overseen mainly by local committees and the Public Instruction Department, being largely relieved of its administrative responsibilities, should conduct periodic inspections only. Though the Select Committee's line of argument was meant to support its recommendations, its observations were at some places critical of Kempsen, with whom, as we know, there was a history of differences with Sir Sayyid Ahmad. Nevertheless, Kempson severely criticized the committee's report, with main contentions that Muslims showed an inherent resistance to allowing their children modern education and that the number of Muslim children enrolled in government schools could sufficiently fulfil the requirements of government offices and legal profession. Rather, Kempson suggested the promotion of conventional (so-called oriental) education, which (according to him) had a genuine demand from the community. This was followed by a stout defence of the strategies for propagating education in the provinces by his department. Noting the tone and tenor of Kempson's expostulations, the Anglo-Indian newspaper *The Pioneer* (17 September 1873) published a long article expressing regret about Kempson's attitudes and recourse to low-level personal attacks on Sir Sayyid Ahmad.[18]

Kempson's disputation had a deleterious outcome, warranting a discussion in this chapter. This rather important aspect of the history of Indian education remains inadequately researched; circumstantial evidence indicates that although the local government ostensibly overruled Kempson's observations, approving the establishment of the institution recommended by the Select Committee at Aligarh – by allotting a 74-acre land – the larger project, namely the establishment of a chain of schools, could not be launched. Arguably, it was the adversarial position of Kempson that led Sir Sayyid Ahmad to concentrate all his efforts on establishing the

---

[18] Iftikhar Alam Khan, *Sir Sayyid Ka Nazariya-e Talim* (Urdu) (Delhi: Educational Publishing House, 2017), pp. 261–6.

Aligarh College without pursuing the larger vision of residential educational institutions in and around important cities. In addition to being capital intensive, the Aligarh College project entailed excessive engagement with the educational establishment of the state, which became inexpedient given the personality clash.

Furthermore, Sir Sayyid Ahmad realized the magnitude of the challenge at Aligarh and deemed it prudent to concentrate all his energy there. Notably, taking on the Aligarh enterprise in the right earnest entailed another sacrifice: the founder gradually, but steadily, disengaged himself from scholarly activities centred on the rational interpretation of Islam, particularly harmonization of Christian and Muslim theologies. Nevertheless, Sir Sayyid Ahmad later publicly disavowed any involvement in the religious instruction and supervision of religious observances of Muslim residents of the hostel to dispel any apprehensions in the minds of parents regarding their wards' orthodox beliefs being tampered by the 'innovative Sayyid'.

In its meeting on 12 May 1872, the Select Committee formally adopted its report and resolved to constitute a College Fund committee. Next, in its meeting on 15 February 1873, the committee resolved to open a college at Aligarh as envisaged by Sir Sayyid Ahmad. Pursuant to the committee's actions, a school with English and Urdu sections or departments was introduced, but with English as compulsory, even in the Urdu departments.[19]

The purpose of this school was to be the feeder for the proposed college, for which the foundation stone was laid by Governor General Lord Lytton in 1877; here, Sir Sayyid Ahmad delineated his mission of the proposed college 'to preach the gospel of free enquiry, of large hearted tolerance, and of pure morality' and indicated that the endeavour was unique because the institution was established as a result of neither an initiative of the state nor an act of individual philanthropy, but that of the effort of a whole community. On this occasion, Sir Sayyid Ahmad expressed his hope that this college will fructify into an autonomous university some day.

Furthermore, in February 1873, in addition to his committee's efforts, Sayyid Mahmud prepared a scheme of a university (*Dar-ul Ulūm*) for Muslims.[20] However, this idea was considered premature – partly because of

---

[19] Sir Sayyid's letter to *Karpardaz*, Director, Department of Public Instruction, North West Provinces, 30 June 1876, Sir Syed Academy Archives, AMU, Aligarh.

[20] Baljon, *The Reforms and Religious Ideas of Sir Sayyid Ahmad Khan*, p. 50. This scheme is detailed in the *Tahzib-ul Akhlaq* 5 (1874): 90–102, described and

hindrances created by Kempson but mostly because of resource constraints. In other words, the coat was cut according to the cloth!

In his later writings and speeches on the college's status and prospects, Sir Sayyid Ahmad emphasized the need for character building and grooming *tarbiyat*, a component not on the agenda of other colleges; however, he regretted that these aspects could not be introduced to the extent he desired owing to the paucity of funds and requirements of the affiliated universities.[21]

Around 1884, the idea of establishing a university at Allahabad, by carving large areas out of Calcutta University's jurisdiction, was first proposed. The proposal was for the university to be modelled on the 'oriental pattern' of the recently established Punjab University. This was a grave concern to Sir Sayyid Ahmad; he felt by whittling down the role of English language in higher education, the qualitative decline in higher education will be imminent.[22] Nevertheless, the Allahabad University established

---

critically examined by Musa Khan Sherwani in 'Muslim University ke bhule hue usul'. Lelyveld (*Aligarh's First Generation*, pp. 126–8) provides details of the Sayyid Mahmud's *Dar-ul Ulúm* scheme, which among many other things, envisaged that a student would enter the residential school at 10 years of age and would do BA; emphasis on natural sciences was relatively less; most distinctive feature was that at the postgraduate level, after having done a dissertation too, he will be provided with a handsome amount of stipend for next 7 years to pursue higher research. Robinson (*Separatism among Indian Muslims*, p. 199) says that this elaborate university scheme eventually acted as a historical resource to upgrade the MAO College into a Muslim university, and that 'the idea of a Muslim University had always been connected with Aligarh'. Macdonnell took it up in 1896; Beck and Morison drew up plans and AIMEC, 1898, Lahore, adopted it. Only then did the campaign for a Muslim university begin (Gail Minault and David Lelyveld, 'Campaign for a Muslim University, 1898–1920', *Modern Asian Studies* 8, no. 2 [1974]: 145–89).

[21] *Writings and Speeches*, ed. Muhammad, pp. 100–1, 123–7.

[22] Ibid., pp. 100–1. For Gurdaspur (Punjab) speech of Sir Sayyid, 27 January 1887, see *Writings and Speeches*, ed. Muhammad, pp. 123–7; and Muhammad Imamuddin, *Mukammal Majmua*, pp. 253–9. Also see Sir Sayyid's essays: 'Hindustan Mein Ala Talim aur Government' and 'Hamari Zubaan aur Hamari Ala Darja ki Talim (Our Language and Our Higher Education, 1881)', in *Tahzib-ul Akhlaq*, 1881, repr. in Ismail Panipati (ed.), *Maqalat-e Sir Sayyid*, vol. 8 (Lahore: Majlis-e-Taraqqi-e-Adab), pp. 29–33 and 42–50, respectively. To this effect he had also written two other essays: 'Vernacular Yani Hamari Zuban',

in September 1887 was based on the tried-and-tested Calcutta University model, much to the relief of the MAO College founder.

It was not as if the Select Committee, steered by Sir Sayyid Ahmad, prepared a model for the institution it considered the best suited or commensurate with the aspirations of its moving soul, the founder; pragmatism and feasibility were counterpoised against the ideal and a practical balance had to be struck.[23]

OBJECTIVE OF EDUCATION: BEYOND PUBLIC EMPLOYMENT AND LAW COURTS

Sir Sayyid Ahmad's venture into movement for educational enrichment of Muslims was driven by his need to ensure the Muslim share in public employment and administration; however, in some of his writings, he has considered other avenues of material advancement. For instance, his essay 'Graduate aur Tijarat' (Graduates and Trade),[24] based on one of his 1895 addresses to the MAO College students, is noteworthy. Herein, he states the unorthodox view that character building and obtaining employment are not the only objectives of higher education and that, as such, there is no reason that university degree holders should shy from the fields of trade and commerce. Sir Sayyid Ahmad noted that neither can all educated individuals

---

Tahzib-ul Akhlaq, 1881, repr. in Panipati (ed.), *Maqalat-e Sir Sayyid*, vol. 8, which has republished it with a changed title, 'Hamari Talim Hamari Zuban Mein', without giving any clarification to that effect. In this essay, Sir Sayyid asserted that experimentation of higher education through translations have been just a wastage of time and resources in the cases of the Fort William College, Delhi College, and even in his own Scientific Society. Same year (1881), another essay that was published, 'Mashriqi Ulum o Funun' (he characterized the Eastern knowledge as dead, *murdah ulum*), in which he had condemned the Senate of the Punjab University for moving towards oriental learning through translations. Also see *Aligarh Institute Gazette*, 19 May 1883, where he stressed that translations cannot enable obtaining higher education.

[23] *Aligarh Institute Gazette*, 12 January 1877. These points were again stressed by Sir Sayyid at the Educational Conference, 1891; see Muhammad Imamuddin, *Mukammal Majmua*, pp. 516, 534.

[24] *Tahzib-ul Akhlaq* 2, no. 4, 3rd series, 1 Muharram 1313 AH (June 1895, pp. 57–61). Earlier too, he had observed that even the Hindus were obtaining modern education mostly to gain public employment and the least for obtaining higher enlightenment; see *Hayat-e Javed*, p. 124.

actually be accommodated in public employment nor can a community make progress with education as the only means of public employment. Even people without a university degree obtain government jobs and are thus not motivated to study further; consequently, university degree holders do not get government jobs. Moreover, understandably, Sir Sayyid Ahmad was persuading traders to become stakeholders in the obtainment and promotion of modern education.

As a pragmatist, he chose a new forum, the AIMEC, to select the brains for the Muslim intelligentsia in order to extend the scope of technical and professional education, which he realized was beyond the scope and resources of the hub at Aligarh. Thus, the concern regarding the increase in the number of quacks and charlatans masquerading as *tabib*s (indigenous physicians) drew the attention of the community to establish formal institutions for imparting knowledge and skills in orthodox Greek medicine (*tibb-e unani*). Hence, in this sphere of general public interest, quality education could be imparted out of the confines of the families of eminent physicians, making standard medical education no longer a cloistered affair.[25] Sir Sayyid Ahmad possibly left modern, so-called allopathic, medicine out of the reckoning because its introduction to the community would have first involved removal of prejudices against a system of therapeutics, the pharmacopoeia of which then involved liberal alcohol use. With regard to technical education as well, while he did not put forward any institutional proposals in the forum of the AIMEC, his assertion was that theoretical education (*ususli ta'lim*) was pointless without practical learning (*a'mali ta'lim*). This drew considerable attention of the Muslim gentry towards education in engineering schools, such as the Thomason Engineering College at Roorkee.[26]

Lately, an impression that Sayyid Ahmad opposed female education has been created. While from a twenty-first century perspective, he could be faulted for not having realized that Muslim women had their own independent and autonomous faculty, yet he was not completely unconcerned about female education. In the 1891 session of the AIMEC, he clarified that no society could educate its women before its men had acquired education.[27] To him, 'no female education' was not an issue,

---

[25] Muhammad Imamuddin, *Mukammal Majmia*, pp. 502–3.
[26] Ibid., pp. 477–89.
[27] Ibid., pp. 494–96.

but only a priority. What is misconstrued as his hostility towards female education could have majorly been his wariness, considering the resistance he encountered when promoting Western education for Muslim men. Another aspect of this wariness was the complete impossibility of educated women taking up jobs in the then-prevalent circumstances.

Therefore, consistent with the spirit of wider pursuits advocated by the Scientific Society and within the severe constraints of innovative action available to him, Sir Sayyid Ahmad tried advancing multiple agendas of wider learning and modern thought. This aspect of Sir Sayyid has been dwarfed by his role as an institution-builder *par excellence* and by his views on the contemporary political scenario from the perspective of someone committed to promote and safeguard Indian Muslims' interests based on his perceptions in the last two decades of the nineteenth century.[28] His enterprise at Aligarh was an integral part, not the entirety of his educational mission – this is clarified by his 'co-curricular' efforts. The inference emerging from a bird's-eye view of his life's work on education is that all of his missions aimed at ushering in a brighter future with better quality of life for his *qaum* in that overall prosperous territory, which by then had become India. Perhaps his rational approach to matters of faith and belief was something that once was his 'first love', which he scuttled to achieve more imperative 'practical ends'.

SUMMING UP

At first, the strands of thoughts and vicissitudes underlying Sir Sayyid Ahmad's initiatives may paint a confused jumble of pictures. As outlined above, although (at times) his thoughts and actions seem to be at odds with each other, their context and purpose can now be explained contemporaneously and understood pragmatically.

In a coherent view, his vision or conception regarding education was utilitarian. Perhaps the pugnacious expostulations of Kempson led him to scuttle a model of institutions replicable using the Aligarh pattern; however, this is a moot point. (Note that in the next century, the passage of the Muslim University legislation was similarly delayed by at least a decade because its promoters insisted on an affiliating Muslim University, and because the

---

[28] Hafeez Malik, *Sir Syed Ahmad Khan and Muslim Modernization in India and Pakistan* (New York: Columbia University Press, 1980).

Government of India was not willing to concede anything beyond a unitary self-governing institution.[29]) The genius of Sir Sayyid Ahmad was that even while factoring in his pragmatic considerations (rather the realities of the age), he did not lose sight of his principles; this is sufficiently evident from his oft-repeated views on using the vernacular as the medium of instruction. His institutional frameworks, pedagogies, and methodologies all aimed to further his *qaum*'s overall well-being.

The ever-active mastermind was mindful of 'higher things' through education: he considered education as part of a 'package deal' – steering his *qaum* towards the new avenues that the British Raj had opened for India's 'sons of the soil' in the aftermath of 1857. For traversing the avenues of the admittedly restricted opportunities, specific skills and attitudes – shaped by several interventions where education, according to the demands of the state, was the most important component of a set (which also had ingredients such as loyalty, family circumstances and the right regional and social makeup) – were required.

Sir Sayyid Ahmad did his best to prepare his *qaum* in taking the most advantage of the package deal. For this, he was required to make constant adaptations and course corrections, dictated by not only the emerging state policies but also his own evolving understanding of the climes – which had radically altered since the time he, the author of *Asar-us Sanadid*, was copying inscriptions on towers and turrets using elevated scaffoldings and penning graphic accounts of the monuments and monumental personages of mid-nineteenth-century Delhi. His plain pragmatism was tempered with 'higher things', as evident from not only his personal scholarly pursuits but also the residential model of his institution; thus, he set a new trend rather than toeing the one followed even by the Presidency towns, which had few competitive advantages. Through the AIMEC, he planned to replicate the Aligarh paradigm of residential colleges for educating younger male Muslims elsewhere in the subcontinent (as well as Burma), which, in general, attests to his vision of education as a stepping stone.[30]

---

[29] Minault and Lelyveld, *Campaign for a Muslim University, 1898–1920*; Syed Yusuf Shah, *Higher Education and Politics in Colonial India: A Study of Aligarh Muslim University, 1875–1920* (Delhi: Renaissance, 1996).

[30] It would be an interesting and useful enterprise of research to find out why could not the AIMEC set up similarly enduring residential colleges in other parts of the subcontinent; why did the AIMEC eventually become more of a political body.

To the purists in pursuit of a standalone educational charter, this may come as a disappointment, but to enable his *qaum* take centre-stage in the public sphere of the late nineteenth-century India, supra-educational tasks requiring much wider interventions were quite efficiently handled by Sir Sayyid Ahmad. He contemplated that the future was not defined by or contingent on education alone and that there was much more to it in terms of the economic, social, and political well-being of his community, which was an important part of the newly defined nation-state of India. An ever-curious, ever-pragmatic mind, he was incessantly active towards attaining his ultimate goal and managed to strike a harmonious balance between what ought to be done and what could be done.

Figure 2 An alumni of Aligarh Muslim University (AMU) and recipient of the Bharat Ratna, Dr Zakir Husain, who later served as the Vice President (1962–7) and the President of India (1967–9), is seen on the AMU campus (note the Jama Majid of AMU in the background) with Dr Rajendra Prasad, the first President of India (1952–62). Courtesy of the Public Relations Office, AMU.

Figure 3 A photograph of some notable personalities at AMU, including the poet Fani Badauni and Maulana Hasrat Mohani. Courtesy of the Public Relations Office, AMU.

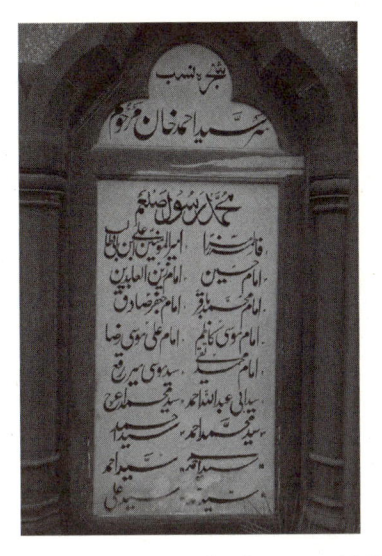

Figure 4 An image of a plaque on AMU campus depicting the family tree of Sayyid Ahmad Khan and showing his lineage to Prophet Muhammad and his daughter Fatima. Courtesy of the Public Relations Office, AMU.

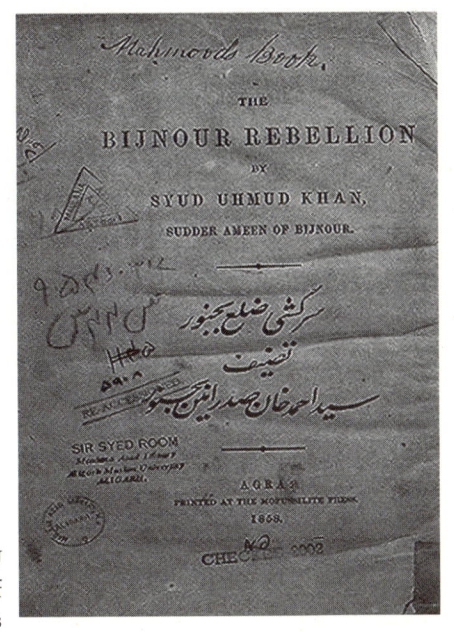

Figure 5 *Bijnor Rebellion* book cover. Courtesy of the Public Relations Office, AMU.

Figure 6 The last message of Sayyid Ahmad Khan, referenced on page 273 in the book. Courtesy of the Public Relations Office, AMU.

Figure 7 Sayyid Ahmad Khan, seated, with four Aligs. One of the rare photographs that show how seamlessly he incorporated Western suit into his persona, the way he adopted Western learning and ideas. Courtesy of the Public Relations Office, AMU.

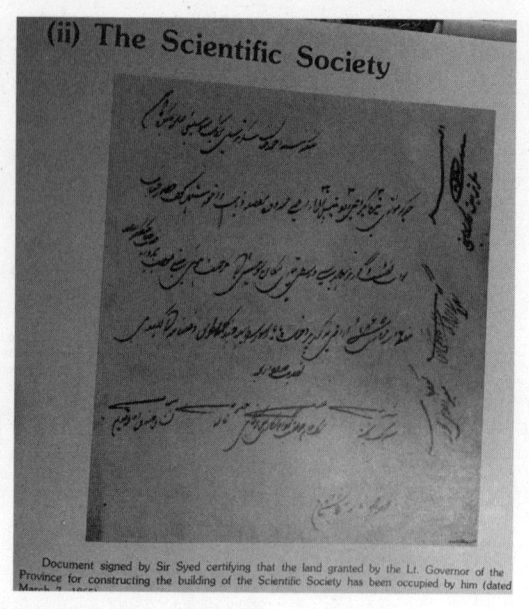

Figure 8 Document signed by Sayyid Ahmad Khan that shows his occupation of the land on which he established the Scientific Society. Courtesy of the Public Relations Office, AMU.

Figure 9 Indian and British staff of the MAO College in a group photograph. Courtesy of the Public Relations Office, AMU.

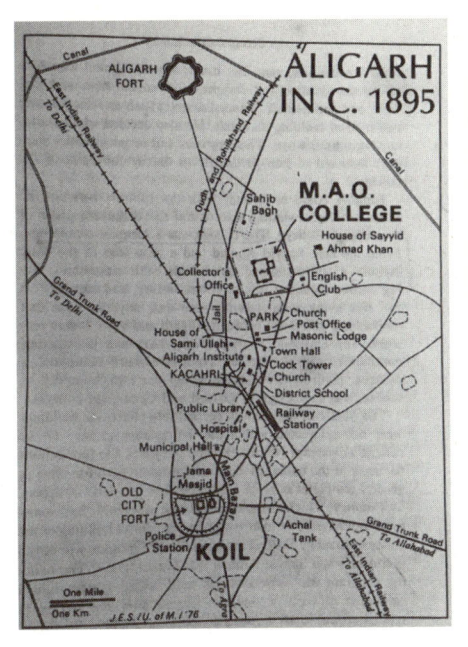

Figure 10 A map of MAO College, Aligarh, in 1895. Courtesy of the Public Relations Office, AMU.

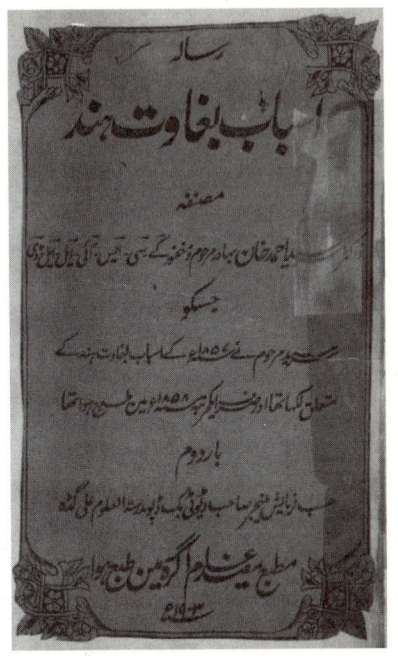

Figure 11 Book cover of *Asbab-e Baghawat-e Hind*. Published by Matba Mufid-e Aam, Aligarh, 1903. Courtesy of the Public Relations Office, AMU.

Figure 12 Dining room of Sir Sayyid Hall in AMU. Courtesy of the Public Relations Office, AMU.

Figure 13 European faculty of the MAO College, along with their wives. Photographed in 1898. Courtesy of the Public Relations Office, AMU.

Figure 14 MAO College football team, 1897–8. Courtesy of the Public Relations Office, AMU.

Figure 15 An early photograph providing an overview of MAO College. Courtesy of the Public Relations Office, AMU.

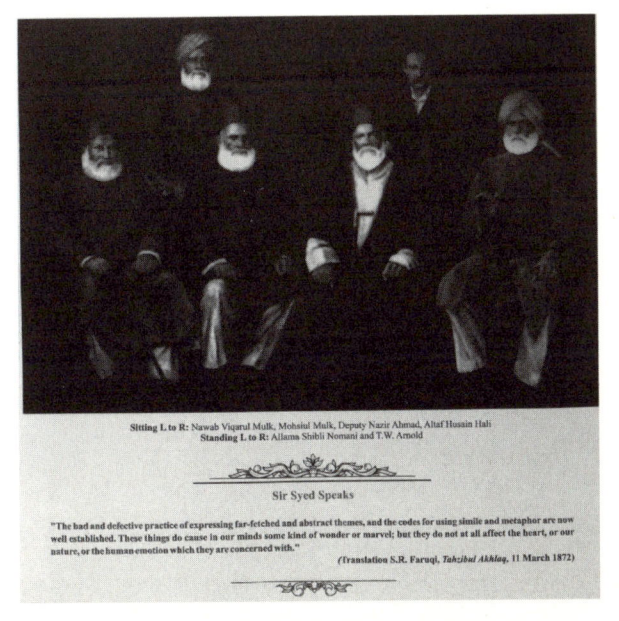

Figure 16 The photograph includes Viqar-ul Mulk, Mohsin-ul Mulk, Deputy Nazir Ahmad, Altaf Husain Hali, Shibli Numani, and T. W. Arnold. Courtesy of the Public Relations Office, AMU.

Figure 17 A facsimile image of *Tahzib-ul Akhlaq*, or *Muhammadan Social Reformer*. Courtesy of the Public Relations Office, AMU.

Figure 18 A group photograph of Sayyid Ahmad Khan with students and staff of MAO. Courtesy of the Public Relations Office, AMU.

Figure 19 Seal of the MAO College, Aligarh. Courtesy of the Public Relations Office, AMU.

Figure 20 Strachey Hall, one of the iconic buildings of MAO College, was the first building to come up on the campus. It was completed in 1885 and named after Sir John Strachey. Courtesy of the Public Relations Office, AMU.

Figure 21 Entrance to Sir Sayyid Hall (North). The entrance Bab-e Ishaque seen in this picture was the main entrance and was named after Nawab Mohammad Ishaq Khan, Secretary of Trustees. Courtesy of the Public Relations Office, AMU.

7 Religion, Science, and the Coherence of Prophetic and Natural Revelation

Sayyid Ahmad Khan's Religious Writings

CHARLES M. RAMSEY

Should religion and science be reconciled? As one of India's foremost public intellectuals of the nineteenth century, Sayyid Ahmad Khan inhabited the great transition, a hinge period in the shift from the Ptolemaic geocentric to the Copernican heliocentric view of the universe. Sayyid Ahmad Khan is highly regarded as the 'Father of Modern Islam' worldwide. His interests spanned across diverse fields of enquiry, and no study of this towering figure can be considered complete apart from a careful evaluation of his religious ideas.[1] However, this is not an easy task. Sayyid Ahmad was a complex thinker living in a complicated context during a period when significant political, social, and intellectual changes occurred. The primary concern of Sayyid Ahmad was to articulate religious knowledge in the light of advancements in science; he attempted this through *necharī* philosophy, which is addressed in detail elsewhere in this volume.

Although numerous insightful studies have been conducted on Sayyid Ahmad's religious writings in general and on his rationalist and naturalist conclusions in particular, the purpose behind this 'social revolutionary's' concern regarding the interrelation of prophetic and natural revelation remains unclear. This concern persisted throughout his extensive literary career. Sayyid Ahmad examined nearly every aspect of religious practice in the light of the Qur'ān and of plain reason. He argued that if the clutter of tradition is removed, then pristine religion would emerge to be consistent with the 'new sciences' and compatible with the highest orders of human intellect.[2] Pure (*thet*) Islam, which was understood and announced by prophets, was revealed through both prophetic and natural revelation. The prophetic revelation of pure Islam never contradicts its natural revelation.

---

[1] Christian W. Troll, *Sayyid Ahmad Khan: A Reinterpretation of Muslim Theology* (Delhi: Vikas Publishing House, 1978), p. 225.

[2] Ibid., p. 99.

Although prophetic messages provide instructions, the original *sharī'ah*, which is the nature's message, is no less recognized for being inarticulate. Then, the prophetic message must harmonize with the nature's message without contradiction. Thus, if a belief contradicted a basic common sense, then it was dismissed. If a scriptural passage contravened a simple reason, then that passage required a figurative rather than a literal interpretation.

Shamsur Rahman Faruqi, a novelist and historian, captured the complexity of this legacy by stating that 'Sayyid Ahmad Khan was a saviour, a sage, and a political-social leader of tremendous credibility. His theology didn't enter into the matter at all'.[3] In other words, although Sayyid Ahmad had troubling views on religion, he was a person of such consequence that he continues to be revered, often despite his beliefs. His conclusions were so profoundly unsettling that Altaf Husain Ḥālī, a biographer and his friend, recounted that 'the great sectarian divides finally had been drawn together in one common cause: too denounce Sayyid Ahmad as an unbeliever, a *kāfir* and *murtad*'.[4] Apparently, there was a boundary, and Sayyid Ahmad Khan had gone too far.

The troubled relationship between science and religion remains an issue of pressing concern. The pursuit to identify and examine hermeneutical tools that can demonstrate the integral coherence shared by natural and prophetic revelation (*waḥy*) was at the heart of Sayyid Ahmad's religious writings. Building on the existing academic literature and on my own study of Sayyid Ahmad's exegetical writings, primarily found in *Tabyīn al-kalām* and *Tafsīr al-Qur'ān*, we will attempt to understand how his 'theology' in actuality shared continuity with a leading Muslim intellectual lineage. By exploring these correlations, we can better understand why Sayyid Ahmad considered the reconciliation of reasons and revelation to be absolutely necessary for the flourishing of the Muslim community in the future. Although his scriptural commentaries, first of the Bible in *Tabyīn al-kalām* (c. 1860–65) and then of the Qur'ān (c. 1877–1904), provide a window into the mind of this vital figure at crucial junctures of his intellectual and spiritual

---

[3] Shamsur Rahman Faruqi, *From Antiquary to Social Revolutionary: Syed Ahmad Khan and the Colonial Experience* (Aligarh: Aligarh Muslim University, 2006), p. 3.

[4] Altaf Husain Hali, *Ḥayāt-e jāved* (An Immortal Life), 6th ed. (New Delhi: National Council for Promotion of Urdu Language, 2013), p. 547. All translations are mine unless otherwise stated.

journey, these commentaries are some of Sayyid Ahmad's least examined works.[5] Considering against the backdrop of his other principal writings, a question that arises is whether Sayyid Ahmad had a clear outlook of conceptualizing revelation. This is highly important in order to understand how Khan reconciled science and faith, or the word and work of God. Let us now consider how he attempted to bring together what others believed must be left apart.

SAYYID AHMAD KHAN AND HIS INTELLECTUAL ENVIRONMENT

To understand Sayyid Ahmad in the realm of intellectual context, it must be noted that significant reforms (*iṣlāh*) in Muslim theology were already underway prior to British hegemony. As rightly cautioned by Daniel Brown, overemphasis on the rupture caused by the onset of European control and influence must not overshadow the continuity shared between Indian thinkers and those from preceding generations.[6] Even those who have appreciated the elements of Sayyid Ahmad's theology have underscored European naturalism's influence on Sayyid Ahmad without adequately recognizing the continuity shared with earlier Muslim thinkers.[7] Sayyid Ahmad certainly was engaged and influenced by interactions with Europeans and by his journey to Britain in 1870; however, the agency of liminal thinkers in this context, thinkers considerably involved at the hinge of this period of significant technological changes, or the ability of thinkers to tackle issues brought forth in this tumultuous period should not be underestimated. Substantive reforms were already underway among Muslim

---

[5] Sayyid Ahmad Khan, *Tabyīn al-kalām fī tafsīr al-Tawrāt wal Injīl ʿalā millat al-Islām* (Aligarh: Sir Sayyid Academy, 2004). I have translated the title as 'Elucidation of the Word in Commentary of the Torah and Gospel According to the Religion of Islam'; however, its author simply referred to the text as 'The Mohamedan Commentary of the Holy Bible'. Instalments were printed and circulated and subsequently compiled and published between 1860 and 1865, although preparations began considerably earlier, possibly as early as 1847 (see *Āthār al-ṣanādīd*, repub. Aligarh: Aligarh Muslim University Press, 2007). *Tafsīr al-Qurʾān*, Parts I–VI (Aligarh: Institute Press, 1880–95), Part VII (Agra: Mufīd-i ām Press, 1904). Hereafter, these are referred to as TK and TQ.

[6] Daniel Brown, *Rethinking Tradition in Modern Islamic Thought* (Cambridge: Cambridge University Press, 1996), pp. 2–6.

[7] Tauqeer Zia, *Sir Sayyid kī dīnī shiūr* (Aligarh: Aligarh Muslim University, 2005), p 57; Fazlur Rahman, *Islam* (Chicago: University of Chicago Press, 1979), p. 30.

religious thinkers prior to colonial hegemony, which predate the seemingly revolutionary ideas of Sayyid Ahmad Khan.[8]

Crucial developments in the seventeenth and eighteenth centuries shaped the trajectory of Muslim religious thoughts in India. Shāh Walī Allāh (1703–1762) is the personality most associated with this period of reform. Being a prolific writer and a Sufi adept of the Nashbandī-Mujaddidī order, Walī Allāh and his companions embodied the blend of juristic and spiritualist ideals, characteristic of this era of the Persianate world.[9] As Jamal Malik convincingly argued, their characteristic 'philosophical scripturalism' brought a new dynamism to religious sciences.[10] Although centred in Delhi, this cluster of thinkers was a part of a diffused network of knowledge that traversed from India to Iran and Syria and over the seas to Hijaz and the Malay archipelago.[11]

During this period, Europe was excelling in mechanical sciences and the Persianate region was reaching a zenith in philosophical or 'natural' sciences (as it was known in English at that time). The writings of great philosophers, such as al-Fārābī, Ibn Sīnā, al-Ghazzālī, Ibn ʿArabī, al-Simnanī, and Mulla Ṣadrā, were actively read, discussed, and challenged across Central Asia. India had a close connection with Iran; therefore, finding leading theorists, such as Walī Allāh, and subsequently Sayyid Ahmad, presenting

---

[8] Rudolph Peters, 'Ijtihad and Taqlid in 18th and 19th Century Islam', *Die Welt des Islam* 10, nos 3–4 (1980): 131–45.

[9] The term 'Persianate' is a cognate of the term 'Islamicate' that signifies proclivities shared by cultural regions, allowing for the nuanced but crucial differentiation between an ideal, such as Islam, and its cultural manifestations. Marshall G. S. Hodgson, *The Venture of Islam, Volume 1: The Classical Age of Islam* (Chicago: University of Chicago Press, 1974). The term 'Persianate' reflects the commonalities of ethos and the worldview shared by various ethnolinguistic groups across the 'Balkans to Bengal complex'. For a robust exposition, see Shahab Ahmad, *What Is Islam? The Importance of Being Islamic* (Princeton: Princeton University Press, 2016).

[10] Jamal Malik, *Islam in South Asia: A Short History* (Leiden: Brill, 2008), pp. 170–1. Walī Allāh was a very senior figure, and almost all contemporary Sunni schools in South Asia, despite their considerable differences, proudly claim to be a part of his lineage. Riffat Hassan, 'Islamic Modernist and Reformist Discourse in South Asia', in *Reformist Voices of Islam: Mediating Islam and Modernity*, ed. Shireen T. Hunter, pp. 159–65 (New York: M.E. Sharpe, 2009), p. 182.

[11] Annemarie Schimmel, *Mystical Dimensions of Islam*, 2nd ed. (Chapel Hill: University of North Carolina Press, 2011), pp. 263–7.

an elaborate and compelling theory of the interrelation of the divinely revealed message and the recipient is not surprising. According to Walī Allāh, the 'primordial ideal' is manifested in a form suitable to the recipient community. The doctrinal application (*shar'īah*) was inherently flexible so that 'its form, beliefs, and spiritual practices can adapt to a nation's customs, previous faiths, and temperaments'.[12] Walī Allāh and the other aforementioned thinkers were Sayyid Ahmad's intellectual predecessors; they had a highly developed metaphysical understanding of the existential connection between history and revelation.[13]

THE CREATOR AND THE CREATION

The ideas of these reformers, as well as those of the chain of thinkers who preceded them, provided the syllabus for Sayyid Ahmad's religious study and the backdrop against which his originality can be assessed. It is essential to note that the vast majority of Muslims in India accepted Muḥyī al-Dīn Ibn 'Arabī's (d. 1240) doctrine of *tawḥīd/waḥdat* as axiomatic.[14] This was

---

[12] Walī Allāh al-Dihlawī, *The Conclusive Argument from God: Shāh Walī Allāh of Delhi's Ḥujjat Allāh Al-Bāligha*, trans. Marcia Hermansen (Leiden: E.J. Brill, 1995), p. 147.

[13] Jamal J. Elias, *The Throne Carrier of God: The Life and Thought of 'Ala' ad-dawla as-Simnani* (Albany: State University of New York Press, 1995), pp. 152–3; Mohammed Rustom, *The Triumph of Mercy: Philosophy and Scripture in Mullā Ṣadrā* (Albany: State University of New York Press, 2012), pp. 65–70; Al-Dihlawī, *The Conclusive Argument from God*, trans. Hermansen, pp. xxiii–xxxvi.

[14] Tahir Tanoli convincingly argued that 'the doctrine of 'unity of being' (*waḥdat al-wujūd* or *tawḥīd al-wujūd*) was often seen as obligatory for all Muslims'. Tahir Tanoli, 'A Forgotten Debate on *Wahdat ul-Wajud* in Contemporary Perspective', in *Mysticism in East and West: The Concept of the Unity of Being*, ed. Heike Stammer, pp. 202–17 (Lahore: Loyola Hall, 2013), pp. 202–4. Abdur Rehman Lucknavi in *Kalimāt al-ḥaqq* (d. 1829), for example, forcefully claimed that the acceptance of this doctrine was obligatory for all Muslims. This position was not seriously challenged, according to Tanoli, until 1897 when Sayyid Mehr 'Ali Shah (d. 1937) composed *Tehqīq ul-haq fī kalimāt al-ḥaqq*. See also the defence of the doctrine put forth by a founder of the Deoband movement, Ashraf 'Ali Thanvi, in *Khuṣūs al-kalim fī al-fuṣūs al-hikam* as recorded in Marcia Hermansen, 'Rewriting Sufi Identify in the 20th Century: The Biographical Approaches of Maulānā Ashraf 'Alī Thānvī and Khwaja Ḥasan Niẓāmī', Occasional Paper 79 (Islamabad: Islamic Research Insitute, 2007), p. 2. For a greater description of this intellectual context, see Bruce B. Lawrence,

the semantic framework used by generations of thinkers to discuss the paradoxical interrelation between the creator and the creation. For example, consider a portion of Sayyid Ahmad's translation of Ibn ʿArabī's seminal words in the introduction of *Tabyīn*:

> If there were not God, or had we not knowledge of God, then what exists would not be. So we are doubtlessly servants (*bande*) and doubtlessly God is our Master (*malik*). And we are indeed that same which our Master is. So when you take the name human (*insān*) then know its essence (*aslīyat*). When they call you human (*insān*) do not be ashamed, because it has been proven to you that you and your Master are one.[15]

The metaphysical quest to understand and experience how the creator is manifested in his creation progressed within the paradigm of *tawḥīd*. This assumed a complex cosmology and theory of emanation that had direct implications on how divine activity enters the human realm.[16] In an intellectual culture that assumed divine imminence and in which an absolute differentiation between the creator and creation was perceived to be a logical impossibility, there was a constant concern to safeguard divine transcendence.

These topics retained their importance in the times of Sayyid Ahmad Khan. For example, Shāh Ismāʿīl (d. 1830), who was a leading source of inspiration for Sayyid Aḥmad Barelvī's (d. 1831) Mujahidin Movement, which Sayyid Ahmad followed closely during this period, carried forward the colloquy and added at least two important points that Sayyid Ahmad subsequently affirmed.[17] First, he posited that the doctrine of *wahdat al-*

Notes from a Distant Flute: The Extant Literature of Pre-Mughal Indian Sufism (Boston: Shambhala Publications, 1979).

[15] *TK*, Part III, pp. 4–5.

[16] The central question was whether 'everything is from Him [God]' (*hama az ust*) or 'everything is Him' (*hama ust*). For a cogent exploration, see William C. Chittick, *In Search of the Lost Heart: Explorations in Islamic Thought*, ed. Mohammed Rustom, Atif Khalil, and Kazuyo Murata (Albany: State University of New York Press, 2012), pp. 71–8.

[17] In *Maktūb-i madanī* by Shāh Walī Allāh and *Takmīl al-Adhhān* by Shāh Rafīʿ al-Dīn (d. 1818), for example, it can be seen that underlying the juxtaposition of the metaphysics of *wahdat al-wujūd* (unity of being) and *wahdat al-shuhūd*

wujūd must be qualified by the assurance that God remains ultimately (`abdiyat*) apart from creation.[18] While attempting to safeguard both 'God's transcendence and the multiplicity of the cosmos' as explained by Faruque, Walī Allāh asserted that 'actual existence' (*wujūd*) belongs only to God and that contingent beings possess only 'borrowed existence'.[19] Sayyid Ahmad Khan took this a step further and indicated that all created matter, including all contingent beings, is both actual and everlasting. We will discuss its significance in the content reported below.

Certainly, the infusion of European questions and ideas stimulated discussions on the merits of rationalist and naturalist theology; however, this did not occur in a vacuum. Delhi was a dynamic intellectual environment, and the *`ulama-e wahdat al-wujūd* provided a conceptual framework that facilitated Sayyid Ahmad's robust intellectual engagement with European sources. This is not to say that Sayyid Ahmad's encounter with the 'new sciences' did not have a tremendous impact on his intellectual journey. He certainly underwent radical reversals (*rajuwāt*) along the way. For example, in 1847, he insisted that the sun orbits the earth, but then in 1848, in *Qaul-e matin dar ibtal-e harkat-e zamin* (Sound Argument in Refutation of the Theory of Revolution of the Earth), he vehemently denounced this previous position.[20] The outworking of these ideas, as recalled later by Sayyid Ahmad, brought about a sense of enlightenment that was nothing short of a conversion (*kabūl kiā*) or a wondrous discovery of the testimony found in the natural order (*hayawān*: more literally the 'animal kingdom') during the period between 1844 and 1849.[21] However, even in this period of dramatic

---

(unity of the apparent), there was an active search to synthesize philosophy and revelation.

[18] Al-Dihlawī, *The Conclusive Argument from God*, trans. Hermansen, p. 13.

[19] Muhammad U. Faruque, 'Sufism contra Shariah? Shāh Walī Allāh's Metaphysics of *Waḥdat al-Wujūd*', *Journal of Sufi Studies* 5 (2016): 27–57, 56.

[20] Suraya Hussein, *Sir Sayyid Ahmad Khan aur us ka `ahad* (Aligarh: Educational Book House, 1992), pp. 59–60.

[21] John W. Wilder, *Selected Essays by Sir Sayyid Ahmad Khan* (Lahore: Sang-e-Meel, 2006), p. 27. Founded in 1817, the School-Book Society supported many of the early experiments with the 'new sciences' in institutions such as Maulvi Aminullah's Calcutta Madrasa where Sayyid Ahmad's grandfather had taught mathematics. Sayyid Ahmad remained actively involved, and the project rendered thousands of pages into several Indian vernacular languages. During this time, Sayyid Ahmad worked extensively with John James Moore and the Agra School-Book Society to make 'thousands of pages' of scientific and agricultural material available in India's vernacular languages.

changes, Sayyid Ahmad consistently filtered ideas through Muslim sources. In this case, as the chosen terminology indicates, inspiration was apparently drawn from *Kitāb al-hayawān* by Abū ʿUthman al-Jāḥiẓ (d. 886). The driving force of al-Jāḥiẓ's text (in seven volumes) was to adduce God's existence through the study of nature.[22] Although not referenced by name (as was often observed in the literature from this time), there are several echoes to al-Jāḥiẓ's writings that can indicate a vital connection, not least of these is the title of Sayyid Ahmad's journal *Tahẕīb al-akhlāq* (The Muhammadan Social Reformer), which is identical to al-Jāḥiẓ's *Kitāb Tahẕīb al-akhlāq*. Furthermore, the title *Tabyīn al-kalām* may hold a degree of inspiration from Jāḥiẓ's *Bayān wa'l tabyīn*.[23] An awareness of al-Jāḥiẓ's works and the progression of scholars before and after him may have contributed to Sayyid Ahmad's unambiguous conviction that *Muslim scientific knowledge stimulated the European enlightenment and is thus rightfully shared in the intellectual legacy of the 'new sciences'*.[24]

Awareness of the intergenerational colloquy on the 'unity of being' provides a backstory to Sayyid Ahmad's rather controversial *necharī* philosophy.[25] He was convinced that all that can be known of the divine nature (*fitrah Allāh*) through prophetic revelation is mediated through

---

[22] Jamāl F. el-ʿAṭṭār, 'The Political Thought of Al-Jahiz with Special Reference to the Question of Khilafa (Imamate): A Chronological Approach', doctoral thesis (University of Edinburgh, 1996), p. 335. See also A. S. A. Haleem, *Chance or Creation? God's Design in the Universe* (Garnet, 1995), p. 22, and Charles Pellat, *The Life and Works of Jahiz: Translations of Selected Texts*, trans. D.M. Hawke (London: Routledge and Kegan Paul, 1969).

[23] There are many possible Muslim examples from where Sayyid Ahmad may have drawn inspiration, and that is precisely the larger point being made. Notable scholars, such as Sheila McDonough and Mushirul Hasan, have identified the writings of Abū ʿAlī ibn Miskawayh (d. 1030) to be of central importance for Sayyid Ahmad Khan, but Miskawayh (and Ibn ʿArabī who, similar to Miskawayh, authored a work titled *Tahẕīb al-akhlāq*) proceeded according to the chain of thinkers who seriously pondered the testimony of what could be observed in creation.

[24] Charles M. Ramsey, 'On Faith: Martin Luther and Sayyid Ahmad Khan' in *Reformation Jubilee of 2017: Luther! 95 Treasures – 95 People*, ed. Benjamin Hasselhorn, pp. 418–20 (Stiftung Luthergedenkstätten in Sachsen-Anhalt, 2017).

[25] *TQ*, Part I, p. 62. Sayyid Ahmad Khan used other labels, such as animal kingdom (*hayawān*) or the law of nature (*qānūn-e qudrat*), but *necharī* (a vernacular transliteration of 'nature') endured as his preferred term to describe this paradigm.

nature (*fitrah*). Earlier Muslim thinkers had considerably more continuance in this domain than that assumed in much of the contemporary academic literature. A more accurate view is that expressed long ago by Hafiz Malik, who was deeply conversant with the broader literature: 'In his [Sayyid Ahmad Khan's] efforts to harmonize the laws of nature with Islam, he acquired the sobriquet of *nechari* (transliterated as naturist, but also pejorative for atheist), but in his outlook he was no more of a naturist than the great *mujtahid* of India—*Shah Wali Allah*.'[26] If that is the case, then let us now consider how Sayyid Ahmad Khan conceptualized prophetic and natural revelation.

HOW DID SAYYID AHMAD CONCEPTUALIZE PROPHETIC REVELATION?

Sayyid Ahmad applied a convincing method to conceptualize prophetic revelation, either by describing the Qur'ān or any other sacred writing. It is important to underscore here the longstanding acceptance of 'polychromatic theism', such as that found in Hinduism and Sikhism, within the boundaries of Muslim thought in this context. As Muhammad Hamidullah explained, in Islam, there is an assumption of prophetically revealed texts that are not mentioned in the Bible or Qur'ān. 'In India, too, some religious scriptures are to be found. Among those holy books are the Vedas, the Puranas, the Upanishads, and others.'[27] Carl Ernst has drawn attention to the multiple facets of these relations and particularly to the means through which this conviviality was preserved. As Ernst explained, 'Qur'anic passages regarding Christians and Jews were at times applied analogously to indigenous faith expressions.' Although the reverence of idols remained a difficulty, the conception allowed for a more encompassing definition of 'unitarian belief' (*tawḥīd*) that could be extended to the universality of religious expression, including the 'Hindu'.[28] Simply stated, there was ample precedent to encompass a broad range of metaphysical positions within the fold of

---

[26] Hafeez Malik, *Sir Sayyid Ahmad Khan and Muslim Modernization in India and Pakistan* (New York: Columbia University Press, 1980), p. 267.

[27] Muhammad Hamidullah, *The Emergence of Islam*, trans. Afzal Iqbal (Islamabad: Islamic Research Institute, 1993), p. 19.

[28] Richard C. Martin and Abbas Barzegar, 'Formations of Orthodoxy: Authority, Power, and Networks in Muslim Societies,' in *Rethinking Islamic Studies: From Orientalism to Cosmopolitanism*, ed. Carl Ernst and Richard C. Martin, pp. 179–202 (Columbia: The University of South Carolina Press, 2010), pp. 186–8.

monotheistic belief. As Shahzad Qaiser summarized, 'Tawḥīd is not a numerical quantity but rather a qualitative symbol of wholeness.' It is the uncreated 'Supreme Unity' manifested in the many.[29]

This allowed for a more encompassing definition of 'unitarian belief' (tawḥīd) that could be extended to the universality of religious expression. It was understood within this intellectual tradition that there is an inherent flexibility in the principles of doctrine (shar'īah) necessary to accommodate the considerable variety of human communities throughout history. Some principles can be applied only in a particular context, and some universal principles can be continuously and recurrently, as Sayyid Ahmad explained, once instituted by 'any prophet, or *avatar*' applied throughout history.[30] But once instituted, shar'īah remains enduringly effective for its respective community of adherents.[31] This is the cornerstone of Sayyid Ahmad's attitude towards prophetic revelation, and it offers a crucial stepping stone to assess his pluralistic view of other faiths.[32]

Sayyid Ahmad applied a specific taxonomy from the science of tradition (`ilm-e ḥadīth) to discuss prophetic revelation (kalām ilāhī) as *matlū* or *ghayr matlū*.[33] Unlike other mechanisms that describe the interrelation between the Qur'ān and Ḥadīth, namely *riwāyat bil lafẓ* and *riwāyat bil mā'anī*, which Sayyid Ahmad used in the earliest portions of *Tabyīn* but not subsequently, this taxonomy was specifically applied to convey the organic equivalence shared by the Qur'ān and Sunnah despite their difference in form. As explained by Abdullah Saeed, the taxonomy recognized the Qur'ān

---

[29] Shahzad Qaiser, *The Metaphysical and Cultural Perspectives of Khawaja Ghulam Farid* (Lahore: Iqbal Academy, 2012), p. 102.

[30] 'Qadīm aur jadīd `alūm', *Tahzīb al-akhlāq* 1 (1879): 63–91, 41–2.

[31] TK, Part II, p. 268. Sayyid Ahmad Khan, *Aḥkām-e ṭa'ām ahl-e kitā*, 1868 (Aligarh: Aligarh University Press, 2011), p. 11.

[32] For a more extensive exploration of this, see Charles M. Ramsey, 'Sir Syed's Religious Foundations for a Pluralist Society', in *Sir Syed Ahmad Khan: Muslim Renaissance Man of India – A Bicentenary Commemorative Volume*, ed. A. R. Kidwai, pp. 288–307 (New Delhi: Viva Books, 2017).

[33] The terms are derived from the works of the eminent jurist Idrīs al-Shafi'ī (d. 820), and these continue in mainstream use today. For a contemporary usage on an international level, see Nāsir al-Dīn al-Albanī (d. 1999); in the South Asian context, see Muḥammad Isma'īl Salafī, *Hujjait-e Ḥadith* (Lahore: Islamic Publishing House, 1981). As Kīlānī explained, the *riwāyat bil lafẓ* and *riwāyat bil mā'anī* construct assumes an inherent difference of authority. Abdurraḥman Kīlānī, *Difā`i Ḥadīth* (Lahore: Dar al-Andalus, 1999), p. 38.

and Sunnah to have equal religioethical authority.[34] Sayyid Ahmad provided greater details by subdividing the category of *matlū* into two additional forms: words (*alfāz*) and subject (*maḍmūn*). In the first subcategory, the recipient rehearsed the 'pure words' spoken by God in revelation. In the second subcategory, the recipient rehearsed the 'pure subject' spoken by God in revelation.[35] However, *Ghayr matlū* revelation was recounted through intermediaries who served as inspired 'sacred historians' (*muqaddas mu'arrikh*).[36]

In summary, Sayyid Ahmad held that prophetic revelation recorded in scriptures has complex histories and these differ in form and content; however, the messages are coherent because they proceed from the same divine source. Sayyid Ahmad's originality can be seen in his application of these existing categories to scriptures other than the Qur'ān.[37] He specified that Muslims must not consider *matlū* revelation to be of greater worth than *ghayr matlū* because these are both of divine origin and 'in matters of religion, both are equal (*dīn kā mu'amlah main, donon barābar hain*)'. In addition, he clarified that in no uncertain terms, 'God protect us [from Satan] (*Na'udhbillāh*)! The revelation of the earlier (*sābiqīn*) prophets is no less

---

[34] Abdullah Saeed, 'Rethinking 'Revelation' as a Precondition for Reinterpretation of the Qur'ān? A Qur'ānic Perspective,' *Journal of Qur'ānic Studies* 1, no. 1 (1999): 93–114. Abdullah Saeed, *Interpreting the Qur'an: Towards a Contemporary Approach* (London: Routledge, 2006), pp. 31–3. Esack, *The Qur'ān*, pp. 111–13. *TK*, Part I, p. 24; Part III, p. 52. See Kīlānī, *Difā'i Ḥadīth*, 38.

[35] *TK*, Part II, p. 349.

[36] The correlation among these is one of the substance (*jawhar*). According to Imām Rāghab Isfāhanī's definition, that which is *mukhtālifūn* is always *ghayr*, but that which is *ghayr* is not always *mukhtālifūn*. Both *matlū* and *ghayr matlū* are *waḥy* and therefore share the same substance. Sunnah is of the same substance (*jawhar*) as Qur'ān because *ghayr* refers to 'another' type of revelation, rather than what is 'other' than revelation.

[37] In this paradigm, the Bible contains a blend of *matlū* and *ghayr matlū* revelation. *Matlū* revelation, whether of word or subject, is classified as *matn*, or text, which is the 'backbone' of content. On the other hand, *Ghayr matlū* revelation also contained contextualizing narrative (*riwāyat*). The Qur'ān is solely *matlū* and is therefore completely *matn*, which can make precise interpretation difficult. However, Sunnah is predominantly derived from *ghayr matlū* sources, which contain a blend of text and contextualizing narrative. Regardless of differences in form and in the function of these texts in religious practice, both *matlū* and *ghayr matlū* are of the same substance (*jawhar*).

than that which was granted to the Prophet Muḥammad.'[38] Sayyid Ahmad, without a doubt, affirmed the finality of the Qur'ān as the culmination of scriptural prophecy; however, he also noted that the Qur'ān assumed its recipient audience to be familiar with other revelation as well. In the first pages of the Genesis commentary, Sayyid Ahmed wrote,

> Without this history, the world would be in darkness, not knowing where it came from or to where it is going. In the first page of this book, a child may learn more in an hour, than all the philosophers in the world learned without it in a thousand years.[39]

Sayyid Ahmad's attitude towards prophetic revelation reflects a pluralistic view of other religious traditions. Having introduced the concept that he applied to conceptualize revelation, we now consider why Sayyid Ahmad embarked on the ambitious enterprise to understand how God's word (kalām ilāhi)—spoken and otherwise—became expressed in the human realm.

WHAT PROMPTED SAYYID AHMAD'S PERSISTENCE IN RELIGIOUS WRITING?

All the religious writings of Sayyid Ahmad were a part of a journey of hermeneutical exploration to understand the universal genius of the Qur'ān. He recognized the need for principles to delineate the 'soundness and unsoundness' of scriptural interpretation. As explained in his letter to Mohsin-ul Mulk, quoted in *Taḥrīr* (1892), such principles, once identified, would constrain discussion and propel interpreters towards a reasonable outcome. 'But as long as the principles are not agreed upon in the manner I have described, objections and writings and questions and answers seem simply futile, and this is waste of precious time.'[40] Sayyid Ahmad was on a mission to unlock the eternal truth contained with the earthen vessels of natural revelation.

It is vital to underscore that Sayyid Ahmad ascribed to the coherence of all revelation, natural and prophetic. He affirmed that creation occurred

---

[38] *TK*, Part I, p. 24.
[39] Ibid., Part II, p. 30.
[40] Daud Rahbar, 'Sir Sayyid Aḥmad Khān's Principles of Exegesis Translated from His *Taḥrīr fī ʿusūl al-tafsīr*', *Muslim World* 46, nos 2 and 4 (1956): 104–12 and 324–35, 335.

by the divine fiat, 'be, and it is' (*kun fāyakūn*), as stated in the Qur'ān. In addition, he asserted, 'God created all at one time.'[41] Taken out of context and read apart from the remaining exposition, these statements would appear to espouse a view of *ex nihilo* creation or signify that Sayyid Ahmad accepted a literal reading of pertinent passages. However, a close reading of Sayyid Ahmad's exposition indicates a considerably different conclusion and discloses an underpinning worldview.

As explained by Sayyid Ahmad, the Divine Will (*irādah*) once spoken – 'be' – will surely be accomplished.[42] However, the timing and progression proceeded through inherent processes (*nechar ke qā'idē ke mutābiq*).[43] Once the law of nature is instated, then the Divine Will proceeds in conformity with this law through cause and effect. All revelation must conform to the boundaries of the created cosmos because it originated from the one word (singular) spoken by the singular divine source that is continually expressed in the processes of creation.

From at least the 1860s, Sayyid Ahmad read the Bible and Qur'ān to affirm the evolutionary process of creation. This shaped Sayyid Ahmad's reading of Genesis 1, for example that recounts the creation of the universe. From among the 'six days of creation', he differentiated those that occurred before and after the 'law of nature' was instituted. Pronouncements prior to the institution were not bound to the common measurements of time. 'Evening and morning' did not refer to a twenty-four-hour period but rather to prolonged phases of development: the 'full courses of darkness and light' necessary for a particular development. It was not until the 'fourth day' when the sun and moon were formed that the present workings took effect. As he understood from Surah al-Furqan (Q 25:2), 'It is He who has control over the heavens and the earth and has no offspring – no one shares control with Him – and who created all things and made them to an exact measure.'[44] However, once this was set in motion, then no further intervention was required and the continual processes of cause and effect proceeded unhindered by supranatural forces.[45]

---

[41] *TK*, Part II, p. 46.
[42] Ibid., p. 114.
[43] Ibid., p. 74. References from the Qur'ān were listed (Q10: 5, 2:189, 6:96–97, and 49:16,18) but no authorial comment was provided by Sayyid Ahmad Khan.
[44] A.S. Abdel Haleem, *The Qur'ān: A New Translation* (Oxford: Oxford University Press, 2004), p. 227.
[45] *TK*, Part II, p. 39.

Commenced by the divine fiat, creation was accomplished gradually in phases through secondary causation. 'Development was affected in a moment; yet, it was necessary that this occur in a manner that advances by degrees.'[46] The Divine Will was expressed through infinitely repeated typological patterns. Once created, 'it pleased the all-independent God to leave to it the future continuation and regularity of his works'.[47] All that was 'needed to be done was done, and nothing remained to be done – all was set in motion'.[48] As summarized by Sayyid Ahmad Khan, 'The divine Essence is the Cause of causes (`ilet al-`ilal) of all things.'[49]

Although no reference was provided, Sayyid Ahmad clearly presented the shorthand of Mullā Ṣadrā's (Ṣadr al-Dīn al-Shirāzī, d. 1640) unique doctrine of 'motion-in-substance (ḥaraka jawhariya)'.[50] By synthesizing the elements of Ibn `Arabī's theosophy, Ibn Sīnā's peripatetic tradition, and al-Suhrawardī's illumination (ishrāqī), Ṣadrā's metaphysics constituted what some have regarded as the pinnacle of Persianate philosophy. Ṣadrā posited that the divine essence is manifested in the created realm as 'Self-unfolding Existence (tashkīk)'.[51] According to Sayyid Ahmad, similar to Ṣadrā before him, all created matter is contingent. The 'Self-unfolding' proceeds through cause and effect, which is the foundational 'law of nature', and progresses without the possibility of being altered by divine intervention, because this is God's first law – never to be abrogated for it is reasonable to assume that God abides by God's own laws.

Sayyid Ahmad understood creation as an ordered and coherent system where the cosmos is endowed with divinely imposed limits. This understanding conforms with his interpretation of scriptures. For example, in the commentary of Genesis 1, Sayyid Ahmad explained that creation was begotten (paidā) through a singular substance (jawhar). The substance progressively divided into increasingly complex variants so that a person eventually can be differentiable from a tree.[52] However, the interrelation

---

[46] TK, p. 52.
[47] Ibid., p. 68.
[48] Ibid., p. 68.
[49] Christian Troll, 'Sir Sayyid Ahmad Khan, 1817–98, and His Theological Critics: The Accusations of `Ali Baksh Khan and Sir Sayyid's Rejoinder', *Islamic Culture* 51 (1978): 1–18, 2.
[50] Fazlur Rahman, *The Philosophy of Mullā Ṣadrā* (Albany: State University of New York Press, 1975), pp. 12–16.
[51] Rahman, *The Philosophy*, pp. 12–13.
[52] TK, Part II, p. 55.

of a human with a tree differs from that of a human with God. In this light, it can be seen that the quote from Ibn ʿArabī in *Tabyīn*, Part III, 'you and your Master are one', was not intended to be read literally or express a monistic view. The composite picture of creation is that of a unified whole, differentiated but coherent, because it is made of one substance that proceeds from one source. Sayyid Ahmad attempted to express the idea that there is an intrinsic relation between God and persons because the creator generated or 'begot' creation.[53]

One can find it helpful to explicate Sayyid Ahmad's view of natural revelation through an analogy. Muhammad Iqbal, a poet-philosopher, once described prophetic mediation (*shafāʿa*) as the seed for bearing the fruit of inductive intellect.[54] I borrow this analogy to elucidate Sayyid Ahmad's description of the process of creation. Consider a seed. Given the right growth conditions, the seed sprouts and the differentiated internal components follow a set growth order, producing the root, stem, and leaf. The intricacy of this simple seed is in a word: miraculous. It grows, produces, and the cycle is repeated infinitely according to the variables of the ecosphere. God's 'work' demonstrates predictable patterns. Likewise, God's 'word' is also composed within an ecosphere and must similarly conform to the variables of time and place. On occasion, it yields 'divine words' derived through dialogue with the prophetic conscious. It also yields inspired ideas or 'divine subjects' transposed through carefully selected words. Original (first) principles can be identified within these prophetic recordings. Such principles are universally applicable and comprise true (*thet*) religion. Created (secondary) principles can also be derived from these recordings. These are useful to establish religious legislation (*sharīʿah*), which is necessary for the promotion of human felicity (to use Chittick's term).[55]

According to Sayyid Ahmad's view, prophecy is a form of revelation; thus, it also conforms to the natural processes established in creation. Prophecy proceeds through human faculties, is intended for guidance, and

---

[53] The most direct translation of the term *paidā* is birthed but can also be rendered as generated, begot, or came forth from. This term is used in the earlierst Urdu translations, and it is linguistically consistent with the pre-existing Persian version translated by Walī Allāh, Shāh ʿAbd al-Azīz, and Shāh Rafīʿ al-Dīn. In Arabic, God made (*khalq*) rather than 'begot' the heavens and the earth.

[54] J. M. S. Baljon, *Modern Muslim Koran Interpretation (1880–1960)* (Leiden: Brill, 1968), pp. 65–6.

[55] Chittick, *In Search of the Lost Heart*, p. 163.

is reconcilable with reason. Hence, prophetic and natural testimonies can be juxtaposed because these proceed from the same source and are constrained by the same forces. Taken together, these records of revelation elucidate the word that has reverberated from the beginning of history. However, it should be recognized that Sayyid Ahmad did not describe the cosmos as devoid of divine activity but rather as permeated with divine attributes and the outworking of the Divine Will commenced at creation.

The originality of Sayyid Ahmad can be observed in the manner in which he delineated essence (*dhāt*) as the impermeable boundary between the creator and creation. He assigned eternality and utter transcendence to the divine essence but ascribed everlasting immanence to divine attributes (*ṣifat*) present in creation. If attributes remain separated from the essence, then the purity (*ikhlās*) of God's transcendence is logically sustained.[56] The distinction allowed divine attributes to be coexistent and operative in nature without collapsing the distinction between the divine essence and the created substance.

In summary, according to Sayyid Ahmad, all that can be known, experienced, or imagined of the divine occurs within nature. This is the reasoning, as he explained in *Tafsīr*, why Shaykh Sirhindī stated that Allah would not actually be seen on Judgement Day. The divine essence exists considerably apart from the dimensions of time and space.[57] That which is described as visible in the Qur'ān is in actuality an imagined emanation. Sayyid Ahmad applied this similar reasoning to conceptualize how the prophet received or rather became cognizant of revelation. As explained by Sayyid Ahmad, the prophet Muḥammad's encounters with the angel Gabriel (*Jibrīl*) were in actuality projections of the imagination. In his conception, the prophetic *habitus* (*malakah-e nubūwat*) was not engendered supranaturally but rather occurred through recurrent natural selection. 'There is a divine deposit in nature (*wadī`at-e fitrat*), a natural inspiration (*ilhāmāt-i ṭab`i*) in every being.'[58] The development of the *habitus*, as explained by Sayyid Ahmad, was exceedingly rare and no longer necessary because all possible prophetic revelation has already

---

[56] Nagendra Kr. Singh and N. Hanif, *God in Indian Islamic Theology* (New Delhi: Sarup and Sons, 1996), pp. 186–90.

[57] Abdollah Vakily, 'Some Notes on Shaykh Ahmad Sirhindi and the Problem of the Mysical Significance of Paradise,' in *Reason and Inspiration in Islam: Theology, Philosophy and Mysticism in Muslim Thought*, ed. Todd Lawson, pp. 407–17 (London: I.B. Tauris, 2005).

[58] Troll, *Sayyid Ahmad Khan*, p. 184.

been granted. However, as seeds have different qualities, different seasons, settings, and conditions are required for germination and fruition. Similarly, a prophet's exceptionality is due to the confluence of natural phenomena. The prophetically endowed developed the capacity under right conditions. They could tap into coded revelation embedded at the beginning of time, which has remained present in the substance (jawhar) of creation. In this manner, one can see how Sayyid Ahmad's assumption of the natural coherence of all substances and the interconnectivity of all creations predisposed the view that prophetic and natural revelation have always worked symbiotically in human history.

As readily can be seen in the present collection of essays, Sayyid Ahmad has contributed significantly to the intellectual history of South Asia. One way to observe this is to note his influence upon the works of subsequent writers. Sayyid Ahmad's religious ideas have been juxtaposed with many of his contemporaries such as Chiragh Ali, Shibli Numani, and Muḥammad Iqbal, to name but a few.[59] However, a gap in the literature can be noted concerning his interrelation with another highly significant thinker in this context, Fazlur Rahman.[60] Although space constraints preclude a substantial exploration, crucial similarities are shared between these on the subject of revelation that are pertinent to our study. In addition, establishing correlations such as these further underscores the continued relevance of studying Sayyid Ahmad Khan.

Considering the context, it is not surprising that Rahman drew from the same basic discourse chain as did Sayyid Ahmad. In other words, they share a continuity of sources, including ibn ʿArabī, al-Fārābī, ibn Sīnā, al-Ghazzālī, Ibn ʿArabī, al-Simnanī, Sirhindī, Mulla Ṣadrā, and Shāh Walī Allāh. Because they were both modernists, a predictable overlap can be observed in many areas; however, a particular similarity can be noted in their view of revelation. Rahman and Sayyid Ahmad applied a similar paradigm to consider revelation in the Qur'ān. Both disliked the 'mechanical or external' description employed traditionally and were in search of a more satisfactory account of the complex process through which revelation proceeds from the 'heart of the Prophet'.[61] Each attempted to find a better way to understand how verbatim revelation – actual words – could originate from God and yet

---

[59] Baljon, *Modern Muslim Koran Interpretation (1880–1960)*, pp. 66–9.
[60] Christian W. Troll, 'Reason and Revelation in the Theology of Mawlana Shibli Nuʿmani', *Islam and the Modern Age* 14 (1982): 19–22.
[61] Rahman, *Islam*, pp. 148–64, 190–204.

be articulated within a particular phase of history in accordance with the language and custom of the time.[62]

Sayyid Ahmad's appeal to Sirhindī, as noted above, offers a key identifying the correlation with Rahman. Fazlur Rahman's study of Ibn Sīnā established a connection between the Prophet's experience of revelation and emanationist psychology. Rahman subsequently traced the development of this line of thinking through works of Mullah Sadra and of Shaykh Ahmad Sirhindī. The result is strikingly similar. According to Sayyid Ahmad, the words recited as Qur'ān came about because 'the [Prophet's] conscience becomes like a mirror outside of the self, and by which God's message comes forth from what is already naturally implanted within'.[63] As Rahman convincingly argued, Ibn Sīnā's medical examinations led to an original conclusion: the imagination is a 'physical faculty'.[64] Trances and dreams (waham) were activities of the mind, rather than departures into another dimension. This was precisely the point intended through Sayyid Ahmad's reference to Sirhindī in Tafsīr, namely that spiritual images are the projections of imagination.

In other words, as Iqbal explained in Reconstruction of Islamic Thought in Islam, the source and origin of revelation lies beyond the reach of human agency, but this is not an 'agency working on things from without'.[65] Rather, the process occurs as an integral part of the agent's (the Prophet's) mind. As explained by Rahman, Iqbal adopted a 'psychological' approach to explain that the 'feeling, the idea, and the word are an organic entity and are born in the mind of the Prophet at once'.[66] This was made possible by

---

[62] Tamara Sonn, 'Fazlur Rahman's Islamic Methodology', The Muslim World 81 (1991): 212–30. Frederick Denny, 'Fazlur Rahman: Muslim Intellectual', The Muslim World 79 (1989): 91–101.

[63] TQ, Part III, pp. 204–8. Reference is given to Sirhindi, Letters III, p. 90. Also found in Bashir Ahmad Dar, Religious Thought of Sayyid Ahmad Khan (Lahore: Institute for Islamic Culture, 1957), pp. 136–8. Aḥmad Sirhindī, Intikhāb-e maktūbāt-e Shaykh Aḥmad Sirhindī, ed. Fazlur Rahman (Karachi: Iqbāl Akādamī, 1968), p. 44.

[64] Lenn E. Goodman, Avicenna (Ithaca: Cornell University Press, 2006), p. 176.

[65] Muhammad Iqbal, The Reconstrution of Islamic Thought (Oxford: Oxford University Press, 1934), p. 29.

[66] Rahman, Islam, pp. 30–1. Annemarie Schimmel, Gabriel's Wing: A Study into the Religious Ideas of Sir Muhammad Iqbal (Leiden: E.J. Brill, 1963), p. 95. 'Iqbal goes back behind the rationalistic commentaries and the mystical speculations to the original Qur'ānic teachings and describes God first and last as Ego: His name Allah, as He calls Himself in the Qur'ān, manifests His personalistc character, and the 112th Surah, the short confession of God's unity

the assumption of contingency: the idea that the substance of all that exists is in constant motion and development and mutually linked. This is the view Sayyid Ahmad expressed long before Rahman or Iqbal, and he did so in the light of the same august thinkers.[67] Ibn Sīnā's view of the imagination stimulated questions concerning the contingency of all matter, and by necessity of the Qur'ān.

Returning to the sources of Sayyid Ahmad's position, it is crucial to note that Sirhindī applied Ibn Sīnā's psychological insights to interpret the Qur'ān. The example provided by Sayyid Ahmad evaluated the possibility of actually seeing God on the Day of Judgement. As recounted by Sayyid Ahmad, Sirhindī concluded that the meaning of Surah al-Qiyama (Q75:23) was not that the faithful will look upon their Lord in physical actuality, but rather they will gaze upon an imagined manifestation of the Lord.[68] Sayyid Ahmad applied this same rationale to account for the Prophet's seeing a figure or spirit on the occasions of revelation. In his understanding, similar to many of the great rationalists who came before, revelation was received through the physical faculty of imagination. The 'angel' was the vehicle of the imagination and a mirror of consciousness. The advent of the Qur'ān is miraculous, but it is not supranatural. Its reception did not necessitate the crossing over between realms because all the relevant content and processes were already present within the substance of nature. The experiences of revelation were real and historical, but these occurred as projections of the Prophet's imagination.

This doctrine was regarded as beyond the intellectual capacities of all but an intellectual elite. It was the view of philosophers, that for most people, the 'letter of the revelation and the materialistic symbols must remain the literal truth'.[69] Sayyid Ahmad had brought this rather concealed view, one held by the leading Sufi-Philosophers, and presented it to a general audience in the vernacular. As disconcerting as this was for many of his readers, it is vital to grasp that Sayyid Ahmad's assessment was drawn from established

---

which is of paramount inportance in Islamic thought, theology and spiritual life, is again a proof of God's being an Ego.'

[67] Rahman *Islam*, p. 237; Oliver Leaman, *The Qur'ān: A Philosophical Guide* (London: Bloomsbury, 2016), p. 266; Zailan Morris, *Revelation, Intellectual Intuition and Reason in the Philosophy of Mulla Sadra: An Analysis of the al-Hikmah al-`Arshiyya* (Abingdon: Routledge, 2003), p. 237.

[68] *TQ*, Part III, pp. 204–8.

[69] Fazlur Rahman, *Prophecy in Islam: Philosophy and Orthodoxy* (Chicago: University of Chicago Press, 2011), p. 42.

sources within this intellectual tradition whose authority was highly esteemed in this milieu. His account of the process of revelation in *Tafsīr* draws our attention to a continuance that he shared with these leading sages of Delhi's Mujaddidī, who were the stalwart elders of today's 'orthodoxy' in South Asia and their global diaspora. Sayyid Ahmad proceeded in a channel cut by these earlier Muslim thinkers, a pathway trodden by others before him, including Sirhindī and Shāh Walī Allāh, and more recently by great scholars such as Muhammad Iqbal and Fazlur Rahman. These areas of similarity between Sayyid Ahmad and Rahman require further study; however, the correlation of their views of revelation again emphasizes the continuity of Sayyid Ahmad's ideas and his sources within the history of Muslim thought.

CONCLUSION

For Sayyid Ahmad, evidence from the 'new sciences' confirmed a pre-existing philosophical paradigm. In his understanding, the European theists and 'Broad Churchmen', whose writings were causing extensive division and even loss of faith, were not breaking new ground but rather coming to terms with ideas that had begun to take shape already in the earlier writings of some Muslim thinkers, though seldom conveyed to the masses. This view of revelation also appears to elucidate the pluralist esteem Sayyid Ahmad expressed for other faiths. If the Qur'ān is not a transcendent intrusion, but rather it came into being within the cosmos – no matter how – then it is easier to see how this revelation is not so different from the Ḥadīth, which came from Muḥammad himself, and from the books of the Bible, which came from a series of authors, or the Vedas, Puranas, or the Guru Granth Sahib. Thus, Sayyid Ahmad does not have as much difficulty in placing the various books, and their respective communities, at the same level as this might at first appear.

According to Sayyid Ahmad, it was untenable for religious thinkers to proceed with unreflected insistence upon earlier positions and expect beneficial progress. In light of our present circumstances, it is wise to enquire 'What route will we travel, what path will we take— that of Cartesian rationalism in search of certitude, of that of humanist not-knowing in search of wisdom?'[70] Through faith, Sayyid Ahmad predicted that in time,

---

[70] Marianne Moyaert, *In Response to the Religious Other: Ricoeur and the Fragility of Interreligious Encounters* (London: Lexington Books, 2014), p. 16.

all would be made clear, but until then, he continues to challenge us to lay hold of the universal principles embedded in scriptures, and through science, he demonstrated that these scriptures contain the resources required for the journey towards the furthest boundaries (*ghāyat hadd*) of human flourishing.[71]

---

[71] *TK*, Part III, p. 110.

8 Defending the 'Community'
Sir Sayyid's Concept of Qaum
FRANCES W. PRITCHETT

Sir Sayyid's long and adventurous life contained two or three ordinary lifetimes full of activity. In the larger societal arena, his beloved Muhammadan Anglo-Oriental College (1878) at Aligarh was his supreme achievement, but in other domains, he consistently saw himself, and was seen, as a mediator between the British and 'native' ideas and interests. Not surprisingly, his literary output was voluminous – he has left us records of his antiquarian interests (*Āsār-ul ṣanādīd*, 1854 [1847]), his religious views (a commentary on the Qur'an), and his journalistic commitments (*Tahżīb-ul aḵẖlāq*), along with numerous letters, essays, reviews, and speeches on a wide variety of topics.

Undoubtedly, the greatest watershed in his life was the Indian Rebellion of 1857. As an East India Company administrator posted in Bijnor, he was emphatically true to his salt, risking his life repeatedly in defense of British lives and interests. Then, in 1858, almost before the rebellion was over, he recorded his personal experiences and local impressions in 'History of the Bijnor Rebellion'. However, the Bijnor account – as fascinating as it is – has always been obscured by his greater achievement during this intensely turbulent year: his famous work, really a sort of long pamphlet, called 'The Causes of the Indian Revolt' (*Asbāb-e baġhāvat-e Hind*).

In writing a work with such a title, at so fraught a time, Sir Sayyid knew that he was courting trouble. Still, he was determined. Once Sir Sayyid had gotten 500 copies of his Urdu pamphlet printed, the result was a dramatic scene:

> When Sir Sayyid resolved to send them to Parliament and the Government of India, his friends forbade him. And Master Ramchandra's younger brother, Ra'e Shankar Das, who at that time was a clerk in Moradabad and was Sir Sayyid's extremely close friend, said to him, 'Burn all these books, and don't by any means put your life in danger'. Sir Sayyid said, 'To make clear all these matters to the government, I consider to be for the welfare of the country and

the community (*qaum*) and the government itself; thus if it would be beneficial to the rulers and the people both, then even if some harm would come to me, that's acceptable'. When Ra'e Shankar Das saw Sir Sayyid's stubborn determination, and when no effect was achieved by his own persuasion, then tears came to his eyes and he fell silent. Sir Sayyid first performed a supplementary prayer, then asked God's blessing, and at once sent off almost all the 500 copies in a single parcel to England. And he sent one copy to the Government of India, and kept some copies in his own possession.[1]

In his biography of Sir Sayyid, *Ḥayāt-e jāved* (An Immortal Life) (1901), Altaf Husain Hali (1837–1914), Sir Sayyid's younger contemporary and great admirer, goes on to tell the full story of how this pamphlet caused some Englishmen to distrust Sir Sayyid as a malcontent, or even a traitor, while others warmly defended him. Over time, Hali reports, his manifest sincerity won the hearts of even the most determined sceptics.

Hali claims that the pamphlet was translated a number of times during the first few years after 1857, but these earlier translations were apparently for internal governmental use and were not disseminated widely. It was not until the 1873 translation by Major-General G. F. I. Graham and Sir Auckland Colvin – 'his two European friends' – that Sir Sayyid's work became well known. This is the only form in which the pamphlet is cited normally, as it was issued with Sir Sayyid's approval.[2]

The pamphlet is full of free-flowing emotions and rife with self-contradictions. The most conspicuous, unignorable contradiction involves Sir Sayyid's shifting attitudes towards what he loyally and possessively refers to as 'our' government. He prefaces his work with a kind of credo: 'An honest exposition of native ideas is all that our government requires to enable it to hold the country with the full concurrence of its inhabitants and not merely by the sword.' Thus, his official stance is extremely sanguine and

---

[1] Altaf Husain Hali, *Ḥayāt-e jāved* (An Immortal Life) (New Delhi: Taraqqi Urdu Bureau, 1982), pp. 93–4. Author's personal translation. See also *Hayat-i-Javed: A Biography of Sir Sayyid*, trans. David J. Matthews (New Delhi: Rupa & Co., 1994).

[2] Sayyid Ahmed Khan Bahadur, C.S.I., *The Causes of the Indian Revolt*, in Urdoo, in the Year 1858, translated into English by his two European friends (Banaras: Medical Hall Press, 1873), ed. Frances W. Pritchett (2005), available at http://www.columbia.edu/itc/mealac/pritchett/00urdu/asbab/translation1873.html (accessed on 27 February 2017).

optimistic. In the introduction, he declares that the recent 'proclamation issued by Her Majesty contains such ample redress for every grievance' that his pamphlet can be of historical interest alone. Still, because no 'native of the country' has publicly expressed their views on the 'disturbances' yet, he will venture to do so.

After passing in review many commonly, but erroneously, ascribed causes of the rebellion, Sir Sayyid provides his own official diagnosis: 'The non-admission of a native as a member into the legislative council was the original cause of the out-break.' This, he describes, as the 'one great cause', while all others being but secondary.[3] He then enumerates five such subsidiary causes, each of which has many 'branches' of its own. Any reader who considers the ramifications of these causes will find Sir Sayyid's official view simply bizarre. Believing that the presence of a single native member in the legislative council could ever have prevented all these grievances from developing or rectified them on their development would be unwise.

In fact, Sir Sayyid himself could not sustain his own official view. As he enumerates the long lists of 'native' grievances, he presents them more and more forcefully and personally, until he actually says, with an engaging show of fairness, 'The English Government had, however, many, very many, good points. I do not condemn it entirely.' He then enumerates the benefits, such as the security of travel, the postal system, and the protection of the poor. Then, lest the reader overrates these, he concludes severely, 'But it must be borne in mind that the benefits derived from the above do not efface the feeling that I have above portrayed.'[4] What a mental and emotional journey – from a small problem (no native in the legislative council) and a sense that 'ample redress for every grievance' is already at hand to the grudgingly concessive 'I do not condemn it entirely!' Nevertheless, Sir Sayyid repeatedly makes this back-and-forth journey, with many bylanes and detours, throughout his long life.

Sir Sayyid's goals in writing the pamphlet, as reported by Hali, were basically threefold: to be of service to the country and people as a whole, to the government, and especially to the (Muslim) 'community', the *qaum*. The government would benefit by understanding the rebellion more accurately; the people, in general, and the Muslims, in particular, would benefit from the (excessive) blame for the rebellion that the government had wrongly ascribed to them. Throughout his pamphlet, Sir Sayyid wrestles with the

[3] Khan Bahadur, *The Causes of the Indian Revolt*, ed. Pritchett, section 0.2.
[4] Ibid., section 3.8.

question of this blame. Because the government had laid the chief share of blame on the Muslims, he tries especially to defend his own religious community. This defence develops along several lines, some of which are mutually contradictory.

In his first line of defence, he states that all Indians in general deserve much less blame for the rebellion than the government has ascribed to them. He argues that under the Company Government, Hindustanis in general have become progressively poorer. Thus, in sections 3.5[5] and 3.8,[6] we learn that 'poverty' induced the poor to work for the rebels and rejoice at the idea of a change in the government. In addition, there is an additional dimension to the situation because the circumstances of the rebellion 'appeared more serious to the authorities than they in reality were':

> It is well known in India that the taking of service is no offence. Whoever pays is served. It is thought wrong not to tender allegiance to a king who may have been proclaimed king in the place of another deposed.[7]

Thus, the government's violent vengefulness and wholesale accusations of 'treason' were an overreaction based on a misunderstanding of what was in fact more like a somewhat haphazard 'mutiny'.[8]

As compared to these general economic and political considerations, however, Sir Sayyid gives far more prominence to religious causes:

> There is not the smallest doubt that all men whether ignorant or well-informed, whether high or low, felt a firm conviction that the English Government was bent on interfering with their religion and with their old established customs. They believed that government intended to force the Christian Religion and foreign customs upon Hindu and Mussulman alike. This was the chief among the secondary causes of the rebellion.[9]

In the analysis of these causes, Sir Sayyid's second line of defence appears, wherein he tries to show that Hindus participated as completely in the

---

[5] Khan Bahadur, *The Causes of the Indian Revolt*, ed. Pritchett, section 3.5.
[6] Ibid., section 3.8.
[7] Ibid., section 4.10.
[8] Ibid., section 5.7.
[9] Ibid., section 4.10.

rebellion as Muslims, so that Muslims ought not to be singled out for special distrust – as, most conspicuously, they had been. He not only emphasizes the extensiveness and centrality of perceived religious grievances but also argues that some of these were particularly significant to Hindus. (One such grievance is an arrangement for shared meals in jails that violates caste rules;[10] another is an act increasing the legal rights of widows, 'opposed to practice of the Hindu religion'.[11])

Near the end of the pamphlet he concludes, 'If the whole facts regarding the rebellion be thoroughly sifted, I feel certain that we shall find that just as many Hindoos were concerned therein as Mahommadans.'[12]

Nevertheless, there is a third line of defence. Even if the Muslims did play a disproportionately large part in the rebellion – as Sir Sayyid himself sometimes explicitly states – he argues that this is understandable because they in fact had a disproportionately large share of grievances. Many of these were based on historical or cultural factors. For instance, in case of the resumption by the government of revenue-free lands, the Muslims had more such lands to lose, so that it was the Muslims 'on whom this grievance fell far more heavily than on the Hindus'.[13]

Even when Sir Sayyid speaks of the difficulties generally faced by 'the Hindustanees', 'who are becoming more and more impoverished every day',[14] he maintains that this 'overwhelming poverty of the Indians' too is 'particularly of the Mohammadans' – for it is they who suffer most from the lack, under British rule, of aristocratic employment opportunities:

> A native's best profession is service. Now although everyone felt the difficulty of getting service, this difficulty pressed most heavily on the Mahommadans. It must be borne in mind that the Hindoos, the original inhabitants of the country, were never in former days in the habit of taking service, but on the contrary they were each engaged in such work as their forefathers had been engaged in before them. The Brahmins never took service, the Vaishyas were always traders and bankers; the Kshatriyas, once lords of the land, never took service, but each kept his own small portion of land.[15]

[10] Khan Bahadur, *The Causes of the Indian Revolt*, ed. Pritchett, section 1.12.
[11] Ibid., section 2.2.
[12] Ibid., section 4.10.
[13] Ibid., section 2.6.
[14] Ibid., section 2.10.
[15] Ibid., section 4.10.

Because the Muslims 'came in the train of former conquerors and gradually domesticated themselves in India', they were 'all dependent on service'. Because of the scarcity of suitably 'honourable' opportunities for 'the higher class of Mahommadans' under British rule, over time, 'they, far more than the Hindoos, were put to much inconvenience and misery'.[16] Because of this aristocratic history, the Muslims have more pride than the Hindus:

> For centuries the Mahommadan's position in India has been an honourable one. There is an element of shame in his disposition. He has no grasping desire for money; he esteems honour above all other things; and there are many proofs on record, which shew that the Muhammadan is not easily brought to do that which, under the influence of temptation, other races (*qaum*) in India will do without compunction.[17]

Ultimately, more central than such economic and social grievances are the religious ones. In these cases as well, Muslims had had more to lose. The last item in Section 1, 'The interference in religious matters more repugnant to the Muhammadans, and its causes',[18] provides an intriguing comparative analysis of Islam and Hinduism, in which Sir Sayyid attempts to distinguish orthodoxy from orthopraxy:

> All these causes rendered the Muhammadans more uneasy than the Hindus. The reason of this, I take to be that Hindu faith consists rather in the practice of long-established rites and forms, than in the study of doctrine. The Hindus recognise no canons and laws, or appeals to the heart and conscience. Their creed does not admit of such things. Hence it is that they are exceedingly indifferent about speculative doctrine. They insist upon nothing excepting the strict observance of their old rites, and of their modes of eating and drinking. It does not annoy or grieve them to see such rites and observances as they consider necessary, disregarded by other men.
>
> Muhammadans, on the contrary, looking upon the tenets of their creed as necessary to Salvation and upon the neglect of them as

---

[16] Khan Bahadur, *The Causes of the Indian Revolt*, ed. Pritchett, section 4.3.
[17] Ibid., section 4.6.
[18] Ibid., section 1.14.

Defending the 'Community' 165

damnation, are thoroughly well-grounded in them. They regard their religious precepts as the ordinances of God. Hence it was that the Muhammadans were more uneasy than the Hindus, and that, as might have been expected, they formed the majority of the rebels.[19]

However, we may feel about the accuracy of these accounts, the Urdū style is flowing and powerful, even if at times determining the exact grammar is hard to pin down. Sir Sayyid's rhetoric not only has Biblical resonances but also cites numerous Biblical passages.[20] It is bracing to hear him speak truth to power. He works hard to defend Indians, in general and his own Muslim 'community', in particular, from British reproach.

Thus, it is even more dismaying to find that almost at the end of his pamphlet, Sir Sayyid offers the government some very explicitly Machiavellian 'divide and rule' advice. According to him, one of the pre-1857 errors the government had made was to include Hindus and Muslims in the same military regiments. Thus, he loyally provides the colonial government his best political advice:

[5.2] If these two castes formed distinct Regiments perhaps the Mahommadans would not have objected to the use of the new cartridges.

Government certainly did put the two antagonistic races (*hindū aur musalmān donoñ qaumoñ ko jo āpas meñ muḵẖālif haiñ*) into the same regiment, but constant intercourse had done its work and the two races in regiment had almost become one. It is but natural and to be expected, that a feeling of friendship and brotherhood must spring up between the men of a regiment, constantly brought together as they are. They consider themselves as one body, and thus it was that the difference which exists between Hindus and Mahommadans had, in these regiments, been almost entirely smoothed away.

[5.3] The employment of Hindus and Mahommadans in the same regiment.

If a portion of the regiment engaged in anything, all the rest joined. If separate regiments of Hindoos and separate regiments of Mahommadans had been raised, this feeling of brotherhood could

---

[19] Khan Bahadur, *The Causes of the Indian Revolt*, ed. Pritchett, section 1.14.
[20] Ibid, section 4.2.

not have arisen, and, in my opinion, the Muhammadan regiments would not have refused to receive the new cartridges.

Nothing in the pamphlet suggests that he finds this advice repugnant or even problematic. This reflects a tripartite scheme of analysis: There are Hindus and Muslims and then there is 'our government'. In the original Urdu text, each of the first two groups is unproblematically referred to as a *qaum*, for which the only 'least marked' translation is 'community'.

After the hardships of 1857, the following three decades were easier for Sir Sayyid. He campaigned tirelessly for his Muslim Anglo-Oriental College (1877) at Aligarh, raising money for it from the people of every community and providing admission to boys from not only Muslim but also other communities (provided they were from 'good' families). He also travelled to England. There, he admired much of what he saw and established warm friendship with many Englishmen. However, seeing him become so theologically liberal, conservative parents stipulated that their sons could attend the Aligarh college only if Sir Sayyid himself did not impart religious education. As always, he had patrons and friends from different religious communities. In *Ḥayāt-e jāved*, Hali tells stories of these years. David Lelyveld has also given us *Aligarh: The First Generation*, to which we all owe so much.

In 1885, however, an event horrified Sir Sayyid – an event that might have seemed at the time to be a tempest in a teapot, but that has loomed much larger over the years. This event was the founding of the Indian National Congress. Despite his own personally liberal, trans-communalist tendencies, this event seemed to rouse him to extreme anger. Rejecting the urgent appeals and remonstrances of Badruddin Tyabji and other friends, he demonstrated furious hostility towards this small nascent organization. He did not merely decline to join it himself or advise his own friends not to join it. He pulled out all possible stops, and opposed it as publicly as possible, with his whole heart and soul.

In Lucknow, on 18 December 1887, Sir Sayyid devoted a major speech to an urgent – desperate-sounding – appeal to the Muslims discouraging them from joining the Indian National Congress. A few months later (14 March 1888), he reiterated his arguments in a second major speech in Meerut. If these speeches did not mark the introduction of the 'two-nation theory' into Indian political discourse, they certainly gave it all the impetus of Sir Sayyid's personal prestige and powerful rhetoric. They did lay down the track and greased the rails, which eventually led straight to the logic of the 'partition'.

The 1887 speech was presented before the Muhammadan Educational Conference. According to the *Pioneer* (Allahabad), upper-class Muslims from all over north India had come for the speech:

> There were present the taluqdars of Oudh, members of the government services, the army, the professions of law, the press and the priesthood; Syeds, Shaikhs, Moghals and Pathans belonging to some of the noblest families in India; and representatives of every school of thought, from orthodox Sunni and Shiah Maulvis to the young men trained in Indian colleges or in England.[21]

Sir Sayyid spoke for an hour and a half, interrupted often by cheers. This speech was a carefully prepared major address. Yet, it is truly surprising and disappointing to read. From our perspective, Sir Sayyid is making arguments of the social classes' snobbishness, ethnic chauvinism, and unabashed religious communalism. His reasoning is slipshod and unconvincing. He is supposed to be, by his own lights, a rational thinker, a liberal reformer, an educator, rather than a demagogue. Why does he so passionately reject the possibility that Indians might fruitfully come together as one group? It will be helpful to consider the nature of his arguments and see how best to explain his position.

I have translated the 1887 talk from the Urdu as literally as I could manage and have made it available on my website.[22] For convenient reference, I have divided the talk into numbered sections. For reasons of space, the whole speech cannot be reproduced here, but it is well worth reading in full (as indeed is the Meerut 1888 speech that forms a kind of sequel to it; also available on my website). For our present purposes, I offer an outline of the main points, based on my own translation (because Sir Sayyid did not officially endorse the translation in *Pioneer*):

1. There is a kind of political tumult today in Hindustan, and I must tell you my views about it.

---

[21] 'Speech of Sir Syed Ahmed Khan at Lucknow (1878)' in *Sir Syed Ahmed on the Present State of Indian Politics, Consisting of Speeches and Letters Reprinted from the 'Pioneer'* (Allahabad: The Pioneer Press, 1888), a modern facsimile version (Lahore: Sang-e-Meel Publications, 1982).

[22] Sir Sayyid Ahmed Khan's Lucknow 1887 speech and Meerut 1888 speech, according to my translation and the *Pioneer* reporter's translation, the original Urdu text, and other relevant materials can be found at http://www.columbia.edu/itc/mealac/pritchett/00islamlinks/txt_sir_sayyid_lucknow_1887.html (accessed on 2 May 2018).

2. The Government has created a Council that makes laws, and has invited knowledgeable administrators and nobles ('Ra'is') to sit on it.
3. It must invite the Ra'is, rather than inviting people on the basis of personal worth, because only the Ra'is can mix socially with the Viceroy and his circle, and only they can be accepted by the upper classes as suitable to rule over the country:
    a. Will the Ra'ises of our land like it if a man of low [adnā] community [qaum] or low rank [darjah], even if he has taken a B.A. degree or an M.A., and even if he is also worthy, would sit and rule over them, would be master of their wealth, property, and honour? Never – nobody at all will like it. (Cheers.)
4. It is our misfortune that our Ra'ises are a worthless lot and can do nothing in Council for the benefit of Hindustan.
5. The Council carefully considers public opinion before promulgating laws.
6. The Government must also fulfill its duty to keep the Queen's rule in Hindustan firm and secure.
7. At present we have full access to our Government – we can express our ideas, and obtain a fair hearing for our claims.
8. Chief among the many demands of the Congress is that all Government posts should be allotted by competitive examination, and that these examinations should all be held in India rather than England.
9. When examinations held in England result in the appointment of people of low birth, such people are of 'no benefit', while 'those of high family honour the Ra'ises and treat them well, and impress upon people's hearts an image of the honour of the English people [inglish qaum] and the justice of the British Government, and are of benefit to the country and the Government'. But at least England is so far from us that we don't know the family backgrounds of the officers who come here. Whereas the 'noble communities [sharīf qaum] of Hindustan will not like it for a Hindustani of low rank, with whose roots and background they are acquainted, to be the master of their lives and property. (Cheers.)'
10. Competitive examinations are suited to countries in which a single community [qaum] lives, or in which various well-integrated communities can compete on a footing of equality. But this is not the state of our country, in which different

Defending the 'Community' 169

communities [*qaum*] dwell. On one side there are the Hindus, on another side Musalmans, and on a third side the Parsis. Even among the Hindus, the Hindus of our region [*mulk*] and the Bengalis of the eastern region and the Marathas of the Dakani region are not one.

These communities are not on an equal footing with regard to competitive examinations:

Now this is the question: has the Musalmans' education and training, and their knowledge of literature, which for the Government's high posts is necessary, reached such a level that it would be equal to that of the Hindus? No, absolutely not. Now, taking the Musalmans and Hindus of our region [*mulk*] together, I ask whether they both can equal the Bengalis. Absolutely not. When this is the situation, then in this country how can competitive examinations be instituted? (*Cheers.*)

11. Competitive examinations would result in government by Bengalis. 'All the communities [*qaum*], not just Musalmans but all the Hindus of this region [*mulk*], the honoured Rajahs and brave Rajputs too who remember their ancestors' swords, will see as their ruler one Bengali, who upon seeing a knife would drop down beneath a chair'. To endure the rule of Bengalis would be 'to suffer shoe-beatings'.

12. The Congress's second request is that members of the Viceroy's Council should be elected. Even assuming this could happen, the Hindus would vote for a Hindu, and the Muslims for a Muslim. Thus, there would be four votes for a Hindu, for every vote for a Muslim. 'And it will be like a game of dice in which the Hindus have four dice and we have one.'

13. If electors were chosen through a property qualification, the Bengalis would entirely dominate the Council, and other, more martial communities would become restive.

14. If a system of proportional representation were adopted, there would still be four Hindu members for every Muslim member.

15. Even if Muslims were given half the seats in the Council, not one of them would be able and willing to do the work.

16. Even if a Muslim were somehow made Viceroy, he could never grant such a request.

17. Even if the whole of Hindustan joined the agitation of the Bengalis, 'then is the Government so weak that it cannot suppress it?' We must remember how quickly the rebellion of 1857 was put down.

18. The Government is wrong to distrust us Muslims, but such distrust is understandable, for we are a martial community. 'We are those who for six or seven hundred years ruled over Hindustan. (*Cheers.*) We are those from whose hands the Government snatched [*chhīnnā*] the country.... We neither eat fish, nor fear that if we eat with knife and fork we might cut our fingers. (*Cheers.*)'
19. A commotion confined to Bengal is not a danger. 'But if you create the same commotion in these regions [*mulk*], and among the Rajputs, or among the Pathans of Peshawar – will you content yourself with the scratching of the pen, or the babbling of voices? At that time, then, the Government will have to send the army, and explain with bayonets what their cure is for this turmoil.'
20. Another foolish Congress request is to have approval of the budget for the Army. 'He who has never seen a battlefield, or seen the mouth of a cannon – he says, "we will prepare the budget for the army"!'
21. Another Congress request is to be able to have representatives sit in the Council and speak, even if they are not allowed to vote. What is the benefit of such 'babble', and what is to be gained from it?
22. Another Congress request is that army schools for officer training should be established in Hindustan, and Hindustani volunteers should be appointed as officers. Indeed, the Government ought to do this, and it is wrong of them to distrust the Hindustanis.
23. Oh brothers! I have blamed the Government in such harsh words – but that time is coming when our brother Pathans, Sadats, Hashimis, and Quraishis, from whose blood comes the scent of the blood of Abraham, will at that time wear glittering uniforms and become colonels and majors in the army. But we ought to wait for that time. The government will certainly attend to this, on condition that you do not permit it to become suspicious.
24. We should continue to show our strict loyalty; only then can we make a claim for appointment as officers.
25. We ought to have patience, and let such military reforms unfold gradually:
26. [For] when you conquered Hindustan, what did you yourselves do? For how many centuries was there the name of not even one Hindu on the list of soldiers? But when the time of the Mughal dynasty came and there was mutual trust between them, it was

Defending the 'Community' 171

these very Hindus who were appointed to high posts in the army. Be just – how many days has the Government been in power? How many days has it been since the rebellion? And that shock that affected the Government, although it was from the ignorant/ barbarous [*jāhil*] and not from the Ra'is – please tell me how many days ago it took place!

27. We should remember that election to local offices and councils will always present a numerical problem for Muslims.
28. Just now in Calcutta a bearded Musalman of very venerable family met me and said this: 'A disaster has taken place! In our city eighteen members were to be elected. Not one Musalman was elected; they were all Hindus. Now I want from the Government, the appointment of some Musalman. I hope that the Government would appoint me.' This is the state of all the cities.... Then how can we walk along that road, on which we are neither capable, nor in control?
29. And in conclusion:
30. Friends! Don't say that I'm like that dyer who because he only knew how to dye things mango-colored, said that only mango color pleased him. But I say truthfully that the thing that will raise you to a high level, is only high education. As long as in our community such people will not be produced, we will remain low [*zalīl*], we will remain below others, and we will not attain such honour as our heart wishes to attain.

Perhaps, the largest internal contradiction in this remarkable speech – one that leaps to the attention of the Urdu reader – is the quite tricky use of the word and concept of *qaum*. In Platts's dictionary, *qaum* is defined as 'a people, nation; a tribe, race, family; sect, caste', which pretty well covers all the bases. However, the problem is that Sir Sayyid's usage here shifts from one sense to another in a very slippery way.

One of his basic assumptions in the Lucknow 1887 speech is that the Hindu and Muslim 'communities' would always feel and act as massive religious blocs. (This is the primary assumption of 'Causes of the Indian Revolt' as well, although therein, Sir Sayyid also shows how easy it is to change the behaviour of 'these two antagonistic races' by, for example, putting Hindu and Muslim soldiers together in the same platoon.)

In Sir Sayyid's rhetoric, a polarized 'two-community' view of Hindus and Muslims is so fundamental that he depicts the situation even more ominously in his Meerut 1888 speech only a few months later. In that speech, he supposes the situation if the British leave:

Then, in Hindustan, who will be the ruler? In such a situation will the Hindus and Muslims, both communities (*qaum*), be able to sit together, with equal rank, on a single throne? Absolutely not. It will certainly happen that one of them would conquer and suppress the other.[23]

He goes on to envision scenarios of escalating military intervention from various Asian and European powers.

Yet, just as in 'Causes of the Indian Revolt', in his Lucknow 1887 speech, he himself offers arguments that contradict this monolithic–bloc view. For example, there are clear regional differences within the 'communities'. In section 9, he observes, 'Even among the Hindus, the Hindus of our region (*mulk*) and the Bengalis of the eastern region and the Marathas of the Dakani region are not one (*ek*).'

Moreover, as he repeatedly emphasizes that there are crosscutting social class differences and that each social class also becomes a *qaum*. In section 3, he invites his upper-class listeners to consider how distasteful it would be if 'a man of low community (*adnā qaum*)' were chosen by competitive examination to preside over their affairs. His listeners respond with cheers. In section 9, he returns to this point, emphasizing the displeasure that the 'noble communities (*sharīf qaum*) of Hindustan' would feel at such degradation. The whole speech assumes this elite perspective, with no point intended for lower-class Muslims.

Most crucially, Sir Sayyid grapples with the problem of the Bengalis, often by differentiating them clearly from 'Hindus' in general. In section 9, he laments that the Muslims do not equal the Hindus in educational attainment, but asserts that the Hindus of north India do not equal the educational attainment of the Bengalis. In his lexicon, all 'Bengalis' are Hindus. He clarifies the point in his Meerut speech: 'If we take the whole of Bengal together, then almost half will be Muslims and a bit over half will be Bengalis.'[24] However, the fact that there is very large number of 'Bengali Muslims' is one that he cannot or will not see.

(Hindu) Bengalis are always the chief objects of his envy and anxiety. They are cowardly: they 'eat fish' and fear that if they would eat with a knife they might cut their fingers.[25] Heightening the contrast, he praises his

---

[23] Shaikh Isma`il Panipati, *Khuṭbāt-e sar sayyid, jild-e duvvum* (Lahore: Majlis Taraqqi-e Adab, 1973), p. 97. Author's personal translation.

[24] Ibid., p. 36.

[25] Ibid., p. 17.

listeners for their own martial heritage and qualities: 'All the communities (*qaum*), not just Musalmans but all the Hindus of this region (*mulk*), the honoured Rajahs and brave Rajputs too who remember their ancestors' swords' would feel that to be governed by Bengalis would be 'to suffer shoe-beatings'.[26] (Again, he depicts conspicuous regional differences among Hindus, so that his fear of them always voting as a monolithic bloc looks increasingly implausible.)

His listeners are to think of themselves as martial – but not too martial. Herein, Sir Sayyid treads a remarkably narrow rhetorical path. The Muslims, the community from whom the British seized Hindustan, retain the martial prowess of their ancestors. Nevertheless, in the aftermath of their major role in the rebellion of 1857, they must not show even an ounce of disloyalty to the government. If they do, then they would be vigorously, understandably slapped down. Because of their abundant martial prowess, they must more carefully demonstrate their nonviolence and allegiance.

All this convoluted and internally contradictory rhetoric – with all its uncharacteristically mean-spirited ethnic sneers and boasts – can only be explained by the urgent need to appeal most viscerally to his audience. For the situation, as he sees it, was dire indeed. Sir Sayyid speaks of situations in which competitive examinations are possible: First, those in which the whole country consists of a single community (*qaum*). Second, those in which 'various communities would live, but those communities would have come together and become almost one community, like England and Scotland'. The third situation for competitive examinations is this: that although in one country different communities may live, still with regard to worthiness, education, and wealth they would all be equal, and to every community the opportunity can be available that through this examination it can obtain equal advantage – even if it might never do so, but the opportunity would be there.[27]

Here, Sir Sayyid summarizes everything he wishes for his community. Yet he is aware of how far his community is from a state of 'worthiness, education, and wealth', which would enable its elite young men to compete on equal terms with those of other communities. He knows the obstacles, chronicled in detail by Hali, against which he has struggled to establish his college at Aligarh. He stresses that Muslims should not join the Indian National Congress and not share in its demands for competitive

[26] Panipati, *Khuṭbāt-e sar sayyid*, p. 10.
[27] Ibid., p. 9.

examinations because the Muslims are not yet prepared to compete as individuals. Supporting voting rights would also be like playing 'a game of dice in which the Hindus have four dice and we have one'. Only through the most cohesive group solidarity can Muslims achieve political potency, thus sustaining themselves until some happy, fulfilling day when they no longer need this kind of crutch.

At the risk of sounding like a dyer who has only one shade of dye, Sir Sayyid concludes his speech by insisting once again, as he has in dozens of speeches before, that 'the thing that will raise you to a high level, is only "high education"'. He is so determined to emphasize the phrase that he gives the English phrase in transliteration and follows it by an Urdu translation. He then predicts solemnly, 'As long as in our community such people will not be produced, we will remain low (*zalīl*), we will remain below others, and we will not attain such honour as our heart wishes to attain.'

9 Understanding Sir Sayyid's Political Thought
MIRZA ASMER BEG

Men make their own history, but they do not make it as they please; they do not make it under self-selected circumstances, but under circumstances existing already, given and transmitted from the past.

– Karl Marx, *The Eighteenth Brumaire of Louis Bonaparte*
(New York: Die Revolution, 1852)

Sir Sayyid considered both Hindus and Muslims as one *qaum* (nation) – arguing that *qaum* should be used to describe the inhabitants of India even if they have individual characteristics.[1] Explaining further, he wrote, 'By the word *qaum* I mean both Hindus and Muslims. That is the way in which I define the word nation (nation).'[2] This is in contrast to his opinion on the Hindi–Urdu debate and the participation of Muslims in the programmes of the Indian National Congress (INC). To understand the rationale underlying the positions of Sir Sayyid, situating his ideas in the context of the developments of his times is essential.

This chapter aims to understand Sir Sayyid's political thought by examining how Sir Sayyid responded to the political concerns of his times and contributed to a broader conversation about society, democracy, and political participation. The attempt is to investigate his ideas on two important issues: his response to the Hindi–Urdu controversy and his position regarding the INC.

The first part of this chapter discusses the Hindi–Urdu controversy. Through the Hindi movement, we discover an important facet of the growth of Hindu nationalism in north India and see how the Hindi movement was

---

[1] Sir Sayyid Ahmad Khan, *'Ta'limaur Ittifaq' Maqalat-e Sir Sayyid: Taqriri Maqalat* (Lahore: Majlis-e Taraqqi-e Adab, 1963), cited in Hafeez Malik, *Sir Sayyid Ahmad Khan and Muslim Modernization in India and Pakistan* (New York: Columbia University Press, 1980), p. 244.

[2] Sayyid Iqbal Ali, *Sayyid Ahmad Khan ka Safarnamah-e Punjab* (Lahore: Majlis-e Taraqqi-e Adab, 1991), pp. 154–86.

successful in differentiating Hindi from Urdu and making Hindi a symbol of the Hindu culture. It also shows how people like Sir Sayyid had practically no option but to oppose this movement.

The second part addresses the political participation of the Muslims of India. Sir Sayyid regarded the INC as a step towards the creation of a more advanced 'nation' of Bengali specifically, not of Hindus in general. Like many others, he considers this a consequence of the asymmetrical impact of colonial policies in different parts of India, which resulted in a significant section of Hindu and Muslim middle classes – including many *zamindar*s and *taluqdar*s – coming together to oppose the INC. Only a short time before this, many of these protesters had been standing against each other on the Hindi–Urdu issue.

HINDI–URDU CONTROVERSY

Since the foundation of the Delhi Sultanate in the thirteenth century until the establishment of British supremacy in the late eighteenth century, Persian was the official language in north India. In 1837, it was replaced by Urdu, which drew its inspiration from Persian. During much of the nineteenth century, many north Indian Muslims and Hindus were familiar with both Urdu and Persian.

The Hindu *kayastha* community was particularly proficient in Urdu. Its members held government positions in large numbers. Along with Kashmiri Brahmins and Khatris, they held a virtual monopoly at public service, which remained largely unchallenged until the final decades of the nineteenth century. A majority of Hindus were at a disadvantage because of the brisk extension of the government educational system and its division into two vernaculars, Hindi and Urdu – with Urdu having the preferential position in administration. Hence, the competition for government service inevitably became linguistically and communally articulated.

Hindi and Urdu share common grammar, based on Khari Boli, the regional Hindi dialect of the western North-Western Provinces (NWP) and Oudh. Only a few insignificant differences, such as the use of Arabic plurals in formal Urdu or the use of Sanskrit suffixes in Hindi, separate the two verbally. However, the greatest and most conflicting difference between the two manifests in their scripts. No writing system may be as diverse as these two. Moreover, each script is associated with the sacred language of each religion: Nagari (Hindi script) is adapted from Sanskrit, the language of Hindu scriptures, whereas Urdu is adapted from Arabic, the language of the Qur'an.[3]

Sir Sayyid began reconsidering his ideas on inclusivity after the dispute over the official language status, which was enjoyed by Urdu hitherto. Urdu language in the Persian script had been the strongest link between the Hindu and Muslim communities of India over a long time. However, when the movement for replacing Urdu with Hindi as the exclusive language of north Indian Hindus started in the 1860s, many eyebrows were raised. Sir Sayyid opined that Urdu was the common heritage of Indians and thus should be continued. He feared that the differences between the two communities would increase with time, having disastrous consequences for the country in the long run. The supporters of Hindi argued that the good of the Hindu majority required the introduction of Hindi, even if the Muslim minority suffered because of the change. During this time, the first signs of differentiation identifying Hindi with Hindus and Urdu with Muslims appeared. Thus, the process of developing a consciousness of a common identity based on language and religion began.

Gradually, two ends of the pole emerged – one represented by those insisting on the use of a more Sanskritized Hindi and the other by those insisting on the use of a more Persianized Urdu. As the movement gained momentum, it put the Hindus who were part of the Urdu-speaking elite in the spot. They had strong economic reasons to be part of the Muslim legacy, but at a cultural level, they could not oppose Hindi and the Nagari script because they were considered representatives of the Hindu heritage. This issue attracted particular attention in 1873, when the supporters of Hindi presented a memorandum to the Provincial Lieutenant Governor, Sir William Muir. Sustained efforts for promoting Hindi began in 1893 after the founding of the Nagari Pracharini Sabha (Society for the Promotion of Nagari) at Banaras. This society organized resources for the growth of Hindi and the Nagari script and could produce literature that glorified the Hindu past.

These developments shook Sir Sayyid. To add insult to injury, Babu Fateh Chand, among others, organized committees at several places with a central office at Allahabad. These committees planned and coordinated the activities of various bodies for promoting Hindi. At the same time, Babu Shiva Prasad – a prominent official of the Provincial Department of Public Instruction – despite being an Urdu writer, pressed his hatred for

---

[3] Christopher King, 'The Hindi–Urdu Controversy of the North-Western Provinces and Oudh and Communal Consciousness', *Journal of South Asian Literature* 13, nos 1/4 (1977–78): 111–20, 111–12.

the former Mughal rule in India and its legacy, Urdu. He even implored the Hindu members of Sayyid Ahmad Khan's Scientific Society to replace Urdu with Hindi as the language of business in the society. Thus, these Hindu members began demanding the publication of the society's journal in Hindi rather than Urdu.[4] For the Hindi movement leaders, language had become a symbol of cultural and religious distinctiveness. They mobilized numerous people. Even a lawyer in the high court of the NWP maintained that the people regarded the recognition of Urdu as the court language as a pure and simple survival of the old Mughal tyranny in India.[5]

Sir Sayyid considered Urdu a mixed language and was not opposed to the recognition of the Nagari script. However, those on the other side, like Saroda Prasad Sandel, argued that Hindi and Urdu were not the same and that Urdu should make room for the more popular Hindi, just as Persian had made room for Bengali and Urdu.[6] In 1868, Babu Shiva Prasad wrote a memorandum favouring Hindi and submitted it to the provincial government. This was followed by other memoranda in 1869, 1872, and 1873. Although these did not lead to changes in the government's language policy, it created apprehension in the minds of people like Sir Sayyid. Even if the memoranda did not ask for a change in the court language or elimination of the Urdu script, it requested that 'the written character of the immense majority of the people (that is, the Nagari script) should be used in the courts, and all summonses, decisions and decrees should be issued in that character'.[7]

During 1867–1890, many Hindus of the NWP agitated through meetings and distributed leaflets; this led to groups of representatives approaching the government, requesting the substitution of Urdu in the Persian script with Hindi in the Nagari script as the official court language. Similar arguments were presented before the common masses mainly through poetry and drama in vernacular literature. In 1882, *The Calcutta Review* carried an article by Babu Shyamacharan Ganguli, who exhorted Muslims to accept that 'Urdu

---

[4] Aziz Ahmad, *Studies in Islamic Culture in the Indian Environment* (Oxford: Claredon Press, 1964), p. 260.

[5] *Education Commission Report by the North-Western Provinces and Oudh Provincial Committee; with Evidence Taken before the Committee, and Memorials Addressed to the Education Commission* (Calcutta, 1884), p. 200.

[6] Correspondence between Sir Sayyid Ahmad Khan and Saroda Prasad Sandel, *Aligarh Institute Gazette* 3, no. 48 (27 November 1868): 757–9.

[7] *Kasi-Nagari Pracharini Sabha Ka Arddhshatabdi Itihas* (Kasi, 1943), pp. 119–20.

is Hindi in its basis, just as they themselves are largely Hindu by race'.[8] During this period, the political conflict between Hindus and Muslims began in NWP. At this time, the leading Muslims of the province organized themselves into a political association to oppose the Hindu demands. Sir Sayyid's Muhammadan Educational Conference, founded in 1886, began defending Urdu in its meetings. Overall, the most crucial issue in NWP during this time was not the spread of English education, but whether Hindi or Urdu should gain prominence as the medium of primary education.[9]

A main concern of the Hindi camp was that because of the continued official importance given to Urdu in the provinces, a large number of Hindus were being assimilated in the cultural language and script of the Muslims in the late nineteenth century. In 1896, all vernacular elementary schools in the NWP and Oudh combined had 50,316 boys studying Urdu and 100,404 studying Hindi. The leaders of the Hindi movement were opposing this process of assimilation in the late nineteenth century, whereas the Muslims in the Aligarh school wanted to continue it.[10] Hindustani or Urdu was said to be a symbol of the 'syncretic culture', but when the social equilibrium on which this culture rested was threatened, Urdu became a symbol of a distinct communal identity.[11]

Regardless of the true motive of the Hindi movement supporters, the fact remained that no issue had previously mobilized Hindus in such large numbers. This was indeed a cause for alarm. For those supporting Urdu, like Sir Sayyid, communal animosity was the basis of all the agitation for Hindi and the Nagari script. Without thinking of the public interest, the Hindus were expressing their religious bigotry. Considering the increasing competition for government service, the Hindi movement made efforts to differentiate Hindi from Urdu, denying any assimilation to cultural traditions associated with the Mughal rule. It glorified a Hindu past, implicitly giving expression to Hindu communalism. For the Hindus, Hindi and the Nagari script looked to different religious and historical traditions than did Urdu and the Urdu script.

---

[8] 'Hindi, Hindustani and the Behar Dialects', *The Calcutta Review* LXXV (1882), p. 36.
[9] Paul R. Brass, 'Muslim Separatism in United Provinces: Social Context and Political Strategy Before Partition', *Economic and Political Weekly* 5, nos 3/5, (January 1970): 167–9, 171–3, 175, 177–9, 181, 183–6.
[10] Ibid.
[11] Alok Rai, *Hindi Nationalism* (Hyderabad: Orient Blackswan, 2001), p. 61.

The pressure on the government to replace Urdu with Hindi continued unabated, with the British official policy also appearing to be receptive to this demand. Urdu was replaced by Hindi first as the written medium of recording in the courts of law in Bihar. During 1872–1873, the same happened in the subordinate offices in the Central Provinces and the Darjeeling district of Bengal. In 1881, the exclusive use of Hindi in the Nagari script was introduced in Bihar.[12]

All this culminated in 1900, when Sir Anthony MacDonnell, the Lieutenant Governor, gave official recognition to the permissive, but not exclusive, use of Hindi in the Nagari script in the courts of NWP. On 4 July 1900, *The Punjab Observer* reported, 'We cannot but characterize it as anything short of a grave political blunder, and history written a hundred years later will have to mourn the mistake made in 1900.' This policy created considerable confusion on the issue of language. In areas where Muslims were more in number or were influential, like Punjab and UP, Urdu remained firmly rooted until India's independence. However, in places where Urdu had no such hold, like Bihar and Central Provinces, Hindi and the Nagari script replaced Urdu.

In 1874, Sir John Strachey, Lieutenant Governor of NWP and Oudh, had rejected the argument that the government should favour Hindi because of the number of Hindi speakers is larger. However, by the end of the century, Sir MacDonnell forwarded the same argument to justify the governmental recognition of Hindi and the Nagari script through a political argument documented in a 22 August 1897 letter addressed to Lord Elgin: '... the strong position of Muslims was a risk to the security. The ratio of Muslims to Hindus should be reduced to three to five.'[13]

Evidence clearly indicates a fundamental contradiction in the British language policy among the United Provinces; precisely, it encouraged the use of Hindi in education along with the preferment of Urdu in administration. This language policy helped create a flood of Hindi textbooks in the Nagari script and a class of people with a vested interest in Sanskritizing them. It also exposed tens of thousands of students to Hindi-medium education using these textbooks, but denied these students equal access to the

---

[12] Abdul Hamid, *Muslim Separatism in India: A Brief Survey 1858–1947* (Lahore: Oxford University Press, 1971, repr. [1967]), pp. 37–8.

[13] Francis Robinson, *Separatism among Indian Muslims: The Politics of United Provinces' Muslims 1860–1923*, Cambridge South Asian Studies (Cambridge: Cambridge University Press, 2007), p. 134.

very government positions (for which they had gone to school), where the knowledge of Urdu was privileged. This glaring inconsistency found no parallel outside the United Provinces, but significantly increased the differentiation between the two forms of Khari Boli.[14]

Sir Sayyid feared that the stance of the Hindi movement leaders and the official language policy was causing a deep rift between the Hindus and the Muslims, but no Hindu leaders paid attention to Sir Sayyid's objections. In addition, when the INC was established in 1885, in the name of the Indian 'nation', it took no position on these divisive official measures or the disquieting Hindi movement. Several delegates to the INC sessions were in the forefront of the movement. During the 1890s, the meetings of the Hindi Sahitya Sammelan were held in the INC *pandal* after the closing of the INC sessions.[15] The way INC leaders associated with the demands for Hindi can be gauged from Lala Lajpat Rai's 1882 confession that he did not know the language (Hindi) at the time but was actively promoting its cause in Punjab and was going to continue supporting the Hindi movement.[16] Rai was an admirer of the British rule and maintained that the British were the liberators from the atrocities and mischiefs of the Muslims. Another prominent INC leader, Madan Mohan Malviya was a member of the Nagari Pracharini Sabha since 1894. He acted as its representative on the delegation supporting Hindi to Sir MacDonnell in 1898. Hindi supporters' sentiments resonate in Malviya's 1897 book *Court Character and Primary Education in NWP and Oudh*.

Apparently, scripts and languages were merely a pretext of the struggle for jobs and access to power. Because these main reasons were not exposed, the arguments paraded in the support of Hindi carried little weight. A major argument of the Hindi movement leaders that Nagari was the script of the masses was not supported by facts – because 97 per cent of them were illiterate at the time.[17] In fact, compared with the Nagari script, the Kaithi script was more widely used then, and thus, democratic arguments favouring the Nagari script carried little weight. The reason that the Kaithi

---

[14] Christopher R. King, *One Language Two Scripts: The Hindi Movement in Nineteenth Century North India* (New Delhi: Oxford University Press, 1994), p. 186.
[15] Sharif Al Mujahid, 'Sir Syed Ahmad Khan and Muslim Nationalism in India', *Islamic Studies* 38, no. 1 (1999): 87–101, 93.
[16] Lakshminarayan Gupta, *Hindi Bhasha aur Sahitya ki Arya Samaj ko Den* (Lucknow: Sahitya Mandir Press, 1961), pp. 258–62.
[17] Rai, *Hindi Nationalism*, p. 58.

script was not considered by the Hindi movement leaders was that this script was somewhat associated with Hindustani, rather than Sanskrit, and was known to both the Hindus and Muslims – which made it not 'pure' enough to create a basis of differentiation. Therefore, the reason underlying the Hindi movement and its consequences was the contest between two elite groups: the entrenched Urdu-wielding Avadh elites (including both Muslims and Hindus) and the emergent and aspirant *savarna* Nagari–Hindi elites.

As the Hindi movement intensified, the situation became so polarized that ignoring their economic interest associated with Urdu, *kayastha*s passed a resolution in the first Kayastha Conference in 1988. The resolution favoured the introduction of the Nagari script in government courts and offices. At its conclusion, a memorandum was sent to the Lieutenant Governor.[18]

As time passed, there grew a deep-rooted hatred of the Urdu script. Raja Shiva Prasad bared his heart out stating that the arguments were specifically directed against the use of the Persian script, not Persianized Urdu – which he himself used with considerable ability. In an 1868 memorandum, he wrote, '... the official script thrusts a semitic element into the bosoms of Hindus and alienates them from their Aryan speech ... to read Persian is to become Persianised, all our ideas become corrupt and our nationality is lost.'[19]

However, in this conflict, both sides demonstrated competitive fidelity by being cautious not to antagonize the British. When Raja Shiva Prasad petitioned the government on behalf of the Nagari script in 1868, he said, 'Never will it be safe to leave any district without a fair-complexioned head. It is not the excess but the dearth of the fair-complexioned that we have to complain of.'[20] The opponents of the Hindi movement were equally prompt in pointing towards the connections among the Hindi movement, the cow protection movement, and the emergent INC. On 18 June 1900, the Urdu periodical *Al Bashir* warned, 'The Hindi–Urdu controversy, the cow protection societies and the system of competitive examinations ... though they apparently seem to be directed against the Muslims, are really appendages of the INC, and indirectly breathe a spirit into the country which cannot possibly be beneficial to the British government.'

---

[18] Charles H. Heimsath, *Indian Nationalism and Hindu Social Reform* (Princeton: Princeton University Press, 1964), pp. 281–3.

[19] Shiva Prasad, *Memorandum: Court Character in the Upper Provinces of India* (Banaras: Library of the Nagari Pracharini Sabha), p. 5.

[20] 'Strictures upon the Strictures of Sayyad Ahmad Khan Bahadur' (Banaras, 1870), p. 16, quoted in Rai, *Hindi Nationalism*, p. 36.

Sir Sayyid foresaw the consequences of the Nagari/Hindi politics, and in a 29 April 1879 letter to his friend Mehdi Ali Khan from London, he expressed his anguish by explaining that 'it would open an unending vista of split and strife between Hindus and Muslims. The rupture would never be healed.... The two communities would be irrevocably rent asunder'.[21]

With these developments in the background, Sir Sayyid argued that status quo should be maintained regarding the language policy. Although this position advantaged the Avadh elite, it emphasized unification of Indians, rather than their differentiation – which the Hindi movement leaders were attempting. Sir Sayyid anticipated the consequences of this movement, and thus, his response was guided by his concern for the Muslim community as well as the larger cause of social amity and harmony. Accusing Sir Sayyid of being communal and exclusivist for advocating the cause of Urdu and exonerating the supporters of Hindi of all charges (for doing exactly the same thing in their support for Hindi) would be a great injustice to Sir Sayyid and his legacy.

The basis of Sir Sayyid's arguments can be understood by looking at the way this issue has played out in the political arena of independent India. As recently as 2014, the UP Government's decision to accord Urdu the status of second official language was challenged by the UP Hindi Sahitya Sammelan in court. The case escalated to the Supreme Court, which eventually ruled that the state's decision was constitutional. The real reason underlying this opposition was not genuine (or imagined) concerns for Hindi, but the communal consciousness present in the public sphere. Even today, Urdu is unpalatable to those who look at the language issue through the communal lens. Even in the twentieth century, these individuals are not ready to shed the political baggage of the nineteenth century.

POLITICAL PARTICIPATION OF MUSLIMS

In the Hindi movement, the communal fault lines in the Indian society were becoming quite visible. Sir Sayyid saw that this movement was leading to majority communalism, which eventually would have marginalized the Muslims, who were in minority and considered the reason for the perceived disadvantages of the majority. Not guided by some exclusivist agenda, his

---

[21] Shaykh Muhammad Isma`il Panipati (ed.), *Maktubat-e Sir Sayyid* (Lahore: Majlis-e Taraqqi-e Adab, 1959), p. 103.

ideas for the political participation of the Muslims were well thought and based on a sound understanding of the situation. A main demand of the INC was that members of the Viceroy's Council should be chosen through election: This was the emphasis in the INC meeting at Madras, presided by Budruddin Tyabji. Expressing his apprehension on this issue, Sir Sayyid argued, '... the power of legislation over the whole country will be in the hands of Bengalis or of Hindus of the Bengali type and the Mahomedans will fall into a condition of utmost degradation.'[22]

Sir Sayyid was aware of the numerical inferiority of the Muslims. Moreover, he was apprehensive of the first-past-the-post system. Long before the system was introduced in India, he could foresee that it would be to the great disadvantage of the Muslims. He explained it in quite clear terms: 'And first suppose that all Mahomedan electors vote for a Mahomedan member, and all Hindu electors for a Hindu member; It is certain the Hindu members will have four times as many, because their population is four times as numerous.'[23] Sir Sayyid's views on the inherent weakness of the first-past-the-post system were much ahead of his time. After studying John Stuart Mill's writings, he was convinced that where the majority vote is a decisive factor in a political system, the electors need to rise above the narrow considerations of race, religion, language, region, and caste. Otherwise, the minorities and marginalized groups would have very little voice and their legitimate concerns and aspirations would be at the mercy of the majority. Appreciating the diverse nature of the Indian society and the communal divide, he anticipated that with the kind of dispensation the INC desired to create in India, the Muslims would be increasingly side-lined. Unfortunately, his fear became reality in 1936, when in popular elections for the Legislative Assembly in UP, the INC won the majority, with most of those elected being Hindus who then became ministers. Held after the enactment of the Government of India Act, 1935, this election gave voting rights to only about 14 per cent of the Indian population. Nevertheless, this was an improvement compared with the Government of India Act,

---

[22] Sir Sayyid's reply to Mr. Badruddin Tayabji's letter published in *The Pioneer* in 1888, quoted in *Writings and Speeches of Sir Syed Ahmad Khan*, comp. and ed. Shan Muhammad (Bombay: Nichiketa Publications Limited, 1972), pp. 240–3.

[23] Sir Sayyid's speech at Lucknow, 28 September 1887, in *Sir Syed Ahmad on the Present State of Indian Politics, Consisting of Speeches and Letters Reprinted from the 'Pioneer'* (Allahabad: The Pioneer Press, 1888), pp. 1–24, a modern facsimile version (Lahore: Sang-e-Meel Publications, 1982).

1919, which gave only 3 per cent of the adult population the voting rights. Eventually, the first-past-the-post system, with universal adult franchise, was operationalized after India's independence.

In April 1890, a petition signed by approximately 40,000 Muslims from nearly 70 cities and towns of India was presented to the House of Commons, through Sir Richard Temple. The petitioners prayed, '... your Honourable House will not introduce the principle of election into the Constitution of the Indian Councils as requested by the Indian National Congress.'[24] This move elicited some support from the British press as well. *The Times* denounced the INC's scheme as a clever devise created by a 'little organized clique of baboos to gain power for itself'.[25] Consequently, the Indian Councils Act, 1890, did not introduce any form of elective government. Sir Sayyid's views on this subject did not change until the very end. In December 1896, on his directions, a scheme dealing with the Muslim representation in the Legislative Council and the Municipalities was drafted. This scheme, crafted by Theodore Beck and Sayyid Mahmud, was presented to the government by the Muhammadan Anglo-Oriental Defense Association.

Sir Sayyid also did not appreciate the intricacies of democracy, mainly because democracy then had not evolved to its present liberal maturity anywhere in the world and was largely a preserve of the rich and propertied class of men. Sir Sayyid based his opposition to participatory democracy in India on a sociological argument. He argued that the English society is made up of free-acting individuals, unrestrained by 'community' allegiance. In India, however, individuals are trapped within institutional communities. In the political arena, they do not act as free individuals. Because the society demands, they support candidates of their own community. A Muslim has to vote for a fellow Muslim, and a Hindu for a fellow Hindu. Sir Sayyid said that this was a fact of the Indian culture. Therefore, until the society and culture individualized, democracy would remain unsuitable for India. He identified that the problem still plagues the Indian polity. He concluded that for the time being, having the British as impartial referees was useful.[26]

The increasing numbers of educated middle class individuals from Bengal in the government jobs posed a challenge to the entrenched Avadh elite. Consequently, they protested against the INC, which they felt was created

---

[24] *The Pioneer*, 12 May 1890.
[25] *The Times*, India, 23 June 1890 (London).
[26] Hamza Alavi, 'Misreading Partition Road Signs', *Economic and Political Weekly* 37, nos 44/45 (2–15 November 2002): 4515–17, 4519–23, 4516.

by the Bengalis to further their own ends. Because Sir Sayyid also belonged to this group of elites, he opposed the INC and founded the United Indian Patriotic Association in 1888. Raja Saheb of Banaras, Raja Bhinga, and Babu Shiva Prasad, all of whom were in the forefront of the Hindi movement, as well as Munshi Naval Kishore, who was earlier with the INC, came together to oppose the INC.

Considering that the British Government had mainly blamed the Muslims for the events of 1857, Sir Sayyid thought that it would be better if the Muslims did not commit any such folly and again become suspects in the eyes of the British, who according to him were going to rule over India for a long time. He argued, 'Leaving this aside, it is not expedient that Mahomedans should take part in proceedings like that of the congress, which holds meetings in various places in which people accuse government before crowds of common men of withholding their rights from her subjects.'[27] He wanted to redeem the Muslim community from the stigma of disloyalty, and through education, prepare it to avail the benefits of British rule. He argued that although the Muslims and Hindus had together risen against the British in 1857, after the rebellion was brought under control, the Muslims were primarily held responsible for daring to rise against the British and thus faced the wrath of the imperialists first. This made Sir Sayyid ask Muslims to stay away from the INC.

As the INC embraced the cause of Hindi, people like Sir Sayyid began weaning away from the INC, because they distrusted the increasingly divisive Hindi movement. Sensing that the cause of Hindi commanded a clear democratic advantage, the emergent INC had taken hold of the Hindi movement. Unsurprisingly, Sir Sayyid, along with many others, opposed the INC for this step. An Urdu daily newspaper reported that a large anti-INC meeting was held in Lucknow on 3 December 1899. Attended by approximately 5,000 gentry, it condemned the INC's support for Hindi.[28] In December 1887, while the INC held its meeting in Madras, Sir Sayyid addressed the Muhammadan Educational Congress in Lucknow. Here, he denounced the INC as an attempt by Bengalis to take over India. The INC had always accused the British for their 'divide and rule' policy, but this attempt to divide Indians on the issue of language failed to draw the attention of the INC.

---

[27] Sir Sayyid's reply to Mr Badruddin Tayabji's letter published in *The Pioneer* in 1888, quoted in *Writings and Speeches*, ed. Muhammad, pp. 240-3.
[28] *Oudh Akhbar*, 3 December 1899 (Lucknow: Nawal Kishore Press).

According to Sir Sayyid, the arguments he advanced for Muslims to keep away from the INC were in the larger interest of the country. His fears regarding any vocal and passionate political mobilization were not meant to depoliticize the Muslims or create a communal consciousness among them. He simply believed that it was not politically wise for the Muslims to join the INC; this was in the best interest of the country. He said, 'There has grown up in India a political agitation and it is necessary to determine what action should be taken by the Muhammedan community with regard to it. Although my own thoughts and desires are towards my own community, yet I shall discuss whether or not this agitation is useful for the country....'[29] He felt that only education could lead the Muslims towards empowerment and choosing political activism over education would make them slip further down the abyss of backwardness. He was convinced about neither the objectives of the INC nor their commitment to their stated objectives. Hence, for him, advising Muslims to join the INC was impossible. However, in the retrospectively constructed nationalist narrative, some have called him a 'separatist' based on his call to the Muslims for nonparticipation in the early INC. Sir Sayyid did have a point, but in this all-pervasive, entrenched nationalist narrative of the twenty-first century, there is a limited chance that many would appreciate his nuanced arguments.

Notably, the INC then was not a body fighting for the independence of the country, but merely a group of loyal elite Indians that would petition the British Government, while ensuring that none of its actions and deeds amounted to antagonizing the government's powers. The INC was convinced of the providential nature of the British rule and hoped for its continuance in India. From the first two decades of its existence until much after Sir Sayyid's demise, the INC did not make any worthwhile contribution to the cause of nationalism. Hence, Sir Sayyid and many others like him disagreed with its *modus operandi*. At that time, neither the INC nor Sir Sayyid and his friends were disloyal to or opposed the British Government. In fact, Sir Sayyid thought that by only making demands to the government without having the required commitment to go to any extent to get these demands met, betrayed the nonseriousness of the INC towards its proclaimed goals. Hence, according to him, the INC's actions did not make much sense: 'What benefit is expected from all this for the country, and what revolution in the government can we produce? The only results can be to produce a useless uproar to raise suspicion in government....'[30]

[29] Sir Sayyid's speech at Lucknow, 28 September 1887.
[30] Ibid.

Notably, not only Sir Sayyid and a handful of Muslims (who did not agree with the INC and its style of functioning) but also several prominent Hindus did not agree with the INC. These people included most Muslim and Hindu *taluqdar*s of Oudh. Sir Sayyid wanted the British Government to appreciate this fact. Furthermore, while he believed that the movement started by the INC was not a national movement, Sir Sayyid was cautious to ensure that no exclusivist message was conveyed by his opposition to the INC. Hence, suggesting that Sir Sayyid wanted to keep the Muslims away from the INC while all other people supported the INC is quite misleading. Sir Sayyid's harshest critics were also Muslim. Thus, apprehensive that the aforementioned perception might gain ground, he argued,

> In India all people-the officials and the public-are well aware of the opposition that has been raised by Hindus and the Muhammedans to the INC. But the supporters of the INC are trying by wrong means to create a false impression on England that the whole of the people of India, Hindus and Muhammedans, are in its favour. Hence it is necessary for us to inform the people of England that the Muhammedans and many influential and powerful Hindus are opposed to it.[31]

Before considering Sir Sayyid a narrow-minded community leader, it would be prudent to consider that he worked with Hindus in the Scientific Society, the Aligarh British India Association, and the United Indian Patriotic Association. He was also supported by several Hindu *zamindar*s and Rajas in his college, and many leading Hindus were members of his college committee. In the early years of his college, there were significant number of Hindu students and teachers. Between 1879 and 1900, there were 1,573 Muslim and 451 Hindu students in the Muhammedan Anglo-Oriental College.[32] Ten Hindu teachers were also appointed.[33]

On the other hand, the symbols, slogans, ideas, phrases, and idioms used to bring the masses towards the INC were majorly Hindu in the

---

[31] Sir Sayyid's letter to the editor of *The Pioneer* in opposition to the Indian National Congress after the formation of the United Indian Patriotic Association, 8 August 1888.

[32] Sayyid Iftekhar Alam, *Muhammadan College History* (Agra: Matba Mufid-e Aam, 1901), pp. 135–6.

[33] Khaliq A. Nizami, *Sir Syed on Education, Society and Economy* (Delhi: Idarah-e Adabiyat, 2009), p. 87.

religio-cultural sense. Although it might have been unintentional, this fact alarmed the Muslims. In 1893, after the Hindu–Muslim riots in Bombay, Tilak started the Ganapati celebrations in Poona. In these processions, songs denigrating Muslim and British rulers were sung. In one case, a procession attacked a mosque, adding communal colour to the whole celebration.[34] In the Bengal Council, Lal Mohan Ghose questioned the propriety of parading the Muharram procession in the streets of Calcutta. Surendranath Banerjee expressed great joy when the cow-killing circular of the Bengal Government was issued. The attitude of the INC leaders and the resurgence of Hindu nationalism embodied in the form of the Bharati Varsha National Association, Arya Samaj, and anti-cow-killing societies, distressed the Muslims. These factors further alienated this community and created suspicions in their minds.

This situation is strikingly similar to the current developments in India, where the strengthening of majoritarian forces and their aggressive intent has intensified the feelings of insecurity and fear among the minorities, particularly the Muslims. These developments are a stark reminder that Sir Sayyid's fears regarding the rise of majoritarianism were not entirely unfounded.

Sir Sayyid also opined that the demands of the INC may disturb the communal amity in the country. He added, 'These proposals of the congress are extremely inexpedient for the country.... To create animosity between them is good neither for peace, nor for the country, nor for the town.'[34] Sir Sayyid is often accused of creating a sense of difference between the Hindus and Muslims. By contrast, he worked tirelessly in search of the points of convergence between the two communities. He further thought that the INC and its demands would never evoke any positive response from the British Government, rather disturb the fragile peace of a country India had become. 'The result of these unrealizable and impossible proposals can be only this: that anger and excitement will spread throughout the people, and the peace of the country will be destroyed.'[35]

On 22 November 1888 in a meeting of the United Indian Patriotic Association, Raja Shiva Prasad tabled a resolution to establish a new central association at Lucknow for opposing the INC, named Indian Loyal

[34] Sir Sayyid's speech at Meerut, 16 March 1888, in *Sir Syed Ahmad on the Present State of Indian Politics, Consisting of Speeches and Letters Reprinted from the 'Pioneer'* (Allahabad: The Pioneer Press, 1888), pp. 29–53, a modern facsimile version (Lahore: Sang-e-Meel Publications, 1982).

[35] Sir Sayyid's speech at Lucknow, 28 September 1887.

Association. He wanted approval for a petition addressed to the government, signed by the Maharaja of Banaras and some others. The petition asked the government to add certain sections to its criminal code for suppressing seditious writings of the INC leaders in the press. This petition required the INC leaders to be charged of sedition, with appropriate legal action. It was a serious petition, which Sir Sayyid did not agree with. For him, the INC was a body of the Bengali elites, with which he had a difference of opinion; however, he did not believe that the organization was disloyal to the government, although it had adopted extremely immoral methods with regard to public affairs. He bore no animosity against the congressmen and disagreed that he 'should undertake the work of trying to have them arrested by the criminal courts. We believe that what they want is very harmful for the Mohammedans, for Rajputs, and especially for the peace of the country.... Let the government do what it thinks fit.'[36] Thus, leaders like Raja Shiva Prasad and Raja of Banaras nursed a deep-rooted animosity towards the INC, whereas Sir Sayyid was opposed to the INC at the level of ideas.

Those with a very insular understanding of the term 'nationalism' often blame Sir Sayyid of being a traitor to the cause of Indian nationalism. On the contrary, Sir Sayyid considered India a country where people of all hues lived together, where a territorial uniqueness still allowed cultural communities their space. His engagement with the traditional Islamic values and history did not deter him from redefining the role of religion in the modern era. Here, he found no qualms in positing religion as a private matter, thus keeping it out of the public sphere. In his Urdu essay 'Mazhabi Khayal Zamana-e Qadeem aur Zamana-e Jadeed mein', Sir Sayyid noted that in the early era, humans were created for the sake of religion whereas in modern dictum, the latter has been created for the former. According to Sir Sayyid, religion in the past dealt both with the spiritual and physical needs of a human society; now it was meant to deal only with the spiritual aspects.[37]

His rational outlook in religious matters also negates his image of an inward-looking community leader – which some analysts have bestowed upon him. Sir Sayyid was the only prominent Muslim disputing the claims of the Khalifa of Turkey and wanted to sever the link of Indian Muslims with the international Muslim fraternity. He argued that Indian Muslims

---

[36] Sir Sayyid's letter to the editor of *The Pioneer*, 24 September 1888.

[37] Panipati, *Maqalat-e Sir Sayyid*, vol. 3 (Lahore, 1963), pp. 24–7, quoted by Iftekhar H. Malik in *Sir Syed Ahmad Khan: Muslim Renaissance Man of India – A Bicentenary Commemorative Volume*, ed. Abdur R. Kidwai, ch. 12 (Mumbai: Viva Books, 2017), p. 214.

had to survive in the Indian situation and not turn to a foreign power for their moral or religious survival. 'His emphasis on *ijtihad* or independent reasoning and disapproval of *taqlid* or adherence to the four authoritative schools of Islamic jurisprudence set him apart from the *ulama* that saw in his modernist intellectual stance a barely disguised attack on their preeminent status in Muslim society.'[38]

In the final decades of the nineteenth century, an Indian nation did not exist. Sir A. O. Hume talked of a congeries of communities.[39] Because the idea of an Indian nation was yet to develop in India, no one then accused Sir Sayyid of dividing the nation – a myth created by some twentieth-century writers.

Sir Sayyid, a person who despite his differences with the INC worked for communal harmony and inclusivity has been condemned as an exclusivist and proponent of the two-nation theory. The predicament of Sir Sayyid is the same as that Indian Muslims are in today. When they talk of their legitimate concerns and rights, their patriotism is suspected. When they protest if pushed against the wall, they are branded as anti-national.

CONCLUSION

In some of the Indian writings, Sir Sayyid's role has been largely misrepresented because of his opposition against the Hindi movement and the INC. He deserves to be judged more objectively. None of the Hindi movement protagonists is loathed currently. Instead, all venom is spewed on Sir Sayyid for advocating the cause of Urdu. Hamza Alavi argues that although Bankim Chandra Chatterjee has been highly acclaimed by some scholars as the pioneer of Indian nationalism, his violent hostility towards the Muslims and his declaration that British were not our enemies are often ignored. Bankim advocated English education and accepted the British rule just as Sir Sayyid did, but Bankim is honoured, whereas Sir Sayyid is hated – for holding the same views.[40] As late as 1894, even Aurobindo Ghosh had this to say about the INC: 'The congress is dying of consumption; annually

---

[38] Ayesha Jalal, 'Exploding Communalism: The Politics of Muslim Identity in South Asia', in *Nationalism, Democracy and Development: State and Politics in India*, ed. Sugata Bose and Ayesha Jalal, pp. 1–21 (Delhi: Oxford University Press, 1998–1999), p. 6.

[39] Sir William Wedderburn, *Allan Octavian Hume, C.B.: Father of the Indian National Congress* (London: Fisher Unwin, 1913).

[40] Alavi, 'Misreading Partition Road Signs', p. 4516.

its proportion sinks into greater insignificance.'[41] However, he is still never characterized as anti-national. These unique differences in assessments reveal the intellectual biases underlying the Indian nationalist thought.[42]

Until he was alive, Sir Sayyid carried the image of a broadminded leader. It was only in the twentieth century that all kinds of accusations began being hurled at him. Sir Sayyid went to Punjab in 1884. Of the hundreds of addresses presented there, the one presented for the Indian Association of Lahore by its President, Sardar Dayal Singh, is particularly noteworthy. It talks about Sir Sayyid's 'liberal attitude towards the section of the country other than your own co-religionists.... Your conduct throughout has been stainless of bigotry'.[43]

Even until his last breath, Sir Sayyid's commitment towards inclusive politics did not desert him. Only one week before his death, Sir Sayyid wrote, 'We should have the courage to accept that the education which is teaching our Hindu youth to hate the Muslims will one day make them understand that until Hindus and Muslims come together and do not learn to respect the feelings of each other, neither of them will get a place of respect under the British rule.'[44] Today, we can understand how prophetic these words were.

---

[41] Niharranjan Roy, 'Nationalism in India', in *Sir Syed Ahmad Khan Memorial Lectures*, ed. Shan Muhammad, pp. 120–230 (Mumbai: Viva Books, 2107), p. 174.
[42] Alavi, 'Misreading Partition Road Signs', p. 4516.
[43] Ali, *Sir Sayyid Ka Safarnamah-e Punjab*, p. 157.
[44] *Aligarh Institute Gazette*, 19 March 1898, Aligarh.

Part III
Sir Sayyid today: Enduring legacies

10 Bridging the Past and the Present
How Sir Sayyid Speaks to the Twenty-First Century Protestors

MOHAMMAD ASIM SIDDIQUI

In February 2017, a heated discussion broke out among a section of Aligarh Muslim University (AMU) students, especially on social media. The issue was of blasphemy following a first information report filed by a member of AMU Students' Union (AMUSU) against Shehla Rashid, a student leader from Jawaharlal Nehru University in New Delhi.[1] Shehla Rashid was invited to an event in Aligarh, organized by AMUSU, which was postponed in the wake of this controversy. Shehla Rashid was accused for one of her Facebook posts, in which she had allegedly used blasphemous language against the Prophet. She had drawn a distinction between hate speech and hateful speech, essentially in the legal perspective, by using sentences about religious figures like Ram and the Prophet to illustrate her points.

The post offended and enraged numerous young Muslim students and many others associated with AMU – many missing the point that these were not Shehla Rashid's opinions about the Prophet or Lord Ram but simply examples of hateful epithets and offensive remarks about the Prophet, which are common on the Internet. Nevertheless, her nuanced distinction between hate speech and hateful speech did find several supporters among AMU students who clearly saw her line of argument.[2]

At the macro level, this incident becomes a metaphor to understand the shrill responses of many Muslims to anything they consider a threat to

---

[1] See Shreya Roy Chowdhury, 'Objections to JNU's Shehla Rashid Prompt Aligarh Muslim University Students to Postpone Event', *Scroll.in*, 17 February 2017, available at http://www.google.com/amp/s/amp.scroll.in/article/829604/objections-to-jnus-shehla-rashid-prompt-aligarh-muslim-university-to-postpone-event (accessed on 24 May 2018).

[2] Nadim Asrar, 'Open Letter to Shehla Rashid, from Former AMU Students Union Leader', *DailyO*, 20 February 2017, available at https://www.google.com/amp/s/www.dailyo.in/lite/politics/amu-jnu-hate-speech-shehla-rashid-shora/story/1/5760.html (accessed on 24 May 2018).

their religion – whether it is the Shah Bano case of 1985 or the more recent debates in India about the practice of triple *talaq*. All hell certainly breaks loose when it comes to the reaction of the Muslims to the real or alleged insult of the Prophet.

How did Sir Sayyid Ahmad Khan, the founder of AMU, react to such situations during his time? He faced many similar issues, including the dishonouring of the Prophet and the charge of irreconcilability of Islam with modernity, but his response to these issues was never emotive, knee-jerk, or irrational. His articles and books written on Islam, the Prophet, and the cultural life of Muslims acquire a prescient quality when seen in the context of many twenty-first century debates.

His responses to the contents of a book or article he considered offensive or blasphemous have relevance beyond his time. In an analytical article titled 'Blasphemy and Conversion Debate and Sir Syed', Shafey Kidwai refers to two incidents from Sir Sayyid's life when he very thoughtfully addressed blasphemy.[3] One incident is related to Sir Sayyid's support to a resolution passed by Muhammadan Educational Congress in 1884 against the book *Establishment of the British Rule in India* by A. Coxe. This book was prescribed in the syllabus of Allahabad University, but contained opinions about Islam and Muslims which were considered offensive by a section of the Muslim community. Sir Sayyid took up the matter with the director of the Office of Public Instructions, North-West Provinces, and wrote a letter to the Registrar of Allahabad University about the issue. Consequently, the book was withdrawn from syllabus and replaced by a different one.

Discussing the other incident from Sir Sayyid's life, Kidwai refers to a 'dispassionate editorial' titled 'Religious Root in Bombay' in *Aligarh Institute Gazette*, written in response to a clash between Muslims and Parsees in Bombay after the publication of a translation of a book containing derogatory remarks about the Prophet. In the editorial, Sir Sayyid laments the lack of understanding between the two communities. He makes a case against deliberately insulting the beliefs of the other community and suggests two possible courses of action if the religious sentiments of a community are hurt: either write a rejoinder or seek a legal remedy by

---

[3] Shafey Kidwai, 'Blasphemy and Conversion Debate and Sir Syed', in *Sir Syed Ahmad Khan: Muslim Renaissance Man of India – A Bicentenary Commemorative Volume*, ed. Abdur Raheem Kidwai, pp. 140–52 (New Delhi: Viva Books, 2017).

approaching the government. He emphasizes that under no circumstances should people resort to violence:

> If it is true, then nobody could claim that writing hatred and ridicule filled book has religious sanction. If publication of such material leaves one community hurt, it may either write back or seek constitutional remedy by approaching the government. One must not try to settle the issue by itself. Our government must put a complete ban on the publication of such nasty books that are aimed at denouncing or despising the other religion. The newspapers and journals carrying religious debates in intemperate language must not be allowed publication. The government must enact strict laws and articles that fanning religious hatred should be treated at par with the act that inflames sedition.[4]

He lived in a different time and faced different circumstances. Still, because Sir Sayyid was not only a writer of distinction but a journalist as well, the comparison of his words with those of many contemporary writers with a modern perspective would yield interesting results. A January 2017 statement issued by Pen International on the anniversary of the *Charlie Hebdo* Attack heavily reprimanded different governments for their repressive measures on the pretext of security:

> This kind of governmental response is chilling because a particularly insidious threat to our right to free expression is self-censorship. In order to fully exercise the right to freedom of expression, individuals must be able to communicate without fear of intrusion by the State. Under international law, the right to freedom of expression also protects speech that some may find shocking, offensive or disturbing. Importantly, the right to freedom of expression means that those who feel offended also have the right to challenge others through free debate and open discussion, or through peaceful protest.[5]

---

[4] *Aligarh Institute Gazette* 9, no. 10 (6 March 1874): 124–125 (trans. Shafey Kidwai).

[5] Pen International, 'On the Anniversary of the *Charlie Hebdo* Attack Dissenting Voices Must Be Protected', 2017, available at http://www.pen-international.org/newsitems/anniversary-charlie-hebdo/ (accessed on 9 July 2017).

Clearly, unlike Pen International's categorical advocacy of freedom of speech, Sir Sayyid was not a votary of absolute freedom, though he carried the motto 'Liberty of the press is a prominent duty of the government and natural right of the subject' on the masthead of *Aligarh Institute Gazette*, a journal edited and published by him. He was not averse to appealing to the government to ban a publication if it preached deliberate hatred, or at least for decency's sake, he does not appear to believe in the right to offend. In other words, he did not consider some self-censorship to be inappropriate.

From today's perspective when freedom of speech and right to offend go hand in hand, seeking government intervention to ban the publication of a book definitely seems problematic. However, just because Sir Sayyid thought of banning hate speech and removing a book from a syllabus by appealing to the government, he cannot be charged as intolerant. His sentiment was against publications fanning religious hatred. He was thus appealing to the government of the day to decide what constituted hate speech. He proposed his demands without fuss or violent demonstrations.

The two aforementioned incidents reveal Sir Sayyid's reluctance to just let go the matter of hate speech and 'blasphemy' if it concerned the Prophet. He practised the two solutions suggested: seeking government intervention for getting a controversial book removed and writing a rejoinder to a book.

Raising objections against a book and petitioning the government to ban it may seem to be a relatively easy task, but writing a rejoinder to a book is a tougher proposition. Sir Sayyid followed this modernist method of refutation in his career many times and intellectually engaged with his opponents. Thus, in a section of his book *Tabyin-ul Kalam* (which shows his unflinching faith in the historical and geographical veracity of the Bible), he responds to Bishop Colenso's objections regarding the unhistorical characters of many stories in the Bible. He also wrote 'Review of W.W. Hunter's Indian Musulman' (1872), wherein he refuted the charges against Islam and Muslims made by Hunter in the book *The Indian Musalmans: Are They Bound in Conscience to Rebel Against the Queen?* (1871). The most famous example of his writing a rejoinder, however, is *Life of Muhammad* (1870), which required painstaking scholarship and an arduous journey overseas.

In general, books on philosophical and religious issues have a longer shelf life than do books on other topics. This is because many philosophical and religious debates refuse to die down. Sir Sayyid's *Life of Muhammad* is a collection of twelve essays and is a book that continues to have an afterlife because the form and manner of Sir Sayyid's responses and the issues he addresses in the book remain relevant even today. This is an exercise in *seerat nigari*,[6] but as Obaidullah Fahad says, 'the material of *seerat* (biography) has been approached from the perspective of analysis and literary criticism'.[7] The book not only is an informed critique of many historical and biographical works on the life and times of the Prophet but also provides a comparative perspective on Islam, Christianity, and Judaism in a very sympathetic manner.[8]

There is a saying that the more things change, the more they stay the same. Even after a century and a half of its publication, the book continues to speak to a twenty-first century audience because the context of writing *Life of Muhammad* keeps reinventing itself. Thus, discussing the context of writing this book and the efforts that Sir Sayyid made to achieve his task becomes essential.

The book was a rejoinder to William Muir's *The Life of Mahomet*. Muir's book, the first and second volumes of which had come out in 1858, and a portion of which had appeared in the form of newspaper articles even before that, was published in 1861 in four volumes. Characteristically subtitled 'From Original Sources', this book adopted the objective tone of a historian, displaying the historian's sceptical attitude towards his material. Muir based his book on four sources: the Qur'an, traditions, contemporary documents, and Arabic poetry. However, contemporary documents and Arabic poetry also depended on traditions. In the book, the material is organized very neatly, making it a good read even today. The discussion of traditions in the book appears so convincing that a person not very familiar with Islam and its tenets may not find anything amiss in Muir's views. However, some major problems exist in the treatment of Islam by Muir. Despite an apparent neutral tone, he frequently invokes the 'we Christians' and 'they Muslims' terminology. More importantly, he questions the Islamic concept of revelation, which he calls 'Mahomet's alleged divine direction', and asks whether the words of the Prophet were

---

[6] As a genre, *seerat nigari* is inspired by the personality, ideas, values, and teachings of the Prophet. Both Muslim and non-Muslim writers have tried their hands at this genre.

[7] Obaidullah Fahad, 'Maaruzat', in *Kutbat-e-Ahmadiyah: Maqalat Seminar KaIntikhab*, ed. Obaidullah Fahad and Lateef Husain Kazmi, pp. 1–2 (Aligarh: Seerat Committee, 2016), p. 2.

[8] See Gulfishan Khan, 'Sir Syed's Life of the Prophet: Eastern Sources', in *Sir Syed Ahmad Khan: Muslim Renaissance Man of India – A Bicentenary Commemorative Volume*, ed. Abdur Raheem Kidwai, pp. 111–30 (New Delhi: Viva Books, 2017).

inspired or revealed.[9] In other words, he incorrectly considers the Prophet the author of the Qur'an. He also implies that the Qur'an was a work of ordinary composition, that the Prophet did the writing and appropriated the Jewish sources.[10] He also questions the organization of the material in the Qur'an. The neutral and objective tone of the historian used in the book often gives way to an evaluative vocabulary reflecting his bias: 'It was a fond conceit of Mohammad.'[11] 'Abrahamic genealogy ... as mere plagiarisms from rabbinical lore.'[12] Despite praising the Prophet for the better part of his book, Muir's representation of Muhammad cannot go down well with most Muslims – conservative or moderate. Muir refers to the Prophet as 'vindictive' with 'unrelenting hatred for his enemies'[13] and as the one who laughed 'immoderately'. He also presents the Prophet as weak and dispirited. Muir's proselytizing instinct gets the better of him at many places in the book. About the Prophet, he writes, 'He might have become Christian.'[14]

Although greatly disturbed by William Muir's account in the book, Sir Sayyid did not think about taking any legal steps against the book for several reasons. First, the book was published in Britain, where no law against blasphemy existed to protect Islam or the Prophet. Second, even if he proved that the book had hurt the sentiments of the Muslims and twisted important facts of their beliefs, the use of the material by Muir for research would not have hurt in any way. This point was not missed by the committee that, sixty odd years later in 1924, framed Section 295(A) of Indian Penal Code, which criminalized malicious acts intended to outrage religious feelings of any class by insulting its religion.[15] Muhammad Ali Jinnah, a member of the

---

[9] William Muir, *The Life of Mahomet: From Original Sources* (1861, repr. New Delhi: Voice of India, 2002), p. 42.
[10] Ibid., p. 102.
[11] Ibid., p. lxii.
[12] Ibid.
[13] Ibid., p. 27.
[14] Ibid., 21.
[15] A look at the legal history of India suggests that Section 295(A), which deals with hate speech, came into existence after very strong protests by the Muslim community against the publication of a book titled *Rangila Rasul* ('The Colourful Prophet') by an anonymous writer in Punjab in 1924. As the book's self-explanatory title suggests, the book slandered the private life of the Prophet very offensively. However, the publisher of the book, Rajpal, was tried in the court of law under Section 153(A) by Justice Dilip Singh of the Lahore High Court. Although the judge found the book very objectionable, he found no concrete evidence against Rajpal and acquitted him. In his judgment

committee that made the act, wrote that 'the fundamental principle that those who are engaged in historical works, those who are engaged in the ascertainment of truth and those who are engaged in bona fide and honest criticisms of a religion shall be protected'.[16]

Third and the most important reason was that as a scholar and a public intellectual, Sir Sayyid decided to channel his anger and hurt in a more positive direction. The thought of writing a response to Muir's book occupied his mind, but only after his visit to England did he finally begin work on his book. In 1869, Sir Sayyid's travelled to England accompanying his son Sayyid Mahmud, who had he won a scholarship to study there. During his seventeen-month stay in England and after working very hard, Sir Sayyid could complete writing his response to Muir's book. Altaf Husain Hali, Sir Sayyid's biographer, writes about the efforts that he made in writing his response:

> He got books from the library of India Office. He collected a lot of information from the library of British Museum. He procured many biographies of the Prophet which were published from Egypt, France and Germany. Many rare Latin and old English books were bought at a very high price from the markets of London. After continuously working day in day out, he wrote 12 essays and got them translated

---

though the judge observed 'that a clause might well be added to section 295 by which the publication of pamphlets published with the intention of wounding the religious feelings of any person or of insulting the religion of any person might be made criminal' (quoted in Shoaib Daniyal, 'A Short History of the Blasphemy Law Used against Wendy Doniger and Why It Must Go', *Scroll.in*, 18 February 2014, available at https://scroll.in/article/656608/a-short-history-of-the-blasphemy-law-used-against-wendy-doniger-and-why-it-must-go, accessed on 9 July 2017). This observation was made in the context of cases of communal violence between Muslims and Arya Samajist groups in Punjab. In view of the deteriorating law and order situation and the fear of communal flare-ups, the British brought into existence Section 295(A). As it now stands, Section 295A of the Indian Penal Code refers to 'Whoever, with deliberate and malicious intention of outraging the religious feelings of any class of [citizens of India], [by words, either spoken or written, or by signs or by visible representations or otherwise], insults or attempts to insult the religion or the religious beliefs of that class, shall be punished with imprisonment of either description for a term which may extend to [three years], or with fine, or both' (https://indiankanoon.org/doc/1803184/, accessed on 9 July 2017).

[16] Quoted in Daniyal, 'A Short History of the Blasphemy Law'.

by a competent Englishman and published them in England itself with the title Life of Mohammad.[17]

In a letter to Mehdi Ali, one of Sir Sayyid's closest associates, written from England, he expresses his reaction to Muir's book and his determination to write its rejoinder:

> My mind is a bit agitated these days. I am looking at Mr William's book about the Prophet and it has disturbed me. My heart is burnt to cinders to see his prejudices and unfairness. I have made a firm resolve, and it was there since long, that I should write a biography of the Prophet. I don't care even if all my money is spent, and I am reduced to beggary. On the day of judgement when asked to present myself I will be introduced as one who died in beggary in the name of his ancestor Muhammad.[18]

Notably, Sir Sayyid Ahmad Khan did not have much knowledge of the English language.[19] His references to spending money and fearing imminent beggary in the aforementioned quote is with regard to his expenses for buying books, paying translators, and travelling to different places.

Many of Sir Sayyid's letters from England indicate his commitment, singleness of purpose, and perseverance, even despite acute economic worries. In a letter to Mehdi Hasan Khan, Sir Sayyid asks Khan to go to a moneylender and borrow one thousand rupees on interest for him. He also tells Khan that he has arranged to sell his books and his other possessions, including the utensils in the house, for raising one thousand rupees.[20] In

---

[17] Altaf Husain Hali, *Hayat-e Javed* (Lahore: Punjab Academy, 1957), p. 492.
[18] Shaikh Ismail Panipati (ed.), *Maktubat-e Sir Sayyid* (Lahore: Majlis-e Taraqqi-e Adab, 1959), p. 62.
[19] In his book, *Sir Sayyid: Daroon-e Khana* (Aligarh: Educational Book House, 2006), pp. 92–3, Iftikhar Alam Khan makes the point that Sir Sayyid read English newspapers regularly, but he could not write in English. He wrote his English speeches in the Urdu script. Historian David Lelyveld also mentions that Sir Sayyid 'had some slight conversational ability in English'; see his *Aligarh's First Generation: Muslim Solidarity in British India* (New Delhi: Oxford University Press, 1996), p. 105.
[20] Panipati, *Maktubat-e Sir Sayyid*, pp. 74–5 (my translation). Iftikhar Alam Khan explains that here the reference is not to Sir Sayyid's rich collection of books, but to his stock of books in Delhi, which he often sold. For an entire account

another letter, Sir Sayyid writes, 'My dreams and sleep are taken away by this book. I am writing Life of Muhammad day in day out. I have given up all other works. Continuous writing has caused me back ache.'[21]

From the beginning, Sir Sayyid knew that he was writing this book for English readers. Hence, the English translation of his text, originally written in Urdu, had to be very good. His concern was genuine. Eventually, his efforts did pay off as the English translation of this book is more accurate than many modern translations of his essays and other writings.

So, what other Muslim scholars of his times were doing, and were they also offended by Muir's book? Unfortunately, no response of other Muslims to Muir's book has been recorded.

People often get offended by the content of a book not by reading it, but by listening to word of mouth about it. One person reads the book and then comments on it; eventually, the word circulates, causing mild to extreme reactions against the book. In 1860s, very few Indian Muslims read English texts; thus, the number of readers who would have read Muir's book would have been negligible in any case. (In fact, the lack of English education among Muslims led to the establishment of Muhammadan Anglo-Oriental College a decade and a half later.) Because Muir's book was written at the height of British imperial power, it had a global impact, including that in several Muslim countries. However, the combined number of English readers in Muslim countries then was not expected to be very large. The discussion of Muir's book was received by an average Muslim through its discussion in the vernacular.[22] Sir Sayyid's decision of writing a rejoinder became important because at a time when there was no dearth of Islamic scholars in the Muslim world, he alone decided to respond to this challenge.

---

of Sir Sayyid's management of his finances during his England visit, see Khan, *Sir Sayyid: Daroon-e Khana*, pp. 118–23.

[21] Panipati, *Maktubat-e Sir*, p. 68 (my translation). Iftikhar Alam Khan does not agree with Hali's view (in *Hayat-e Javed*) that a reason for Sir Sayyid's visit to England was to collect material to write a response to Muir's book. The thought of writing this response occupied his mind – maybe since 1858 – but he was silent for almost a decade. It was only when he reached England that he decided to write his rejoinder, reasoned Khan in a personal interview with the author (1 July 2017).

[22] In his *Review on Dr. Hunter's Indian Musalmans: Are They Bound in Conscience to Rebel Against the Queen?* Sir Sayyid reveals that unlike works of English literature, anything on subjects such as 'the state of feeling of the English to the natives, religious questions, or matters affecting taxes' reaches the common people of India (Lahore: Premier Book House, n.d., p. 5).

William Hemingway defines courage as grace under pressure. Sir Sayyid displayed grace under pressure while he wrote a response to Muir. In various ways, his decision to join issues with Muir was courageous. In his prolegomenon to *Khutbat-e Ahmadiya*, Shaikh Ismael Panipati writes:

> The world is full of timid, cowardly and flattery-loving people and they are present in all eras. Therefore, when it became known that Sir Sayyid Ahmad Khan was going to England to write a response to William Muir's book, many of Sir Sayyid's acquaintances tried to discourage him from doing this. They invoked the unsuitability of times and told him that the occasion, time and expediency did not ask for this kind of extreme step. ' Why on earth do you risk your life'; you will lose your job and freedom; Not only do you risk imprisonment but, it is quite possible, you could even be hanged; the Revolt is just past you and the anger of Englishmen has not subsided; you will burn in the fire of this anger; you just escaped death when you wrote *Causes for the Revolt of India* and endangered your life; you are repeating that silly mistake and are inviting a new trouble(for you) by writing another book.[23]

Undeterred by fear or by the thought of expediency, Sir Sayyid wrote *Life of Muhammad*. Therein, he responds to not only Muir's arguments but also those of other Orientalists, who had written about Islam. He addresses contentious issues like polygamy and slavery. He does not engage with Muir in every passage, but attacks his main objections against Islam and the Prophet in different chapters of the book. In the preface, Sir Sayyid clarifies that he is a believer of Islam, without compromising the spirit of critical inquiry and investigation whatsoever: 'As far as my own search after true religion is concerned, I sincerely and conscientiously assert that I have found Islam to be most undoubtedly the true religion, that is, its genuine and chief principles are in perfect harmony with that true one which I have defined to be true religion.'[24]

---

[23] Quoted in Abu Sufian Islahi (trans.), 'Khutbat-e Ahmadiyah: Tahlil-o Tajziya', in *Khutbat-e Ahmadiyah: Maqalat Seminar Ka Intikhab*, ed. Obaidullah Fahad and Lateef Husain Kazmi, pp. 25–68 (Aligarh: Seerat Committee, 2016), pp. 29–30. I am grateful to Abu Sufian Islahi for his help in locating important sources in Urdu for this article.

[24] Sayyid Ahmad Khan, *Life of Muhammad* (1870, repr. New Delhi: Cosmos Books, 2002), p. xvii.

However, while writing this biography of the Prophet, Sir Sayyid unambiguously advocates the need of a 'process of a severe and critical examination'[25] for examining *hadith*s – be they in *Sahih Muslim* or *Sahih al-Bukhari*, two of the most authentic *hadith* collections to understand the Prophet's life. Sir Sayyid considered many other sources – generally used by the biographers of Muhammad, such as Ibn Ishaq, Ibn Hisham, Tibree, Secrati Shamee, Al Waqidi, Abulfeda (Sir Sayyid praises him liberally), and Mawahib Ladonneyah – 'a confused collection of indiscriminate and uninvestigated traditions'.[26] In fact, more than Muir, Sir Sayyid was fully convinced that thoroughly interrogating and establishing the authenticity of *hadith*s was required. Through his different writings, he reiterates this subject.

In *Life of Muhammad*, he also considers the work of many other European writers who had written about the Prophet. He praises Edward Gibbon, Godfrey Higgins, Thomas Carlyle, and John Davenport for their positive account of the Prophet. Among the other European writers on the Prophet, he finds Sprenger's biography as being 'warped by prejudice and bigotry'.[27]

Sir Sayyid certainly knew a thing or two about how not to make a public refutation unpleasant. The detailed discussion of the blind spots in Muir's book is preceded by Sir Sayyid's high praise for his work: 'The best of all biographies of Muhammad from the pen of foreign authors, and the one which is executed in the most learned manner, is the *Life of Mahomet* by Sir William Muir.'[28] Nonetheless, Sir Sayyid's critiques that 'the simplest and plainest facts connected with Islam and Mohammed had been strained and twisted and distorted ... subjected to the Procrustes' process in order to make them the indices or exponents of the author's prepossessions and prejudices'.[29] The reasons Sir Sayyid advances for the weaknesses in Muir's work are related to both the intentions and methodology of Muir. As for the intentions, Muir undertook the work at the insistence of C. G. Pfander, a Christian missionary, whom Sayyid calls a Christian apologist. As such, Muir's work had its beginning in a missionary's prejudice against Islam. This is followed by a more serious charge about the sources Muir used for writing the book. Among the Islamic sources, Muir heavily depended on

---

[25] Sayyid Ahmad Khan, *Life of Muhammad*, p. xviii.
[26] Ibid., p. xix.
[27] Ibid., p. xxii.
[28] Ibid., p. xxiii.
[29] Ibid., p. xxv.

Al Waqidi (747–823 CE), whom Sir Sayyid calls 'the worst author of all, and of the least credit, and all Mohammedan doctors and divines have declared him not to be, in the least degree, of any authority, as being the least entitled to credit'.[30] Muir cites Al Waqidi liberally in his book, whereas Sir Sayyid repeatedly describes him as unreliable in his rejoinder.

For his disagreement with Muir's arguments on Islamic history and the life of the Prophet, Sir Sayyid often uses a highly evaluative vocabulary to articulate his sense of hurt. He maintains a fine balance between irony and understatement while commenting on the methods by which Muir has presented the history of the rise of Mecca and its religion. He accuses Muir of resorting to 'conjectures' and 'gratuitous fictions', comments on his 'fertile brain' and his 'airy' and 'active' imagination. Muir's account of the history of Mecca appears so fanciful that Sayyid dismisses it with one evaluative sentence: 'But as these emanations from his quill are neither historical facts, nor local traditions, nor scripture [sic] truths, but the mere offspring of Sir William's wonder-working fancy, and destitute as they are of all support and corroboration from reliable authority, we do not think it worthwhile to give them a place in our Essay.'[31] As is obvious from this sentence, Sir Sayyid's attacks on Muir are directed at Muir's failure to use reliable sources and his reliance on conjectures and his imagination to fill gaps in his account.

By using reasoning and logic, Sir Sayyid counters many of Muir's arguments, particularly the discussion of some Islamic traditions. He states a generally acceptable opinion that authenticity of a tradition has to be established through careful investigation, but chides Muir for considering the Islamic traditions 'mere fabrications or inventions of the narrators and other persons.'[32] He then considers this assertion of Muir to be a hasty generalization – 'a mere assertion without proof' superseding 'argument altogether ... cutting the Gordian knot, instead of untying it'.[33] With regard to Muir's discussion of some specific traditions, Sir Sayyid counters his description that the Prophet was born circumcised as an occurrence 'contrary to the usual course of nature'.[34] Referring to examples of hermaphroditism and lusus naturae, Sir Sayyid explains how 'an occasional deviation from

---

[30] Sayyid Ahmad Khan, *Life of Muhammad*, p. xx.
[31] Ibid., p. 145.
[32] Ibid., p. 301.
[33] Ibid., p. 188.
[34] Ibid., p. 191.

nature's natural course is by no means uncommon; a fact which at once accounts for Muhammad's being born minus a prepuce'.[35] His reasoning also includes a reference to the sacred Arab custom of circumcision and the historical fact that 'circumcision was never performed on him'.[36]

Sir Sayyid's reasoning spirit finds its best expression in his discussion of the Prophetic seal. On the authority of Safia, a wife of the Prophet, Muir says that the Prophetic seal 'was written upon his (Muhammad's) back, in letters of light'.[37] Sir Sayyid does not attach any importance to this and explains in simple terms that the Prophetic seal was the result of Muslim devotion to the Prophet:

> The real fact appears to be that, as everything connected with the Prophet was regarded with reverence, his followers, thinking that it would be rather derogatory to the Prophet himself, as well as a want of respect and consideration on their part to call the fleshy excrescence of his body with the common name of mole or wart, figuratively designated it by a more exalted appellation of the 'prophetic seal'.[38]

Sir Sayyid was puzzled to know that not only Muir but almost all Christian writers had written that the Prophet suffered from epilepsy. On setting out to correct this historical inaccuracy, Sir Sayyid discovered that this misconception has arisen because of 'mistranslation into Latin, by Dr Pococke, of some of the passages in Abulfeda's work'[39] as well as the superstitions of the Greek, who attributed epilepsy to some god or evil spirit. Sir Sayyid approvingly quotes Gibbon who called the alleged epilepsy of the Prophet 'an absurd calumny of the Greeks'.[40] Through further research, backed by his reasoning, Sir Sayyid wonders how Muir could believe that his 'epileptic swoons ... gave him the idea of his divine mission'.[41] He reasons that it was impossible for people to consider an epileptic individual a Prophet, particularly when he destroyed idolatry of his people.

Sir Sayyid defends the organization of material in the Qur'an and believes that Muir misses this point because of his failure to see the literary quality of

---

[35] Sayyid Ahmad Khan, *Life of Muhammad*, p. 191.
[36] Ibid.
[37] Ibid.
[38] Ibid.
[39] Ibid., p. 199.
[40] Ibid., p. 201.
[41] Ibid., p. 204.

the holy book. He also rejects Muir's view that part of the Qur'an may have been lost – a point which appears in many Orientalist accounts. Similarly, he rejects Muir's view of the existence of a second recension of the Qur'an during Khalifa Usman's period. He emphasizes the role of memory and the extreme care taken in the *Isnad* tradition to preserve the original word of the Qur'an. The concept of *Nasikh-Mansookh*, whereby some verses are abrogated and cancelled, may apply to earlier scriptures, but not the Qur'an, which was revealed after the Torah and the Bible and thus is complete in all respects.

At times, Sir Sayyid quotes the Christian scriptures to counter many of Muir's arguments. Thus, when Muir levels the charge of severity and sternness against the Prophet in not praying for his mother's salvation, Sir Sayyid brings in the authority of Athanasian Creed: 'And this is the Christian faith, which, except a man believe, he cannot be saved'.[42] Similarly, he quotes a passage from Matthew xiv to counter Muir's disbelief in the Prophet's family being satisfied with its meal when he shared it with them.[43]

As such, although Sir Sayyid was potentially badly hurt by the contents of Muir's book, his rejoinder was aimed to make only sound arguments. Therein, Sir Sayyid emerges a sane argumentative Indian man in his stance. Unsurprisingly, after this, his relationship with Muir remained cordial, despite these serious disagreements.

How does one explain the tone, tenor, and form of Sir Sayyid's response in the book? How did he acquire this spirit of inquiry, this rational thinking, and this modernist method of refutation and debate in public sphere? All these aspects of his thinking are not confined to his response to Muir. They can be seen in almost all his works on politics and religion, most prominently in his articles in *Aligarh Institute Gazette* and *Tahzib-ul Akhlaq*. His interpretation of the Qur'an, *Tafsir al-Qur'an wa al Huwa al-Huda was al-Furqan*, written later (in 1891), did not go down well with the 'ulama, for he has used excessive reasoning and logic in the book.

This rational approach of Sir Sayyid came from his thoughtful mind, his deep reading of the works of many Islamic thinkers and philosophers, and his exposure to Western ideas. These two strands in his thought, the influence of a long philosophical tradition in Islam, and a keenness to learn from the West characterized his thinking and actions throughout his life. Always receptive to new ideas, his approach was anything but dogmatic. He could

---

[42] Sayyid Ahmad Khan, *Life of Muhammad*, p. 205.
[43] Ibid.

change his views on reflection or finding new evidence. For instance, in his early writings he held the view that Sun revolves around Earth, he gradually came to accept the Copernican view of the revolution of Earth around Sun.

After thorough research, Christian W. Troll comprehensively describes the development of Sir Sayyid's theological views in the book *Sayyid Ahmad Khan: A Reinterpretation of Muslim Theology*. Therein, he identifies three early influences on Sir Sayyid – Naqshbandiyah Mujaddidiyah, Shah Wali Ullah's thoughts, and the Mujahidin movement. The *Sufi* influence in Sir Sayyid's life was more in the nature of inner purification than in the niceties of Islamic law. Shah Waliullah's discussion of *taqlid* and *ijtihad*, his harmonization of different traditions in Islam, his sense of history, and his efforts to establish the relevance of Islamic law exerted some influence.[44] The Mujahidin movement's emphasis on the Qur'an and the Islam of the Prophet also appealed to Sir Sayyid.

Before writing his commentary on the Qur'an, Sir Sayyid read different commentaries on the Qur'an and *hadith*s and found most of them unsatisfactory. He was well read in Mu`tazilite philosophy, which laid great emphasis on rationalism and sought harmony between faith and reason. His denial of miracles shared commonalities with the Mu`tazilite philosophy. He bore the influence of Fakhruddin Razi and Ibn-e Rushd in his strong belief in rationalism. He and Razi shared common links – their reasoning about the authenticity of *hadith*s and their reliance on the use of intellect in all matters were similar. Sir Sayyid's most discussed dictum of seeking harmony between the word of God and the work of God – a key aspect of his rationalism, which appears in all his works, including *Life of Muhammad* – has some similarity with Ibn Rushd's reconciliation of religion and science. In case of any conflict between the two, as Troll puts it, the meaning of the scripture 'must be interpreted metaphorically'.[45] There is also something common between Sir Sayyid's ideas and those of his contemporary Egyptian scholar Muhammad Abduh, especially regarding their startlingly radical views on angelology, Satan, Adam, and miracles.[46] In fact, very little in Sir Sayyid's rational approach to Islam had not been attempted before by

---

[44] Christian W. Troll, *Sayyid Ahmad Khan: A Reinterpretation of Muslim Theology* (New Delhi: Vikas Publishing House, 1978), pp. 30–1.
[45] Ibid., p. 170.
[46] See Abdur Raheem Kidwai, 'Sir Syed's Tafsir Al-Quran', in *Sir Syed Ahmad Khan: A Centenary Tribute*, ed. Asloob A. Ansari, pp. 69–89 (Delhi: Adam Publishers and Distributers, 2017), p. 89.

Muslim philosophers and thinkers, but to his credit, he forcefully brought these points in the new context of the challenge coming from the West, so as to show that Islam and modernity were not irreconcilable.

Although the influence of Mu'tazilites and other traditions in Islamic philosophy on Sir Sayyid is fairly obvious, the influence of the West on his worldview – clearly reflected in his decisions, actions, and ideas – is not backed by concrete evidence. The influence of the West on him resulted from the currency and ascendancy of Western ideas in India, his interaction with the English people, and his visit to England when he experienced and saw many things first-hand. Troll refers to C. F. Andrews' memoir of Maulvi Zakaullah, in which the author outlines the spread of modern education in Delhi, particularly the education of science, and its impact on the educated sections of Delhi.[47] Andrews uses the term 'Delhi Renaissance' to emphasize the nature and influence of this scientific education, distinguishing it from the literary nature of 'Bengal Renaissance'. As a Delhi man who was always abreast of his times, Sir Sayyid was certainly exposed to these ideas.

Asloob Ahmad Ansari conjectures that Sir Sayyid was influenced by eighteenth-century rationalists and Lockean empiricists during his stay in England:

> His son, Sayyid Mahmud, himself a prodigy of Nature in virtue of his superb and enormous cognitive powers, and staying with him at that time, may well have been instrumental in Sir Sayyid's getting acquainted, however, superficially, with the Western modes of thought, which left him overwhelmed.[48]

Sir Sayyid's firm belief in the law of causality and the infallibility of reason, very much evident in *Life of Muhammad*, owes greatly to his exposure to eighteenth-century English rationalist philosophy. Ansari sees parallels between Sir Sayyid's conception of God and the British Deists:

> Sir Syed tries to explore religious truth and the nature of the Deity or Allah by looking up for inspiration and sustainment, to the eighteenth century British Deists, the leading spirits among whom were John Toland, Matthew Tindal, Anthony Collins and William Woodstan

---

[47] Troll, *Sayyid Ahmad Khan*, p. 150.
[48] See Asloob A. Ansari, 'Sir Syed Ahmad Khan: An Apologist for Rationalism', in *Sir Syed Ahmad Khan: A Centenary Tribute*, ed. Asloob A. Ansari, pp. 271–90 (Delhi: Adam Publishers and Distributors, 2017).

who believed in religion but did not quite recognize the need and validity of revelation, and made short shrift of its supernatural machinery and Sir Sayyid appeared to follow them at close heels.[49]

Although Sir Sayyid did not deny revelation, his emphasis on reason as his guiding principle explains his distrust of miracles and angelology.

Sir Sayyid certainly admired the all-round progress of England during his visit, but he did not create a good East–bad West binary – which characterized the approach of both his admirers and critics. Because he advocated the universal message of Islam, harmonizing the good qualities of the West with the virtues of Islam was not difficult for him. In a very strong defence of Sir Sayyid's rational approach, which potentially influenced Iqbal and Maulana Maudoodi greatly in the twentieth century, Syed Asim Ali asserts, 'He discovered it as a lost Islamic value via West. In his approach, interestingly enough, *maghribiyat* (the Western) appears much closer to the original Islam than *mashriqiyat* (the Eastern).'[50] In other words, Sir Sayyid could discover true Islam – which seemed lost in obscurantism and blind adherence during his time – in Western emphasis on education, reason, progress, and scientific spirit.

Taken together, Sir Sayyid's engagement with the West – both at the level of its intellectual influence on his thought and his sympathetic and thoughtful adoption of its strength – suggests that abundant content in his oeuvre resists any attempt to localize him within his time and his geographical location. A revisionist reading of his work and actions reveals him to be a thinker on the world stage.

Based on this entire discussion of Sir Sayyid's intervention in the religio-political controversies of his time and their relevance to the present times, some conclusions can be drawn. When Sir Sayyid takes recourse to hard work and incisive scholarship for responding to works he disagrees with, focus on modern education in his other ventures, preach restraint in the face of extreme provocation, and speak against violence under all circumstances, he was taking a line against the thoughtless assertion of Muslim identity. This thoughtless assertion of identity is a very common phenomenon in the twenty-first century. The call for banning a book or film because its subject hurts the religious sentiment of some groups often results in fiery protests

---

[49] Ansari, 'Sir Syed Ahmad Khan', p. 287.
[50] See Syed Asim Ali, 'Sir Syed's Attitude to the West', in *Sir Syed Ahmad Khan: A Centenary Tribute*, ed. Asloob A. Ansari, pp. 308–21 (Delhi: Adam Publishers and Distributors, 2017), pp. 371–2.

on the street, loud demonstrations, and even, terrorist activities directed against the authors, publishers, or producers. Some of the examples include the ban on *The Satanic Verses*,[51] the *fatwa* against Salman Rushdie, and the Danish cartoon controversy, leading to the terrible murder of Theo Van Gogh.[52] Moreover, in a protest over the bad representation of the Prophet in the film *Innocence of Muslims*, more than fifty people lost their lives. The brutal killing of about a dozen people associated with *Charlie Hebdo*, a self-proclaimed irreverent French magazine, for publishing offensive cartoons of the Prophet is another major example of violence for the honour of the Prophet. All such incidents invariably trigger heated debates on the differences between hate speech and freedom of expression.

How should ordinary Muslims behave when they encounter deliberate or unintended provocation? With growing Islamophobia in many parts of the world and with technology ruling daily lives of people, the instances of disrespect to the Prophet and their easy spread have not only increased but cannot be prevented by laws alone.[53] Despite their belief in the right to offend, many mainstream publications do not publish material that is supposedly offensive to religious groups – not because they try to appease some religious groups, but because it is an editorial decision. Nevertheless, other publications like *Charlie Hebdo* may adopt a completely different editorial policy. On the Internet, any kind of opinion can find a place without any restriction whatsoever – be it offensive remarks against the Prophet or against anyone else's sacred beliefs.

---

[51] The history of protests over books and their banning by the powerful groups is very old. It is not specific to any particular group. In different times in history books as varied as Milton's *Aeropogetica* and Mark Twain's *Adventures of Huckleberry Finn* were banned. More recently A. K. Ramanujan's *Three Hundred Ramayanas* and Wendy Doniger's *The Hindus: An Alternative History* offended right-wing groups in India. In fact, countless books that supposedly offended people and were banned can be easily exemplified.

[52] See Ataullah Siddiqui, 'Sir Syed Ahmad Khan and the Honour of the Prophet: The Danish Cartoon Crisis in Perspective', in *Sir Syed Ahmad Khan: Muslim Renaissance Man of India – A Bicentenary Commemorative Volume*, ed. Abdur Raheem Kidwai, pp. 308–21 (New Delhi: Viva Books, 2017).

[53] Two recent incidents in India resulted from offensive Facebook posts. There were widespread demonstrations by Muslims in different cities following an offensive post by a small-time Hindu Mahasabha leader, Kamlesh Tiwari. In the second incident, a post by a teenager in Baduria region in West Bengal led to clashes and shutdowns.

The need for Muslims to exercise restraint was never greater than it is in the twenty-first century. With the rapid advancement of information technology, no news item today has a merely local significance. In this world, even a small incident can provoke reaction in distant parts of the world, generating meanings far beyond their original signification. Many such incidents can be easily engineered with ridiculous ease. A Facebook comment, a tweet, an impressionistic painting, a speech in an election rally, or a fake news item – all have the potential of becoming a headline on any news channel.

Emotional expression of public anger does not sit harmoniously with the liberal arguments about freedoms of speech and expression and right to offend. The exaggerated reaction of many Muslim groups has helped their opponents and has led to Muslims' being typecast as irrational, unreasonable, and intolerant to other viewpoints. The stereotype draws its force from its representation in popular media, journalism, literature, and street talk. The skewed perception – often strengthened by incidents of mindless violence committed in the name of Islam – shapes the common sense of people almost all over the world.

Sir Sayyid's method of engaging with his opponents in intellectual terms, his skill in carrying out reasoned debates, his perspicacity in not closing the possibility of dialogue, and his willingness to understand the other viewpoint have become more urgent than ever. His interest lay not in asserting Muslim identity but in strengthening it through education, clear thought, reform, reasonable conduct, and faith in the law of the land. His politics was the politics of dialogue and negotiation, rather than that of confrontation and conflict. This pragmatism was the result of the aftermath of the events of 1857 and his realization that the British power in India was there to stay. Strengthening Muslim identity through education, reform, and reasonable conduct, rather than assertion of identity through kneejerk reaction, shrill protest, provocative demonstration, and violent action, are the need of the hour for the twenty-first-century Muslims. Sir Sayyid bridges the gap between the past and present – between his turbulent period and ours in the twenty-first century.

11 Darwin or Design?
Examining Sayyid Ahmad Khan's Views on Human Evolution

SARAH A. QIDWAI

In an 1896 article in the Urdu journal *Tahzib-ul Akhlaq*, titled 'Adna Halat se Aala Halat par Insaan ki Taraqqi' (The Stages of Human Development from an Inferior to Superior State),[1] Sir Sayyid Ahmad Khan (1817–1898) wrote, 'The monkeys that exist today, orangutans and apes, are quite similar to humans in many ways. Darwin claims that middle chains are missing or extinct, but even if we found them, they would only prove similarities among kinds.'[2] Here, Sir Sayyid's reference to the English naturalist Charles Darwin (1809–1882) was not to discredit or defend Darwin's theory of evolution, but to support his own position on the topic, outlined in 'Adna Halat'. In the article, Sir Sayyid argued that humans evolved overtime from a common animal ancestor and this process is guided by a divine creator.[3] He also believed that this process was not antagonistic towards Islamic beliefs and the Qur'an. Overall, this position tied in with his general approach to the relationship between science and Islam, one where science was a part of Islam; the other part being the Qur'an.[4] Although most of Sir Sayyid's views on evolution have appeared in various articles he wrote over the

[1] Sayyid Ahmad Khan, 'Adna Halat se Aala Halat par Insaan ki Taraqqi' (The Stages of Human Development from an Inferior to Superior State), *Tahzib-ul Akhlaq* 2, no. 11 (1 Sha'baan 1313 Hijrah): 41–47, repr. in *Maqalat-e-Sir Sayyid*, ed. Muhammad Ismail Panipati (Lahore: Majlis-e Taraqqi-e Adab, 1962).
[2] Sayyid Ahmad Khan, 'Adna Halat se Aala Halat', unpublished translation by Sarah Qidwai.
[3] Darwin presented readers with two major arguments that living things have evolved or descended with modification from a common ancestor and that natural selection was the mechanism of this process. Natural selection is simply a process, where organisms that adapt to their environment tend to survive and produce more offspring.
[4] Sayyid Ahmad Khan, *Tabyin-ul Kalam* (The Muhammadan Commentary on the Holy Bible) (Ghazipur: Private press of the author, 1865), p. 44.

course of his life, 'Adna Halat' presents a detailed summary of his perspective regarding the origin and development of living things, including humans, from a common animal ancestor.

Today, the theory of evolution by natural selection is officially accepted by scientific establishments worldwide, including countries with a Muslim majority, but many people remain unconvinced or apprehensive about this theory.[5] While the scientific community continues to discuss and debate issues in the field of evolutionary biology, such as the role of genetics in the evolutionary process, some individuals are attempting to disprove the evolutionary thought all together.[6] Some of these individuals go back to Darwin and point out flaws in his theory of natural selection, like the lack of adequate understanding of inheritance, while others claim that life is too complicated to have developed by chance and to support various views of divine creation.[7] Providing evidence against a scientific theory backed with empirical observation and evidence is one thing, but discrediting it based on misinformation may lead to greater issues in the public sphere, including how evolution is taught in schools. Currently, this issue is even more apparent. For example, in August 2017, Turkey banned any mention of human evolution from high school curricula and textbooks, even though science foundations from numerous Islamic countries, including Turkey, in

---

[5] Salman Hameed, 'Bracing for Islamic Creationism', *Science* 322, no. 5908 (2008): 1637–8.

[6] In 2014, several experts published a debate in the journal *Nature* titled 'Does Evolutionary Theory Need a Rethink?' The sides were not debating the legitimacy of evolution, but whether the focus of research in the field required any changes. The side that argued to keep the field as it is said that a focus on genetic inheritance and process that change gene frequency was sufficient. The group that argued for a rework of the field claimed that the current framework was too narrow. They put forward a theory called extended evolutionary synthesis. For them, 'important drivers of evolution, ones that cannot be reduced to genes, must be woven into evolutionary theory'. They argued that organisms are constructed in development, not only by genes, and that embryology should be integrated with molecular genetics. See Kevin Laland, Tobias Uller, Marc Feldman, Kim Sterelny, Gerd B. Müller, Armin Moczek, Eva Jablonka, John Odling-Smee, Gregory A. Wray, Hopi E. Hoekstra, Douglas J. Futuyma, Richard E. Lenski, Trudy F. C. Mackay, Dolph Schluter, and Joan E. Strassmann, 'Does Evolutionary Theory Need a Rethink?' *Nature* 514, no. 7521 (2014): 161–4.

[7] *Creationism* refers to the position that a Divine Being (God) created the heavens, earth, and all living things. Creationists generally refer to the Bible, particularly the early chapters of Genesis and the creation story.

2008 signed a statement by the Interacademy Panel supporting the inclusion of evolution in school curricula.[8] In many cases, evolution is perceived as a Western, materialist concept, imported to Muslim countries, but this is not the case. In fact, Muslim philosophers have been proposing various theories of evolution from as early as the ninth century.

Sir Sayyid's arguments supporting human evolution offer two important interventions. First, he draws on, in my view, a legacy of Islamic scholars before him, who have presented the very idea, to make his arguments. Second, his approach to evolutionary thought presents some pedagogical advantages to teaching evolution today. With regard to the first intervention, a bulk of the scholarship in the field of the history of evolutionary biology limited itself to the origin of European evolutionary thought, its development and subsequent dissemination from the continent to the rest of the world. Of these works, a survey of early Islamic intellectuals and their theories of human development and evolution were left out.[9] This particular trend has led scholars to comment on evolution in response to Darwin and created a perception of the Eurocentric nature of evolutionary thought when actually the theory has developed over centuries, with numerous contributions from Muslim philosophers.[10] As for the second intervention about teaching evolution, Sir Sayyid's views on the topic presents another way to approach controversial scientific theories and address topics that seem contradictory to religious beliefs.

In this chapter, I argue that Sir Sayyid's views on human evolution are not only vital for discussing human evolution and shedding light on his perspectives on science and Islam, but also important in examining the legacy of Islamic scholars and their views on human development – an area that has been relatively ignored in discussions of evolution. Sir Sayyid's approach to human evolution can also be an important tool in teaching evolutionary biology, even in religious settings, if we focus on

---

[8] Kareem Shaheen, 'Turkish Schools to Stop Teaching Evolution, Official Says', *The Guardian*, 23 June 2017, available at https://www.theguardian.com/world/2017/jun/23/turkish-schools-to-stop-teaching-evolution-official-says (accessed on 5 September 2017).

[9] Recently, Marwa Elshakry's book *Reading Darwin in Arabic* has highlighted some aspects of evolutionary thought in the Middle East. She has also highlighted some older theories laid out by Islamic philosophers. See Marwa Elshakry, *Reading Darwin in Arabic* (Chicago: University of Chicago Press, 2013).

[10] See Eve-Marie Engels, Thomas F. Glick and Elinor S. Shaffer (eds), *The Reception of Charles Darwin in Europe* (London: Continuum, 2008).

this legacy in the Islamic context and the role of science in societies. Academic writings about Sir Sayyid generally focus on three aspects of his life: Some portray him as a leader of Indian Muslims and the father of Muslim nationalism in India, whereas others portray him as a prominent Islamic thinker; Moreover, many describe his educational reform agenda and the origins of Aligarh Muslim University (AMU).[11] Currently, we do not have a complete understanding of his views on scientific theories, such as the theory of evolution, and their effects on his reform agenda. To address this, the first part of this chapter is a summary and analysis of Sir Sayyid's article 'Adna Halat'. Next, I draw on certain arguments from the article and relate them to both Islamic scholars and Darwinians and then discuss how evolutionary thought was an importance part of reform agendas for Muslims in the nineteenth century. Finally, I address how we can use Sir Sayyid's approach on the topic in the field of education. Overall, in this chapter, I blend older Islamic theories with some developments in the history of biology by using Sir Sayyid as a guide.

SIR SAYYID'S THEORY OF EVOLUTION

Although Sir Sayyid has alluded to his views on evolution and the origin of living things in numerous texts throughout his life, 'Adna Halat' synthesizes his position on the topic and outlines a mechanism to account for human evolution. At this point in his life (1896), he was managing the Muhammadan Anglo-Oriental College (founded in 1875), coordinating the Muhammadan Educational Conference (established in 1886), and continuing his critique of the Indian National Congress.[12] However, he was aware of the evolutionary thought and Darwin well before this time.

One of the earliest indicators that Sir Sayyid was aware of Darwin's theory appears in 1864. In a letter to Sir Sayyid in response to his public address, C. A. Elliot Esquire, a member of the Scientific Society, founded in 1864, wrote, 'Darwin's *Origin of Species* is a book that should be read by the scholars in the society.'[13] Ultimately, members of The Scientific Society decided not to translate *Origin of Species*, but this letter confirms that Sir

---

[11] Christian Troll, *Sayyid Ahmad Khan: A Reinterpretation of Muslim Theology* (New Delhi: Vikas Publishing House, 1978), p. 3.

[12] David Lelyveld, *Aligarh's First Generation: Muslim Solidarity in British India* (Princeton: Princeton University Press, 1978), p. 305.

[13] Shan Muhammad (ed.), *The Aligarh Movement: Basic Documents, 1864–1898* (Meerut: Meenakshi Prakashan, 1978), p. 22.

Sayyid was aware of Darwin's theory of evolution and some arguments in *Origin* at this point. Interestingly, he, unlike many Europeans, did not seem concerned with the implications of Darwin's theory. In fact, in his 1865 publication *The Muhammadan Commentary on the Holy Bible*, Sir Sayyid presented the idea that humans were composed of a similar substance to all created things. He wrote:

> It is this, that all created things have but one source of existence and owe their being to the same substance or essence. The stone, the tree, the animals all share equally with ourselves in this respect. The only difference between us and them is in the diffusion among us of the substance which we all have in common in a proportionately greater or less degree.[14]

This quote indicates that Sir Sayyid was already thinking about the origin of life, but did not explain it in much detail. A few articles later on articulated some aspects of his position on development. For example, in 1891, he published an article titled 'Creation of Men According to the Qur'an', wherein he argued that the process of development for humans began with lifeless matter. He referred to the fermentation of clay in the Qur'an to support his argument.[15] In the article 'When was the World Created', published in 1893, he mentioned the emergence of humans in the tertiary period (a geological period from 65–2.58 million years ago), but did not express an argument supporting the origin of humans from a lower form.[16] In 'Adna Halat', he came out explicitly and stated his views on the topic in great detail.

In 'Adna Halat', Sir Sayyid covers a wide range of related topics on evolutionary thought and the origins of life. First, he presents the readers with the notion that all things on Earth were part of three types of things: animals, plants, or minerals. Second, he elaborates that the changes in plants and animals were due to both internal and external factors. Plants and animals grew to reach a final or superior state; on reaching this state, growth stopped. By contrast, minerals had no internal growth. Humans were part of the evolutionary process of animals, but were the highest form.

---

[14] Khan, *Tabyin-ul Kalam* p. 66.
[15] Martin Riexinger, 'Responses of South Asian Muslims to the Theory of Evolution', *Die Welt Des Islams*, vol. 49, no. 2 (2009): 212–47, available at http://www.jstor.org/stable/27798302 (accessed on 25 August 2018), p. 219.
[16] Ibid., p. 219.

He goes on to explain why humans developed and how this process was compatible with Islamic theology.

A key idea in this article was the notion of continuity and order of things in a chain. Sir Sayyid used observations to illustrate his point about this. He wrote about plants and trees:

> If we look at plants and trees, initially they are seeds and then they grow into weak plants. Following this step, twigs form and leaves grow. Eventually, flowers bloom and different fruits grow on different trees. The plant or tree eventually reaches a superior stage after which it can no longer improve. [...] There are different kinds of trees such as date trees and palm trees. Once placed they were placed in order of resemblance, the trees of the world will resemble the one closest, but not one that might be five to ten types away from it.[17]

Here, after establishing that each type of things has a superior state, after which there is no growth, he argues that everything is linked in a chain of development. He uses the same logic for animals: Some animals appear similar and can produce a hybrid offspring, but a lion can never become a dog. He then claims that humans – although the highest form of animal – share a common original animal ancestor. Then, Sir Sayyid explains how similarities between humans and monkeys originated. He explains that matter was composed of certain elements. All things of the universe came into being by the composition of those elements at different ratios. Different ratios compose different things. He places heavy emphasis on the role of a Divine Being in this process and argues for the overall compatibility of human evolution and development with Islamic doctrine.

The last paragraph of this article ties together his point and presents his mechanism for evolution:

> Man at the beginning was inferior, but the force of progress bestowed by God (which is present in all animals) was instilled and is still present in their generation (given that external factors do not go against them). Then slowly, due to *tarbiat* (training), which I mentioned earlier, we progressed so that humans reached the level they are at today. God only knows, how much progress man has yet to make. From Adam to Noah, when did man learn to build an ark?

---

[17] Khan, 'Adna Halat se Aala Halat'.

The Old Testament measures this span of time by 1657 years. This is amusing![18]

This quote highlights that the growth of humans from one generation to the next is driven by both God and the external world. Sir Sayyid states that each generation improved from the previous one – indicating that he embraced a teleological view of the process. For him, in case of the mechanism of evolution, two types of change occur: the first is an external set shaped by the environment and the second is the God-given desire to grow to the highest form. Humans still have not reached their full potential. Furthermore, he points to the timespan between Prophets Noah and Adam. He believed that progress occurred even between those two stages because man learned to build an ark, and perhaps, this is evidence of training and development over time. He ends the article by taking a jab at the idea that Adam and Noah were separated by less than two millenniums in the Old Testament, thus pointing to the idea of deep time again.

CONTEXTUALIZING SIR SAYYID'S EVOLUTIONARY VIEWS

Sir Sayyid's views on human evolution in 'Adna Halat' were not novel, but they were also not in support of Darwinism exclusively. He incorporated many ideas proposed by prominent Islamic scholars before him. These theories were not popularized, often losing favour to the idea of 'creatio ex nihilo' (creation out of nothing) of humans. Nevertheless, they existed from as early as the eighth century. A few of those who professed these ideas included some Mu`tazilites, such as al-Jahiz (776–869), the Ikhwân al-Safâ' (the Brethren of Purity), Ibn Khaldun (1332–1406) and even in the political thought of Shah Wali Allah (1703–1762). In addition to Islamic scholars' views, Sir Sayyid reached certain conclusions about the role of a Divine Creator that were similar to those of some Darwinians, such as the famous American botanist Asa Gray (1810–1888), who held a theistic view of evolution. In short, Sir Sayyid's views on human evolution not only shed light on alternative theories and the legacy in a non-European context but also reflect the response of religious individuals in Europe and North America who supported evolution of humans.

The first point raised by Sir Sayyid, the universe being composed of *hajr* (rocks or minerals), *shajr* (trees/plants), and *haivan* (animals), can be traced to Aristotle (BCE 384–322), which has re-emerged in works of Medieval

---

[18] Khan, 'Adna Halat se Aala Halat'.

Islamic philosophers, such as Ibn Sina (980–1037), Ibn al-Farabi (872–951), and the aforementioned Ikhwân al-Safâ', all of whom have translated and commented on Aristotle's theories. Thus, Sir Sayyid's views were not directly influenced by Europe, but a more complex diffusion of knowledge in which Muslims played a critical role and requires further investigation. Considering that plants and animals are linked in a chain of development and that humans are superior to other animals but share a common ancestor, there are several links between Islamic philosophers and Darwinians. Plants, animals, and minerals were often split into three categories, but many a time a fourth category, humans, was added.

A detailed theory of development was written by the Ikhwân al-Safâ', a secret society of Muslim philosophers in Basra (modern Iraq). In *Rasâ'il Ikhwân al-Safâ'*, (Treatises of the Brethren of Purity), they lay out a theory of development in tenth century.[19] One of the treatises outlines how humans developed from animals:

> The natural world is made up of three kingdoms: the mineral, plant, and animal kingdoms. Evolution rests on the view that every kingdom constitutes the primary matter and nourishing material for the next higher kingdom. Accordingly, the mineral kingdom must have come into existence long before that of plants. The plants came into existence before the animals; sea animals before the animals on land; the less developed before the more developed; and all animals were in existence ages before man.[20]

This theory of development also lays out a timeline for each type. First, the kingdom of minerals, then plants, and finally animals. There is also a notion that each subsequent kingdom is dependent on the previous one. These short examples show that Sir Sayyid's composition was not some recent idea that he developed or picked up, neither was it a 'Western' theory.

Another example is that of Ibn Khaldun (1332–1406), a north African Muslim scholar of religious and natural science. He worked as a judge, lawyer, administrator, and teacher in various areas of the Muslim world

---

[19] This book is an Islamic encyclopedia consisting of fifty-two treatises. Split into four sections, it covers topics from math to theological sciences. The treatises aimed at collecting the intellectual thoughts of the time. See Nader El-Bizri, *Epistles of the Brethren of Purity: The Ikhwan al-Safâ' and Their Rasa'il: An Introduction* (Oxford: Oxford University Press, 2008), p. 5.

[20] Ibid.

and commented on the topic of development.[21] His book *Muqaddimah* (Introduction), published in 1377, is a diverse intellectual work that brings together differing commentaries, such as Islamic theology, political theory and biology. In his translation, Franz Rozenthal outlines the descent of humans:

> One should then look at the world of creation. It started out from the minerals and progressed, in an ingenious, gradual manner, to plants and animals. The last stage of minerals is connected with the first stage of plants, such as herbs and seedless plants. The last stage of plants, such as palms and vines, is connected with the first stage of animals such as snails and shellfish which have only the power of touch. The word 'connection' with regard to these created things means that the last stage of each group is fully prepared to become the first stage of the next group. The animal world then widens, its species become numerous, and, in a gradual process of creation, it finally leads to man, who is able to think and to reflect. The higher stage of man is reached from the world of the monkeys, in which both sagacity and perception are found, but which has not reached the stage of actual reflection and thinking. At this point we come to the first stage of man after (the world of monkeys). This is as far as our (physical) observation extends.[22]

There are many similarities between what the Ikhwân al-Safâ's theorized and Ibn Khaldun's ideas. There is a hierarchy of development and a final goal in the process for each type. Furthermore, humans are a higher form of animal, originating from the world of monkeys. Because Ibn Khaldun had a small following, his ideas were not popularized, but intellectuals were aware of them.[23] However, the similarities among his ideas, those of the Ikhwân al-Safa, and Sir Sayyid's own views are clear. The three kingdoms play a crucial role in certain Islamic schools of thought. Sir Sayyid, however, does not specify if the three kingdoms are connected the way Ibn Khaldun considers them to be, but he reiterates that they are all composed of the same ingredients; this he argues based on verses from the Qur'an.

---

[21] Farid Alatas, *Ibn Khaldun* (New Delhi: Oxford University Press, 2013), p. 98.
[22] Ibn Khaldūn and Franz Rosenthal, *The Muqaddimah: An Introduction to History* (New York: Pantheon Books, 1958), p. 138.
[23] Alatas, *Ibn Khaldun*, p. 100.

Returning to 'Adna Halat', after explaining the process of improvement and arguing for similarities among types, Sir Sayyid argues that humans are in the same category of animals as monkeys, but they are still the highest form. At this point, he refers to Darwin. He claims that if 'missing links', or transitional fossils, are uncovered, they would only prove Darwin right. This reference to Darwin in the text is important because a popular argument used to disprove Darwin's theory of evolution by natural selection was the idea of an incomplete fossil record. By replacing a Divine Creator with a natural process, Darwin's theory challenged the position of theology in Western society. This was significant in the Europe and North America because natural theology served as an organizing concept in science at the time.[24] Many opponents of Darwin argued that the fossil record did not provide the evidence of transitional species between those inhabiting the ocean and the land, or in other words, prove the existence of transition between the two. While this was a common concern at the time, well before, the Ikhwân al-Safa' described fossils as remains from sea creatures. Arguing early on that there was a link between sea creatures and land creatures. Sir Sayyid thought that if more fossils were discovered, they would only prove Darwin correct, thus suggesting again that he had no issues with Darwin's theory.

After referring Darwin, in the article, Sir Sayyid questioned how similarities among animals and humans were possible. He states that matter (*madah*) is composed of similar ingredients and that all things in the universe came into being by a composition of these ingredients. He went onto explain how humans appeared similar to monkeys and why they have developed one way while other animals have not. The reason for him is simple: God bestowed upon humans the internal desire to grow. This was one of the features that set them apart from everything else. Another Islamic philosopher, Al-Jahiz (776–869), a Mu`tazilite,[25] articulated one of the first theories that explained the struggle for existence. In his *Book of Animals* (*Kitab al-Hayawan*), he combines the knowledge of animals written before him in Arabic, Persian, and Greek. He also studied over 300

---

[24] Edward J Larson, *Evolution: The Remarkable History of a Scientific Theory* (New York: Modern Library, 2004), p. 90
[25] The Mu`tazilah, a major theological school of Islam, held reason above scripture and other sources of religious knowledge. See Racha el Omari, 'Mu`tazilah', in *The Oxford Encyclopedia of the Islamic World*, Oxford Islamic Studies Online, available at http://www.oxfordislamicstudies.com.myaccess.library.utoronto.ca/article/opr/t236/e1073 (accessed on 7 May 2018).

animals and described and classified them into categories.[26] In this book, he writes about the struggle for existence in detail.[27] In particular, he argues, 'All animals, in short, can not exist without food, neither can the hunting animal escape being hunted in his turn. Every weak animal devours those weaker than itself [...] And in this respect, men do not differ from animals, some with respect to others, although they do not arrive at the same extremes.'[28] This particular passage shares some similarities with what Sir Sayyid wrote. Sir Sayyid related humans to animals as well and linked them in a chain of development. Al-Jahiz's views are quite similar to some of the ideas in Thomas Malthus' 'Essay on the Principles of Population' (1798), a publication that influenced Darwin's *Origin of Species*. In his essay, Malthus argues that all species reproduce at high rates and there is a lack of food to go around. This would eventually result in a competition for survival.[29] The concept was developed overtime, but a particular paper proved influential to Darwin.

For Darwin, the process of evolution was random. Thus, it removed the need for a creator. Sir Sayyid, on the other hand, believed that a Divine Being guided the evolutionary process. This is key because Sir Sayyid's views are aligned with other Darwinians, who also relied on the existence of God as the driving force behind the process of evolution. It is important to note that many of Darwin's colleagues were deeply religious and made similar leaps as Sir Sayyid did, while defending human evolution. For example, Asa Gray published *Darwiniana*, a collection of essays that defended the theory of evolution from the perspective of botany and theology as well.[30] Gray defended Darwin's ideas from a theological standpoint by arguing that the two were not mutually exclusive. A Divine Being guided the evolutionary process by causing beneficial variations that selection acted on.[31] Thus, just because Sir Sayyid did not deny the role of a God in the evolutionary process, does not mean he was against Darwin's theory. The difference here is that Darwin considered evolution a random process, but Sir Sayyid,

---

[26] Seyyed Hossein Nasr and Roland Michaud, *Islamic Science: An Illustrated Study* (London: World of Islam Festival Publishing Co. Ltd), p. 62.
[27] Conway Zirkle, 'Natural Selection before the "Origin of Species"', *Proceedings of the American Philosophical Society* 84, no. 1 (1941): 71–123.
[28] Ibid.
[29] Jerry A. Coyne, *Why Evolution Is True* (New York: Viking, 2009), pp. 10–11.
[30] John Hedley Brooke, *Science and Religion: Some Historical Perspectives* (Cambridge: Cambridge University Press, 1991).
[31] Larson, *Evolution*, p. 86.

and those like Gray, held that there was a final goal or evolution was a teleological process.

Overall, Sir Sayyid never abandoned his religious beliefs. Even in 'Adna Halat', he argues that his views were not going against Islamic beliefs. 'Adna Halat' opens a discussion of evolutionary thought in the South Asian and Islamic world. Some claim, 'Muslims do not appear to have reacted to specific scientific discoveries, including Darwinism, though there is evidence of unease among some about the fundamental autonomy presupposed by science.'[32] Through his writings, Sir Sayyid not only offers a way for Muslims to discuss evolutionary thoughts but also demonstrates the awareness of Muslims in India, alongside Hindus, to new scientific theories.[33] Studies on evolutionary thought are reframed to account for Islamic evolutionary thought and not just look for a reaction to Darwin.

SIR SAYYID AND HIS CONTEMPORARIES

On 4 March 1888, drawing a crowd of a thousand at a *mela* (state fair) in the north Indian town of Meerut, Sir Sayyid delivered a lecture identifying the deteriorating social conditions of the Muslims in India.[34] This lecture further outlined his solutions to improve these conditions, which included reforms in education and strong alliance with the British Government. In this speech, he said, 'Why should we not be obedient and faithful to those white-faced men whom God has put over us?'[35] His view here reflected his perspective of differences among civilizations. This influenced his call for better relations with the British Government, who according to him were a 'highly evolved and organized race'.[36] By understanding Sir Sayyid's view on human evolution, and, in turn, the progress of civilizations, scholars can understand his pro-Imperialist position to a greater extent. He was influenced by the notions of civilizational progress and believed that Muslims were behind Europeans, but had to follow their template to modernity. Even here,

---

[32] David Gosling, 'India's Response to Darwinism', in *Science and Religion: East and West*, ed. Yiftach J. H. Fehige, pp. 70–87 (London: Routledge, 2016), p. 77.

[33] For more on Hinduism and Darwin, see Mackenzie Cheever Brown, *Hindu Perspectives on Evolution: Darwin, Dharma, and Design* (London: Routledge, 2012).

[34] Sir Sayyid Ahmad Khan, *The Present State of Indian Politics* (Lahore: Sang-e-Meel, 1982), p. 53.

[35] Ibid., p. 65.

[36] Ibid., p. 68.

in a political discussion, evolutionary thought plays a significant role, but he was not the only Islamic reformer to reach these conclusions.

In 'Adna Halat', Sir Sayyid explained differences among different kinds of humans. He acknowledged that some similarities among different *qaums* (nations) existed and he discussed the idea that the offspring of two different *qaums* could produce a mixture of the two. He also stated that differences existed among *qaums* because of different climates. He claimed that like plants and animals, different *qaums* could also be placed in a chain of development. These ideas appear to be extensions of some theories posed by Shah Wali Allah (1703–1762), who wrote extensively on *irtifaqat* – the idea that the human civilizations go through different stages towards development.[37] He argues that humans have the urge for development towards this by attaining knowledge. According to him, there were four steps in this process. First, man was a nomad. Then, by gaining the ability to speak, he formed civilized towns. Third, he eventually formed city-states. Fourth, he attained universal presence was oneness with God.[38] Because of the close relationship between Sir Sayyid's grandfather and Wali Allah's son, Shah Abdul Aziz (1746–1824), Sir Sayyid's early theological training was in this school of thought.[39] Sir Sayyid did not dwell on this too much, but he did present a view regarding the evolution of civilizations; one that was related to not only some ideas originating from Europe but also the political thought of prominent Islamic leaders.

Other Islamic reformers drew conclusions similar to those of Sir Sayyid. In the Middle East, in *Reading Darwin in Arabic* (2014), Marwa Elshakry presents a compelling story of numerous individuals who engaged with evolutionary thought and applied it to their reform agendas. Two examples include Muhammad Abduh' (1849–1905) and his teacher, Jamaluddin al-Afghani (1838–1897). Exiled from Egypt in 1882, Abduh' later returned and rose to the ranks of Grand Mufti (highest official of religious law). In his early years, Abduh' was a political activist. In 1879, he took control of a national gazette, where he spread anticolonial ideas and demands for religious reform. The cause of his exile was his support of Ahmed Orabi, an

---

[37] See Muhammad al-Ghazali, *Socio-political Thought of Shah Wali Allah* (Delhi: Adam Publisher, 2004).

[38] Ibid., pp. 51–76.

[39] Muḥammad Ikrām Cughtā'ī, *Sir Sayyid Ahmad Khan, 1817–1898: A Prominent Muslim Politician and Educationist* (Lahore: Sang-e-Meel Publications, 2005), p. 354.

Egyptian nationalist, who in 1879 had led a revolt against the government.[40] While exiled in Paris, he published a journal with al-Afghani called *al-Urwah al-Wuthqa* (The Firmest Bond). This journal was anti-British and opposed outside colonial governance in the Middle East.[41] On his return from exile in 1888, Abduh began a legal career. He also founded a religious society and advocated for the revival of Arabic sciences. He stopped promoting anticolonial sentiments and decided to work with the British administration to govern and reform Egypt. He frequently argued that science and Islam were compatible and evolutionary thought was another justification for this.[42] He was interested in the scales of civilization or in the rise and fall of empires and argued that Arabs could learn from the West on how to improve their own conditions. For Abduh', it was not about the theory of how species changed, but the application of ideas in terms of improvement for civilizations. This was another take on how evolutionary thought was implemented in reality.

Abduh's teacher, al-Afghani, also thought that the evolution of civilizations played a big part in the narrative. Al-Afghani is frequently characterized as a critic of Sir Sayyid and his reform agenda. Al-Afghani branded him as a *nayshiriya* (naturalist).[43] The meaning of the term *nayshiriya*, according to Marwa Elshakry, was vague enough 'for Afghani to group such people (Sir Sayyid and his followers) together with atomists, evolutionists, nihilists, and materialists as "enemies of religion" and "destroyers of civilization"'.[44] According to Elshakry, al-Afghani used the term to refer to Sir Sayyid's search for the sources of a 'natural religion', not because of his views on 'matter and life'.[45] Interestingly, both Sir Sayyid and al-Afghani acknowledged that embracing new scientific developments was an integral to the progress of civilization. In 'Adna Halat', Sir Sayyid expressed his view in terms of the chain of development. In 'Answer to Renan', according to Nikki Keddie, al-Afghani writes, 'All nations emerged from barbarism and marched towards a more advanced civilization.'[46] Keddie

---

[40] Elshakry, *Reading Darwin in Arabic*, p. 165.
[41] Ibid., p. 19.
[42] Ibid., p. 165.
[43] Ibid., p. 120.
[44] Ibid., p. 120.
[45] Ibid., p. 120.
[46] Nikki R. Keddie, *An Islamic Response to Imperialism: Political and Religious Writings of Sayyid Jamāl ad-Dīn 'al-Afghānī'* (Berkeley: University of California Press, 1983), p. 183.

continues, 'Christianity preceded the Muslim religion in the world by many centuries.' Here, al-Afghani according to Keddie is suggesting that Muslims were on the verge of a similar path. Sir Sayyid shared this view as well.

Overall, Sir Sayyid's view of civilizations and human evolution influenced his reform agenda and attitude towards British Imperialism to an extent. This aspect has been left out of numerous studies regarding Sir Sayyid's political agenda. Moreover, he was not the only one, other Islamic reformers like Abduh' and al-Afghani in the Middle East shared this notion as well.

PUBLIC EDUCATION IN MUSLIM COUNTRIES AND THE TOPIC OF HUMAN EVOLUTION

So far, I have outlined Sir Sayyid's views on human evolution and placed some sources, both Islamic and European, in dialogue with Sir Sayyid's views. However, the overall issue is regarding the relevance of his position on human evolution to contemporary issues. For those unfamiliar with modern theory of evolution, it is easy to comprehend. It can be summarized, according to Jerry Cohen, in a single sentence:

> Life on Earth evolved gradually beginning with one primitive species – perhaps a self-replicating molecule – that lived more than 3.5 billion years ago; it then branched out over time, throwing off many new and diverse species; and the mechanism for most (but not all) of evolutionary change is natural selection.[47]

This summary outlines the simplicity underlying the theory of evolution. However, it still appears to be radically divisive to some individuals.

There are only a handful of studies on how Muslims have interacted and reacted to the theory of evolution and this does not capture the entire picture. In a study in 2010, Anila Asghar, Jason R. Wiles, and Brian Alters investigated the attempts to reconcile science and religion in Pakistan's public school curriculum.[48] In their study, titled 'The Origin and Evolution of Life in Pakistani High School Biology', they analysed high school

---

[47] Coyne, *Why Evolution Is True*, p. 3.
[48] Anila Asghar, Jason R. Wiles, and Brian Alters, 'The Origin and Evolution of Life in Pakistani High School Biology', *Journal of Biological Education* 44, no. 2 (2010): 65–71.

textbooks and curricula in biology and concluded that the Pakistani national education policy supported the inclusion of Islamic religious principles in the curricula. Islamic beliefs and Qur'anic scripture were interwoven with science in Pakistan. Topics in evolution were not covered extensively but they did exist. Although the biology textbooks contained several verses from the Qur'an, they promoted a conciliatory language. In another sociological study, in Muslim countries, conducted in 2006, researchers posed a question on evolution. The respondents were asked, 'Do you agree or disagree with Darwin's theory of evolution?' Only 14 per cent of the Pakistanis and 8 per cent of the Egyptians agreed that Darwin's theory probably or most certainly is true.[49] These studies suggest that religion is still shaping the reception of evolutionary thought to a great extent. Therefore, in case of teaching evolution, even with the limited studies on Muslim perspectives on the topic, there are issues that require a resolution. Although some might simply be misinformed about the topic, many do not encounter the topic at all. Some people think Darwin meant that humans evolved from apes but fail to understand the mechanism by which they share a common ancestor.

Overall, human evolution is a controversial topic even today. Furthermore, by framing it as a 'Western' or 'materialist' theory and ignoring centuries of contributions by Islamic philosophers, discussions about the theory have adopted a certain degree of cognitive dissonance among many Muslims. Consider the justification Turkey provided for banning the teaching of evolution in high schools. In an online address, Alparslan Durmus, the head of Turkey's national education board, said, 'We are aware that if our students don't have the background to comprehend the premises and hypotheses, or if they don't have the knowledge and scientific framework, they will not be able to understand some controversial issues, so we have left out some of them.'[50] Durmus seems to believe that students would not be able to cope with the reality of the theory itself, but by understanding the history and development of the actual theory of evolution, we can begin to tackle the issue of teaching it in an Islamic setting because it is not a 'Western' import.

---

[49] Hameed, 'Bracing for Islamic Creationism', p. 1637.
[50] Tuvan Gumrukcu, 'Turkey to Stop Teaching Evolution Theory in High Schools: Education Board', *Reuters*, 23 June 2017, available at https://www.reuters.com/article/us-turkey-education-evolution/turkey-to-stop-teaching-evolution-theory-in-high-schools-education-board-idUSKBN19E1RA (accessed on 12 October 2017).

Another issue to address is the lack of evolutionary thought in the original curriculum at the Muhammadan Anglo-Oriental (MAO) College in 1875. When the MAO College was established, evolutionary biology was not a part of the curriculum. The most apparent reason is the anachronism here; the field of evolutionary biology emerges around the 1930s. However, Lelyveld put forth another argument regarding the lack of focus on science, technology and empirical research in general. He wrote, 'In making this choice [to gravitate towards the Oxford-Cambridge example], he [Sir Sayyid] was abandoning the encouragement of science, technology and empirical research.'[51] In short, evolutionary thought was not excluded from the MAO College, or even from the Scientific Society mentioned earlier, because it was problematic, but because it did not meet the goals of the society or institution at the time, which focused on, according to Lelyveld, 'moral perfection'.[52] As the MAO College evolved to become AMU, the Zoology Department incorporated several themes from evolution in their courses. This includes an elective on evolutionary biology that covers everything from population genetics to origin and evolution of man.[53] What the short account of AMU demonstrates is that educators continuously revise their pedagogical approaches depending on the context.

Instead of students waiting to specialize in zoology, they should be taught the history of evolutionary biology at an earlier stage. A revised history of evolutionary biology textbook or curriculum should include some discussion of ideas from Islamic philosophers and other backgrounds like Buddhism or Hinduism. It should also include developments in other fields, such as geology and palaeontology. This will allow students to understand how scientists arrived at the theory of evolution. Besides the historical study of the theory of evolution, contemporary issues should be discussed. Many have claimed that the theory of evolution is in crisis. Although it is true that since its inception, the theory of evolution has faced its challenges, some who seem to sensationalize or refute the issues do not account for modern developments in research. For one, Darwin, unequipped with modern theories of inheritance, did not provide a viable mechanism by which evolution occurred. Such concerns were alleviated through modern

---

[51] Lelyveld, *Aligarh's First Generation*, p. 116.
[52] Ibid.
[53] Aligarh Muslim University, 'Department of Zoology', 5 October 2017, available at https://www.amu.ac.in/departmentpage.jsp?did=43 (accessed on 24 August 2018).

synthesis, the reconciliation of Darwin's ideas with Mendelian genetics in the nineteenth century, and our modern field of evolutionary biology formed.[54] If there is an issue with the theory after learning its history and modern issues, the next step would be to step into the field and conducting experiments. Only by going into the laboratories, conducting scientific experiments, and approaching peer-review journals can we begin to debate and uncover more about this topic. The key is engaging with the topic without fear of persecution.

CONCLUSION

In this chapter, I introduced readers to Sir Sayyid's position on the topic of human evolution, outlined its continuity with previous Islamic theories of development, and compared his position to the theory of evolution by natural selection. Although Sir Sayyid relied on a Divine Being as an explanatory factor for the evolutionary process, he had no problem accepting the idea that humans have developed from an original animal ancestor. He also refuted several claims of creationists, such as the relatively young age of Earth and special creation of humans. Finally, he did not deem Darwin's theory as false, but he went a step ahead to demonstrate how human evolution is compatible with Islamic doctrine – an idea, as I have argued before, was a continuation of previous theories developed by Islamic scholars. These short examples have just scratched the surface of what some prominent Islamic scholars have postulated with regard to human development and evolution, but it is apparent that Sir Sayyid wanted to demonstrate that these ideas were consistent with developments on the topic in the nineteenth century. Here, the idea that the theory of evolution is not a foreign or 'Western' concept is important, not the evolution or creation debate.

Since its inception, Darwin's theory has transformed significantly. Then, why is Sir Sayyid's position on human evolution important for contemporary issues? The answer is simple. How Sir Sayyid approached the topic in relation to Islam and the Qur'an is significant. He did not attempt to find evidence of Darwin's theory from versus in the Qur'an nor did he attempt to disprove it, but simply fit the data to the best available theory. While scientists continue to study topics in evolutionary biology, many

---

[54] Modern synthesis is a theory about how evolution works at the level of genes and phenotypes. In addition to natural selection, it recognizes several other mechanisms of evolution, such as random genetic drift.

are still unaware of the theory of evolution. Also, due to the monopoly of Darwinism in the evolutionary discourse, the legacy of evolutionary thought by Muslim scholars has been relatively absent in general. Only after going back and revising the history of evolutionary biology and integrating the rich history of Islamic philosophers and their views on development can we begin debating and discussing the future of evolution in countries with a Muslim majority. One place to start is definitely the history of evolutionary biology, and more importantly, how other Muslims, like Sir Sayyid, approached the topic of science and religion historically. Universities such as AMU are already incorporating the scientific side of it, but the historical side is a significant part of the narrative as well.

12 Loss and Longing at the *Qila Muʿalla*
Ās̱ār-us Ṣanādīd *and the Early Sayyid Ahmad Khan*
MRINALINI RAJAGOPALAN*

BEGINNINGS

In 1846, Sayyid Ahmad Khan (1817–1898), a young *munsif* in Delhi, took on the ambitious task of documenting all of the city's monuments. The result of his labour was a 600-page encyclopaedic survey of Delhi's monuments and biographical excerpts of the city's major personalities titled *Ās̱ār-us Ṣanādīd* (Traces of Noblemen; hereafter *Ās̱ār*).[1] Nothing as comprehensive had been attempted before and it took another seventy years for the Archaeological Survey of India (ASI) to produce a comparable list of Delhi's historic structures. By bearing witness to Delhi's urban heritage, Sayyid Ahmad Khan struggled with reconciling past and present, tradition and modernity, science and myth, materiality and poetics, observation and belief. The importance of *Āṣār* as a thorough survey of Delhi's built environment cannot be overstated, especially given that many of the structures discussed in the book were destroyed by the British military during and after the Indian Rebellion of 1857. Yet *Āṣār* occupies an ambivalent position in Sayyid Ahmad's larger oeuvre. His work on the built environment and material culture of Delhi appears as an outlier to his later rich philosophical and political contributions and his social reform programmes following the events of 1857.

Keeping with the mandate of this volume, I offer an interpretation of *Āṣār* as an early example of Sayyid Ahmad's experimentations with key motifs

---

* I would like to thank Eric Beverley for his comments and suggestions on this chapter. All shortcomings and any errors that remain are my own.

[1] Sayyid Ahmad Khan, *Āṣār-us Ṣanādīd*, 1st ed. (Delhi: Maṭbaʿ Sayyid al-Akḫbār, 1847). The title *Āṣār-us Ṣanādīd* has also been translated as *The Remnants of Ancient Heroes* in Rana Safvi's forthcoming translation of the book. See Sayyid Ahmad Khan, *Āsar-us Sanadīd* (*The Remnants of Ancient Heroes*), trans. Rana Safvi (New York: Columbia University Press, 2018).

of modernity and modernization. I define modernity as the eighteenth- and nineteenth-century phenomena where individuals struggled to articulate their singular place within a long arc of history. Modernity was seldom a neatly defined project that delivered resolution, but rather a messy and incomplete process with unexpected outcomes. It also did not travel linearly from a European core to the global South.[2] Modernization, I define, as the material changes to built environments and social organization that followed in the wake of the Industrial Revolution. In the words of Marshall Berman:

> To be modern is to live a life of paradox and contradiction. It is to be overpowered by the immense bureaucratic organizations that have the power to control and often to destroy all communities, values, lives; and yet to be undeterred in our determination to face these forces, to fight to change their world and make it our own. It is to be both revolutionary and conservative: alive to new possibilities for experience and adventure, frightened by the nihilistic depths to which so many modern adventures lead, longing to create and hold on to something real even as everything melts.[3]

It is this paradox of modernity – a palpable excitement for new futures coupled with a profound alienation from the present – that is the leitmotif of Sayyid Ahmad's *Āṣār*. As an early project in which Sayyid Ahmad invested considerable time, resources, and energy, *Āṣār* reveals much about the author's perceptual and processual engagement with his urban environment and his effort to extrapolate both philosophical, historical, and social meaning from the same. While it is true that Sayyid Ahmad produced *Āṣār* for a European audience, this comprehensive work on Delhi's historic architecture cannot be reduced to a mere token of colonial ingratiation. Instead, *Āṣār* signals the beginnings of Sayyid Ahmad's lifelong commitment to creating a seamless historical continuum between a vibrant Islamic heritage and modernization facilitated by European intervention. Delhi's surfeit of Islamic architecture provided the urban milieu for Sayyid Ahmad to imagine and articulate such a grand continuum where the firm bedrock of Islamic aesthetics and history would be the foundation for a modern efflorescence.

---

[2] For broad discussions of modernity that de-centre its Eurocentric biases, see Dilip Gaonkar (ed.), *Alternative Modernities* (Durham, NC: Duke University Press, 2001).
[3] Marshall Berman, *All That Is Solid Melts into Air: The Experience of Modernity* (Middlesex, UK: Penguin Books, 1988), pp. 13–14.

In this chapter, I offer a close reading of descriptions of the Red Fort, or as Sayyid Ahmad referred to it, the *qila mu'alla* – the imperial fort. As a site, the Red Fort signified Sayyid Ahmad's vexations with both history and modernity. On the one hand, the aesthetics and technological aspects of the fort signified the glory of the Mughal Empire. On the other hand, the contemporary dilapidation of the fort represented the impotency of the Mughal Emperor as well as the empire's increasing isolation from the modern world. As such, Sayyid Ahmad's interpretation of the Red Fort provides valuable insights into his later articulations of Islamic culture's place within a long arc of historical progress.

ĀṢĀR

Āṣār, the first comprehensive survey of the monuments of Delhi, included Hindu, Jain, and Sikh architecture alongside the Islamic heritage of the city.[4] In terms of its documentary scope, its only worthy, if abridged, competitor would be the ASI's 1919 English-language catalogue on the built heritage of Delhi.[5] When he wrote the first edition in 1847, Sayyid Ahmad was a thirty-year-old employee of the British administration in northern India.[6]

---

[4] In its comprehensive scope and focus on architectural objects, *Āṣār* had few precursors but was nevertheless followed by urban histories of other cities in the late nineteenth century, such as *Mumbaiche Varnan* (Description of Mumbai) (1863), written by Govind Narayan, in Marathi. For an English translation, see Murali Ranganathan (ed.), *Govind Narayan's Mumbai: An Urban Biography from 1863* (London: Anthem Press, 2009). Two histories of Lahore seem to have drawn direct inspiration from *Āṣār*: *Tahqīqāt Chishtī: Tarīkh-e Lahor ka Encyclopedia* (Chishti's Inquiries: An Encyclopedia of Lahore's History) (1867, repr. Lahore: Al-Fasl Nashraan-o-Tajran Kitab, 1996) by Noor Ahmad Chishti and Sayyid Muhammad Latif's *Lahore: Its History, Architectural Remains, and Antiquities, with an Account of Its Modern Institutions, Inhabitants, Their Trade, Custom, etc.* (1892, repr. Lahore: Sang-e-Meel, 1994). For a critical analysis on the two urban histories of Lahore, see William Glover, *Making Lahore Modern: Constructing and Imagining a Colonial City* (Minneapolis: University of Minnesota Press, 2008), pp. 185–201.

[5] Maulvi Zafar Hasan, *Monuments of Delhi: Lasting Splendour of the Great Mughals and Others*, ed. J. A. Page (New Delhi: Aryan Books International, 1919, repr. 2008).

[6] Although India would not officially become a colony of the British Empire until 1858, the English East India Company had instituted an elaborate system of revenue extraction, resource management, and military administration that positioned them as the *de facto* government of a large part of north India.

Already a prolific writer, his earlier books had focused on topics, such as the political history of Delhi, imperial genealogies, and an administrative manual.[7] Dr Aloys Sprenger, Secretary of the Vernacular Translation Society, Principal of the Delhi College (1845–1847), and founder of the college's printing press Matba`-ul `Ulum, claimed that he had encouraged Sayyid Ahmad to compile Āṣār.[8] Sayyid Ahmad spent eighteen months completing his ambitious survey of the city's monuments, a task for which he enlisted the help of Maulvi Imam Baksh Sahba`ī, Head of the Persian Department at Delhi College, and two draftsmen, Faiz Ali Khan and Mirza Shah Rukh Beg.[9]

When it was published in 1847, Āṣār was well received by some members of the Asiatic Society (est. 1784), such as Arthur Austin Roberts, who was then Collector of Delhi. Roberts convinced Sayyid Ahmad to simplify the elaborate prose of the book and correct the discrepancies of the original before beginning an English translation.[10] Although the translation was

---

The Mughal Emperor was himself in the pay of the Company, and his role had been reduced to that of a mere figurehead. A historical account of this sociopolitical climate can be found in Narayani Gupta, *Delhi between Two Empires, 1803–1931: Society, Government and Urban Growth* (Delhi: Oxford University Press, 1981).

[7] Before writing Āṣār, Sayyid Ahmad had authored six books, the first of which was an imperial history of Delhi. For more on the larger oeuvre of Sayyid Ahmad and Āṣār-us Ṣanādīd's place within his other works, see C. M. Naim, 'Syed Ahmad and His Two Books Called Asar-al-Sanadid', *Modern Asian Studies* 45, no. 3 (2011): 669–708.

[8] M. Ikram Chaghtai, 'Dr Aloys Sprenger and the Delhi College', in *Delhi College: Traditional Elites, the Colonial State, and Education Before 1857*, ed. Margrit Pernau, pp. 105–24 (Delhi: Oxford University Press, 2006). It should be noted that Sayyid Ahmad himself does not mention Sprenger in his acknowledgments in either the 1847 or 1854 version of Āṣār.

[9] Not much is known about the draftsmen Faiz Ali Khan and Mirza Shah Rukh Beg. Maulvi Imam Baksh Sahba`ī, however, was an important intellectual in Delhi at the time and was a close friend of Sayyid Ahmad as well as his collaborator on Āṣār. For more on him and how much influence he may have exerted on the style of Āṣār, see C. M. Naim, 'Shaikh Imam Bakhsh Sahba`i: Teacher, Scholar, Poet, and Puzzle-Master', in *Delhi College: Traditional Elites, the Colonial State, and Education Before 1857*, ed. Margrit Pernau, pp. 145–85 (Delhi: Oxford University Press, 2006).

[10] Christian W. Troll has provided a detailed account of the reception of the first edition of Āṣār and the dialogue that surrounded its translation into English

never completed, the revised manuscript appeared as a second edition in 1854.[11] The differences in language and content between the first and second editions of *Āṣār* are so radical that some scholars, such as C. M. Naim, have referred to the two editions as separate books named identically.[12] Other scholars, such as David Lelyveld, have suggested that the first edition celebrated the living cultures of Delhi, particularly its position as a centre of Urdu literature, whereas the second edition was created within a more rigid archaeological framework.[13] Whether as a site of cultural efflorescence or as an urban example of civilizational teleology, Delhi provided a rich imaginative space for Sayyid Ahmad's early articulations of history and modernity.

In the analysis that follows, I look at the textual and visual descriptions of the Red Fort, which comprised the second section of *Āṣār* (the book was divided into four sections), and suggest that two modalities emerge in the arrangement of historical evidence and observation.[14] First, Sayyid Ahmad's thick descriptions of the Red Fort reveal a politics and poetics of anticipation, in that, the Red Fort's glorious past and contemporary decline make it a talisman for a new society yet to come. What this new order would be Sayyid Ahmad could not know, neither could he predict the violent rupture through which such newness would manifest itself a mere ten years later, but throughout *Āṣār*, Sayyid Ahmad is convinced that massive change was both inevitable and imminent. The frisson between the material gravitas of the past, evident in every stone of the city, and the intangible but certain signs of change are most evident in Sayyid Ahmad's

---

in his 'A Note on an Early Topographical Work of Sayyid Ahmad Khān: "*Āṣār al-Ṣanādīd*"', *Journal of the Royal Asiatic Society of Britain and Ireland* 2 (1972): 135–46.

[11] Fatima Quraishi mentions that although Sayyid Ahmad had begun working on the English translation of *Āṣār*, the institutionalization of archaeology in the 1860s and the regular publication of preservation and excavation reports made such a translation unnecessary. See Fatima Quraishi, '*Āṣār-ul-Sanadid*: A Nineteenth-Century History of Delhi', *Journal of Art Historiography* 6 (2012): 6FQ-1.

[12] Naim, 'Sayyid Ahmad and His Two Books'.

[13] David Lelyveld, '*Sauda Sulaf*: Urdu in the Two Versions of Sayyid Ahmad Khan's *Āṣāru's-Sanadid*', *The Annual of Urdu Studies* 26 (2011): 21–38.

[14] The four sections of *Āṣār* elaborate on (a) buildings outside the walled city of Shahjahanabad, (b) the various buildings within the Red Fort complex, (c) buildings within the walled city of Shahjahanabad, and (d) *tazkirah* or biographical accounts of Delhi's important personalities.

treatment of the Red Fort. They also run through *Āṣār* as a broader theme. As such, the book captures the latent energy of Delhi as a city perched on the cusp of change; the future is both seductive in its promise and frightening in its unpredictability.

The second modality is the posture of Sayyid Ahmad as the recorder of Delhi's built environment. He casts himself as a surveyor – one who is able to hold the entire city in his expansive gaze – but mostly as a witness to the past and present of the city. This is an important distinction from the other forms of urban writing, such as the *shahr-āshob* – poetic lamentations about the social and urban decline brought on by the erosion of Mughal power.[15] Despite being written for a largely European audience, *Āṣār* deviates from the more clinical archaeological approaches championed by organizations such as the Archaeological Society of Delhi (ASD, active 1847–1854). Instead, *Āṣār* traffics between thick empirical description and sensory appraisals of the environment. Fact and observation are woven with the affects of sound, feeling, sensation, and memory to create a corporeal knowing of Delhi's architecture. Sayyid Ahmad positions himself not simply as a detached observer but as an immersed witness, perhaps even an accomplice, to the city's changing fortunes.

In the following paragraphs, I first look at the use of empirical data, particularly architectural facts that Sayyid Ahmad used to anchor the Red Fort within a strong arc of history. The next section looks at the topographical drawings of the Red Fort in *Āṣār*, which tend towards a sterile minimalism paring the monument down to its stark architectural definition. The last section of the chapter wrestles with the conspicuous absence of the Mughal Emperor Bahadur Shah Zafar's body from *Āṣār*. This deliberate elision of embodied power is perhaps the most evocative of Sayyid Ahmad's politics of anticipation and his role as a witness to a new coming order. The urban arena was a crucial locus for Sayyid Ahmad to forge his thoughts on past histories and future modernities – juxtapositions that would preoccupy him for many years after he wrote *Āṣār*.

THE WEIGHT OF HISTORY

To this day, Sayyid Ahmad's textual description of the Red Fort remains a reliable and the most thorough account of the imperial complex before

---

[15] For an explanation of the *shahr-āshob* genre and its many variations see Frances Pritchett, 'The World Turned Upside Down: Šahr-Āšōb as a Genre', *Annual of Urdu Studies* 4 (1994): 37–41.

it was besieged and destroyed by the British military, during and after the 1857 rebellion. After the sacking of Delhi by the Persian Nadir Shah in 1789 and the Anglo-Maratha wars (1803–1804), this royal complex had fallen into considerable disrepair. By 1846, when Sayyid Ahmad was composing *Āṣār*, its dilapidation signalled the eroded Mughal court and the emperor's dependence on the British to maintain its basic infrastructure. In Sayyid Ahmad's description, the fort is thus both an architectural feat in terms of technological and artistic achievement and a ruin haunted by the spectre of a fallen empire. The architecture of the fort was the debris of that lost glory, but Sayyid Ahmad suggests that it may become the foundation for a new renaissance.

For Sayyid Ahmad, the true regnal protagonist of the *qila muʿalla* was the Mughal Emperor Shah Jahan. Indeed, the emphasis on the size, strength, and beauty of the fort could be read as a representation of the Mughal Empire during its cultural apogee in the seventeenth century. To establish the creation of the Red Fort as a unique moment in time, Sayyid Ahmad provides a surfeit of empirical facts and dates related to its construction. For example, based on an astrological chart from the time of the establishment of the fort, he concludes that ground was broken on a Friday evening at twelve minutes past five o'clock in the first month of autumn (*Urdi*) on 1049 Hijri (1638) (Figure 22). Sayyid Ahmad's attention, rather insistence, on recording such granular details of the Red Fort continues with naming the architects (*mimar*) Ustad Hamid and Ustad Ahmed as well as the various superintendents (*ahtamam*) Izzat Khan, Alwardi Khan, and Mukkarmat Khan, along with the length of their service. The construction of the fort cost five million rupees. An additional five million was spent on the various individual apartments within the fort compound. Other details included the dimensions of the foundation: eleven *gaz* in depth, tapering from fifteen *gaz* in breadth at the base to ten *gaz* at the top,[16] and the moat, which was twenty-five *gaz* wide and ten *gaz* deep, the type and provenance of the stone used for constructing the outer ramparts of the fort, and the number and type of bastions and gates leading in and out of the fort.

---

[16] A *gaz* was a unit of measuring length prevalent in the Indo-Persian world. Its measurements varied historically over time and region. For example, in the mid-eighteenth century, a *gaz* in the region of Delhi would have been 28.5 inches, whereas by the mid-nineteenth century or during the time *Āṣār* was written, it would have become identical to the English yard or 36 inches.

240 Mrinalini Rajagopalan

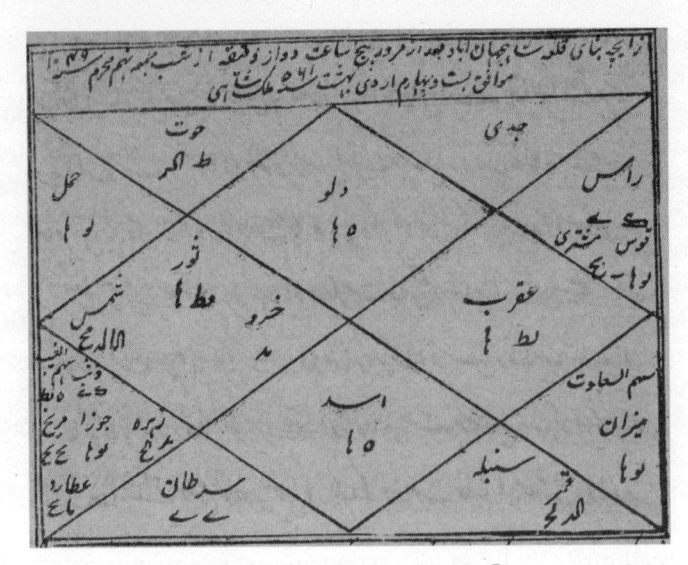

Figure 22 Astrological chart for the Red Fort from *Āṣār-us Ṣanādīd* (DS486.D3 A618470). Courtesy of the Bancroft Library, University of California, Berkeley.

As mentioned, it was important for Sayyid Ahmad to create an archival record of Delhi's monuments that would appeal to his largely European audiences, particularly Thomas Theophilus Metcalfe, British Agent at Delhi, whose patronage he was eager to attract. At this time, archaeological and architectural data provided the necessary scientific basis for establishments such as the ASD to acknowledge and accept Sayyid Ahmad's survey as a veritable historic text. Sayyid Ahmad's insistence on recording the dates, times, dimensions, contractors, and materials associated with the building of the Red Fort was not, however, mere pandering to a possible patron. This archival weight of the facts and figures was a means to fill the power vacuum that was the defining feature of the Red Fort amidst its dilapidation – the ruins of the Mughal Empire and the seat of a weakened king. Sayyid Ahmad's description may be considered textual archaeology – an excavation of the minutiae of a monument that while in dilapidated conditions stood as a powerful representation of Islamic rule in the subcontinent. This moment of Islamic creative and cultural surplus is, however, short-lived as Sayyid Ahmad's narrative moves quickly to a series of ill-fated interventions in the Red Fort.

Sayyid Ahmad positions the demise of the Red Fort as starting in the post-Shah Jahan era with Emperor Aurangzeb's period of rule (1658–1707). For example, he recounts Aurangzeb's decision to destroy the two large elephant statues on either side of the Delhi Gate (southern gate), which he considered idolatrous. Sayyid Ahmad earlier describes these statues as almost life-like representations. He later clarifies his admiration for them as part of the larger aesthetic programme of the Red Fort. Another account of Aurangzeb's aggressive intervention concerns his building of barbicans in front of the Delhi and Lahori Gates. The gates originally did not have such massive screens in front of them and thus would facilitate views back and forth between the interior of the fort compound and the city. In fact, the Lahori Gate provided a clear line of sight from the Chandni Chowk to the Diwan-e `Am (Hall of Public Audience) and the major commercial artery of the city also acted as an extended court of the Mughal Emperor through rituals of procession. For example, Sayyid Ahmad tells us that nobles were required to dismount from their horses at Fatehpuri Masjid (which was at one end of the Chandni Chowk) and walk on foot to the Lahori Gate (which marked the other end of the Chandni Chowk). Emperor Aurangzeb, however, found this fluidity between the fort and the city – the royal complex and quotidian urbanism – inappropriate (*nāmunāsib*) and thus had both barbicans built, truncating the line of sight between the fort and the city.[17] Such interventions were the first steps to isolating the Red Fort from its larger and vibrant urban context.

To clarify the historical rupture wrought by Aurangzeb's changes to the Red Fort, Sayyid Ahmad narrates the following anecdote. Shah Jahan, imprisoned at the time in Agra by his son Aurangzeb, hears of these changes to his imperial fort and remarks: 'Oh my beloved son, you have taken the Red Fort as your bride and removed her veil.'[18] The reference to the son's (Aurangzeb's) illegitimate or forcible appropriation of the fort (and by extension Shah Jahan's imperial throne) and to his lust for power (insinuated by the aggressive alterations to the Red Fort) is clear here. The gendered metaphor of an unveiled bride is interestingly cryptic in that although Aurangzeb's addition of the barbicans increased the privacy of the Red Fort, screening it from the gaze of a broader public, Shah Jahan accuses him of the reverse – that his 'bride' is now publicly exposed and thereby humiliated. Although Sayyid Ahmad employs a neutral tone in recording the dramatic architectural interventions made by Aurangzeb to the Red Fort, the melancholic mien of this episode signals its decline and by extension that of the Mughal Empire. Shah Jahan's plaintive assessment of Aurangzeb's

---

[17] Khan, *Āṣār-us Ṣanādīd* (1847), Part II, p. 7.
[18] Ibid.

changes to the Red Fort becomes the opening note to an extended coda of imperial and architectural recession.

Āṣār also records more recent changes to the Red Fort sponsored by the British government. In the early nineteenth century, the drawbridges over the moat at Delhi and Lahori Gates were replaced by permanent bridges financed by the English East India Company. The marble inscription on the Delhi Gate's bridge credited the rebuilding of the bridge in 1811 to the British who were acting on the orders of Emperor Akbar Shah II.[19] As he does in many other places in Āṣār, Sayyid Ahmad indicates that the British are now the custodians of Delhi's architecture – making interventions of the scale and importance once made by the Mughal Emperors Shah Jahan and Aurangzeb. That Akbar Shah II appears only as a facilitator of British agency in this inscription on the public façade of the Red Fort is an omen of Mughal imperial weakness and anticipates the change of guard that was to come a mere decade after Sayyid Ahmad wrote these words. The history of the Red Fort in Āṣār is one of glory followed by decline: Its Shah Jahani origin, exemplifying exceptional creativity and technological ambition, is followed by a period of aggressive reorganization based on religious orthodoxy, and later by ambivalent power relations between the British government and their puppet Mughal Emperor seen in modest infrastructural maintenance. Taken together, the history of the Red Fort betrays Sayyid Ahmad's affective mourning for a glorious but lost empire coupled with his hope that the demise of the older order must surely also lead to a new modernity.

VISUAL REORDERING

The section of Āṣār (Bāb doosra) dedicated to the Red Fort carries sixteen images of the Red Fort and the various structures within its walls.[20] The

---

[19] Khan, Āṣār-us Ṣanādīd (1847), Part II, p. 8.
[20] The images, in order of appearance, depict the following: a wide view of the Delhi Gate from the southern part of the city; the Naqqar Khana (ceremonial entrance pavilion); the Diwan-e `Am (Hall of Public Audience); exterior and interior of the Rang Mahal (pleasure pavilion); the Khwabgah Mussaman Burj (private chambers of the king or the zenana); two views of the Hamam (royal baths); Heera Mahal (royal quarters); Moti Mahal (royal quarters); Moti Masjid (Pearl Mosque, built by Aurangzeb); the fountains; Zafar Mahal and the tank of Mehtab Bagh (royal quarters built by Emperor Bahadur Shah Zafar within the royal tank); Sawan (monsoon pavilion); the Shah Burj (royal tower/lookout); and panorama of Red Fort from the river Yamuna.

Loss and Longing at the Qila Muʿalla 243

first three images include the view of the south-facing Delhi Gate (Figure 23) (which, Sayyid Ahmad notes, can also be seen as a substitute for the west-facing Lahori Gate, owing to the nearly identical form of the two barbicans), the Naqqar Khana or the drum house (a ceremonial entrance where passage was reserved for nobility and the emperor), and the Diwan-e ʿAm. The other images of the Red Fort are of its various pavilions, baths, royal quarters, and the Moti Masjid – a small mosque constructed by Emperor Aurangzeb in 1659.

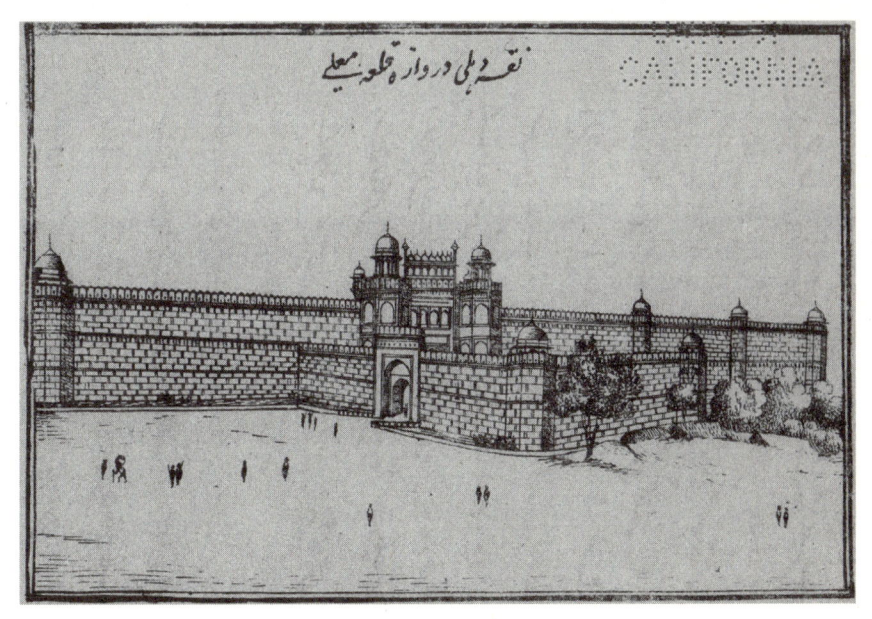

Figure 23 Delhi Gate of the Red Fort from *Āṣār-us Ṣanādīd* (DS486.D3 A61847). Courtesy of the Bancroft Library, University of California, Berkeley.

The urban axis coming from the Chandni Chowk passed through the Lahori Gate and the Naqqar Khana to arrive at the Diwan-e ʿAm. As the emperor passed through the ceremonial gateway of the Naqqar Khana, musicians on the top stories would herald his passage in and out of the Red Fort. Yet the perspective of the Diwan-e ʿAm offered by Sayyid Ahmad stops short of providing a clear view of the empty throne at its centre. Instead, the draftsman, Mirza Shah Rukh Beg, offers a wide view of the structure with its interior shrouded in deep shadow (Figure 24). Indeed, the emphasis in this drawing is on the large public forecourt (defined by the red sandstone railing, which served as both the symbolic and physical boundary between

244   Mrinalini Rajagopalan

nobility and commoners) and the rhythmic cadence of the nine-arched Diwan-e `Am, anchoring a motley jumble of lesser structures on either side. Conspicuous by its absence in the images of the Red Fort in *Āṣār* is the Diwan-e Khās (Hall of Royal Audience), the architectural and imperial counterpart to the Diwan-e `Am. While the more public business of the empire was conducted in the Diwan-e `Am, the Diwan-e Khās was where the inner court met with the emperor.

Figure 24   Diwan-e `Am of the Red Fort from *Āṣār-us Ṣanādīd* (DS486.D3 A61847). Courtesy of the Bancroft Library, University of California, Berkeley.

The images for *Āṣār* aim for an architectural accuracy and most of them are devoid of any signs of human activity, ritual, or ceremony. In the section pertaining to the Red Fort, all extraneous detail is mercilessly edited out to present architectural views existing outside the human context and certainly imperial traces (*Āṣār*) that were the foundation for the Red Fort. When a few perfunctory human figures are included in the drawings, they only function to emphasize the scale of the monuments. J. P. Losty has chronicled the various drawing techniques through which the Red Fort was depicted in the first half of the nineteenth century when Indian artists produced images of monuments in Delhi and Agra mostly for the European patrons. Two modes of architectural representation prevailed during this time in north

India: a topographical style of drawing favoured by draftsmen from Agra, which insisted on documenting buildings free of context with perspectival details, and another picturesque style showing monuments as they were used and within their broader urban contexts. The two styles were not entirely exclusive and often artists operated between a spectrum of topographical precision and picturesque affect.[21] The drawings in *Āṣār* pertaining to the Red Fort, however, follow the topographical tradition of architectural representation alone. While the images are accurate architecturally, they say little of the sociality of these spaces. Thus, these images may even be seen as privileging the technological and aesthetic qualities of the monument over its lived reality.

The clinical tenor of the Red Fort's images in *Āṣār* is often in stark contrast to the rich affect of the corresponding monument's textual description. For example, consider the image of the Naqqar Khana (Figure 25) with Sayyid Ahmad's description of it:

> The western part of the courtyard that leads to the Diwan-i ʿAm has a very large gate that rises to meet the skies. Adorned with several hundred alcoves, which impart great pleasure to the viewer, the music of kettledrums sound day and night from the gate at the appointed time. All the pain and anguish in the world disappears upon hearing the sound of these drums. Beast and bird, man and spirit, the meek and the brave, rejoice when they hear this musical invitation. The noble and courageous draw life breath from its sound, while their enemies flee in terror from the same. Made entirely of red sandstone, and topped with four beautiful domes, this structure in the Red Fort is known as the Naqqar Khana.[22]

---

[21] Jeremiah P. Losty, 'The Delhi Palace in 1846: A Panoramic View by Mazhar ʿAli Khan', in *Arts of Mughal India: Studies in Honor of Robert Skelton*, ed. Rosemary Crill, Susan Stronge, and Andrew Topsfield, pp. 286–302 (Ahmadabad: Mapin Publishing Ltd., 2004). See also Peter Gottschalk, *Religion, Science and Empire: Classifying Hinduism and Islam in British India* (New York: Oxford University Press, 2013).

[22] Khan, *Āṣār-us Ṣanādīd* (1847), Part II, p. 10. The epigraph is excerpted and translated from the description of the Naqqar Khana as it appears in Sayyid Ahmad's book. He refers to the structure as Naqqar Khana – a portmanteau of the terms *naqqar* (sounding of drums) and *karkhana* (workshop or in this case atelier).

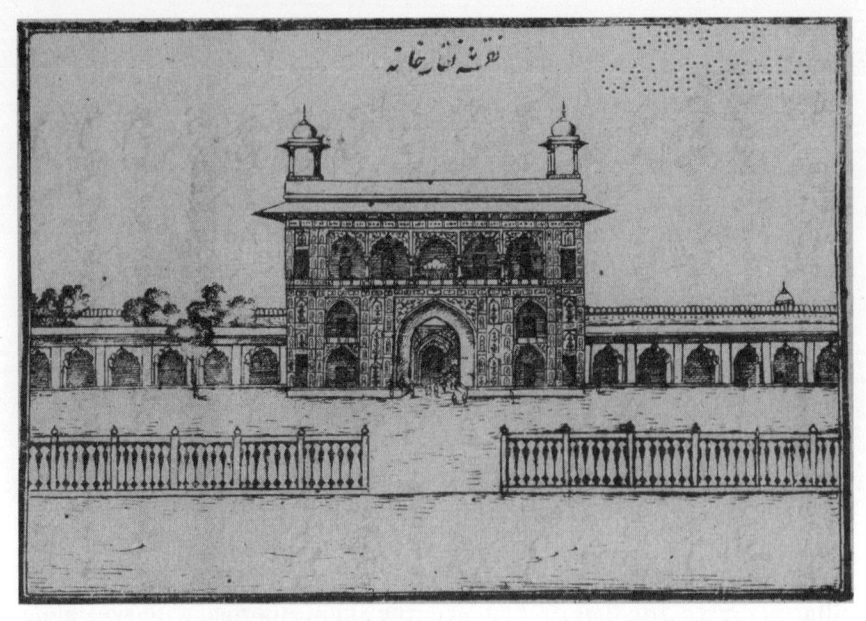

Figure 25 Naqqar Khana of the Red Fort from *Āṣār-us Ṣanādīd* (DS486.D3 A61847). Courtesy of the Bancroft Library, University of California, Berkeley.

What accounts for such discrepancy between the rich sensorial description of the Naqqar Khana and its sterile visual depiction devoid of any signs of human life save a few shadowy figures passing through its gates? When image and text are read together the visual 'silence' of the pomp and circumstance that once surrounded these structures casts an eerie pall over the Naqqar Khana. It appears as a historically mute (both literally and figuratively) yet precious object within the imperial fort complex. Lying dormant, it awaits reactivation of its ceremonial and ritual power – the empty courtyard beckoning a new order of imperial pomp and procession.

The stark depictions of the Red Fort are in contrast to the other excerpts in *Āṣār*, where the images convey the rich urbanism surrounding Delhi's monuments. For example, in his description of the Jama Masjid, Sayyid Ahmad details the delightful urban practices thriving on the four major entrances to the imperial mosque. Each doorway is populated with a unique cast of characters that seem to make up a microcosm of Delhi's society. For instance, the southern doorway and steps leading from Bazaar Chitli Qabr were well known for their *faluda* vendors and *kebabchi*s. The celebration of Nauroz brought out 'angel-faced' boys who were known for their beauty as well as their wily ways.[23] The northern doorway to the mosque was famous for its storytellers and performers, especially the *dastan-go* who narrated the stories of Amir Hamza to a rapt audience of old and young men. The eastern door that leads off to Khās Bazaar, which was originally the ceremonial and imperial entrance to the mosque, was now home to petty merchants who sold textiles. They draped their colourful fabrics on the walls of the mosque so that it looked like a garden in bloom. Pigeon-sellers and horse-traders wandered about yelling the prices of their merchandise. The image accompanying this description of the Jama Masjid certainly does not represent the bustling urbanism described in the text. Nevertheless, the grand southern entrance to the mosque is shown populated by an urban sociality that spills from its steps to the street and the city below.

The drawings of the Red Fort may also be contrasted with an image of the central courtyard of Quwwat-ul Islam mosque, where a man is shown trying to wrap his arms around the Iron Pillar (Figure 26). The fifth-century Iron Pillar was brought to and placed within the central courtyard of the mosque in the twelfth century by the Sultanate rulers of Delhi. The depiction of the pillar in the *Āṣār* references the popular urban myth that those who could meet their arms around the pillar received blessings and the reverse awaited those whose arms did not touch. By deliberately choosing to represent the lived rituals surrounding certain monuments, Sayyid Ahmad roots these monuments within a broader canvas of urban sociality and imagination. By contrast, the images of the Red Fort perform the reverse. They encourage the separation between the fort and the city, between the viewer and the image, between the past and the present.

If the textual depictions of the Red Fort were weighted with historical detail and the precision of dates, measurements, and facts, the visual representations of the fort isolated it from its contemporary sociocultural context. Sayyid Ahmad anticipated a new social and political order by redacting the current dilapidation of the Red Fort and restoring the fort's architectural integrity in the images. In other words, Sayyid Ahmad 'makes room' in the visual representations of the Red Fort for a modernity – the arrival of which he believed was imminent. While the text of *Āṣār* may be infused for a longing for a glorious past, the images are more determined

---

[23] Such triangulated descriptions of commerce, youthful male beauty, and urban space seem to be a motif borrowed from the *shahr āshob* poetry in the Indo-Persian world. For more on this topic see Sunil Sharma, 'The City of Beauties in Indo-Persian Poetic Landscape', *Comparative Studies of South Asia, Africa, and the Middle East* 24, no. 2 (2004): 73–81.

in their stance as impressive relics of a past that must be co-opted into a new future.

Figure 26 Iron Pillar at the Quwwat-ul-Islam Mosque from *Āṣār-us Ṣanādīd* (DS486. D3 A61847). Courtesy of the Bancroft Library, University of California, Berkeley.

AN EMPTY THRONE

A profound (perhaps deliberate) absence in *Āṣār* is that of the reigning Mughal Emperor, Bahadur Shah Zafar. Although Sayyid Ahmad credits him for a few newer structures in the *qila mu`alla*, such as the eponymous Zafar Mahal and Hira Mahal (both are illustrated), the Mughal Emperor's persona and his embodied power are relegated to these peripheral structures on the margins of the political court. Sayyid Ahmad's decision to introduce Bahadur Shah Zafar as a bit-part player in the history of the imperial fort is most clear in his description of the marble *jharoka*[24] (royal throne) in the Diwan-e `Am. The section on the Diwan-e `Am begins with the

---

[24] The term *jharoka* refers to a covered balcony or a baldachin, but in the Mughal style came to be associated with the canopied throne in the Diwan-e `Am. Sayyid Ahmad himself does not use the term *jharoka*, opting instead for the term *pesh-taq* (an arched building or cupola) or *nishiman* (mansion) to describe the structure. I have used *jharoka* here as this is the term commonly used for this particular architectural form.

observation that, in the past, when the emperor held court, the *jharoka* was the structure in which he would present himself to the public. The marble railing around the Diwan-e ʾAm, that once was decorated with beautiful engravings and topped with delicate finials, has now fallen into ruin (*tūta-phūta bāqi hain*).[25] Another railing made of red sandstone that defined the large forecourt in front of the Diwan-e ʾAm, where the court would gather and stand according to rank, was also in similar disrepair until it was recently refurbished by Bahadur Shah Zafar. By referring to the function of the *jharoka* in the past tense and the derelict condition of the boundary between imperial seat and the wider world, Sayyid Ahmad sets up the Diwan-e ʾAm as the empty seat of a now hollow crown. The Mughal Emperor's agency in repairing not the actual structure of the Diwan-e ʾAm but the outer railing further emphasizes his feebleness. The vacant *jharoka* appears as a taunt of the Mughal Emperor's absence and the symbol of collapsed Mughal power.

The textual description of the *jharoka* is as richly rendered as any other structure in the Red Fort. Sayyid Ahmad refers to the royal throne in the Diwan-e ʾAm as the *nishiman zille-illāhi* (mansion in the shadow of God), the *takht-i-shāhi* (royal seat), and *aurang zille-illāhi* (throne in the shadow of God). He describes the *jharoka* as made entirely of marble and resembling a small *bangla* (a vernacular house) because of its four pillars, open sides, and curved roof. The entire structure is covered with exquisite inlay work of floral motifs (a reference to the *pietra dura*) as well as many different animals and birds, including the image of Orpheus playing the lute to the lion and the lamb that adorns the back of the *jharoka*. Sayyid Ahmad describes the *jharoka* as an object of aesthetic excess – its materiality (white marble contrasting with the earthy red sandstone) and artistry (its delicate *pietra dura* work and allegorical imagery) signifying the opulence of the Shah Jahani era.

In terms of procession as well, the *jharoka* was the jewelled terminus at the end of a long axis that stretched from the Fatehpuri Mosque at one end of Chandni Chowk to the interior of the royal palace. As Sayyid Ahmad notes earlier in the section, until Aurangzeb had built the barbican of the Lahori Gate, nobility proceeding towards the Red Fort dismounted from their horses in front of the Fatehpuri Mosque and walked the length of the Chandni Chowk and then entered the *qila muʾalla* to finally reach the Diwan-e ʾAm. City and royal fort were thus united by the bodily practices of procession

---

[25] Khan, *Āsār-us Sanādīd* (1847), Part II, p. 11.

and ceremony. At the Diwan-e ʿAm, these norms of bodily submission to the emperor were manifested in the proportion of the architecture. For example, Sayyid Ahmad notes that the base of the *jharoka* is taller than the heads of most men so that the emperor was always elevated above the nobles and petitioners. Those approaching the emperor with a petition had to climb on a small marble step in front of the *jharoka* to present their request; even then, they would remain at a lower level from the emperor. Similarly, the courtiers standing in the large forecourt in front of the Diwan-e ʿAm (defined by the red sandstone railing) would be arranged by rank and assume a posture of submission by standing with their hands folded in front of the emperor. Commoners were not allowed within the precinct defined by the red sandstone railing.

In other words, when the Diwan-e ʿAm was used as it was in the past, it represented the perfect order of the empire: the emperor at the magnificent centre of a well-organized court, with the nobility and his subjects arranged concentrically around him. By documenting the *jharoka* as an unoccupied structure, Sayyid Ahmad mourns the loss of such imperial organization. Unsaid in this description is Sayyid Ahmad's personal history of having been offered a position at the court, continuing the legacy of his maternal grandfather who had served under the Mughal Emperor with the title of *Jawwad-ud-daulah Arif Jung*. Sayyid Ahmad had chosen the service of the English East India Company instead.[26] His less than flattering description of the Diwan-e ʿAm might also be read as a further assertion of his own separation from the Mughal court.

The art historian Ebba Koch explains the Hindu and Islamic ritual aspects of Shah Jahan's *jharoka* in the Diwan-e ʿAm. She argues that the daily ritual of the emperor of presenting himself to his court and the broader public framed in an arched console can be seen as a form of *darshan* – the Hindu ritual of devotees 'seeing' or 'gazing upon' their deities in the daily acts of worship. To this end, the architecture of the *jharoka* mimics the shrine-like interiority of the Hindu temple, where the deity is enshrined in the *garbagriha* (sanctum sanctorum), a building within the larger building of the temple. Like the *jharoka*, the axial pathway of the Hindu temple proceeds from public (and profane) to increasingly sacred and least accessible terminus of the *garbagriha*. In addition to these Hindu practices, the architectural form of the *jharoka* simulates Islamic sumptuary rituals, especially the daily

---

[26] H. Khan Sherwani, 'The Political Thought of Sir Sayyid Ahmad Khan', *Indian Journal of Political Science* 5, no. 4 (1944): 304–28.

act of bowing in front of the *mihrab* – the blind arch in mosques that faces Mecca and signifies the prostration of the faithful to Allah. In the Diwan-e ʾAm, Hindu and Muslim subjects reiterated such bodily acts of prostration, devotion, and submission in front of the *jharoka*, the only difference was that the *mihrab* or the *garbagriha* now held the emperor's body. The *jharoka* thus allowed both access and separation: it allowed intimacy with the emperor while reinforcing his demigod status.[27] An absent emperor, however, meant an empty *jharoka* denuded of its symbolic affect.

Sayyid Ahmad closes his description of the *jharoka* and the Diwan-e ʾAm as follows: 'It has been many days since a court was held here. This hallowed structure, where once even the ambassadors of powerful kings did not have the good fortune to enter, now lies desolate (*veerān pada hua hain*). Royal guards lounge about in it day and night.'[28] The imperial *jharoka* and the Diwan-e ʾAm lay unoccupied and vacant; this is clearly more than a matter of pragmatic disuse to Sayyid Ahmad. Indeed, the very hollowing out of the Mughal Empire is apparent in its inability to command authority over the court, no matter its vast dominions. By describing the desolation of the Diwan-e ʾAm, Sayyid Ahmad definitively calls the end of the Mughal Empire. In *Āṣār*, this is both a moment of textual and visual crisis, where the Red Fort is the site of mourning and its substantial architectural heft cannot make up for the hollowing out of imperial power.

READING *ĀṢĀR* TODAY

In recent scholarship, Sayyid Ahmad is rightly acknowledged as a reformer (especially in the field of education) – a champion of modernization – for his philosophical views on religion, nation, and naturalism and his contributions towards Urdu. Less has been said about Sayyid Ahmad's vision of modernity and historical progress as it was shaped by the urban environment. I argue that although *Āṣār* is in stark contrast to his preceding and subsequent writings, it aided Sayyid Ahmad's formulation of modernism that would profoundly shape his later works. In the section dedicated to the Red Fort analysed here, one can already detect Sayyid Ahmad's struggle with the dissonant components of modernity. For example, his struggle to reconcile the glorious history of the Red Fort with its current dilapidation begs the

---

[27] Ebba Koch, *Mughal Art and Imperial Ideology: Collected Essays* (New Delhi: Oxford University Press, 2001).

[28] Khan, *Āṣār-us Ṣanādīd* (1847), Part II, p. 13.

following question: Does the embrace of modernity (which Sayyid Ahmad clearly saw as a European import) require a clean, if painful, rupture from the past? Similarly, his discomfort with the impotency of the Mughal Empire and the concomitant demise of orderly governance illustrate his belief in a new form of political economy based on rational adjudication and centralized leadership. Most importantly, *Āṣār* is evidence of Sayyid Ahmad's belief that his fellow countrymen were capable of scientific thought and rational arbitration, and the proof of this was provided by the architecture of Delhi. By explaining the technological aspects of the Red Fort and more than hundred other structures in Delhi, Sayyid Ahmad clarified that Islamic culture had been innovative in scientific method and material progress. In other words, Delhi's architecture helped prove Sayyid Ahmad's view that the current impoverished state of Delhi was due to the lack of a political and intellectual infrastructure, rather than an inherent incapacity of Islam to keep pace with modernity. This defence of Islamic consciousness and his belief that Islam could thrive besides and profit from European modernity would become the leitmotif of Sayyid Ahmad's later writings, his advocacy, and, of course, his founding of the Muhammadan Anglo-Oriental College in 1877.

Cities have proven important loci for mediating modernity indexed by South Asian context. William Glover showed that in case of Lahore, various genres of urban writings (encyclopaedic surveys, fictions, and histories with particular emphasis on colonial improvements) emerged in the mid to late nineteenth century as a way to contend with modernization and change. As Glover demonstrates, urban writing became one way in which abstract conceptualizations of progress, political upheaval, and new moralities could be materialized or recorded through the landscape of cities such as Lahore.

As with European cities, dramatic urban change was indexed by the South Asian intellectuals to a new moral order.[29] For example, the genealogical links between the material culture of Delhi's buildings and the *tazkirah* or the biographical description of the city's important protagonists in *Āṣār* was taken up by the Lahori historian Noor Ahmad Chishti in his *Tahqiqāt Chishti: Tārīkh-e Lahor ka Encyclopedia* (1867).[30] Sayyid Ahmad entirely dispensed with the *tazkirah* in the second edition of *Āṣār*, leaving the monuments to perform the work of historical actors as well as archaeological structures. One personality, however, continued to dominate the description

[29] Glover, *Making Lahore Modern*.
[30] Ibid.

of Delhi's built environment in both editions of *Āsār* – Sayyid Ahmad himself. His gaze negotiated the past and present of Delhi through the urban environment. His voice narrated the poetics and excavated the sciences of Delhi's urbanism. He was the chronicler of Delhi's past, and as the city stood on the cusp of massive change, he became a cartographer of its future. As such, Sayyid Ahmad's articulation of modernity was ineluctably bound up with that of Delhi and embodied the vexed currents between the past and the present, religion and science, and the nostalgia of a bygone empire and the seduction of a modern future. The irreconcilable vectors of modernity are made evident in Sayyid Ahmad's struggle with the Red Fort as an icon of the Mughal past and potential catalyst for future change.

CONCLUSION

It is tempting to read Sayyid Ahmad today and see him as prescient, forecasting the events of the 1857 rebellion when the imperial power at the Red Fort changed dramatically from the Mughals to the British. Indeed, one might even go so far as to say that in a purely discursive sense, *Āsār* almost prepares the ground for the British occupation of the *qila mu`alla* by casting a melancholic pall on the Red Fort and predicting the radical caesura between the Mughal and British Empires. However, how Sayyid Ahmad saw the future, especially how centrally the *qila mu`alla* would figure in the changing fortunes of Delhi during and after 1857 remains unknown. Given his explanation in the *Asbāb-e Baghāwat*, Sayyid Ahmad could not have predicted the opprobrium that would befall the Muslim community after the 1857 rebellion. What is clear, however, is that confronting Delhi's rich built heritage was key to Sayyid Ahmad's lifelong commitment of recovering the Islamic cultural past and securing it within a timeline of impending modern innovation.

Not content to confine Delhi's Islamic, particularly Mughal, architecture to the mute status of ruins or relics, Sayyid Ahmad recuperated value from Delhi's largely Islamic built environment by detailing its architectural successes and technological achievements for posterity. Concomitantly, however, he recognized the need for a new realm of scientific and industrial change – a change that was both inevitable and necessary for progress. Therefore, some of his plaintive descriptions of the *qila mu`alla* should not be misunderstood for an uncritical yearning for a precolonial past or a simplistic rejection of contemporary order and possibility. Instead, *Āsār* can most productively be read as Sayyid Ahmad's first attempt to reconcile the many seemingly paradoxical elements of modernity into a seamless narrative of historical development and progress. It is not difficult to imagine Sayyid Ahmad hoping that the *qila mu`alla* would become the site of such a syncretic modernity – a fruitful conjugation of Islamic traditions and European modernity, representing a graceful and unbroken arc from Mughal imperial power to rational political organization. History, however, unfolded differently in 1857. Although stationed in Bijnor during the rebellion, Sayyid Ahmad no doubt heard of the wanton destruction of the Red Fort by the British army during 1857 and its conversion into a military camp. Despite being a prolific author, Sayyid Ahmad would never write again about the built environment.[31] Perhaps a return to Delhi, particularly the Red Fort, in its state of destruction, was too painful for him to contemplate. Perhaps, Delhi had already served as the catalyst for his articulations of modernity and provided fodder for his many intellectual schemes to come. Yet, inarguably, the Sayyid Ahmad that we see emerging in *Āṣār* is a modern intellectual attempting to reconcile the dissonant notes of modernity – a project that would occupy him for the rest of his life in one form or another.

---

[31] In his biography of Sayyid Ahmad, Altaf Hussain Hali mentions that Sayyid Ahmad wrote a history of Bijnor when he was stationed there between 1854 and 1856. This manuscript was lost in the 1857 rebellion and it is impossible to know how much or how little the built environment may have figured in that narrative of history. See Altaf Husain Hali, *Hayat-e Javed: A Biographical Account of Sir Sayyid*, trans. K. H. Qadiri and David J. Matthews (Delhi: Idarah-e Adabiyat-e Delli, 2009 [1979]).

13 A Living Legacy
Sir Sayyid Today
AMBER H. ABBAS

In one of the first interviews I conducted in Aligarh, retired Aligarh Muslim University (AMU) professor of English Asloob Ahmad Ansari described Sir Sayyid Ahmad Khan 'as the greatest benefactor of the Muslims in the last several years'.[1] He quickly edited the scope of his comment by adding, 'or centuries, I should say'. This temporal slip of the frame is more than incidental, and it reappears in much of the current thinking among those sympathetic to Sir Sayyid's educational mission. It captures the perception that Sir Sayyid's work is temporally transcendent – it was born of his moment and remains relevant to the current one. He represented the Aligarh ideal – faithful, educated, generous, dedicated to the cause of Muslim uplift, and progressive – as he pushed against lurking conservatism within the Indian Muslim community. In the Muhammadan Anglo-Oriental (MAO) College, which became AMU in 1920, Sir Sayyid sought to cultivate Muslim men, who embodied these characteristics and were well prepared for public life.

The lasting legacy of Sir Sayyid's work is best exemplified by AMU, as one respondent said, 'He IS AMU.'[2] When graduates and well-wishers of AMU reflect on the role and legacy of Sir Sayyid, his objective of Muslim uplift seems as vital to Indian Muslims today as it was when he founded MAO College in 1875. Responses from surveys and oral history interviews with former students and professors demonstrate that Sir Sayyid's mission to develop a modern educational system for Muslims was both visionary

---

[1] Asloob Ahmad Ansari, interviewed by Amber H. Abbas, Aligarh, India, 5 July 2008, interview in author's possession. Ansari was born in Delhi in 1925. He completed his education from Intermediate through his Master of Arts at Aligarh Muslim University by 1946. He then earned an Honors degree in English language and literature from Oxford University and became a reader and later a professor at AMU. He retired in 1987 and currently lives in Aligarh.

[2] Syed Ali Rizvi, response to online survey, August 2016.

and resilient.[3] While the university has been indispensable in advancing the cause of Muslim education, through their attachment to the need to advance Sir Sayyid's educational agenda continually, these former students suggest that his goals remain unfulfilled.

AMU graduates, distinguished by the appellation, 'Alig,' are spread among all South Asian states, and indeed, the world.[4] The oldest surviving generation of Aligs comprises those who were students during the upheavals of independence and partition in the 1940s, who settled in the newly independent states. The younger generations of Aligs, since the 1960s, are primarily Indian or they are from outside the subcontinent. Since the 1950s, few Aligs have been from Pakistan or Bangladesh. No matter where they have settled, Aligs often seek each other out and form alumni associations – known as 'AMU Old Boys' Associations' (AMUOBAs) – wherever they land and use these organizations to network, seek assistance, and find a meaningful community.[5] As Zakir Ali Khan, the General Secretary of the Pakistan AMUOBA from 1960 until his death in 2012 emphasized to me, 'If you have been educated in Aligarh and if you come to know, you need no introduction. You can straight away go to England and [Aligs] say, "What do you need? What are your requirements?" You have got friends in U.K. and America.'[6] During my own research on AMU, this global network helped me to locate the 1940s graduates in India, Pakistan, and Bangladesh

---

[3] In addition to seventy longer oral history interviews conducted between 2005 and 2010, I conducted an online survey in 2016 and advertised it through two different listservs frequented by AMU graduates and well-wishers: *AMU Network* and *World of Aligs*. Fifteen respondents participated directly through the survey or email communication with me.

[4] Rizvi, response to online survey.

[5] The blog *Aligarh Nama* offers a guide on 'How to Spot an Aligarian' that includes traits such as 'someone who greets people with a loud "Salam Alaikum" without feeling shy about revealing his identity'; 'looks graceful in appearance'; 'respects seniors, older people irrespective of their economic status'; 'addresses other unknown people of his age with "partner"'. Available at https://aligarhnama. blogspot.com/2009/02/how-to-spot-aligarian.html (accessed on 15 May 2018).

[6] Zakir Ali Khan, interviewed by Amber H. Abbas, Karachi, Pakistan, 10 August 2006. Unless otherwise noted, all interviews are archived in the *Sites of Disturbance: Oral History and Memories of Partition*, Oral History Project, Louie B. Nunn Center for Oral History, University of Kentucky Libraries. Khan graduated from AMU in 1948 with a degree in civil engineering. He migrated to Pakistan in 1949 where he served first as an assistant and later as a chief engineer in the Karachi Metropolitan Corporation. He lived in Karachi and died in 2012.

and included me in discussions with the later ones. Both the generations of Aligs, the older and the younger, have emphasized different features of Sir Sayyid's legacy, but illuminated the aspects of his mission that have inspired their priorities today.

The older generation – whether in India, Pakistan or Bangladesh – highlighted the historic atmosphere of inclusivity and tolerance in AMU. Sir Sayyid's efforts to rejuvenate Muslims had the potential to benefit non-Muslims as well. Since the time of Sir Sayyid's first Scientific Society, retired Aligarh professor Iftikhar Alam Khan told me, '... it was a symbol that in our society, no one has any relationship to religion.'[7] Pushing the point further, Ather Siddiqi, a retired AMU professor still living in Aligarh, argued that Sir Sayyid's efforts to raise the status of Muslims were akin to taking care of a 'handicapped child'. He further stated, 'But he was not anti-Hindu. He was not opposed to any other community.'[8] During the 1940s, anti-imperial movements, including the Muslim League's demand for Pakistan, animated the campus. Former students from this period were particularly keen to demonstrate to me that AMU was not 'communal'. While pro-Muslim, it was not anti-Hindu. Pakistani Major General Ghulam Umar told me, '[The Hindu students still] dressed exactly the same as I dressed.... One of the things was, if you found a Hindu student and myself, you could not distinguish. He was wearing the Turkish cap, he was wearing that *sherwani* and he was behaving exactly [as we were].'[9] Even in the aftermath of the 1947 partition, Majid Ali Siddiqi told me, 'There is no

---

[7] Iftikhar Alam Khan, interviewed by Amber H. Abbas, Aligarh, India, 6 June 2009. Iftikhar Alam Khan arrived in Minto Circle School in 1949 and completed high school in 1952. He graduated from AMU and became a professor of Museology there. He is an expert on Aligarh's architectural history and has written several books on the subject.

[8] Ather Siddiqi, interviewed by Amber H. Abbas, Aligarh, India, 11 May 2009. Ather Siddiqi is originally from Saharanpur. He took admission in AMU in 1947 for his Intermediate, where he also completed his Master of Science. He earned his doctorate in Zoology in the United States and became a professor in AMU. He is currently retired from AMU and lives with his wife and fellow academic, Zakiya Siddiqi, in Aligarh.

[9] Ghulam Umar, interviewed by Amber H. Abbas, Karachi, Pakistan, 8 August 2006. Major General Ghulam Umar completed all his education in AMU before joining the Indian Army in the early 1940s during World War II. He served in Pakistan's army during both the 1965 and 1971 wars. After he retired, he was involved in people-to-people diplomacy with India. He passed away in January 2009.

question that even Hindu–Muslim *thinking* was not there at Aligarh, at that time.'[10] The university, its faculty, and staff have been fiercely protective of its history of inclusivity. In our interviews, they deployed this narrative to show that Aligarh was not a separatist institution. Despite its contentious history of association with the Muslim League's demand for Pakistan and the involvement of many – not all – of AMU students in electioneering work on behalf of the League, this narrative resists the aspersion that AMU is not fully Indian.[11]

Later generations, having studied in Aligarh after independence, focussed more acutely on the impact that AMU had in advancing education for women and for Muslims belonging to lower social classes. As Shenaz Khan suggested in her response to an online survey I conducted in 2016, those 'who otherwise wouldn't have the opportunity to avail higher learning, thank Sir Syed Ahmad Khan every day for giving them the opportunity to higher education by founding/establishing AMU'.[12] Like the older narrators, these later graduates emphasize Sir Sayyid's role in developing a modern Muslim education, and particularly the confidence that an AMU education offers to Muslims. As the university has grown to approximately thirty thousand students, including thousands of women at the undergraduate and postgraduate levels, its importance in ensuring that Muslims can pursue higher education cannot be underestimated. The greatest challenge they reveal, however, remains the one that Sir Sayyid originally recognized: the tension between conservative and progressive forces in Indian Muslim communities. Although the university still comes under attack for suspicions of being 'communal', later generations of AMU graduates have focussed more intently on the internal challenges – especially factionalism among Indian Muslims – that the university faces in upholding Sir Sayyid's mission.

---

[10] Majid Ali Siddiqi, interviewed by Amber H. Abbas, Lucknow, India, 2 October 2009. Majid Ali Siddiqi was born in 1935 in Gorakhpur, India. He arrived at AMU in 1952 to study engineering. He was also involved in sports – hurdles and hockey – at AMU. He completed his Bachelor of Science in civil engineering from AMU in 1956. He lives in Lucknow.

[11] Though Aligs were active in advancing the cause of Pakistan in the 1940s and were particularly active in election work, I argue that their activism itself must be considered separately from the creation of Pakistan. Amber H. Abbas, 'The Solidarity Agenda: Aligarh Students and the Demand for Pakistan', *South Asian History and Culture Special Issue, Defying the Perpetual Exception: Culture and Power in South Asian Islam* 5, no. 2 (2014): 147–62.

[12] Shenaz Khan, response to online survey, August 2016.

All of the respondents confirmed that Sir Sayyid's educational agenda remains meaningful and necessary today. Within the global Muslim community, respondents indicated that the university's reputation for its 'rich Muslim culture' is as important for attracting students as the fact that it is one of India's Central Universities.[13] However, Muslims in India face many of the same challenges that Sir Sayyid sought to alleviate: They are underrepresented in public services and employment, but overrepresented in jails. In addition, compared with the non-Muslims, they perform moderately on examinations, have an overall lower level of educational achievement, and experience higher rates of poverty.[14] In 2018, Muslim representation in the Lok Sabha 'is at an all-time low', reported Shoaib Daniyal, with just '22 MPs in the 545-strong current House'.[15] These conditions may help to explain the persistence of a narrative of 'relative deprivation' that is key to the politics of rejuvenation engendered at AMU.[16] Although Sir Sayyid's values were embedded in the current politics of his time, they have become the model by which Aligarh partisans relate to other Indian Muslims as members of a permanent minority in India. Aligs extolled Sir Sayyid's formidable legacy when they suggested – as one respondent did – that they were 'indebted to him' as well as when they advanced a narrative of decline as a defining feature of the Indian Muslim experience.[17] Both features of Sir Sayyid's legacy have motivated Aligs to establish new institutions that claim to advance his educational goals (and often bear his name) throughout the subcontinent and the world.

LEGACY: A BRIEF HISTORY OF AMU

Visitors enter AMU through the Bab-e Sayyid, an ornate red sandstone gate delineating the campus of the university from the city surrounding it. Once

[13] Shenaz Khan, response to online survey.
[14] Justice Rajinder Sachar, *The Sachar Committee Report: Social, Economic, and Educational Status of the Muslim Community of India* (New Delhi: Prime Minister's High Level Committee, Cabinet Secretariat, Government of India).
[15] Shoaib Daniyal, 'Saffron Paradox: Hindutva Supporters Seem Determined to Prove Jinnah was Right', *Scroll.in*, 8 May 2018, available at https://scroll.in/article/878126/permanent-minority-did-jinnah-predict-the-political-marginalisation-of-muslims-in-todays-india (accessed on 10 October 2018).
[16] Gail Minault, *Secluded Scholars: Women's Education and Muslim Social Reform in Colonial India* (Delhi, New York: Oxford University Press, 1998), p. 50.
[17] Shenaz Khan, response to online survey.

inside his eponymous gate, visitors meet Sir Sayyid again in nearly every room, where his bearded visage gazes down on students and administrators alike. Sir Sayyid's gaze links everyone associated with the institution together in a shared experience – one that ties them both to the university and each other. Graduates of AMU – Aligarh Old Boys (even if they are women!) or Aligs – continue to carry his mantle and seek to further his original agenda of Muslim uplift from a period of decline.

Sir Sayyid came to see that traditional systems were losing social currency in the changing environment of British India after the Indian Rebellion of 1857, which brought a formal end to Mughal power. British schools taught English and were spreading quickly after 1860, but the majority of their students were Hindu. Muslims were sceptical of these schools that promised 'enlightenment', fearing that English education would be instrumental in 'creating disbelief of religion in the minds of the pupils'.[18] Therefore, if Muslim students were to study English, Sir Sayyid would have to convince their families of not only its utility in public life but also its consistency with their faith and traditional values. His first moves towards educational reform involved establishing scientific societies and supporting the translation of Western scientific texts into Urdu and then making English the language of instruction in MAO College.

These reforms were intended to counter the pattern identified by W. W. Hunter's 1871 *The Indian Mussalmans*.[19] However, Hunter's evidence of Muslim alienation applied most specifically to the Muslims in Bengal, and evidence does not support a narrative of actual decline of the north Indian Muslim elite – who were the focus of Sir Sayyid's attentions – prior to 1947.[20] Still, the perception of deprivation spurred a shoring up of elite Muslim values after 1857. Anxiety over Muslim decline helped Sir Sayyid to generate support for his ideas.

---

[18] Sayyid Ahmed Khan, 'Translation of the Report of the Members of the Select Committee for the Better Diffusion and Advancement of Learning among Muhammadans of India', in *The Aligarh Movement: Basic Documents, 1864–1898*, ed. Shan Muhammad, vol. 2, pp. 337–80 (Meerut: Meenakshi Prakashan, 1978), p. 341.

[19] W. W. Hunter, *The Indian Musalmans: Are They Bound in Conscience to Rebel against the Queen?* (London: Trubner and Co., 1871).

[20] Anil Seal, *The Emergence of Indian Nationalism: Competition and Collaboration in the Later Nineteenth Century* (London: Cambridge University Press, 1968), pp. 304–5. See also Sachar, *The Sachar Committee Report*.

During his lifetime, Sir Sayyid's educational agenda was often met with controversy because he sought to draw the Muslim service gentry closer to the prevailing British power. As David Lelyveld demonstrates, the institution in Aligarh preserved the basic tenets of a Muslim education, but as a chronogram composed to commemorate the inauguration of MAO College notes, 'Both kinds of education – worldly and religious are indispensable for the students. It is as if the body of the madrasa is made of English, but its soul is religious education.'[21]

Riazur Rahman Sherwani, who was a student at Aligarh during the 1940s, offered some perspective on this:

> The main Aligarh Movement, it was mainly for modernizing the thinking of the Muslims. Sir Sayyid wanted to modernize the thinking of the Muslims in every sphere of life. His religion, his politics, in literature, in social life... And he thought that only through Western education this aim can be achieved... But, on one condition. He always said, that I want that the Muslims should remain Muslims and remaining Muslims they should achieve these things. Not by giving up their religion.[22]

Thus, the hallmark of the Aligarh experience was, according to 1944 graduate Wajahat Husain, a retired Major General in the Pakistan Army, 'a very tolerant, advanced, progressive Muslim society and education'.[23] The environment that the early leaders in AMU sought to cultivate prioritized

---

[21] Rafi Ahmad Alavi, *Translation of Hayat-i-Jawed: A Biographical Account of Sir Syed Ahmad Khan by Altaf Husain Hali* (Aligarh: Aligarh Muslim University Press, 2008), pp. 108–9.

[22] Riazur Rahman Sherwani, interviewed by Amber H. Abbas, Aligarh, India, 6 July 2008. Riazur Rahman Sherwani began his schooling in Minto Circle School in Aligarh in the 1930s. He went on to complete his Master in Arts and obtain his doctorate in Arabic from AMU. He then taught at both AMU and Kashmir University. He is retired and currently lives in his family home Habib Manzil, Aligarh.

[23] Wajahat Husain, interviewed by Amber H. Abbas, Lahore, Pakistan, 13 June 2005. Wajahat Husain was born in Aligarh. He did his early schooling in Minto Circle School and the Muslim University City High School before he began his university education at AMU. He graduated from AMU in 1944 and volunteered for the Air Training Corps in 1945. He opted for Pakistan and rose to the rank of Major General in the Pakistan Army. He lived in Lahore and passed away in 2013.

the brotherhood of students residing within its walls.[24] Sir Sayyid articulated an early version of his vision in 1871 when he argued,

> ... the children of the noble, and well-to-do Muhammadans should be kept at a distance from their homes ... they should be brought up and educated in a particular manner, and under special care.... Boarding houses should be opened in healthy localities ... with a garden and play ground attached; that there should be a mosque with a Muazzin ... belonging to each house; all of the boys should be compelled to learn and say their prayers and all of them should be made to wear one and the same dress.[25]

Sir Sayyid cautioned that unless boys were 'brought up in the manner above referred to, they will always remain ignorant, worthless, and exposed to all sorts of evils'.[26] As Vice Chancellor Aftab Ahmad Khan wrote in 1926, the residential system was the

> ... most distinctive and the most important feature of our institution from its very start.... Hundreds of young men, coming from different and distant parts of the country, and representing all sorts of ideas and manners, virtues and vices, if kept under proper control and effective discipline, gradually evolve a corporate life and character which leads to success.[27]

Indeed, the moral community of Aligs was defined by solidarity of social status and experience, not merely religious confession. As Abdul Rasheed Khan and many others argued, 'character building was the most

---

[24] The most thorough examination of the early years of the MAO College is David Lelyveld, *Aligarh's First Generation: Muslim Solidarity in British India* (Princeton: Princeton, University Press, 1978). It is complemented by his article 'Three Aligarh Students: Aftab Ahmad Khan, Ziauddin Ahmad, and Muhammad Ali', *Modern Asian Studies* 9, no. 2 (1975): 227–40.

[25] Ahmed Khan, 'Translation of the Report of the Members of the Select Committee', pp. 371–2.

[26] Ibid., p. 372.

[27] Aftab Ahmad Khan, *Note by Aftab Ahmad Khan on His Work and Experience During the Last Three Years of His Office as Vice-Chancellor of AMU: Addressed to Members of the University Court* (Aligarh: Aligarh Muslim University, 1926), pp. 54–5.

emphasized of all'.[28] This 'character building' foregrounded unity among Aligarh students. While the most salient aspect of this unity was Muslim identity, the other persistent aspects of AMU's culture – respect for elders, guidance of juniors, traditions of dress (the uniform of the *sherwani*), and greeting – are all products of the residential culture that forged the Aligarh man irrespective of his heritage. These features defined the Aligarh *mahol* (atmosphere) and remained meaningful even in the minds of graduates who ultimately opted to migrate to Pakistan, leaving Aligarh and fellow Aligs in India.

Although these narrators emphasized the absence of Hindu–Muslim strife within the institution during the 1940s, this period was transformative in the university's history as politics became a key aspect of daily life on the campus. Muhammad Ali Jinnah frequently visited the campus during the 1940s and lauded Aligarh boys as 'the arsenal of Muslim India'.[29] The siren song of Pakistan, with its echoes of the tradition of Muslim solidarity so deeply embedded on the campus, drew many AMU students into its thrall. The outcome of the Pakistan demand, the creation of a separate Muslim state, damaged AMU's reputation in India, although the university has remained a stalwart advocate for Muslim equality and advancement.

EDUCATION AND POLITICS

During his lifetime, Sir Sayyid urged young men to stay out of politics and to focus on their studies. Still, there has been a persistent tension between education and politics on the campus. Muhammad Ali, a member of Aligarh's first generation, a leader of the Khilafat Movement, and a founder of the Jamia Millia Islamia, recognized that Sir Sayyid's advice to students to 'concentrate their energies and attention on education' was appropriate for

---

[28] Abdul Rasheed Khan, interviewed by Amber H. Abbas, Karachi, Pakistan, 10 August 2006. Abdul Rasheed Khan was born in Saharanpur. He completed his matriculation and started at AMU in 1944. As a student at AMU, he worked for the elections in 1945–1946 and later he migrated to Pakistan in late 1947. He has now retired from the Karachi Development Authority and serves on the faculty of the Sir Syed University of Engineering and Technology in Karachi.

[29] Muhammad Ali Jinnah, 'Speech at the Muslim University Union, Aligarh, March 10, 1941', in *Some Recent Speeches and Writings of Mr. Jinnah*, ed. Jamil-ud-din Ahmad, 5th ed., 2 vols, vol. 1, pp. 225–32 (Lahore: Sh. Muhammad Ashraf, 1952), p. 268.

its time.[30] However, as Ali's own experience reveals, AMU students rarely heeded this advice and were often motivated to discuss politics and engage in political behaviour. The anti-imperial resistance that led to the founding of the Jamia Millia Islamia in the Aligarh Mosque in 1920 demonstrates how students' enthusiasm can lead to transformative change.[31]

By the early 1940s, AMU students were again attracted to national politics and engaged in efforts to resist British power. In contrast to the Sir Sayyid's injunctions against getting involved in politics, Wajahat Husain argued that an AMU education 'prepared them to take part in the social and political and national affairs'.[32] For him, an AMU education offered all the tools for his own political participation, and the Muslim League's demand for Pakistan seemed to embody Sir Sayyid's goals of developing solidarity among Muslims.[33] Indeed, although Sir Sayyid never could have envisioned a separate homeland for Muslims, many in Pakistan have claimed Sir Sayyid's mantle and honoured him as an intellectual founder of Pakistan.[34]

By contrast, Riazur Rahman Sherwani, who, as a student, supported the Indian National Congress, lamented that Sir Sayyid's goals were diluted by the intrusion of politics:

The Aligarh Movement was a vast movement. Actually politics, when politics became dominant here, it lost many things. The main purpose for which this institution was established and what was the main object of Sir Sayyid, it went back. Politics came forward.

[30] Muhammad Ali, 'Mohammad Ali on the Muslim League and the Indian National Congress', *The Comrade*, December 1925, repr. in *The Indian Muslims: A Documentary Record 1900–1947*, ed. Shan Muhammad, vol. 8, pp. 42–51 (New Delhi: Meenakshi Prakashan, 1985).
[31] Gail Minault and David Lelyveld, 'The Campaign for a Muslim University, 1898–1920', *Modern Asian Studies* 8, no. 2 (1974): 145–89.
[32] Wajahat Husain, interview, 11 June 2006.
[33] Abbas, 'The Solidarity Agenda'.
[34] The Nazaria-e Pakistan Trust has advanced this narrative. During an event celebrating Sir Sayyid's bicentennial birthday, which coincided with Pakistan's 70th year, the President of Pakistan acknowledged Sir Sayyid's role in the educational development of Muslims. Javed Iqbal, 'Sir Syed Laid Pakistan's Foundation', *The Nation*, 11 January 2017, available at https://nation.com.pk/11-Jan-2017/sir-syed-laid-pakistan-s-foundation-mamnoon (accessed on 10 October 2018).

[Politics] was not in the interest of the institution because it was basically established for spreading education among the Muslims. Among Indians! Particularly among the Muslims.[35]

While Sherwani and Husain were rough contemporaries at AMU and both appealed to Sir Sayyid's founding ideals, the India–Pakistan border runs between their divergent perspectives.

Immediately after the 1947 partition, Mohammad Amin, a former professor of History at the University of Delhi, told me that any association with AMU was considered a 'black mark' on one's record.[36] Within a few months, the institution undertook a nationalist turn, which is reflected in many of the narratives from that era's students, as they eschewed the association with the politics of the Muslim League. The 1948 issue of the *Aligarh Magazine* opened with an image of the recently assassinated M. K. Gandhi and a panegyric obituary urging AMU students to uphold the 'ideals of universal human brotherhood and peace for which he lived so single-mindedly'.[37] Sherwani was moved by these ideals and was careful to note that Sir Sayyid's efforts were intended to benefit 'all' Indians. It was especially important that his agenda not appear too parochial in an independent India in which Muslims were always going to be a minority. Many narrators emphasized the role of Prime Minister Jawaharlal Nehru in appointing an Aligarh Old Boy, Zakir Husain, as Vice Chancellor during this tumultuous period, and therefore, 'saving' the university.[38] Still, the university continues

---

[35] Riazur Rahman Sherwani, interview.

[36] Mohammad Amin, personal communication with Amber H. Abbas, 1 November 2009. Mohammad Amin, born in 1928, was a student in AMU during the 1940s but was not active in Muslim League election work. He later became a professor in St. Stephen's College of Delhi University, where he taught medieval history for over forty years. He was awarded the Padma Bhushan, India's third highest civilian honour, in 2012; he passed away later that year.

[37] Syed Zainul Abedin, 'In Memoriam', *Aligarh Magazine*, 1948, p. ii.

[38] Irfan Habib, interviewed by Amber H. Abbas, Aligarh, India, 28 June 2009. Irfan Habib (b. 1931) grew up primarily in Aligarh where his father, Mohammad Habib, had been a professor since the mid-1920s. He was a leftist student leader at AMU and became a professor of history there after completing his Doctor of Philosophy at New College, Oxford. He retired in 1991.

Also, Iftikhar Alam Khan, interviewed by Amber H. Abbas, Aligarh, India, 6 June 2009. Iftikhar Alam first arrived in Aligarh's Minto Circle School in 1949 after his father was arrested, shortly after the partition. Both he and his brother, Iqtidar, were active in leftist student demonstrations. He became a

to chafe against the perception that it harbours potentially disloyal elements because of its past association with the Muslim League and Pakistan.

Today, AMU is a Central University of India and has a responsibility to include students and faculty of all faiths and backgrounds. Still, tension around the question of the institution's all-India or 'Muslim' identity is a persistent feature of the university's relationship with independent India.[39] The AMU community itself is not unified in its perspective on the value of whether the institution should be considered a minority institution, possessing 'minority character.'[40] Some AMU Muslims would seek to blend into India's broader secular public by limiting the demands they place as a community on the central government, but others suggest that they are already marked as different, even ambivalently Indian, by virtue of their faith, and therefore, deserve special protection and services from the government.

Here, the tension has been present in various guises since the earliest years of MAO College when there was no consensus on the value of maintaining a close tie with the British Government. Some Aligarh partisans admired the system of financial support developed in Deoband, where the institution was supported purely by donations from the Muslim community and was independent of the government.[41] The debates and disagreements over government loyalty came to a head during the demand for AMU, and it was the incorporation of AMU by an act of the Parliament during the height of the nationalist movement that remains at the heart of the current debate.[42]

---

professor of museology in AMU and directed the Aligarh Museum and the Sir Syed Academy.

[39] Violette Graff, 'Aligarh's Long Quest for "Minority" Status: AMU (Amendment) Act, 1981', *Economic and Political Weekly* 25 (1990): 1771–81.

[40] The former registrar of the university has recently appraised the legal wrangling of the controversy around 'minority character'. Ajaz Ashraf, 'Attorney General Has Got It All Wrong about Aligarh Muslim University Minority Status: Ex-Registrar', *Scroll.in*, 16 January 2016, available at https://scroll.in/article/801890/attorney-general-rohatgi-has-got-it-all-wrong-about-aligarh-muslim-university-former-registrar (accessed on 10 October 2018).

[41] Minault and Lelyveld, 'The Campaign'. See also Barbara Metcalf, *Islamic Revival in British India: Deoband, 1860–1900* (Princeton: Princeton University Press, 1964).

[42] Kailash Nath Wanchoo, Ranadir Singh Bachawat, Vaidynathier Ramaswami, Gopendra Krishna Mitter, and Kawdoor Sadananda Hegde, *S. Azeez Basha and Anr Vs. Union of India on 20 October, 1967* (New Delhi: Union of India, 1967).

The proponents of minority character defend it because they do not see any other institution making an effort to support and sustain Muslim education. As Theodore Wright has noted, 'admitting students and recruiting faculty for Aligarh strictly on "merit" would mean swamping it with non-Muslims without any compensating improvements in Muslim access to other institutions of higher education'.[43] For them, the preservation of AMU's minority character would preserve Sir Sayyid's legacy to provide an environment dedicated to uplifting downtrodden Muslims.

Throughout the debates on minority character that have waxed and waned periodically over the last fifty years, AMU's situation has been uniquely problematic. Other institutions have been granted privileges of minority character. Even the Jamia Millia Islamia, founded in part by AMU Old Boys, led for many years by an Alig, Zakir Husain, was awarded minority character in February 2011.[44] The National Commission for Minority Educational Institutions deemed the Jamia Millia Islamia's appeal to be legitimate because

> the Jamia Millia Islamia Act 1988, codified, declared, confirmed and encapsulated the continuous and preexisting factual and legal position of the Jamia by incorporating the existing institution formally under the Act as a central university.... Thus, the evidence on record clearly proves that since its inception, administration of the Jamia remained in the hands of Muslims.[45]

The commission clarified that AMU's appeal, on the other hand, has repeatedly been denied in the wake of the Azeez Basha case, in which the Supreme Court determined that 'MAO College had lost its identity by its conversion into AMU, which was established by the AMU Act, 1920 [whereas] the Jamia never lost its identity'.[46] Notably, Jamia Millia

---

43 Theodore Wright, Jr., 'Muslim Education in India at the Crossroads: The Case of Aligarh', *Pacific Affairs* 39, nos 1/2 (1966): 50–63.
44 Aarti Dhar, 'Jamia Millia Islamia Declared Minority Institution', *The Hindu*, Online Edition, 23 February 2011, available at http://www.thehindu.com/news/national/Jamia-Millia-declared-minority-institution/article15454893.ece (accessed on 10 October 2018).
45 Justice M.S.A. Siddiqui, *Order in the Matters Of: Case No. 891 of 2006, Case No. 1824 of 2006, Case No. 1825 of 2006* (New Delhi: National Commission for Minority Educational Institutions, 2011), p. 52.
46 Dhar, 'Jamia Millia Islamia Declared Minority Institution'.

Islamia, unlike AMU, has an unsullied nationalist pedigree, and although it has sometimes come under suspicion of harbouring extremists, it has no material connection to the separatist politics of India's partition or the taint of British loyalism.

This vexed history has exposed AMU, as Sir Sayyid's most visible legacy, to threats and actual violent attacks by right-wing Hindu activists who argue that the university, like other Muslim institutions in India, illegitimately occupies Hindu space.[47] During the disruptions of the 1947 partition, when Hindu–Muslim tensions were extremely high, the university campus was never attacked. In 2018, however, right-wing militants attacked the university during a visit of India's former Vice President, Hamid Ansari. He was to be inducted as a lifetime member of the Aligarh Union, an honour earlier bestowed on M. K. Gandhi and M. A. Jinnah, among others. The activists demanded the removal of Jinnah's portrait and clashed with AMU students and police. Several students and police were injured, but the former Vice President remained unharmed.[48] Such episodes reveal that despite Sir Sayyid's efforts to prepare Muslims for full participation in Indian life and the efforts of Aligs to project the value of Sir Sayyid's reforms on all Indians, even in his two hundredth year, Indian Muslims face serious challenges of belonging.

Nonetheless, the former Aligs in India, Pakistan, and Bangladesh, who spoke to me, have been mainly concerned about how the quality of AMU and the legacy of Sir Sayyid since independence has been affected by the tensions among Muslims within the institution, rather than by any force attacking

---

[47] Vasudha Venugopal, 'R.S.S. Plans to Convert 4,000 Christian and 1,000 Muslim Families to Hinduism', *Economic Times*, 10 December 2014, available at https://economictimes.indiatimes.com/news/politics-and-nation/rss-plans-to-convert-4000-christian-1000-muslim-families-to-hinduism/articleshow/45442684.cms (accessed on 10 October 2018). See also Niha Masih, 'Mass Conversion in U.P. Sparks Outrage in Parliament, Government Asked to Explain', *NDTV*, 10 December 2014, available at https://www.ndtv.com/agra-news/mass-conversion-in-up-sparks-outrage-in-parliament-government-asked-to-explain-711218 (accessed on 10 October 2018).

[48] Anuja Jaiswall, 'Right Wing Activists Try to Take Down Jinnah Portrait, Clash with AMU Students', *Times of India*, 2 May 2018, available at https://timesofindia.indiatimes.com/city/agra/-right-wing-activists-try-to-take-down-jinnah-portrait-clash-with-amu-students/articleshow/64005482.cms (accessed on 10 October 2018).

the university from the outside.[49] The foe that most AMU respondents and narrators identified was the force of conservatism within the Muslim community, which, they suggested, works contrary to Sir Sayyid's goals to develop a progressive community.

Some respondents claim that the university has been taken over by forces of Muslim conservatism that contravene Sir Sayyid's emphasis on 'free enquiry [and] large-hearted toleration'.[50] In fact, in response to the question 'What is still required to achieve Sir Sayyid's goals for Muslims?' respondents focussed their attention on the need to 'protect [their] university' from being taken over by hypocrites or by those who would not sustain the mission of the university and are only concerned with wealth and status.[51] The enemies of AMU are those who waver from Sir Sayyid's mission to modernize education for Muslims to prepare them to serve India and their own community.

CARRYING SIR SAYYID'S TORCH

Sir Sayyid's lessons extend beyond the boundaries of independent India, resonating with Muslim students worldwide and through networks of Old Boys. Every year, to commemorate Sir Sayyid's birthday on 17 October, Aligs in the university and around the world, honour his legacy by celebrating with food, fellowship, and poetry recitation.[52] While this event unifies Aligs globally in a shared experience, some question the extent to which their colleagues and peers have incorporated Sir Sayyid's legacy. Even as

---

[49] I have argued elsewhere that during the Pakistan Movement, efforts to rally Aligs against outside threats helped define its borders and identity in stark contrast to the non-Muslim city surrounding it. After 1947, the institution made a 'nationalist turn' and embraced Nehru's agenda of 'composite culture'. In the following decades, differences emerged between those identifying as 'progressives' – often leftists – and those who sought to 'preserve' the traditions of AMU through an emphasis on Islam. Amber H. Abbas, 'Disruption and Belonging: Aligarh University and the Changing Meaning of Place since Partition', *Oral History Review* 44, no. 2 (2017): 301–21.

[50] Khaliq Ahmad Nizami, *History of the Aligarh Muslim University (1920–1945)* (Karachi: Sir Syed University Press, 1998), p. 255.

[51] Arshad Islam, Shaheer Khan and Ali Rizvi, responses to online survey, August 2016.

[52] Dr Jawed Aziz lamented that no Aligarh student knew the date of Sir Sayyid's death, only his birthday. Response to online survey, August 2016.

individuals insist that they personally carry on his legacy through efforts at educational development for other Muslims, charities, educational foundations and schools, they imply that the others are falling short. While one respondent emphasized that 'most of AMU alumni owe to Sir Sayyid for their education and success in their life [sic]', another lamented that despite this, most only 'remember him through Sir Syed's Dinner Day once a year that's it'.[53] In fact, several sheepishly acknowledged that while Sir Sayyid's legacy is crucial to understanding the role of AMU, few have read his works. Others urged that Aligs must "study his works" if they want his goals to be fulfilled.[54] Respondents sometimes took on an attitude of self-criticism, arguing that the neighbouring countries (read: Pakistan) have 'schools by the name of Sir Syed, even Universities', but India does not.[55] Although Pakistanis often represent Sir Sayyid as an intellectual founder of Muslim nationalism and therefore Pakistan, Ather Siddiqi resisted that narrative when he cautioned, 'People think he was the instigator or initiator of the Two Nation Theory and for Pakistan; they also think that he laid the foundation. I do not believe that. Sir Sayyid realized that the Muslim community was backward and they needed support and they needed to get education.'[56] Although Aligs of all generations argue that the relevance of Sir Sayyid's teachings extends beyond their application to Indian Muslims, they lament that his 'torch' has not shone more brightly in India, particularly since 1947.

There is almost consensus among respondents on one point: the need to carry his torch by contributing to educational development and outreach. Individual Aligs have taken on the educational mission by running small charities and schools to provide opportunities for those less fortunate.[57] They note that his teachings offered 'inspiration to think for our Community Welfare/Education' and 'to fulfil his dream for socio-cultural and economic uplift of Muslims'.[58] These efforts have survived the upheavals of history: Habibur Rahman of Dhaka told me that when the Old Boys' Association was

---

[53] Anonymous, responses to online survey, August 2016.
[54] Syed Ali Rizvi and, Gulfishan Khan, responses to online survey, August 2016.
[55] This criticism from Dr Jawed Aziz, however, is not true. There are several schools incorporated under Sir Sayyid's name, although they are not affiliated with AMU. In addition, in 2010, AMU developed affiliated institutions in Bihar, Kerala, and West Bengal.
[56] Ather Siddiqi, interview.
[57] Anonymous, response to online survey, August 2016.
[58] Arshad Islam and anonymous, responses to online survey, August 2016.

registered, in East Pakistan in 1956, the article of registration stated that it was for the development of cultural and religious activities of the Muslims. However, after the independence of Bangladesh in 1971, he and other leaders argued, 'We want a development of not only the Muslims. If we can live together amicably, just delete this clause. Say this is for the development of the people.'[59] This change, he felt, encapsulated Sir Sayyid's original intent to be non-communal in his approach to educational reform. Zakir Ali Khan explained to me that the goals of the Pakistan AMUOBA were 'exactly what Sir Sayyid has taught us: to establish educational institutions, to impart education, to make education available to those who cannot afford to pay'.[60] Pakistan AMUOBA started the Sir Sayyid University of Engineering and Technology, where Sir Sayyid is a watchdog over the lives of students and administrators as he is in Aligarh itself. In fact, all students are issued a copy of Zakir Ali Khan's book *Riwayat-e Aligarh*, so that 'he may become an Aligarian'.[61] AMUOBA in Dhaka, Bangladesh, has purchased land for a similar project.[62]

In both oral histories and the online survey responses, the former students give credit to Sir Sayyid and the educational institution he founded for the successes they have experienced in their lives. In deeply personal testimonies they affirm, 'I will always be indebted to him, till my last breath. [I am] what I am now because of this great seat of learning [in which] I had the opportunity to avail my degrees and hone my Muslim culture at the same time.'[63] Their gratitude and devotion does not stop there. Rather,

---

[59] Habibur Rahman, interview with Amber H. Abbas, Dhaka, Bangladesh, 20 February 2010. Habibur Rahman was born on 1 January 1925. He matriculated at AMU in 1944 and lived in Sir Sayyid Hall. After completing his education, he settled in East Pakistan and became a lawyer. He went on to become active in the Awami Movement for the independence of Bangladesh.

[60] Zakir Ali Khan, interview.

[61] Ibid.

[62] Significantly, although each of these associations is known as AMUOBAs, there is little, if any, connection between them. AMUOBA in Dhaka was interested and surprised to learn that the Pakistani Association had built an educational institution, as they were hoping to do, and asked me to facilitate a connection for them. There is a somewhat closer connection between AMUOBA Pakistan and Aligarh University. In 2008, Zakir Ali Khan was awarded the first Sir Syed Ahmad Khan International Award for lifetime achievement in support of the ideals of Sir Sayyid Ahmad Khan. Survey responses from former Aligs also advocate for building more schools to combat illiteracy among Muslims.

[63] Shenaz Khan, response to online survey.

they are determined that their efforts should advance his efforts through the creation of new educational institutions and resistance to the forces of conservatism and division that they believe have restricted Muslim access to power in India.

CONCLUSION

Since Sir Sayyid's death more than a century ago, the institution he founded, the MAO College, has become AMU, a Central University of India. Its student body has grown from a few hundred to nearly thirty thousand. It now offers dozens of degree paths and has several colleges. Its History Department is recognized as one of the best in the country. Its student body includes men and women from all walks of life and from all over the world. It has served as a model for educational institutions in Pakistan and Bangladesh and inspired educational leadership among its former students globally. All this might suggest that Aligs would tell a story of the overwhelming success of their founder's mission.

Sir Sayyid's legacy survives in the lives of Aligs, particularly those active in sustaining his commitment to modern education, who continue to narrate the history of the institution through a lens of decline. As long as Muslims remain in need of reform, there is a need for AMU and Sir Sayyid's reformist objectives. He may be seen as an intellectual leader, even a 'founder', in Pakistan, but in India, this logic makes him appear anti-Indian. Although Jawaharlal Nehru recognized that Sir Sayyid 'wanted to reconcile modern scientific thought with religion by rationalistic interpretations and not by attacking basic belief' and that 'he was in no way communally separatist', Sir Sayyid's legacy for Indian Muslims has been closely linked to the fortunes of AMU.[64] The recent attack on the university was ostensibly a protest against a portrait of its Lifetime Union Member Muhammad Ali Jinnah, which has been hung in the Union Hall since 1938, alongside the portraits of Gandhi, Nehru, and others. This suggests that AMU still struggles to distance itself from its past. This history has limited Sir Sayyid's appeal in India, and he has not received worldwide recognition outside of the Muslim community. Just as it was in his own time, the 'relative deprivation' of Indian Muslims continues to be central to Sir Sayyid's legacy in a country where Muslims will always be a minority. As important as it has been for Indian Muslims, Sir Sayyid's work is never done.

---

[64] Jawaharlal Nehru, *The Discovery of India* (Delhi: Oxford University Press, 1989), p. 345.

Conclusion

YASMIN SAIKIA AND M. RAISUR RAHMAN

'I aged before my age, I lost my hair, my eyesight, but not my vision. My vision never dimmed, my determination never failed. I built this institution for you and I am sure you will carry the light of this institution far and wide till darkness disappears from all around.'[1] These last words of Sayyid Ahmad Khan to the students of the Muhammadan Anglo-Oriental (MAO) College – now Aligarh Muslim University (AMU) – are enshrined at an entrance of the university, reminding the obligation to expand the realm of knowledge within and outside the institution. Sayyid Ahmad feared that without knowledge, a community would remain steeped in ignorance and denial. He urged Indians – Muslims and Hindus alike – to embark on the journey of modern education to stop their fall into the abyss of poverty. His pioneering thoughts, ideas, and actions in the field of education, cultural awakening, and social reform produced immediate and positive result during his lifetime, and their overall impact reverberates even today in the India–Pakistan subcontinent. Indeed, this is a rare legacy that the memory of a person can transcend the divides of the South Asian nation-states and bring people together in his memory. Sayyid Ahmad is this figure of unity.

Sayyid Ahmad's name is synonymous with modern Muslim education. His embrace of Western secular learning coupled with the adoption of English language arguably was the most powerful and radical model for Muslim education in nineteenth century India. No one before him had ventured in this direction, in spirit or in magnitude. It was a path plagued with obstacles. Muslim and Hindu opponents attacked, opposed, and reviled him. Despite severe criticisms, he pursued his dream of introducing modern, secular education and founded the MAO College at Aligarh. The benefits of modern education have reached a much larger community, larger than the network of alumni and students of AMU, the Aligs. It embraces everyone – be it Muslims or non-Muslims, Aligs or non-Aligs – who incorporates balanced scientific approach and rational thought with an awareness of religion and cultural practices. Sayyid Ahmad's life and his ideas depict a

---

[1] A plaque at Aligarh Muslim University memorializes these words.

unique blend of tradition and modernity, rooted in Indian culture with the flexibility to adopt and adapt with Anglo-western culture. However, the 'modern' project that Sayyid Ahmad inaugurated for Muslims was not an effort to become British-like. In fact, he did not ascribe to the notion that 'modern' belonged exclusively to the West. He advocated it as a capacity to change. Thus, he remained committed to Indian heritage and history while simultaneously calling for change to adapt to the current times. In the current political climate, his vision serves as an example offering an alternative version of moral Muslim modernity that is free from rigid and extreme political and cultural positioning.

Education, in Sayyid Ahmad's approach, was not the narrow-bound knowledge, confined to books. He was of the opinion that 'higher education is not obtained through reading a few books and memorizing like a parrot and taking exams and saying "A'i tali tel" [I tell a tale] in English'.[2] He was not unaware of the pragmatic considerations of education, but his vision of education at the MAO College was founded on a larger philosophical and humanistic platform. He approached education as a stepping-stone to improve understanding and imbibing the value of one's rights while appreciating the rights of others, overcoming moribund traditions with rational interpretations, creating understanding between communities through dialogue and accommodation, claiming ownership of the present with knowledge of the past, and resolutely shaping the future for progress and advancement. Unique to his approach of education was seeing and developing it as a site for friendship among different groups coming together and pursuing a common endeavour towards progress. Education became the site for creating unity. The MAO residential college that Sayyid Ahmad conceived and developed made history and became a pioneering effort for forging unity among the Indians. Sayyid Ahmad did not impose any system of ownership of this education but created it as a pathway for Muslim modernity after the revolt of 1857 and extended it as an invitation for others to emulate. The values he ascribed to secular education is exceptional. Sayyid Ahmad is a beacon of this possibility. We hope the readers of this *Companion* have developed an intimate knowledge of this iconic nineteenth-century figure and can engage his ideas, thoughts, and actions with greater appreciation for their historical and cultural worth.

---

[2] Sayyid Ahmad Khan, 'Hindustan mein ala ta'lim aur gavarment', repr. in Maulana Muhammad Ismail Panipati (ed.), *Maqalat-e Sir Sayyid*, Part VIII (Lahore: Majlis-e Taraqqi-e Adab, 1962), p. 30.

Sayyid Ahmad was Indian Muslim by origin, but his persona transcended a fixed community or nation. He was a champion of Indian unity and this historical consciousness is evident in every aspect of his work – be it education, community building, inter-faith discussion, or political mobilization. Popular perception and politics have tried to slot and fit him within the narrow box of a 'Muslim reformer' in India. Some have associated him with the founding of Pakistan. These are myopic representations, as we have demonstrated in this volume. Sayyid Ahmad was an astute observer of the colonial rulers and their methods of control; he developed pragmatic thinking to empower Indians to overcome colonial mental enslavement. Freeing the mind from captivity was his passionate goal. He etched new pathways through education and social reform for achieving the unimagined and unthought. It was not a Muslim or non-Muslim pathway, rather a trailblazing effort aimed at enabling a radical imagination of freedom through education, as a possible future. One of his core contributions was his capacity to generate consciousness about self and group rights. The emergence of a large number of modern and educated Muslims from AMU, the assertive demand for political rights and shared governance of Indians subsequently championed by the Indian National Congress, and the Muslim League's successful founding of Pakistan are the obvious end products associated with Sayyid Ahmad's efforts. The larger issue that encompassed in these concrete outcomes was decolonization, which was foundational in Sayyid Ahmad's thoughts and actions. This *Companion* has highlighted this fundamental aspect.

A productive comparison of Sayyid Ahmad's life and work can be made with two other nineteenth- and early-twentieth-century reformers – Raja Ram Mohan Roy (1772–1831) and Rabindranath Tagore (1861–1941), both from colonial Bengal. Roy preceded Sayyid Ahmad by several decades, whereas Tagore followed him a few decades later. Like Roy who was a fervent advocate of English education and had fought relentlessly against the Bengali Hindu community to overcome mindless superstitions, Sayyid Ahmad impressed on Muslims the value of modern English education and undertook the work of social reform in the face of extreme opposition from the orthodox Muslim mullahs who declared him an apostate. On the other hand, Sayyid Ahmad was a forerunner of Tagore in innovative education and academic institution building. Tagore founded his school at Shantiniketan extending education beyond the classroom. In 1921, it became the Vishwa Bharati University. Sayyid Ahmad laid the foundation of the foremost centre of modern secular education, the MAO College, which followed an innovative curriculum of extracurricular activities, ethics, and character building, along with the study of sciences and arts in a residential campus. The purpose of this expansive education as David Lelyveld has shown in *Aligarh's First Generation* was the development of a moral person. When MAO College became AMU in 1920 it continued the ethos of education for moral and human development.

A comparison at a global scale allows for a deeper appreciation of Sayyid Ahmad Khan. His contemporaries in the Muslim world were the modernist Jamaluddin al-Afghani (1839–1897) and the rationalist Muhammad Abduh (1849–1905). Both were inspirational figures generating new thinking among Muslims for decolonization. Their approach was political resistance against Western colonialism, whereas Sayyid Ahmad adopted the strategy of empowerment through accommodation equipping Muslims with the tools for advancement through modern education. Sayyid Ahmad was a forerunner of the Ottoman Muslim theologian Bediuzzman Said Nursi (1877–1960). Like Sayyid Ahmad, Nursi promoted modern sciences and rational thinking alongside the teaching of secular sciences in religious schools and religious sciences in secular schools. Nursi's ideas gave rise to the Nurcu Movement in Turkey that combined religious revival with modernism. Sayyid Ahmad's work inspired the Aligarh Movement that resonates across the subcontinent and its reach is now global as AMU alumni have spread out throughout the world carrying the message of empowerment through education in their local communities. Secular thought, religious reform, modern education, and cosmopolitan values were and continue to be the hallmarks of the Aligarh Movement.

This *Companion* offered a window into Sayyid Ahmad's multifaceted contributions. Each chapter focussed on an aspect of his work. Although these chapters are not exhaustive, reading them together, we hope, has provided the reader with a comprehensive picture of the circumstances and conditions that shaped Sayyid Ahmad's life and his ideas. A critical focus of this *Companion* is a close reading of the historical and political events of the late nineteenth century. The horror of the 1857 rebellion had a deep impact on Sayyid Ahmad. This turning point generated new and original thinking in him at many different levels, as several of the chapters have described. At one level, it required him to move from antiquarian subjects of history, which was his original interest, to a more practical social awareness for addressing issues of contemporary relevance in his time. At another level, he had to rethink the scope and project of Islam. He beseeched the Muslims to embark on the path of a transformed and modern outlook towards religion, while he worked tirelessly to educate the British colonial masters on the common heritage of Christianity and Islam with the hope of representing Muslims as their friends, not enemies. Several chapters in this volume emphasized Sayyid Ahmad's catholic thinking on religion and its value for building relationship between communities.

The chapters on education at the MAO College, along with Sayyid Ahmad's views regarding electoral politics, the caliphate, nature, Urdu and Hindi language controversy, evolution and Darwinism, women's education, as well as his relationship with Christian and Muslim opponents and their outlook towards Islam and Muslims, reveal his erudite mind and breadth of interests in diverse topics accompanied by good manners and tolerant consideration of others' views. Tolerance and friendship, values that guided Sayyid Ahmad, are a running theme connecting all chapters. Sayyid Ahmad's friendship with different groups of Muslims, Hindus, as well as Englishmen and Englishwomen defined his hallmark trait of inclusivity. The spirit of friendship with different others that he encouraged endures even today across divided boundaries of nation-states in South Asia, enabling the people of India, Pakistan, and Bangladesh to come together in the shared memory of Sayyid Ahmad. This is expressed in both personal and intellectual associations that individuals and groups foster with AMU, as the last chapter in the volume has shown.

In undertaking the task of putting together the *Companion*, we were encouraged and challenged in many ways. Sayyid Ahmad was a prolific writer. He is a historian's delight because he left behind a copious amount of writing. This massive compilation of original material also posed a challenge to us. What should we include and what must we sacrifice? Sayyid Ahmad had produced voluminous writings on religion – Islam, Christianity, and Hinduism. However, his erudite mind did not limit the study of religion to theological matters alone. He researched and wrote on the compatibility of religion with science calling for mutual respect and sharing between the two realms of knowledge, which some of his essays have discussed at length. The connection between history, politics, and culture and bringing them together for emphasizing peaceful coexistence between the Muslims and Hindus in India was another subject he wrote about extensively, and this was addressed in several of the chapters. Education and social reform kept him preoccupied and both of them found expression in his journals – *The Aligarh Institute Gazette* and *Tahzib-ul Akhlaq*. Personal and official letters, pamphlets, magazines, speeches and notes, diaries, and so on, were on offer to sift and work through. We had to study his multifaceted writings and probe the driving factors that motivated him. It became clear that Sayyid Ahmad was not only a formidable thinker but also an activist. He considered everyone he encountered important to engage them for their ideas, and he generously shared his own thoughts and opinions with them.

We had to respect his convictions but select only a few to include here. We highlighted the patterns that we found were consistent throughout his life as a thinker and social reformer and presented them as representative of the ones we had to omit. One thing that stood out and emerged as Sayyid Ahmad's passionate concern: all the essays discussed his untiring work to advance his *qaum* (community/nation).[3]

Sayyid Ahmad offers an original voice of the Muslim condition in colonial India, but it is not exclusive to a single community. His voice represents the quest of the Indian people living under the British rule. As a Muslim in north India, Sayyid Ahmad's cultural outlook was fashioned by the *ganga–jamuni tahzib*, a fusion of Muslim and Hindu cultural sensibilities, but he was also equally committed to serve as a bridge between Muslim communities in India and co-religionists beyond the subcontinent. Nonetheless, unlike al-Afghani, Nursi, and many other Muslim intellectuals of his time, who championed pan-Islamism, Sayyid Ahmad was a self-proclaimed *Musalman-e Hind* (Muslim of India) and offered concrete thinking for the improvement of the Muslim condition in India. He believed and worked for this possibility through an East–West cooperation. His approach was practical and effective, and his social alignment with the British colonial masters proved useful because it was the need of the hour. This should not lead one to assume that he exonerated the British for their failure to provide just governance. He called upon them to make a genuine effort to understand

---

[3] The issue of the Muslim *qaum* in India became a matter of some discussion in a recently concluded event on 19 September 2018, 'Bhavishya ka Bharat: A Rashtriya Sevak Sangha (RSS) Perspective'. Mohan Bhagawat, the RSS chief, commented on one of the speeches Sayyid Ahmad made in Punjab where he discussed his concept of a unified Hindustani *qaum* to a mixed audience, including several Arya Samaj members. He shared an abiding friendship with Dayanand Saraswati, the founder of the Arya Samaj (an ideological Hindu movement, precursor to the RSS) and so the Arya Samaj members welcomed Sayyid Ahmad who was in Punjab to raise money for his MAO College. Although Sayyid Ahmad, in this and other speeches, emphasized the close relationship between the different groups in India – Hindus, Muslims, and Christians – constituting one *qaum*, he did not make an appeal to absorb the Muslims under the Hindu *quam*'s umbrella, as Mohan Bhagawat's speech suggests. Sayyid Ahmad encouraged his audience to become involved in enabling the improvement of the other groups, and the Muslims being the most downtrodden *qaum* were in the greatest need for improvement through education, he appealed. The advancement of Muslims, he opined, would be good of the country, which is common to all.

the grievances of Indians, in general, and Muslims, in particular, and prove their capacity to govern through cooperation and goodwill. His friendship with the British strengthened his forceful voice against unjust colonial rule. He thus developed an unusual position of rooted Indianness with an inclusive cosmopolitan outlook, as we have shown in this *Companion*.

In history books taught in India, Sayyid Ahmad receives, at best, a cursory mention, whereas in Pakistan, the emphasis on his sartorial presentation as a Mughal nobleman and his long flowing beard allow for making him into an early Muslim leader instrumental in founding Pakistan. Bollywood's myth making of different heroes and critical moments in colonial India that circulates as popular history in the public domain does not include Sayyid Ahmad, and, thus, he has disappeared from public memory in India. No more than a handful of people may be aware that he was the first Indian to produce an eyewitness account of the Indian Rebellion of 1857 and the transformation of India into a colony.

However, at one place, Sayyid Ahmad lives and is fresh in everyone's memory – in AMU. Here, he is the indisputable hero. On 17 October 2017, AMU celebrated Sayyid Ahmad's bicentennial birth anniversary. Aligs – men and women, young and old alike – from all over the world assembled at the university to mark this occasion. Some were returning after several decades, some were fresh graduates, and some were current students at the university. Around the world, AMU alumni associations solemnized similar events. None of them had met or known Sayyid Ahmad personally. Yet it was for him that they had gathered. Each one of them knew he had invested in them more than a hundred years ago and made them beneficiaries of the wealth of education. They came together as pilgrims and inheritors to carry forward this dream in the twenty-first century. For them, Sayyid Ahmad is a continuous living inspiration, not a distant figure in history. In each person's thinking, he is their personal mentor. He is at the centre of the collective, binding them together in a common pursuit to empower the marginal, the vulnerable, and the less privileged. Sayyid Ahmad did his work at Aligarh, and now Aligs are spreading it throughout the world on a larger canvas. Fulfilling this responsibility is an injunction from Sayyid Ahmad: 'To go throughout the length and breadth of the land to preach the message of free inquiry, large-hearted toleration and pure morality that is possible only with modern education.'[4] The ability to

---

[4] Sayyid Ahmad's speech on the occasion of the foundation of the MAO College on 8 January 1877. See Shan Muhammad (ed.), *The Aligarh Movement: Basic Documents, 1864–1898* (Meerut: Meenakshi Prakashan, 1978), pp. 469–73.

step into this living history of inspiration and embark on the task is an appeal for one and all.

Sayyid Ahmad's call to improve the human condition is a need of our time. His search for a better world, in our dystopic times, serves as a passionate call. The road to this goal is not straightforward. Neither was it for Sayyid Ahmad. Nonetheless, journeying on this pathway for humanity and human progress is a historical necessity. Sayyid Ahmad was its living example and he etched a pathway for others to follow. The history he made at Aligarh continuously evolves and inspires. His gift is a resource that gestures empowerment and advancement for now and in the future. Indians – Muslims or Hindus – are richer because of it. Maulana Altaf Hussain Hali's beautiful eulogy encapsulates the living spirit of Sayyid Ahmad and his inspiration even today:

> After Sir Sayyid's death, it was not only by words but also by actions that the people proved their love and respect for his high ideals. Almost at once, some people began to press for the foundation of Muslim University. The movement spread all over India and abroad and people started raising money for Sir Saiyad's finest memorial. Even in England students raised money for the Muslim University. People were surprised to see the interest of Englishmen and their efforts to collect money to fulfill the dream of Sir Sayyid to make MAO College as Aligarh Muslim University. There is an old saying that a good friend is like a leafy tree. For when a tree is in full bloom one has the pleasure of its shade and the enjoyment of its fruits, and when it withers, its wood is put to many uses. Sir Sayyid was such a friend to the Muslims. When he was alive, he laboured for them with his body, his words, his pen and his money. When he died he left the memory of his love and work imprinted on their hearts so that they might come together and build on the foundations he has laid.[5]

---

[5] Maulana Altaf Hussain Hali, *Hayat-i Javed: A Biographical Account of Sir Sayyid*, trans. K. H. Qadiri and David J. Matthews (Delhi: Idarah-e Adabiyat-e Delli, 1979), p. 238.

Suggested Further Readings

PRIMARY SOURCES

In English

Nizami, Khaliq Ahmad, ed. and trans. *Sir Sayyid Speaks to You*. Aligarh: Sir Syed Hall, 1968.
Sayyid Ahmad Khan papers, 1875–1887. New Delhi: National Archives of India.
Sir Syed Ahmed on the Present State of Indian Politics, Consisting of Speeches and Letters Reprinted from the 'Pioneer'. Allahabad: The Pioneer Press, 1888.

In Urdu

Abbas, Asghar, ed. *Shazrat-e Sir Sayyid*, Part I: *Aligarh Institute gazette se intikhab*. Azamgarh: Dar-ul Musannefin Shibli Academy, 2017.
Ahmad Khan, Sayyid. *Intikhab-e mazamin-e (Aligarh Institute Gazette)*. Lucknow: Uttar Pradesh Urdu Academy, 1982.
Ahmad Khan, Sayyid. *khutoot-e Sir Sayyid: Sir Sayyid Ahmad Khan marhum ke cand zati khutoot*. Aligarh: Nasreen Mumtaz Bashir, 1995.
Haq, Abdul, *Sir Sayyid Ahmad Khan*. Delhi: Urdu Markaz, 1960.
Masud, Ross, ed. *Khutoot-e Sir Sayyid*. Badaun: Nizami Press, 1924.
Suroor, Al-e Ahmad. *Intekhab mazameen Sir Sayyid*. Aligarh: Muslim University, 1927.

SECONDARY SOURCES

In English

Abbas, Asghar. *Print Culture: Sir Syed's Aligarh Institute Gazette, 1866-1897*. Delhi: Primus Books, 2015.
Alam, Shaista Aziz. 'Sayyid Ahmad Khan and the "Ulama": A Study in Sociopolitical Context'. Unpublished master's thesis, McGill University, 1992.
Ali, B Sheikh. *A Leader Reassessed: Life and Work of Sir Syed Ahmad Khan*. Mysore: Sultan Shaheed Education Trust Publication, 1999.
Bhatnagar, Shyam Krishna. *History of the M.A.O. College, Aligarh*. Bombay: Asia Publishing House, 1969.
Dar, Bashir Ahmad. *Religious Thought of Sayyid Ahmad Khan*. Lahore: Institute of Islamic Culture, 1957.

Malik, Hafiz. 'Religious Liberalism of Sir Sayyid Ahmad Khan', *The Muslim World* 54, no. 3 (July 1964): 160–9.
Qadir, Abdul. 'Sir Syed Ahmad Khan', in his *Famous Urdu Poets and Writers*, pp. 71–87. New Delhi: Seemant Prakashan, 1977.
Reetz, Dietrich. 'Enlightenment and Islam: Sayyid Ahmad Khan's Plea to Indian Muslims for Reason', *The Indian Historical Review* 4, nos 1–2 (1980): 206–18.
Siddiqi, Mazheruddin. 'The Religious Thoughts of Sir Sayyid Ahmad Khan', *Islamic Studies* 6, no. 3 (September 1967): 289–308.

Index

Abduh, Muhammad 209, 226, 276
Abdullah, Shaikh 66–7
ʿAbd-ul-Raziq, ʿAli 45–6
Abulfeda 205, 207
Aga Khan 35–6, 93
Aga Khan III, Muhammed Shah (Sir Sultan). *See* Aga Khan
Ahkam-e Taʾam-e Ahl-e Kitab 41
ahl-e jannat 82
Ahmad, Fariduddin (Khwaja) 56, 73, 107, 110
Ahmed, Aziz 17
Ain-e Akbari 4
Akbar, Emperor 4, 43
Al Bashir 182
Al Waqidi 205
al-ʿAbd Allah ʿUmar-ul Hanfi, Jamal ibn 41
al-Afghani, Sayyid Jamaluddin 83–4, 103, 226–8, 276, 278
Alavi, Hamza 191
Allahabad University 124
al-Fārābi 141, 154
al-Ghazzāli 141, 154
al-Simnāni 141, 154
Ali, Ahmed 37
ʿAli, Chiragh 43, 49–50, 154
Ali, Mohamed. *See* Ali, Muhammad
Ali, Muhammad 64, 104, 263
Ali, Mumtaz 60–2, 66–7; and publishing career 62
Ali, Sayyid Ameer 102–3
Ali, Sayyid Imdad 98
ʿAli, Sayyid Mehdi (Nawab Mohsin-ul-Mulk) (Maulawi) 10, 35, 43, 75, 89, 91, 93–4, 104, 119, 149, 202
Ali, Sayyid Mumtaz. *See* Ali, Mumtaz

Ali, Shah Ghulam 56
Ali, Shaukat 64
Ali, Syed Asim 211
Aligarh Girls' School 66; founders 66. *See also* AMU (Aligarh Muslim University), Women's College of
Aligarh Institute Gazette 33, 74, 92, 98, 105, 109, 118, 125, 196, 198, 208, 277
Aligarh Movement 10, 36, 63, 67, 89, 91, 98, 109, 261, 264, 276
Aligarh Muslim University (AMU) 7, 10, 13, 19, 89, 195–6, 255–61, 265–70, 272–3, 275–7, 279–80; social media discussion of 195; Women's College of 67
Aligarh Scientific Society (1864) 7, 74, 78, 98, 101, 117–18, 125, 127, 178, 188, 217, 230
Alig (alumnus of Aligarh Muslim University [AMU]) 7, 12, 256–7, 259–60, 262, 267–73, 279
Al-Islam wa Usul al-Hukm 45
al-Jāhiz, Abu Uthman 145, 220, 224; *Book of Animals* by 223
Al-Khilafa aw al-Imama al-ʿUzma 44
All India Muhammadan Educational Conference (AIMEC) 93, 118, 126, 128
Allāh, Shāh Walī 141–2, 144, 146, 154, 157, 220, 226
Allah, Zakaʾ 43
Allahabadi, Akbar 36
All-India Muhammadan (later, Muslim) Educational Conference 61
Al-Razi 81
al-Safāʾ, Ikhwân 221–3

al-Simnanī 141, 154
Alters, Brian 228
al-Urwah al-Wuthqa 227
AMU Act 267
AMU Old Boys' Associations (AMUOBAs) 256, 271
AMU Students' Union (AMUSU) 195
Andrews, C. F. 210; 'Delhi Renaissance' of 210
Anglo-Maratha wars 239
Ansari, Asloob Ahmad 210, 255
Ansari, M. A. 95, 104
anti-cow-killing societies 189. See also cow protection movement; cow-killing circular
Arkoun, Muhammad 39
Arya Samaj 189, 278
Arya Samajists 100, 201
Āṣār-us Ṣanādīd 1, 5, 128, 233, 240, 243–8, 251–4
Asbāb-e-Baghāwat. See *Asbab-e Baghawat-e Hind*
Asbab-e Baghawat-e Hind 5, 24, 41, 104, 112, 133, 159, 253
Asbāb-e sarkashi-e Hindustān 71
ashraf (elite) 3, 33, 108, 111, 113, 120–1, 168, 172–3, 182, 186–7, 260. See also elites
Ashraf, K. M. 17
Asman Manzil, construction of 92
Aurangzeb, Emperor 43, 241–3, 249
'Auraton ke Huquq' 57, 62
Azad, Abul Kalam (Maulana) 36, 89, 104
Aziz, Shah Abdul 226

Bahadur, Kunwar Narindra 105
Basha, Azeez 267
Bakhsh, Ali (Maulvi) 79, 95
Banerjee, Surendranath 7, 189
Barelvī, Sayyid Aḥmad 143
Bazaar (Chitli Qabr) 246
Beck, Theodore 12, 99, 185
Beg, Mirza Shah Rukh 236, 243
Begam, Abadi Banu ('Bi Amman') 64, 66

Begam, Abdullah 66–67
Begam, Ashrafunnissa (Bibi Ashraf) 65–6
Begam, Azizunnissa 56, 63
Begam, Muhammadi 62, 66–7
Begam, Sultan Jahan 64
Begum, Shahjehan 99
Bhagawat, Mohan 278
Bharati Varsha National Association 189
Bhinga, Raja 105, 186
Bible 11, 21, 34, 41, 71, 72, 139, 140, 146, 148, 150, 157, 198, 208, 215, 218
Bijnor 24–5, 27, 29, 41, 159, 254; Hindus and Muslims plundering in 28
Bijnor Rebellion 5, 26, 159. See also 1857 rebellion
bin Sayyid Muhammad Mutaqqi, Sayyid Ahmad Taqvi. See Mutaqqi, Mir; also see Khan, Sayyid Ahmad (Sir)
Book of Animals 223
British power 4, 19, 84, 261, 264
British Raj (rule) 38, 41, 43, 84, 99,128, 163–4, 181, 186–9, 191–2, 278; rulers 5, 20, 22, 25–6, 28, 30–1, 90, 189
British–Muslim relationship 20, 27
Brooke, S. 99
Brown, Daniel 140
Bustan 56

Calcutta University 125
caliphate 38–40, 44–6, 49–50, 277; Ottoman 45. See also Khalifa
Carlyle, Thomas 75, 205
Causes for the Revolt of India, The/ The Causes of the Indian Revolt 5, 24–7, 30, 32, 71, 104, 159, 161, 164, 171–2, 204
Chand, Babu Fateh 177
Chand, Rao Sahib Lakshmi 101

Chandni Chowk 241, 243, 249
Charlie Hebdo, 211–12, attack of 197
Chattopadhyaya, Bankim Chandra 25
Chaudhris of Halduar 28
Chishti, Noor Ahmad 252
Christian missionaries 31, 48–9
Christianity 21, 41, 48, 70–1, 82, 114, 199, 228, 276–7
Christian–Muslim disputations in Agra 71
civil services 5, 7
Collins, Anthony 210
Colvin, Auckland (Sir) 160
commentary: on the Bible 10–11, 21, 41, 72–3, 76, 80, 139, 159, 208, 222; on the Qur'an 209; on Sura Yusuf 80
communalism 17, 183
community reform movement 18
conservatives 89, 96
conversion 31, 144, 254, 267
cow protection movement 182. See also anti-cow-killing societies;
cow-killing circular 189. See also anti-cow-killing societies
Coxe, A., *Establishment of the British Rule in India* by 196

Danish cartoon controversy 212. See also *Charlie Hebdo*, attack on
Daniyal, Shoaib 259
Dar-ul Islam 41
Dars-e Nizami 96
Darwin, Charles 76, 214–15, 217, 223–5, 229–30; evolutionary thought of 216; Mandelian genetics and 231; *Origin of Species* by 217
Darwinism 12, 220, 225, 232, 277
Das, Ra'e Shankar 159–60
Dass, Jaikishan 100–1
Davenport, John 205
Day of Judgement 80, 98, 153, 156, 202. See also *qiyāmat*
de Lessups, Ferdinand 74, 77

decolonization 275–6
Dehlavi, Nazir Ahmad (Maulvi) 63
Delhi Gate 241–2. See also Red Fort
Deobandis 95–6
Derrida, Jacques 20
Devji, Faisal 77, 80
dialogic process 24
Dilli Kalij (Delhi College) 110, 125, 236
divine creator 214, 220, 223
Divine Will 150–1, 153
Diwan-e 'Am 241–5, 248–51
Diwan-e Khās 244

East India Company 1, 4, 108, 110, 159, 242, 250
education 103, 108, 274 (see also under English); for 'domestic happiness' 57; domiciliary 110, 112; European pattern of 119; formal 57, 110, 114, 121; for Muhammadan females 55; Shibli Numani on 97; vision of 116
Education Commission (Hunter Commission) 55, 60, 120
1857 rebellion 3, 5, 18–20, 23–7, 30, 41, 99, 104, 111, 159, 169, 173, 233, 239, 253, 260, 276, 279; causes of 112; treatises on 26
elites: Avadh 182, 183, 185; Bengali 190; children of 120; intellectual 156; Muslim 111, 120; Urdu 116, 177
Elliot Esquire, C. A. 217
Elshakry, Marwa 226–7
English: education 5, 7, 12, 98, 102, 105, 107, 179, 191, 203, 275; knowing Muslims 107; language 97, 110, 113–14, 116, 124, 202, 273; study of 102, 113
Ernst, Carl 146
Essays on the Life of Mohammed and Subjects Subsidiary Thereto 42
Etawah 91, 93

Europe 74, 83, 85, 99, 221, 226; journey to 73; mechanical sciences in 141
evolution 12, 45, 98, 214–21, 223–2, 277; of civilizations 226. See also al-Afghani, Sayyid Jamaluddin

Fahad, Obaidullah 199
Fariduddin, Khwaja 73, 110
Faruqi, Shamsur Rahman 139
Fatehpuri Mosque 249
fatwa 7, 41, 95, 98, 211
Fikr-o-Nazar 89
Firangi Mahalli, Nizamuddin (Mulla) 96
Fazal, Abul 4
female: education 55, 98, 126; empowerment 31
Fort William College 125
freedom of speech 198

Gandhi, M. K. 8, 85, 268, 272; assassination of 265
ganga–jamuni tahzib 278
Ganguli, Babu Shyamacharan 178
Ghalib, Mirza 4
ghayr matlū 148
Ghose, Lal Mohan 189
Ghosh, Aurobindo 191
Gibbon, Edward 75, 205, 207
Glover, William 252
good governance 6, 21, 23, 27, 30, 34–5
Government of India Act 1858 113, 184
Graham, G. F. I. 12, 118, 160
Gray, Asa 220, 224–5
Gulistan 56
Gupta, Rajani Kant 25

Habib, Irfan 26
Hadith 45, 49, 96, 147, 205, 209
Hali, Altaf Hussain (Khwaja) 26, 63, 81–2, 84, 97–8, 104, 139, 160–1, 166, 173, 201, 280; *Majalis un-Nissa* by 63; natural science and 82
Hamid II, Abdül (Ottoman Sultan) 46, 49
Hamid, Ustad 239

Hamidullah, Muhammad 146
Hamza, Amir, stories of 247
Hasan, Mushirul 17
Hayat-e Javed (An Immortal Life) 26, 160, 166, 203
Hemingway, William 204
Higgins, Godfrey 205
Hindi movement 175–6, 178–9, 181–3, 186, 191
Hindi Sahitya Sammelan 181, 183
Hindi–Urdu language controversy 8–9, 175, 182. See also Nagri/Hindi politics
Hindu nationalism 175, 189
Hindu–Muslim: relations 25; riots 189; tensions 268; thinking 258; unity 1, 8
'Hindustan ki Auraton ki Halat' 59. See also Khan, Sayyid Ahmad (Sir)
Holy Kaaba 49
home-schooling 112. See also education; female, education
Horne, Thomas Hartwell 72
Hume, A. O. (Sir) 191
Hunter Commission 93, 120. See also Education Commission
Hunter, W. W. 33–4, 42–3, 99–100, 198, 260
Huquq un-Niswan 61–2
Husain, Mushtaq (Nawab Viqar-ul Mulk) 9, 89, 91–4
Husain, Sayyid Karamat 61, 66
Husain, Wajahat 261, 264
Husain, Zakir 265, 267

Ibn `Arabī 141–3, 151–2, 154
al-Fārābī 141, 154, 221
Ibn Hisham 205
Ibn Ishaq 205
Ibn Khaldun 220–2; *Muqaddimah* by 222
ibn Sīnā 81, 141, 151, 154–6, 221
Ibn-e Rushd 209
ijtihad 36, 52, 191, 209

Ikhwân al-Safâ' 220–1; *Rasâ'il Ikhwân al-Safâ'* (Treatises of the Brethren of Purity) 221
ilm-ul kalam 11
imamate 49
imperialism 85
inclusivity 21, 177, 191–2, 257–8, 277, 279
Indian Loyal Association 189. See also Indian National Congress (INC)
Indian Musalmans, The, 42, 99, 198; Hunter on 99
Indian Muslims 4–5, 12–13, 18–21, 33–4, 36–7, 43–6, 48–9, 102–4, 190–1, 258–9, 272
Indian National Congress (INC) 8, 20, 35–6, 89, 102, 105–6, 166, 173, 175–6, 181–2, 184–91
Indian Rebellion of 1857. See 1857 rebellion
Industrial Revolution 234
insurgents 41, 43
Iqbal, Muhammad 84, 104, 152, 154–7, 211
Iron Pillar 247
Islam 38, 43, 52, 114; as state 53
Islamic: civilization 58; governance 38, 40; law 48, 50, 57, 62, 208
Islamic State 38, 40, 44–5, 50, 52
Ismail, Shāh 143
izzat 31

Jackson, (Dr.) 100
Jah, Asman (Sir) 92
Jalal, Ayesha 17
Jama Masjid 246–7
Jamia Millia Islamia 263–4, 267
Jawwad-ud-daulah Arif Jung 250
Jennings, Midgeley John (Rev.) 40
jihad 27, 30, 33
Jinnah, M. A. 8, 200, 263, 268; Lifetime Union Member 272
Judgement Day. See Day of Judgement
Jung I, Nawab Salar 92

kafir (infidel) 7, 11, 98
kayastha 176, 182
Keddie, Nikki 227–8
Kempson, Simon Mathews Edwin 115, 120–2, 124, 127
Khalifa: of Turkey 190; Usman 208. See also caliphate
Khan, Abdul Rasheed 262
Khan, Aftab Ahmad 66
Khan, Ali Bakhsh 98
Khan, Allama Tafazzul Husain 73
Khan, Alwardi 239
Khan, Faiz Ali 236
Khan, Iftikhar Alam 122, 257
Khan, Izzat 239
Khan, Mehdi Ali 183
Khan, Mehdi Hasan 202
Khan, Mohomed Inayat Ullah 100
Khan, Mukkarmat 239
Khan, Nawab Mahmud 28
Khan, Sayyid Ahmad (Sir) 1–13, 17–50, 54–63, 69–128, 138–67, 159–67, 171–9, 183–93, 190–2, 195–228, 230–43, 245–65, 267–80; 'Adna Halat' by 214, 217–18, 220, 223, 225–7; al-Afghani on 83; childhood of 56; communal animosity of 179; *Creation of Men According to the Qur'an* by 218; death of 2; and documenting monuments of Delhi 233; dreams and 80; and female education 126; *Graduate aur Tijarat* by 125; and knowledge 76; life of 120; *Life of Muhammad* by 42, 76, 78, 104, 198–9, 201–5, 209–10; 'Mashriqi Ulum o Funun' by 125; 'Mazhabi Khayal Zamana-e-Qadeem aur Zamana-e-Jadeed main' of 190; and modernist philosophy 96; *Musafiran-e Landan* by 9, 99; as *naicari jōgī* 83; on religion and politics 43;

on *ruh* 81; speech in translation 167–71; *Strictures upon the Present Educational System in India* by 116, 119; as subordinate judge 4; *Tabyin-ul Kalam* by 11, 21, 41, 139, 143, 145, 147, 152, 198; *Tafsir-ul Qur'an* (Qur'anic exegesis) by 8, 11, 139, 153, 155, 157, 208; *Tahzib-ul Akhlaq* of 10, 20–1, 62, 78, 81, 92, 94–6, 98, 109, 145, 159, 208, 214, 277; theories of interpretations of 79; translation of *Tabyīn* 143; truth and 76
Khan, Shenaz 258
Khan, Zakir Ali 256, 271; *Riwayat-e Aligarh* by 271
Khari Boli 176, 181
Khilafat Movement, the 45, 263
Khutbat-e Ahmadiya 204
Kidwai, Shafey 196
Kilkelly, Charles 74
Kishore, Naval (Munshi) 186
Kitāb al-hayawān by Abū ʿUthman al-Jāḥiẓ 145, 223
Knight Commander of the Order of Star of India (KCSI) 7
Koch, Ebba 250

Ladonneyah, Mawahib 205
Lahori Gate 241, 243, 249. See also Red Fort
land tax policies 31
Lapidus, Ira M. 52
Lawrence, Lieutenant 70, 82, 84
Lawrence, the Collector 100
Lelyveld, David 12, 69–70, 72, 74, 76, 78, 80, 95, 98, 107, 230; 'practical technology' 118
Life of Mahomet, The 41, 199, 205. See also Muir, William (Sir)
Life of Muhammad 42, 76, 78, 104, 198–9, 202–5, 209–10. See also Khan, Sayyid Ahmad (Sir)

London 9, 78
lower-class Muslim rebels 33
Loyal Muhammadans of India, The (1860) 6, 24, 26–7
loyal Muslims 27, 111
Lucknow 71, 73, 97, 166, 171–2, 186, 189
Lutfullah 95
Lytton, Lord 9, 123

MacDonnell, Anthony (Sir) 180–1
madrasa 93, 96–7, 111–13, 261; in Ghazipur 113
Mahdi, Sayyid 79
Mahomedan/Muhammadan Commentary on the Holy Bible 41, 72, 218
Majeed, Javed 82, 84
Malik, Hafeez 17
Malik, Jamal 141
Malthus, Thomas 224
Malaviya, Madan Mohan 181
Martyn, Henry (Reverend) 40
Marx, Karl 175
Matbaʿ-ul ʿUlum 236
Maudoodi (Maulana). See Mawdudi, Abu'l ʿAla
Mawdudi, Abu'l ʿAla 45, 211
Mayo, Lord (Viceroy) 42
McDonough, Sheila 19
middle classes 176
Mill, John Stuart 184
Minto, Lord 36
Mirʾat-ul ʿUrus 63
missionary schools 112
Mitra, Kishan Chandra 25
Mizan-ul Haqq 40
modern sciences 12, 79–80
modernism 49, 103, 251, 276
modernity 84–5, 96, 110, 196, 209, 225, 233–5, 237–8, 242, 247, 251–4
modernization 18, 22, 234, 251–2
Muhammadan Anglo-Oriental Defense Association 185

Muhammadan Anglo-Oriental (MAO) College, Aligarh (1877) 3, 19, 78, 90, 108–9, 166, 188, 217, 230, 252, 255, 273–4; later became AMU 10, 93
Muhammadans 27, 31, 34, 190. *See also* Muslim
Mughal Empire 3, 5, 25, 235, 239–41, 251–2
Muhammad, Prophet 21, 47, 58, 76, 149; writings on suffering of 207
Muhammad, Shan 17, 94, 105
Muhammadan Educational Conference 93, 118, 167, 179, 217; Women's Education Section of 66
Muhammadan Educational Congress 186, 196
Muharram procession 189
Muir Central College in Allahabad 97
Muir, William (Sir) 41, 75, 97, 104, 118, 177, 199–200, 203–8; controversy over book of 199–203, 205, 207; *The Life of Mahomet* by 41, 199, 205
Mujaddidī 157
Mujahidin Movement 143, 209
Mukherjee, Sambhu Chandra 25
Mulla Ṣadrā 141, 151, 154–5
munshi 1, 4, 115, 186
Musaddas-e Hali. See *Musaddas-e Madd-o Jazr-e Islam*
Musaddas-e Madd-o Jazr-e Islam 98
Musalman-e Hind 12, 34, 278
Muslim: communal self 29; conspiracy 24; identity 17, 211, 213, 263, 266; modernization 2; reform 2, 10, 17, 19–20, 37, 43, 275; societies 10, 36, 38, 50, 52, 191; sovereign 47, 49; violence 28
Muslim Anglo-Oriental College (1877). See Muhammadan Anglo-Oriental (MAO) College
Muslim communities, development among 1; suspicion of 38

Muslim League 1, 36, 257–8, 264–6, 275
Muslim University 280. *See also* Aligarh Muslim University (AMU)
Muslim University Foundation Committee 93
Muslim youth 36, 100; education to 119; higher education for 109
Muslim–British interaction 21
Muslims and Parsees, clashes between 196
Mutaqqi, Mir (father of Sayyid Ahmad Khan) 7, 110. *See also* Khan, Sayyid Ahmad (Sir)
Muʿtazilites 209, 220, 223

Nadir Shah 239
Nagari Pracharini Sabha 177, 181
Nagari script 177–82; in Hindi textbooks 180
Nagari/Hindi politics 182–3. *See also* Hindi–Urdu language controversy
naicari (naturalist) 8, 73, 78–81, 83, 89, 98
Naim, C. M. 237
Naoroji, Dadabhai 7
Naqqar Khana 243, 245–6
Naqshbandiyah Mujaddidiyah 209
Nashbandī-Mujaddidī order 141
Nasikh-Mansookh, concept of 208
National Commission for Minority Educational Institutions 267
nationalism 187, 190. *See also* Hindu nationalism
natural sciences 72, 74, 82, 84, 113, 141, 221
Nauroz, celebration of 246
Nehru, Jawaharlal 8, 272
Neville, Henry Rivers 112
Nizami, Khaliq Ahmad 11–12, 89, 101, 106

Northbrook, Lord 10
North-Western Provinces (NWP) 176, 178–81
Numani, Shibli (Maulana) 36, 43, 97, 104, 135, 154
Nurcu Movement, Turkey 276
Nursi, Bediuzzman Said 276

oppression 31, 33, 60
Oriental learning 91
Osella, Filippo 38
Ottoman Empire 46, 52, 117; Christians in 46
Oudh 176, 179–80, 188
Oudh Punch 83
Oxbridge system (education system) 9, 95, 99, 109, 120

Pakistan 1–2, 17, 45, 90, 228–9, 256–58, 263–4, 270–3, 275, 277, 279
Panipati, Shaikh Ismail 204
pan-Islamism 44, 92, 97, 103
Pasha, Khayr al-Din 103
Pasha, Khedive Tewfiq 103
Patiala 10, 36
Pen International 197
Pershad, Kunwar Durga 105
Persianized Urdu 177, 182
Pfander, C. G. 40, 205
pluralism 2, 11–12
Pococke 207
politics and religion 43, 208
Prakash, Gyan 84
Prasad, Ishwari 3, 100
Prasad, Raja Shiva 25, 115, 177–8, 182, 186, 189–90. *See also* Indian Loyal Association
Pritchett, Frances 82
private press 74
public anger, expression of 213
public services 109, 176, 259
Punjab Observer, The 180
Punjab University 124–5
purdah 56–60, 64

Qaiser, Shahzad 147
Qaul-e matin dar ibtal-e harkat-e zamin 144
qaum (community/nation) 4–6, 35, 37, 109–11, 127–9, 159–61, 164, 166, 168–9, 171–3, 175, 226, 278
qiyāmat 80. *See also* Day of Judgement
Queen Victoria 20
Qur'ān 8, 34, 45, 47, 49–50, 63–5, 78–80, 146–50, 153–7, 199–200, 207–9, 214, 216, 222, 229, 231; interpretations of 81
Qutb Minar 1, 37
Quwwat-ul Islam mosque 247

Rahman, Fazlur 154–7
Rahman, Habibur 270
Rai, Lala Lajpat 181
Rai, Pundit Harsookh 101
rajuwāt 144
Rasâ'il Ikhwân al-Safâ'. *See* Ikhwân al-Safâ'
Rashid, Shehla 195
rationalism 5, 11–12, 98, 208–9
Razi, Fakhruddin 209
rebellion of 1857. *See* 1857 rebellion
Red Fort (*qila mu`alla*) 233, 235, 237–49, 251–4
reform 7, 29, 33, 55, 59–60, 63, 96, 98, 107, 140–1, 213; reform from below 7. *See also* social reform
religion 11; as journeys 3; meaning of 52; and politics 50; and science 89, 158
religious: authority 51–2, 79; thinkers 12, 141, 157
restraint 211; need for 212
Rida, Muhammad Rashid 44
Risalah Khair Khawahân Musalmanân 24, 41
Risalah-e Asbab-e Baghawat-e Hind 24, 41, 112. *See also Asbab-e Baghawat-e Hind*

rituals 59, 65, 241, 244
Roberts, Arthur Austin 236
Robinson, Francis 17, 121
Roy, Ram Mohan 4, 11, 275
Rozenthal, Franz 222
Rushdie, Salman, *fatwa* against 212

Saeed, Abdullah 147
Sahba'ī, Baksh (Maulvi Imam) 236
Sahih al-Bukhari 205
Sahih Muslim 205
Sandel, Saroda Prasad 178
Sanskritized Hindi 177
Sarwar, Muhammad 35
Satanic Verses, The 211
Savarkar, V. D. 24
science and technology 8, 10–11, 69–75, 77–8, 81–5, 138–9, 209, 214, 216–17, 229–30, 232–3
science of tradition 147
Scientific Society 6, 8, 10, 74, 78, 101, 117–18, 125, 127, 178, 188, 217, 260. *See also* Aligarh Scientific Society
Scientific Society Magazine 10
secularism 43, 50
Sen, Sachin 24, 36
Shah Bano case 196
Shah II, Akbar 242
Shah Jahan, Emperor 43, 239–42, 250
shahr-āshob 238
Shakespeare, Alexander 29
Shamee, Secrati 205
sharif. See *ashraf*
sherwani 257, 263
shariah 53, 79, 139, 142, 147
Sherwani, Riazur Rahman 35, 257, 261, 263–5
Sh'ia rituals 65
Siddiqi, Ather 257, 270
Siddiqi, Majid Ali 257
Sindhi, Obaidullah (Maulana) 35
Singh, Chaudhri Jodh 28
Singh, Chaudhri Nain 28

Singh, Gobind (Rani Raja) 101
Singh, Sahib Sarpati (Raja) 101
Singh, Sardar Dayal 192
Singh, Uday Pertap 106
Sinha, Ajay 17
Sipahi Yuddher Itihas 25
Sir Sayyid Memorial Fund Committee 93
Sir Sayyid University of Engineering and Technology 271
Sir Syed's Dinner Day 270
Sirat-e Faridiyya 55–6
Sirhindī, Shaykh Ahmad 153–7
Skinner, Quentin 39, 51
Smith, Bosworth 104
Smith, W. C. 8
Soares, Benjamin 38
social reform 6, 12, 19, 21, 79, 107, 233, 273, 275, 277. *See also* reform
social scientists 42, 53–4
Sprenger, Aloys 236
Strachey, Sir John 180
Sufis 39, 56
Sultan, Ottoman 49
sultanate 49, 176, 247
Sunnah 147–8
Supreme Unity 147
Surah al-Furqan 150
Surah al-Qiyama, meaning of 156
Syria 38, 97, 141

Tabyin-ul Kalam (Commentary on the Bible) 11, 21, 139, 143, 145, 147, 152, 198. *See also* Khan, Sayyid Ahmad (Sir)
Tafsir-ul Quran (Quranic exegesis) 8, 10, 139, 153, 155–6, 208. *See also* Khan, Sayyid Ahmad (Sir)
Tagore, Rabindranath 275
Tahzib un-Niswan 62
Tahzib-ul Akhlaq 10, 20–1, 62, 78, 81, 92, 94–6, 98, 109, 145, 159, 208, 214, 277; as *Muhammadan Social Reformer* 78; Sir Sayyid on

human development in 214. *See also* Khan, Sayyid Ahmad (Sir)
talim 121
taluqdar 101, 105, 167, 176, 188
taqlid 191, 209
taqriz 4
tarbiyat 119, 121
Tarikh-e Sarkashi-e Bijnor 5, 23, 41
tawḥīd/waḥdat, doctrine of 142–3, 146–7
Temple, Richard (Sir) 185
theological sciences (*ilm-ul kalam*) 11
theory of evolution 11, 98, 214–18, 223–4, 228–32
Thomason Engineering College at Roorkee 126
tibb-e unani 126
Tibree 205
Tilak, and Ganapati celebrations 189
Tindal, Matthew 210
Tiwari, Kamlesh 212
tolerance 21, 123, 277; in AMU 257
Toland, John 210
Translation Society 113–15
Troll, Christian W. 17, 208–9
Trump, Donald 38
two-nation theory 1, 166, 175, 191, 270
Tyabji, Badruddin 105–6, 166, 184

Uddin, Khwaja Zain 73
ulama 41, 90, 95–6, 191, 208
Ullah, Shah Wali 76–7, 81, 208
ulum-e jadida 79
Umar, Ghulam 257
United Indian Patriotic Organization (1888), renamed as Muhammadan Defence Association 8, 186, 188–9
university education 118; model of 119
Urdu Defense Association 94
Usman, Khalifa 207
ususli ta'lim versus *a'mali ta'lim* 126

Van Gogh, Theo, murder of 212
vernacular 8, 97, 109, 113–21, 128, 144–5, 156, 176, 178, 179, 203
Vernacular Translation Society 236
Vernacular University 116, 121
Viceroy's Executive Council, nomination to 7
Vijeanagur, Raja 101
Viqar-ul Mulk, Nawab Mushtaq Husain. *See* Husain, Mushtaq (Nawab Viqar-ul Mulk)
Vishwa Bharati University 275
Vizianagaram 10, 36

Wahhabism 99. *See also* Wahhabis
waḥdat al-wujūd, doctrine of 143–4
Wahhabis 33, 39, 42–3, 80
Western: education/learning 2, 5, 18–19, 22, 91–2, 96, 108–9, 113, 127, 261; educational institutions at Moradabad 108; societies 38, 223
Westphalian sovereignty 48
Wiles, Jason R. 228
Williams, Raymond 77
Wolff, Joseph (Reverend) 40
women: education 55–7, 60–3, 66–7, 277 (*see also* female: education; *see also under* Khan, Sayyid Ahmad [Sir]); English 60, 110, 277; as equals 57; home education of 59; Indian 59–60; in labour 59; well-being 58, 61
Woodstan, William 210
Wright, Theodore 267

Yoosuff, Mohomed (Moulvi) 100

Zafar II, Bahadur Shah (Mughal Emperor) 3, 5, 19, 41, 238, 248–9; exiled to Rangoon (Yangon) 5
Zaka Ullah/Zakaullah (Maulvi) 97, 209
Zakaullah (Munshi) 115
Zaman, Muhammad Qasim 96
zamindar 176, 188